Women in the Civil War

Women in the
Civil War

by
Mary Elizabeth Massey

Introduction to the Bison Book Edition by
Jean V. Berlin

University of Nebraska Press • Lincoln

First Bison Book printing: 1994
Most recent printing indicated by the last digit below:
10   9   8   7   6   5   4   3   2   1

Library of Congress Cataloging-in-Publication Data
Massey, Mary Elizabeth.
[Bonnet brigades]
Women in the Civil War / Mary Elizabeth Massey; introduction to the Bison
Book edition by Jean V. Berlin.
p.   cm.
Originally published as Bonnet brigades: New York: A. A. Knopf, 1966.
Includes index.
ISBN 0-8032-8213-3
1. United States—History—Civil War, 1861–1865—Women.   2. Women—
United States—History—19th century.   I. Title.
E628.M3   1994
973.7′15042—dc20
93-45580   CIP

Reprinted by arrangement with Alfred A. Knopf, Inc. The original title of
this book was *Bonnet Brigades*.

∞

Gratefully and affectionately

dedicated

to

ALLAN NEVINS

and

BELL I. WILEY

Introduction to the Bison Book Edition

by Jean V. Berlin

Scholars generally agree that the Civil War was as important a watershed in the history of American women as it was in the history of the nation. The responsibilities women undertook, the jobs they held, the privations they endured, and the heartbreak and sorrow they suffered changed them at least as much as war transformed the country. Women both North and South were never the same after four years of conflict, but it would be one hundred years before a sustained, scholarly account of their experiences would appear. A number of sectional eulogies to the work and sacrifice of women appeared in the years immediately after the war, and in 1936 Francis Simkins and James Patton published a study of the women of the Confederacy, but no one historian tried to tell the story of the women of both sections until the 1966 publication of Mary Elizabeth Massey's *Bonnet Brigades,* reprinted here as *Women in the Civil War.*[1]

Mary Elizabeth Massey was born in Morrilton, a small town in central Arkansas, in 1915. She graduated from Hendrix College in Conway, Arkansas, taught high school in her hometown from 1937 to 1939, and then embarked on graduate study at the University of North Carolina–Chapel Hill, studying Southern history with Fletcher Green. She earned her M.A. in 1940 and her Ph.D. in 1947, and began her college teaching career at Flora Macdonald College in Red Springs, North Carolina, later moving to Washington College in Chestertown, Maryland. In 1950, she accepted a position at Winthrop College in Rock Hill, South Carolina, a four-year, liberal arts college for women— like many female scholars of both her own and previous generations, she remained single and taught at a women's college. Here she spent the remainder of her career, which culminated in her appointment as Distinguished Professor in 1965 in recognition of both her scholarship and her popularity with the student body. She maintained a high profile in national and Southern scholarly circles: she was a member of the Advisory Council to the National Civil War Centennial Commission from 1961 to 1965 and a prominent member of the Southern Historical Association, in which she held several posts.[2]

Massey always thought of herself as a social historian. The dislocations in society caused by wars particularly interested her, perhaps because of the effect of World War II on her own life. Her first book, *Ersatz in the Confederacy,* was published in 1952 and bore the strong imprint of the problems of the American home-front economy from 1941 to 1945. It explored the inventiveness of women of an earlier generation faced with chronic shortages in food and other supplies and examined the political imperatives behind the scarcities. After twelve more years of exhaustive research, she published *Refugee Life in the Confederacy* in 1964, a definitive and sympathetic look at the pain and heartache of the civilians whose lives and homes were destroyed by armies both blue and gray in the course of the war. By now it was clear that Massey's scholarly focus was on women and their lives, and she became both the only woman and the only Southerner to contribute to "The Impact of the Civil War" series, published by Alfred A. Knopf, when Allan Nevins invited her to prepare the volume which would become *Women in the Civil War.*[3]

Massey set out to write "an account of the impact of the war on women, not of women on the war," and concluded that the conditions imposed by a civil war marked a turning point in the development of American women (p. xi). Massey's women of the Civil War were far from weak: they were lively, self-reliant, truculent, and brave. She found that women on both sides of the Mason-Dixon Line stepped up to take the place of absent men and support families by running farms and businesses or taking paid employment outside the home. Some women went further and fought for their countries directly or indirectly, or did their best to defend their homes and property against marauding forces. She delineated their lives in loving detail in her book and presented us with unforgettable portraits.

Massey depicted the range of jobs women took outside the home, a range that was far wider during the war than before. She contended that the industrial machine of the North, deprived of male labor, offered more women employment. Other Union women served as nurses, or teachers, or even joined the growing ranks of civil service workers and became a permanent presence in the federal government. Black women, she pointed out, served in all these positions and also organized associations to bring relief to their newly-freed sisters in the South. When she turned to the stories of Southern women, she found that they did not have as many choices as their Northern counterparts; the region's blighted agricultural economy and lack of industry limited those women who sought work for pay. Some served as nurses; others found work as teachers in areas which had relied on men and Northern women for these positions before the war. In Richmond, women worked as clerks for the Confederate government, but these jobs were surrendered with Lee's army in April 1865. She further maintained that slave women faced more limited choices than any other females, black or white—they were either hired out by their owners or, if they sought the protection of Federal lines, found they had to scratch out a precarious living as best they could.

Massey then described the experiences of women who took direct roles of one kind or another in the war. She estimated that some four hundred women served in both armies as soldiers, and that many other women followed their husbands, sons, or fathers to the front (pp. 65–86). Yet another group was composed of the daring women who chose to act as couriers and spies, certain "that their sex would make them immune to punishment," and Massey recorded in detail their shock and outrage when their activities led to their arrest and close confinement by both governments (p. 234). But Massey found that most women participated in the war unintentionally, and here the burdens and privations of the war fell heavily, but by no means solely, on Southern women. Female householders refused to leave their property in spite of reiterated warnings that they would soon find themselves and their families either in the middle of a battle or behind enemy lines. Hoping to protect their property and belongings, these women found instead

ix

that soldiers from both sides commandeered fence rails, cows, hogs, horses, chickens, molasses—anything they could carry. What they could not take they destroyed to keep it out of enemy hands. These women, Massey contended, were at the epicenter of a "total war" such as had never before been seen by Americans. But even though the bitter nature of the war had become clear, they expected that they would be accorded the respect and gentle treatment that had been theirs in peacetime and were perpetually outraged by the behavior of Yankees and Confederate troops. Massey related these stories, showing how the women of Vicksburg were incredulous when Federal troops continued their bombardment of the city in spite of the presence of the fair sex and how the women of Atlanta reeled under the shock of Sherman's mandatory evacuation of their city.[4]

Massey did not, however, state outright that when women stepped outside their traditional roles, civil and military authorities no longer treated them as ladies. She could easily have supported the statement that the reactions of governments and armies to women's direct and indirect participation in the conflict made it clear that they must accept the consequences when they were taken seriously as enemies and threats to security. Benjamin Butler's infamous order concerning the women of New Orleans, issued in May 1862 in response to their intransigent hostility towards the occupying Federal troops, was a case in point. American women discovered that new rights brought new responsibilities.[5]

There are other women whose stories Massey did not tell fully or at all in *Women in the Civil War*. Her treatment of Northerners was not as deep or knowledgeable as her treatment of Southerners. Her reliance on both published and unpublished narratives, diaries, and letters skewed her story sample to the experiences of the well-off and educated. Missing are accounts of the war's impact on yeomen farm women, middle- and lower-class city and town dwellers, and the factory workers of the North. One of the only hints she gave us about the experience of the underprivileged was her comment that poor women believed that their menfolk were more needed at home than at the front (p. 30). Perhaps this observation should have led her to see that the Civil War was perhaps a rich woman's war and a poor woman's fight.

The most obvious omission is that of black women, slave and free. Although Massey does include a chapter on "Women and Negroes," her narrative concerns the reactions of well-to-do white women to emancipation as much as the experiences of slave women during their activities in the war and after the arrival of Federal troops. She did not discuss their emotions and feelings during the conflict in any depth. Her treatment of free blacks was even briefer. All this was particularly puzzling in light of the interviews with former slaves taken down by WPA workers during the Great Depression as well as other published autobiographies and contemporary histories. These documents could have given her as much anecdotal material from which to fashion a fuller story of the experience of African-American women as did the memoirs, journals, and correspondence she relied on for her stories of white women. She also accepted at face value many of the statements of her white sources as to the post-emancipation behavior of their former bondswomen. To give Massey her due, this lack of satisfying narrative about African-Americans, as well as white "everyday folk," may be attributed to some extent to the time at which she wrote. In the 1960s, social history, which has greatly broadened our knowledge of these groups, was in its infancy, and for us to expect Massey to have employed its unfamiliar, difficult, and often time-consuming methods in addition to her other research is perhaps unrealistic.

After detailing the changes in women's lives, Massey wrote that many of their new wartime opportunities disappeared in the spring and summer of 1865. Returning menfolk, victorious or defeated, expected their women to resume their antebellum lives without a murmur. She depicted the plight of widows or wives of disabled soldiers who desperately needed to keep their paying jobs but who found themselves forced out in favor of returning veterans. Such women became bitter, she declared; the male politicians who had started the war did little or nothing to alleviate the troubles of the families of the men who had borne the brunt of the fighting. Other women, not in such dire straits, resented the fact that their sacrifices and contributions were easily dismissed and forgotten. Still others missed the excitement and satisfaction of their new jobs and responsibilities. Massey theorized that these factors led to an entirely unintended and unexpected politicization of American women. The strength of the suffrage and temperance movements grew accordingly; so did the momentum behind other reform crusades in which women would play a prominent part. She also demonstrated that the behavior of male reformers was also to blame. For example, when Frederick Douglass and others counseled their female associates that "this was the Negro's 'hour'" to get the vote and that they should wait their turn for suffrage, women rebelled and pushed for enfranchisement, regardless of blacks (p. 357). Some women, including Elizabeth Cady Stanton and Susan B. Anthony, would even resort to racist rhetoric in the hopes of provoking female resentment at the fact that "another ignorant class of voters [was] placed above their heads." All of these factors, Massey continued, had made women realize that silent partnerships and quiet sacrifices would not get them the rights and privileges they craved: they would have to make themselves heard.[6]

Intent on proving how the war changed women, Massey did not discuss those women who were seemingly unaffected by the war, who embraced a return to the prewar status quo and relinquished their wartime responsibilities with relief and pleasure. At first, these women do not seem to be a part of the story, but of course they are; for the reasons that cause any one group to reject new ideas and new patterns of behavior are just as significant as those which lead others to embrace them. The conservatism of some women is as significant as the growing radicalism of others in the suffrage and reform movements. She also made no real attempt to analyze the differences in political awareness between Northern and Southern women. We would expect, especially after Massey's contention that the privations of the war fell most heavily on Southern women, some sustained effort to determine what retarded their politicization in comparison to that of their Northern sisters.[7]

Another point Massey failed to make with sufficient rigor is that life changed for women in ways that cannot be quantified. The large number of Union and Confederate dead ensured a generation of spinsters, widows, and fatherless children, the latter two groups often dependent on the charity of government and individuals. Economic hardships aside, the psychological toll brought about by the national grieving for the dead was as devastating as the loss of this generation. Even when men returned, women found that the war had altered their fathers, husbands, sons, and lovers irretrievably. Those men who did not bear physical scars often bore psychic ones and were strangers to their loved ones. It sometimes took years to reestablish the family circle, and in some cases it could never be rebuilt. These experiences are also a part of the impact of the war on women.[8]

Contemporary critical reaction to *Women in the Civil War* was positive, although not widespread in academic presses. The reviewer for the *Journal of Southern History* wished for more analytical rigor, but admired the way Massey rescued the stories of women's wartime careers and ordeals from obscurity and endorsed her conclusions.[9] Similar opinions prevailed for some time as historians continued to agree that Massey had done a good job of encompassing the range of women's lives during the war.[10] But as some historians have begun to examine the question of women's impact on the war, they have come to question the idea that women were generally loyal to their section and worked hard for their country, an important tenet of much of Massey's book. George C. Rable and Drew Gilpin Faust have both recently questioned the nature of Southern women's support of the war effort and have theorized that their disillusionment with war may have helped to bring about the fall of the Confederacy.[11] It remains to be seen what new viewpoints these questions, along with the advances in women's and social history, will bring to bear on the story of women and the Civil War.

But all in all, Massey's was a coherent, intelligent, and entertaining account of the "women's war" from 1861 to 1865. Since the publication of *Women in the Civil War,* no other historian has been brave enough or rash enough to take on the job. The amount of research and work Massey put into her book is impressive and even daunting. Her familiarity with the sources and the breadth and depth of her knowledge gave her a great expertise on which she drew freely. The stories she chose to illustrate her points were entertaining and moving; we come to care deeply about her women and what happened to them. Her narrative flowed smoothly and displayed an ease not often seen in academic writers then or now. While she sometimes eschewed theory for anecdote, her desire was to present the spectrum of female experience as graphically as possible: her ideology tended to be implicit.

Women in the Civil War was Massey's last book. In 1972 she became the third woman president of the Southern Historical Association, succeeding John Hope Franklin, the first black president of the association. Two years later, after a long illness, she died of heart and kidney disease at Duke Hospital. Her last published work, her presidential address to the Southern Historical Association, was "The Making of a Feminist," an introductory article on the life and career of Ella Gertrude Clanton Thomas. This article pointed to Massey's new interests. It was clear that she had become committed to writing women's history, and in particular was interested in how the life and experiences of Thomas, a postwar Southern feminist and reformer, were both a symbol for and an indication of how the Civil War and Reconstruction had led women to step outside the domestic sphere and challenge men for a share of political control. Undoubtedly, she had been influenced by Anne Firor Scott's groundbreaking book, *The Southern Lady: From Pedestal to Politics, 1830–1930* (1970). Massey mused briefly on the research and writing of women's history, partly in response to her critics: "Because women's history is a currently popular topic and popular topics have invariably spawned countless volumes masquerading as history, sacrificing depth for breadth and specifics for generalities, those writing on this subject should make a special effort to avoid superficiality. Two challenges therefore confront the historian: to recognize individuals heretofore neglected and to be satisfied with nothing less than a scholarly presentation."[12] In *Women in the Civil War* she met her own criteria, rescuing the stories of women from obscurity in a well-written and thoroughly-researched book that continues to teach and entertain more than twenty-five years after its first appearance.

In spite of her work, Massey is not much cited in works on Southern women's history specifically or women's history generally. Although many of her writings were not explicitly women's history, there can be no doubt that her brand of social history was women's history. After all, the perils and privations of home-front life in the wartime Confederacy fell upon the women in undue proportion. But when Anne Firor Scott listed the "handful of established historians of women" still working in 1970, Massey's name was not among them.[13] Like many women of her generation who had achieved success in academia in spite of or through manipulation of the "old boy network," Massey was ambivalent about the increasingly militant feminist movement of the 1970s. One colleague said "she rather enjoyed being one of the few prominent women in a profession dominated by men."[14] She believed that moderate statements and moderate goals, rather than tough talk and mandatory quotas, would go further to win male support and redress the inequities of rank and pay in the profession.[15] This conservative attitude may have united with the fact she had no graduate students to carry on her ideas, leaving her work isolated from the scholarly mainstream. But as women's history matures and Civil War studies in fields outside of military and political history proliferate, new generations will come to appreciate her pioneering contributions.

NOTES

1. See L. P. Brockett and Merry C. Vaughan, *Women's Work in the Civil War* (Philadelphia: Ziegler, McCurdy and Co., 1867); Francis W. Dawson, ed., *Our Women in the War: The Lives They Lived, the Deaths They Died* (Charleston, S.C.: News and Courier Co., 1885); Frank Moore, *Women of the War: Their Heroism and Self-Sacrifice* (Hartford, Conn.: S. S. Scranton, 1868); and Francis Butler Simkins and James Welch Patton, *Women of the Confederacy* (Richmond, Va.: Garrett and Massie, 1936).

2. Frederick M. Heath, "Mary Elizabeth Massey," in "The Three Women Presidents of the Southern Historical Association," *Southern Studies* 20, no. 2 (1981): 116, 118–19; Thomas S. Morgan, obituary of Mary Elizabeth Massey, *Journal of Southern History* 41 (May 1975): 292–93.

3. Thomas S. Morgan, obituary of Mary Elizabeth Massey, 293.

4. Recent work on gender and the Civil War has echoed many of Massey's contentions about women while raising new ones; see, for example, Catherine Clinton and Nina Silber, eds., *Divided Houses: Gender and the Civil War* (New York: Oxford University Press, 1992).

5. Mary P. Ryan's analysis of Benjamin Butler and his General Order No.

28 makes this point; *Women in Public, Between Banners and Ballots, 1825–1880* (Baltimore: Johns Hopkins University Press, 1990), 3–4, 143–45. Drew Gilpin Faust's recent work leads to the notion that the assumption of new responsibilities was an important factor in the erosion of Southern women's support for the war; "Altars of Sacrifice: Confederate Women and the Narratives of War," *Journal of American History 76 (March 1990): 1200–1228*. See also Faust, *The Creation of Confederate Nationalism: Ideology and Identity in the Civil War South* (Baton Rouge: Louisiana State University Press, 1988).

6. Elizabeth Cady Stanton and Susan B. Anthony, quoted in Wendy Hamand Venet, *Neither Ballots nor Bullets: Women Abolitionists and the Civil War* (Charlottesville: University Press of Virginia, 1991), 157. Venet and other historians have taken up Massey's contention that some women were radicalized by the events of the war and its immediate aftermath.

7. This point was explored by Anne Firor Scott in *The Southern Lady: From Pedestal to Politics, 1830–1930* (Chicago: University of Chicago Press, 1970).

8. For recent, preliminary speculations on this subject, see Amy E. Holmes, "Such Is the Price We Pay: American Widows and the Civil War Pension System," in Maris A. Vinovskis, ed., *Toward a Social History of the American Civil War: Exploratory Essays* (Cambridge: Harvard University Press, 1990), 171–95; Suzanne Lebsock, *The Free Women of Petersburg: Status and Culture in a Southern Town, 1784–1860* (New York: W. W. Norton & Company, 1984), 237–49; and George C. Rable, *Civil Wars: Women and the Crisis of Sectional Nationalism* (Urbana: University of Illinois Press, 1989), 265–88.

9. Anne Firor Scott, review of *Bonnet Brigades, The Journal of Southern History* 33 (July 1967): 410–11.

10. See, for example, Anne Firor Scott, "Historians Construct the Southern Woman," *Making the Invisible Woman Visible* (Urbana: University of Illinois Press, 1984), 243–58; and H. E. Sterkx, *Partners in Rebellion: Alabama Women during the Civil War* (Rutherford, N.J.: Fairleigh Dickinson University Press, 1970).

11. George C. Rable, *Civil Wars*, and Drew Gilpin Faust, "Altars of Sacrifice: Confederate Women and the Narratives of War."

12. Mary Elizabeth Massey, "The Making of a Feminist," *Journal of Southern History* 39 (February 1973): 3.

13. Anne Firor Scott, "A Historian's Odyssey," in *Making the Invisible Woman Visible,* xxiii, xxiiin.1.

14. Heath, "Mary Elizabeth Massey," p. 119.

15. *Ibid.,* 120.

Introduction

by Allan Nevins

"The women of the South had the spirit of Spartans," said a New York attorney; "the women of the North had the spirit of Romans." He meant that the Southern struggle specially demanded the valor of endurance, while the Northern effort especially awakened a determination to conquer against all obstacles. But was this a valid distinction? In Miss Massey's rich book, so full of careful research and warm understanding, we may find an answer to the question—and to many others. North, West, and South, the Civil War was a contest not of armies but of embattled peoples. All were caught up in the whirlwind that during four years possessed the land, and it was the feminine half of the population that, as the Southern historian Robert Selph Henry has stated, bore "the harder part of the war." For the first time we have in this energetic yet sensitive volume a thorough, comprehensive, and impartial history of the enormous work the women did while the guns sounded, and the steps they meanwhile took toward the sweeping transformations that followed Appomattox.

Actually, as Miss Massey shows, the women of the South and those of the North showed almost precisely the same spirit. They were alike in blood, in breeding, and in essential education. The successors of Eliza Pinckney and Martha Washington did not differ greatly from those of Abigail Adams and Mercy Otis Warren. The people of the South, men and women, were closer to the frontier and farther from industrialism than those of the North. The Northerners were the more acutely aware of social and economic problems as distinguished from political issues. In conducting and enduring a terrible war, however, these differences were of no vital importance. Each side fought for its special civilization. Southern women battled for the civilization of Willam Byrd, John C. Calhoun, and Paul H. Hayne; Northern women for the civilization of Alexander Hamilton, Daniel Webster, and Ralph Waldo Emerson. Women less than men were actuated by selfish considerations. Idealizing their respective causes, they gave intense devotion and strenuous labor to the support of the warriors and the war effort.

Completely realistic in her handling of facts, Miss Massey does not conceal the less creditable aspects of the record written by women of Civil War time: Princess Salm-Salm in the days of General Hooker's command found the Army of the Potomac "teeming with women," many of them camp followers, and Charles Francis Adams, Jr., has recorded that the atmosphere of Hooker's headquarters was much too licentious for his taste. Adventuresses abounded. The best of them were girls who longed for the role of a Joan of Arc and were courageously prepared to run all the risks of the battle area, like Belle Boyd, "the Secesh Cleopatra," who once made a nocturnal ride of sixty miles in the Shenandoah to carry the stolen plans of General James Shields to Stonewall Jackson; the worst of them were dangerous alike to supposed friend or ostensible foe. Miss Massey leaves the story of "Major" Annie Jones, the attractive young Massachusetts girl "commissioned" by General Julius Stahel, who linked her name with Custer's, shrouded in mystery. She tells as much of the precise truth as can be ascertained, however, about such famous figures as Mrs. Rosa Greenhow and Eugenia Phillips, who were as skillful as they were unscrupulous; and she gives us convincing portraits of the brassy if able Anna E. Dickinson and the pathetic actress Pauline Cushman, whose brief career of wild adventure was followed by long years of miserable poverty.

The general record, however, possesses the heroism that we have been taught to associate with the subject. During the war at least 3,200 women held paid positions as army nurses, North and South, an impressive figure. Not one of them became a great organizer like Florence Nightingale; but the South will never forget Fannie Beers and Kate Cumming, just as the North can never forget Mary A. Livermore and Clara Barton, who truthfully boasted that she "went in while the battle raged." So, too, the West will always see Mother Bickerdyke, whom Grant ranked even above Lincoln, as one of the most heroic figures of the Mississippi Valley. Into government offices in both capitals poured a cohort of earnest workers, those in Richmond even braver than the civil servants of Washington in their willingness to face scorn and defamation. Long before the war ended, women schoolteachers were flocking south to teach in the schools organized by the Freedmen's Bureau. Already many Southern women had turned, despite the deep prejudices of the section, to schools and to business pursuits; and some of them were ready to give the Negro a helping hand. As writers, civil servants, estate managers, as the managers of small businesses, they were soon active agents in the New South.

Great as was the courage of those who found it a heroic task, in all sections, just to keep themselves and their families alive during years of privation and trial, the era was not one of fortitude alone. It was an era of change and growth. This was especially true in the North, and Clara Barton exaggerated very little when she said that the war had left women at least fifty years in advance of the position they would have held if peace had endured. The grounds for this statement are varied and significant, and Miss Massey's book—one of the most original contributions we have had to the literature of the Civil War—expounds them lucidly and completely.

Preface

Had every woman and girl of the 1860's described the ways in which she was affected by the Civil War, no two accounts would have been alike. Some might have said they were scarcely aware that a conflict raged, most would have noted varying degrees of stress, and many would have reported direct involvement in the horrors of war. Rich and poor, young and old, white and colored, slave and free, Confederate and Unionist were all caught in the turbulence, but included also were the middle classes and those with no deep-seated political convictions or loyalties. To be found in all areas were selfless, dedicated, energetic, courageous, virtuous women as well as the self-centered, selfish, indifferent, cowardly, lazy, and immoral. In Union and Confederacy alike the very finest and the very worst traits of American womanhood came to the surface during the war years.

It has not been easy to knit together the story of more than fifteen million women, each with her own peculiar inheritance, environment, and experiences. For every generalization in this study there were thousands of exceptions—how many one can never be sure, for not all extant manuscripts could possibly be studied, and even if they had been, questions would arise regarding the millions who left no records. Yet it is from the letters and diaries of the war generation that the historian obtains the clearest insight into individual attitudes, and the author has delved into the varied records of more than a hundred persons who lived in the period. Especially frustrating has been the need for only casual mention or entire omission of scores of stories rich in human interest. Although by no means all manuscripts, newspapers, or other sources used have been cited, all contributed to my conclusions and interpretations.

When invited to make this study I first decided what I would not do. I would not romanticize, idealize, or debunk the women of either North or South or attempt to prove or disprove the theses of any school of history. If I have done any of these things it has been unintentional, for my only purpose has been to show how the Civil War affected American women. I have tried to avoid giving greater attention to one section than to the other, yet conditions were different in each. Partly because of these differences there were more constructive developments in the Union than in the Confederacy. Southern women's contact with the destructive forces of the conflict and bitterness of defeat caused a more negative approach to life.

Two conclusions merit mention at this time. First, the women of the war generation were no different from those of any other. It is true that they lived in a difficult period and encountered grave problems, but they reacted as would women of any age and in so doing evidenced both their frailties and strengths as human beings. Secondly, and despite contrasting conditions, the women of North and South had far more in common than they realized at the time. (Because most studies heretofore have been confined to the women of only one area, a comparison has rarely been made.) They shared many of the same fears, gave vent to the same emotions, voiced the same doubts, and supported their separate causes in much the same way. (Whatever distinctive characteristics women displayed were to be found within any group and were not drawn according to sectional lines. It is interesting to speculate what the feminine reaction might have been had the enemies realized how much they had in common.)

The Civil War compelled women to become more active, self-reliant, and resourceful, and this ultimately contributed to their economic, social, and intellectual advancement. With few exceptions no attempt has been made in this volume to trace the war's impact beyond the nineties, although it is obvious that even today its effects are still in evidence; but such is the case in social revolutions, and the Civil War was in part a social revolution. In an effort to get as close to the women of a century ago as possible and to convey their attitudes, ideas, and reactions, I have included quotes which may be offensive to some, but in many instances they describe feelings more realistically than the author could hope to do. I trust they will afford greater insight into women of the war generation and perhaps make them appear more "human." In trying to be objective, which is itself the goal of an idealist, it is my hope that I have not become objectionable. Finally, I ask the reader to remember that which I have had to remind myself repeatedly in the preparation of this book—this is meant to be an account of the impact of the war on women, not of women on the war. I trust it is.

Mary Elizabeth Massey
January 15, 1966

Contents

Illustrations

The illustrations are grouped after page 168

Women in the Civil War

I

Leaped from Their Spheres

THE THIRTY YEARS preceding the Civil War were marked by
the nation's physical growth and expansion, economic
diversification, democratic advancement, intellectual progress,
and tragic sectional hostility. Time-honored traditions, attacked
from all sides by exponents of new ideologies, were just as deter-
minedly defended by spokesmen of the *status quo.* Women were
affected either directly or indirectly by the challenges and
changes, but most were too busy being wives and mothers to
participate actively in any movement which would take them
beyond the home and church. Yet an ever-increasing number
were becoming economically self-sufficient, better educated, and
more demanding, and these were the women who, according to
Maria Weston Chapman, had "leaped from their spheres," much
to the consternation of the "lords of creation."[1] There were very
few who could be classified as "strong-minded" crusaders for
woman's rights and they were confined primarily to Northeastern
urban areas, but the few were exceedingly noisy. Others showed
signs of being restless but by no means rebellious, and the overwhelming majority were completely indifferent to the movement.

[1] Elizabeth Cady Stanton *et al: The History of Woman Suffrage*
(Rochester, N.Y., 1881), I, 82–83.

3

Most American women readily conceded authority to some man, usually the father until he was replaced by a husband, or if a widow or spinster, to another male relative. Whether or not they were contented depended on individual circumstances, but personal records give no indication that they were less satisfied with their lot than their ancestors or descendants. Except for professional feminists, women did not brood about being second-class citizens, for their world centered around their family. If called to take over a man's responsibilities, most women rose to the occasion, but it was necessity and not preference that converted them. The fact that women left public affairs to their menfolk did not necessarily imply that they hesitated to express themselves in private or that they had no convictions, but the extent of their influence on men is uncertain and to assess it is, as Harriet Martineau said, like trying "to dissect the morning mist." For wherever this ardent British feminist journeyed she was told that while American women had not obtained the right to vote, they nevertheless wielded great political "influence . . . [on] man through the heart."[2] Like Miss Martineau, the woman's rights advocates too often construed a wife's agreeing with her husband as acknowledgment of inferiority, but usually she honestly viewed political matters as he did. If she did not agree, she may have said nothing either because she saw no reason to report the matter to others or because she was wise enough to realize that it was to her advantage to preserve domestic tranquility.

Of all women's new activities, none contributed more significantly to her "emancipation" than increased economic opportunities. Since most were familiar with household chores it might be assumed that those in need of work would first be attracted to domestic service, but they actually had a deep-seated antipathy for it. In the twenties Frances Trollope was surprised to discover that, unlike English girls, the Americans were horrified at the thought of being servants, and Harriet Martineau made a similar observation in the thirties, while in the fifties Fredrika Bremer concluded that the prejudice left the field open to immigrants.[3]

[2] Harriet Martineau: *Society in America* (London, 1881), I, 205.
[3] Frances Trollope: *Domestic Manners of America* (New York, 1949), pp. 117–18, 53–57; Martineau: *Society in America*, II, 34; Fredrika Bremer: *The Homes of the New World, Impressions of America* (New York, 1854), II, 58.

In the North thousands of Irish and German women took advantage of this opportunity, but in the South poor whites were unable to compete with Negro slaves.

Many uneducated Northern women who shunned domestic service did not hesitate to seek jobs in the rapidly expanding industries. By 1860 there were more than 270,000 female operatives, the vast majority being employed in Northern textile, shoe, clothing, printing, and publishing establishments. Over 135,000 worked in the New England factories and composed 65 per cent of the region's industrial labor. In the eleven states later included in the Confederacy, only 12,000 women worked in factories, 10 per cent of the area's industrial wage earners. Although the South had one-third of the nation's people, including slaves, it had only 10 per cent of the industry, and its exceedingly small number of trained women factory hands later posed a problem for the Confederacy. Because agriculture was emphasized at the expense of industry and public opinion frowned on women's work outside the home, Southern girls had limited opportunity.

Foreign travelers were exceedingly curious about the country's industrial development, and the women were especially interested in female operatives. Early observers were enthusiastic, Harriet Martineau being especially impressed by their dress, hair styles, and thrift. She was amazed that many of those working in the Waltham factories were paying off the mortgage on the family farm, some were sending younger brothers and sisters to school, and others were "rapidly accumulating their independence." Fifteen years later, when Fredrika Bremer toured the country, conditions had worsened and she reported poorly clad workers in the same mills but was pleased to hear that employers insisted that only girls of "good character" be hired, for the public as yet often questioned the propriety of working and living away from parental observation.[4] Although factory conditions deteriorated, seamstresses working fourteen or more hours a day for manufacturers endured even greater hardships than the operatives. They sometimes stitched garments in their homes but more often in poorly ventilated and lighted sewing rooms, seldom earning more than twenty-five cents for a long day's work. Introduction of the

[4] Martineau: *Society in America*, II, 246–49; Bremer: *The Homes of the New World*, I, 210–11.

sewing machine somewhat altered conditions, but thousands of women continued to sew by hand long after the Civil War. Although seamstresses catering to individual customers were often underpaid, they usually had more pleasant working conditions and personal contacts.

Women fought their way into the typesetting trade and were first challenged by men in 1835, when it was reported that they were being trained to replace striking males in Philadelphia. This proved only a rumor, but eighteen years later four women trained to replace New York strikers were employed setting type for the *Day Book,* and in 1854 the National Typographical Union protested that woman's place was in the home. Horace Greeley reminded the critics that the women did not choose to support their families, but their "drunken, loafing, good-for-nothing menfolk" left them no alternative. Herman J. Redfield, who favored women's employment because he thought it encouraged virtue, suggested to Secretary of State William L. Marcy that he use the *Day Book* for publication of laws since this would indicate his support of women's right to work. He also told Marcy that women were paid approximately one-half as much as men.[5] Although there were relatively few openings for female compositors in the fifties, women sought this work because they could earn eight to ten dollars a week, four to five times the wage paid most factory operatives.

It was primarily because women were willing to work longer hours for less pay that they were able to take over men's jobs, and their protests seldom improved the situation. The first all-woman strike took place in Dover, New Hampshire, in the twenties, when textile workers demanded higher wages and shorter hours, and a few years later in the same community 800 struck for the same reasons. In the thirties women operatives in Lowell, Massachusetts, protested a wage cut and the firing of one of their colleagues, who started the strike in a typically feminine manner. By prearranged agreement, after her unsuccessful hearing before officials, she threw her bonnet into the air, and the operatives immediately walked out, held a rally, denounced the manage-

[5] New York *Tribune,* July 17, 1854; Herman J. Redfield to William L. Marcy, Feb. 27, 1854, William L. Marcy Papers, Manuscript Division, Library of Congress.

6

ment, and heard a speech on woman's rights. Similar strikes occurred elsewhere in the thirties and local unions were formed, but the depression of 1837 temporarily halted the labor movement. In the forties interest was renewed as feminine labor leaders stepped forward, among them Sarah Bagley who helped organize the Lowell Female Labor Reform Association. Under her leadership association members protested against unfair management practices and petitioned the Massachusetts legislature to establish a ten-hour day and investigate the working conditions of women in industry. The investigation failed to remedy conditions because the press and public opinion opposed it, and the employers freely used their right to dismiss "trouble-makers." Conditions were not generally improved during the forties and fifties, but women showed they could protest if sufficiently aroused.

Business opportunities were more limited than those in industry, and society questioned the propriety of women's catering to the general public and working alongside men. Opponents argued that women could not endure the strain without serious impairment of health, and that they lacked the necessary mental qualifications and talent to engage in business. Sarah Josepha Hale, editor of *Godey's Lady's Book,* was credited with persuading A. T. Stewart "to try the experiment of employing sales women" in his New York store, and there were a few women clerks in other establishments, but sales work was discouraged except when women assisted in family-owned businesses.[6]

Typical was the opposition encountered by Elizabeth McClintock in 1849 when she applied for a position in the Philadelphia import firm of Edward M. Davis and Company. She was qualified to fill the vacancy, having clerked in her father's store, and needing employment, she turned to Davis who had long been a personal friend. Everything was in her favor; everything, that is, except her sex. Elizabeth Cady Stanton encouraged her to apply, certain that if Davis rejected the request his mother-in-law, Lucretia Mott, would force him to reconsider. News of Miss McClintock's application spread along Market Street "like wildfire," and men gathered to discuss this alarming development.

---

[6] Ruth Elbright Finley: *The Lady of Godey's: Sarah Josepha Hale* (Philadelphia, 1931), pp. 238–39.

They wondered what Davis would do since he had advocated woman's rights, but now confronted with the possibility of being the first man in the wholesale district to employ a lady, he hedged while Mrs. Mott brought pressure from one side and businessmen from the other. Davis solved the problem by shifting the responsibility to his staff, who he felt sure would oppose the appointment. The men argued that women were physically, mentally, and emotionally unsuited for the work, and one candidly remarked that the presence of a woman in the offices would lessen the men's "attention to business." Speaking last, Davis reiterated his belief in the theory of woman's right to work but opposed this particular appointment. The matter was settled but not closed.

It was left to Mrs. Mott to notify Miss McClintock that her application had been rejected, but she chose to direct the sad tidings via Mrs. Stanton. Included in the envelope was the firm's official statement, a masterpiece of double-talk, inconsistencies, clichés, and apologies which closed with the assurance that the applicant would not enjoy the work because it was "a miserable circle of antagonisms." Elizabeth Stanton forwarded the communication to Miss McClintock and disgustedly added, "What fools these Quakers be. . . . Lucretia needs a new inspiration." Mrs. Mott had appealed to the men but reported receiving the "Ye know not what ye ask" type of response.[7]

Businesswomen "of sorts" were to be found in every state during the antebellum period, and while most managed or clerked in small shops, a few owned and administered large concerns. One was Sarah Tyndale, whose successful china and porcelain business in Philadelphia made her a wealthy woman. They also managed hotels, boardinghouses, saloons, and other enterprises. Those responsible for making farms and plantations efficient, and plantation mistresses who shared the responsibility, needed a knowledge of business principles. After the death of James K. Polk his widow managed the family plantations in Tennessee and Mississippi, and her instructions to the overseers indicate that she was an efficient businesswoman. While not numerous, others supervised farm property; for example, two elderly spinsters whom Fredrika Bremer was surprised to find on an

[7] Elizabeth McClintock Folder, Garrison Family Papers.

island-plantation off the South Carolina coast where they directed the work of 300 slaves.[8]

Woman's employment in the Washington government offices dates officially from the Civil War, but in the late fifties Clara Barton and a few other women worked as clerks and copyists in the Patent Office. They were a thorn in the flesh of Secretary of Interior Robert McClelland; and Charles Mason, who appointed them, was in constant trouble with his superior because of his daring experiment. McClelland expressed the opinion of most men when he said, "There is such an obvious impropriety in the mixing of the sexes within the walls of a public office, that I am determined to arrest the practice." Arrest it he did, but during her tenure Miss Barton received an annual salary of $1400— more than twice that later paid the wartime government girls. Yet the money scarcely compensated her for the insults and ridicule of male colleagues who "lined up in the halls, stared, blew smoke in the women's faces, spat tobacco juice, and gave cat-calls or made obnoxious remarks."[9] Other women served the government elsewhere, and in 1860 there were approximately 400 postmistresses, the "dean" being Jennet McNair of Cowper Hill, North Carolina, who had held her commission since 1828. Women were also employed by the Interior Department as teachers of Indians in Michigan, Wisconsin, Minnesota, California, and Washington and served as lighthouse keepers and as attendants in the government-supported mental institution in Washington.[1]

It was never easy for women to pioneer in any field, but those who wished to enter the medical profession encountered seemingly insurmountable obstacles. Although there were midwives and unlicensed women practitioners before Elizabeth Blackwell received her medical degree in 1849, this determined lady was the first trained woman physician. Although better qualified than many men to enter medical school, for she had studied privately with a Charleston physician, Miss Blackwell applied at more than twenty-five institutions before being admit-

[8] Bremer: *The Homes of the New World*, I, 390.
[9] Blanche Colton Williams: *Clara Barton: Daughter of Destiny* (Philadelphia, 1941), pp. 55–60.
[1] New York *Herald*, July 20, 1862; *Register of Officers and Agents, Civil, Military, and Naval in the Service of the United States, 1861* (Washington, 1862), pp. 82–90, 99–100.

9

ted to Geneva Medical College, and even here it was the student body and not the faculty or administration that voted to accept her. Her greatest discouragement came, however, when she tried to establish a practice in New York City and discovered that she was not wanted as doctor, colleague, neighbor, or tenant. Only after innumerable heartbreaking experiences did she find a few friends who helped her found the New York Infirmary for Women in 1857, just in time to train the nurses so desperately needed a few years later.

Because women were usually refused admission to medical schools, a few special ones were established for them, the more notable being the Female Medical College of Pennsylvania and the New England Medical College. Dr. Ann Preston was director of the former and Dr. Maria Zakrzewska was associated with the latter. When the Civil War started there were several licensed women physicians, including Emily Blackwell and Mary Walker. Harriet Hunt was addressed as "Doctor" and had received an honorary degree from the Female Medical College in Philadelphia, but she was a physiotherapist. Louisa Shepard was the first woman to graduate from a Southern medical school, Graefenberg Medical Institute in Dadeville, Alabama, which closed in 1861. Discouraged by hostile public opinion, she did not long try to practice. Occasionally Northern-trained women opened offices in the South but seldom overcame the prejudice against them. Dr. Elizabeth Cohen maintained a fairly successful practice "for ladies only" in New Orleans but shocked staid residents when she rode alone through the streets and into the country making night calls, though she always carried a small ivory-handled pistol.[2]

Women were discouraged from entering other professions, none having been admitted to the bar and few to the pulpit prior to the Civil War. Olympia and Antoinette Brown, unrelated to each other, were the most prominent ordained ministers, but most sects forbade the ordination of women. The Society of Friends, however, accorded women the right to speak at meetings, and from this faith came many of the feminists. Women's

[2] Ray Turner: "Graefenburg: The Shepard Family's Medical School," *Annals of Medical History*, V (1933), 548–60; Elizabeth Bass: "Pioneer Women Doctors in the South," *Journal of the American Medical Woman's Association*, II (1947), 559.

greatest professional opportunity was in teaching, but here too they encountered discrimination, for male teachers were generally preferred, especially as instructors of boys. Women teachers received smaller salaries than men, and it was because they demanded less that they were able to invade the profession. Among the many outstanding nineteenth-century women who moved from the classroom to the public arena were Susan B. Anthony, Mary Livermore, Lucy Stone Blackwell, Antoinette Brown, Clara Barton, and Dorothea Dix.

The public assumed that no woman would teach school unless dire poverty drove her, and she was therefore an object of pity; yet if one had to work, all agreed that teaching was a ladylike pursuit. Those conforming to the mores of the community encountered little opposition, but a nonconformist soon discovered that her sex did not immunize her against criticism or even brutality. One certain path to trouble was to defy community views on the education of Negroes. In the South, state laws forbade the teaching of slaves to read or write, but some were surreptitiously taught, often by the planters' children who conducted mock classes with themselves as teacher and the little Negroes as pupils. In the North racially integrated schools provoked the greatest controversy, for most Northerners opposed them on any level. Oberlin was much maligned when it admitted both Negroes and women, coeducation being frowned upon as much as integration. Prudence Crandall's unfortunate experience in trying to integrate her fashionable Connecticut girls' school is well known. White students were indignantly withdrawn by their parents and mobs threatened, stoned, and insulted Miss Crandall and so damaged her home that she abandoned her scheme rather than place her remaining pupils in jeopardy.

White women who taught in all-Negro schools were sometimes mistreated, as in the case of Myrtilla Miner, a Mount Holyoke graduate who opened her school in 1851. She had earlier resigned her tutorial position on a Mississippi plantation after being denied permission to teach slaves and with the help of Northern friends, established a school for Negroes in Washington. While abolitionist senators led by Henry Wilson praised her work, Southern solons led by Jefferson Davis denounced it. The violent demonstrations which closed the institution before the war were led primarily by ruffians.[3] Creditable Northern schools for Negroes included the successful Institute for Colored Youth in Philadelphia under the auspices of the Society of Friends. In the five years preceding the Civil War, nineteen were graduated from this academy, and two of the seven girls who finished continued their studies at Oberlin. In 1861, four of the seven were teaching colored children and the remaining three were trying to find similar positions.[4]

A few women teachers, among them Susan B. Anthony, agitated against the discriminatory practices in the profession, but the majority accepted their lot. Yet women who were educators as well as teachers used a quieter, more positive approach; they sought to improve the training of girls, thus making them so superior that they would eventually win favor from their most caustic critics. Emma Willard, Catherine Beecher, and Mary Lyon, three outstanding pioneers in education, were not active in the woman's rights movement and Miss Beecher denounced it, but they calmly assumed the powers needed to carry through their respective projects. After failing to persuade the New York legislature to establish a teacher-training institute for women, Emma Willard obtained support from the Troy Town Council and in 1821 opened her academy. The school was soon known throughout the nation for its unconventional curriculum which included higher mathematics, thought to be too difficult for feminine comprehension, and physiology, considered indecent. No "nice" young lady would dare discuss the human body, said conservatives, and certainly she should not be exposed to illustrated lectures on the subject! When Paulina Wright Davis later lectured to older women on physiology, the introduction of charts and drawings of the female body and its functions invariably resulted in shocked ladies withdrawing while others hid their faces.

Catherine Beecher, one of the outstanding educators of the century, was frustrated by public indifference. After the success

[3] Myrtilla Miner Papers, Manuscript Division, Library of Congress; Henry Wilson: *History of the Rise and Fall of the Slave Power in America* (Boston, 1872), II, 582. See also Ellen O'Connor: *Myrtilla Miner, A Memoir* (Boston, 1885), *passim;* Sadie St. Clair: "Myrtilla Miner: Pioneer in the Teacher Education of Negroes," *Journal of Negro History,* XXIV (1949), 30–45.

[4] *Annual Report of the Board of Managers of the Institute for Colored Youth for the Year 1861* (Philadelphia, 1861), pp, 2–3.

of her Connecticut school, she dreamed of establishing teacher-training centers throughout the country, and while meeting with only partial success in Iowa and Illinois, her crowning achievement in the Midwest was a school in Milwaukee which thrived and later became the basis for Milwaukee-Downer. Most of her students were trained in the Connecticut institution which she personally conducted and were in great demand as instructors. Miss Beecher had chosen to teach because "it was the only vocation open to young women" at the time, and until her death in the seventies she emphasized teacher training, nursing, and home management. She told her girls that if all young women would prepare for one of these "there would be no female factory hands" toiling endless hours for starvation wages.[5]

Mary Lyon, founder of Mount Holyoke Female Seminary, determined to offer ambitious girls from all economic backgrounds as comprehensive an education as that afforded boys in the best men's schools. With Amherst as her pattern, Miss Lyon accepted no student under sixteen, the age when most terminated their formal schooling, and she required all to pass an entrance examination. Once enrolled they subscribed to the rigid liberal arts course and participated in a domestic training program.

Sallie Eola Renau did not receive the national recognition accorded these Northern women, partly because she failed to achieve her dream of a state-supported institution where Mississippi women might be trained as teachers. In the fifties she pleaded with the legislature to found the school, and in 1856 one was chartered but no funds were appropriated. Yet Sallie Renau merits remembrance because she spoke out in an area hostile to women crusading for any cause.

During the prewar decades female seminaries sprouted like mushrooms throughout the nation, and within these cloisters thousands of young ladies received a finishing-school type of education. Wealthy and middle-class parents enrolled their daughters after they had been instructed in elementary subjects, but whether they continued their studies after graduation depended on the individual and the available libraries. Girls from poor families sometimes had the advantage of a public school

---

[5] Willystine Goodsell (ed.): *Pioneers of Woman's Education in the United States* (New York: 1931), pp. 131–38. See also Catherine Beecher: *Educational Reminiscences and Suggestions* (New York, 1874), *passim.*

education, but this was more often afforded in Northern towns than in the rural areas. The South lagged in developing public education, primarily because its people were scattered and its planters were uninterested or hostile to tax-supported schools. Yet progress was made in the twenty-five years preceding the war and many of the South's schools compared with those elsewhere.

The practice of employing tutors for the children of Southern planters opened innumerable opportunties for Northern teachers, and despite the mounting hostility between the sections, most "schoolmarms" in the South in 1860 were Northern-born and -trained. Very few came South to crusade for abolition, although after secession this charge was hurled at them. Most either accepted the institution or were silent on its evils, but an impressive number, including some from Northern abolitionist families, married Southern planters and later became staunch supporters of the Confederacy. Mary Ashton Livermore was one of the exceptions. Leaving her home in Massachusetts despite her father's protest, she spent three years on a Virginia plantation and became "a pronounced abolitionist." After returning to Massachusetts she subscribed to the *Liberator,* refused to listen to any "apology for slavery," and was soon publicly crusading against the institution.[6]

An increasing number of women chose to express themselves with their pens, and so many were writing professionally in the thirty years preceding the Civil War that only a few can be named here. The most staid conservatives agreed that a woman might write if she had the time, but not all accorded her the right to publish and most who did thought she should do so anonymously. Male writers were often caustic about the "d – – – d scribbling women," as Hawthorne once referred to them, yet even the critic occasionally excepted an individual who produced something to his liking. When "Fanny Fern" (Sarah Willis Parton) published the bitter, semi-autobiographical *Ruth Hall,* Hawthorne was among the first to praise her, saying that she wrote "as if the Devil was in her, . . . the only condition under which a woman ever writes anything worth reading."[7]

[6] Mary Ashton Livermore: *The Story of My Life* (Hartford, 1899), pp. 146, 206–10, 364–65.

[7] Fred Lewis Pattee: *The Feminine Fifties* (New York, 1940), pp. 110–11.

Most women were content to dabble in romantic fiction and poetry, but judging from their sales they were giving the reading public what it wanted. Susan Warner's moralistic *The Wide, Wide World* went through fourteen editions in two years, and Maria Cummins's *The Lamplighter* sold more than 70,000 in twelve months, but it was Harriet Beecher Stowe who set the record with 300,000 copies of *Uncle Tom's Cabin* in one year. By 1861 this one work had converted thousands to the anti-slavery cause, aroused the indignation of infuriated Southerners, and won the author an international reputation as it was immediately translated into ten languages. Caroline Lee Hentz, born in Massachusetts but resident in the South, "answered" *Uncle Tom's Cabin* with *The Planter's Southern Bride*, the story of a slave-holder who married an abolitionist and converted her and her family to his views on slavery. Before the publication of this book, Eliza Nevitte Southworth's anti-slavery novel *Retribution* had been so well received that she left the teaching profession for a literary career and soon became one of the South's most prolific writers. Augusta Jane Evans, the best-known Southern-born woman author, first attracted national recognition with her second novel, *Beulah*, which sold over 20,000 copies in one year. Not a great work by any standard, its major importance lay in its rather shocking unorthodox theme. Its characters debated the questions of faith versus reason, but since religious fundamentalism emerged victorious the author was considered radical only by those who felt that a Southern lady should refrain from discussing the subject.

An impressive number of books, tracts, and articles on controversial issues were being written by women, many of whom were editors of or regular contributors to reform journals. Abolitionists were among the first to use the pen, and in the thirties the South Carolina expatriate Angelina Grimké made herself forever *persona non grata* in her native Charleston with the publication of *An Appeal to the Christian Women of the South*. She urged Southern women, many of whom she knew opposed slavery, to speak out, and despite her failure to reach the audience to which she spoke, hers is one of the significant abolitionist writings. In the same decade Catherine Beecher published *An Essay on Slavery and Abolition with Reference to the Duty of American*

Women, challenging her sex to eradicate the institution, and Angelina Grimké's sister Sarah focused attention on the inferior status of both woman and the Negro in *The Equality of the Sexes and the Condition of Women*. The two groups were being brought together in a dual crusade, often behind the same leaders, which partially, but only partially, explains why Southern slaveholders were hostile to the woman's rights movement.

Lydia Maria Child assisted her husband in editing the *National Anti-Slavery Standard*, and once when William Lloyd Garrison was out of the country she edited the *Liberator*. Jane Grey Swisshelm was probably the most famous abolitionist editor of her sex, but if not the most famous she was certainly the most feared. The columns of her *Pittsburg Saturday Visiter* [*sic*] bristled with sarcastic, belligerent attacks on slavery, other "evils," and specific individuals. Both friend and foe squirmed uneasily, wondering if they would be next, and the male editor was so unnerved that, as Mrs. Swisshelm said, he "sprang to his feet and clutched his pantaloons" on hearing that a woman had invaded his field. Mrs. Swisshelm became an effective weapon for blackmail when one individual threatened to expose another by giving the outspoken lady a story. During the McClintock-Davis affair Elizabeth Stanton indicated that she was considering just such a move, and it was a distraught Lucretia Mott who hopefully asked, "You aren't serious about giving the story to Jane Swisshelm, are you?"[8]

The feminist crusade was slowly gaining momentum despite the opposition of most men and indifference of most women. Its advocates reasoned that they must establish their own journals since most male editors attacked the cause and were unwilling to give them space for rebuttals. Nor could they expect support from one of the foremost women editors in the country, Sarah Hale of *Godey's Lady's Book*, for while she was intensely interested in greater economic and educational opportunities for her sex, she did nothing to advance the woman's rights cause. Her brand of crusading was best illustrated in her battle to rid the vocabulary of the term "female" as applied to women. Then, ac-

---

[8] Jane Grey Swisshelm: *Half a Century* (Chicago, 1880), p. 113; Lucretia Mott to Elizabeth Cady Stanton, Nov. 27, 1849, Garrison Family Papers.

cording to Mrs. Hale, women would be elevated above animals. She was not permitted to forget that most of the subscribers to *Godey's* were dignified, decorous, conservative women from all parts of the country and to retain them she must weigh carefully her words and published ideas. Paulina Wright Davis, an ardent feminist recognizing the need for a journal, personally financed and edited the *Una*, a monthly publication devoted entirely to reports of woman's rights conventions and activities and to essays and serials stressing the movement, but it was in existence for only three years. The *Woman's Advocate*, financed and printed by women and edited by Anna McDowell, was the official organ of woman's rights during the prewar period.

It was the practice of women to found a journal dedicated to a single cause, and the typical lady crusader would soon turn to a host of reforms, all advocated in the publication. The *Lily*, edited for a time by Amelia Bloomer, was begun as a temperance paper and within a matter of months was championing both dress reform and woman's rights. The *Sibyl*, edited by "Doctress" (the term she used) Lydia Sayer, was the official organ of the Dress Reform League, but it also advocated woman's rights, temperance, and the anti-tobacco crusades. Reflected in their journals and activities was the tendency of women to become professional reformers, seldom restricting themselves to a single cause. Because a few affiliated with many groups the reforming women appear more numerous than they actually were.

In addition to *Godey's Lady's Book* scores of girls' and women's magazines were born and most succumbed in the antebellum period. Ann S. Stephens, one of the more prominent editors, was associated with *Peterson's Ladies National Magazine, Frank Leslie's Gazette of Fashion, Ladies Companion* and *Graham Magazine,* and she wrote the first of the Beadle "dime novels," *Malaeska,* published in 1860. Among the Southern women editors were Eleanor Spann (*Texian Monthly Magazine*) and Caroline Howard Gilman, who edited the children's publication *The Rosebud.* Southern women also contributed to regional publications, including the *Southern Literary Messenger* and *DeBow's Review,* but if they advocated anything in particular it was educational or humanitarian, and more often they published romantic stories, emotional poetry, or domestic essays.

For several years the intellectual Margaret Fuller edited the *Dial,* a transcendentalist publication, and she later had the distinction of being the first woman on the editorial staff of the New York *Tribune.* An able editor and brilliant conversationalist, this controversial lady repeatedly expounded woman's superiority, and in her *Women in the Nineteenth Century* she maintained that if given the same opportunities as men, women would prove her theory. Prior to the war Sarah Hale published the first volume of *Woman's Record, or Sketches of Distinguished Women,* which differed in scope, tone, and purpose from Margaret Fuller's work in that it consisted of biographical sketches of great women. When completed after the war, it stood as one of woman's major nineteenth-century literary undertakings.

Lydia Maria Child stands out because of her diverse interests, most of which were reflected in her writings. In addition to novels and poetry, Mrs. Child published a stirring "Appeal in Favor of that Class of Americans Called Africans," *The History on the Conditions of Women in Various Ages* in two volumes, and several cookbooks and home guides, among which *The Frugal Housewife* went through forty editions. She edited a children's periodical, *Juvenile Miscellany,* and wrote of social problems in New York City, including prostitution. Her desire to assist John Brown during his imprisonment provoked a bitter correspondence with Governor Henry Wise, Mrs. M. J. G. Mason, and other Virginians. Mrs. Mason vehemently attacked Mrs. Child for her interest in Brown and abolition, the letters being first published in Greeley's New York *Tribune* and later in pamphlet form for use as propaganda.

The impatient advocates of woman's rights were dissatisfied with trying to approach the public through the press, not only because it was slow but because millions could never be reached in this way. The more daring decided they must air their complaints from the rostrum, knowing full well that society frowned on their speaking to mixed audiences and that if they persisted in defying public opinion they might be greeted with shouts of protest and flying objects. But none more often met with hostile reception than Susan Anthony, who seemed determined to be the first of her sex to address any and all groups. Throughout the fifties she was shouted down in teachers' and temperance meetings, and while conducting a series of anti-slavery meetings in New York in 1861 she was mobbed, hissed, and pelted with rotten eggs. According to one of her friends, a man "who got tired of Susan's address" rose and shouted for her to sit down "as there were several interesting speakers who might like to be heard."[9] And when she spoke in Albany, the mayor sat beside her with a pistol on his lap and police patrolled the hall. Although women had been speaking before mixed audiences since the days of Frances Wright in the twenties, they had by no means won public approbation in 1861.

Nearly all the outspoken feminists had been schooled in the abolition movement, and for this reason they were suspect in the South, where society was conservative, patriarchal, and insistent that ladies live in a kind of earthly limbo. Yet their lives were not far different from those of upper-class women elsewhere, for modesty and decorum were the order of the day. The difference lay in the South's absolute refusal to tolerate critics of its peculiar institution, and it was assumed that almost any idea supported by an abolitionist was necessarily evil. When Southern women voiced their disapproval of slavery they usually did so only in their diaries, many of which are as yet in manuscript form. They could offer no solution for the problem, although they were virtually unanimous in believing it would work a hardship on Negroes and whites alike if all slaves were immediately freed without preparation for liberation. But many Northern women who had never set foot in the South were of the same opinion, as was Fredrika Bremer who prayed for gradual emancipation. Miss Bremer was pained when she heard from Southerners that mistresses were often more cruel to slaves than masters, and that this was especially the case when the slave was a young mother of mulatto children, for the white woman's cruelty was usually a manifestation of her opposition to this disagreeable aspect of slavery.

Gertrude Clanton Thomas, daughter and wife of Georgia planters and a graduate of Wesleyan Female College in Macon, was an atypical Southern woman who frankly admitted that she could express her views nowhere but in her diary. She opposed slavery and read abolitionist writings, including *Uncle Tom's*

[9] Martha Wright to Ellen Wright, Feb. 10, 1861, Garrison Family Papers.

Cabin and *Caste*, but her chief grievance against the system was the immoral relations between white men and Negro women. She realized that it was "thought best for women to ignore" this situation, but she worried constantly about "the standard of morality in . . . Southern homes" and boldly proclaimed, "Southern women are all at heart abolitionists." Mrs. Thomas often heard the Negro Sam Drayton preach. She considered him "an intellectual . . . having a fine command of the language . . . a man of extraordinary talent," and of his wife she said, "She is one of the most ladylike persons I have ever seen." Mrs. Thomas also read and thought about the woman's rights movement and in 1856 concluded, "I am a Woman's Rights Woman in the northern sense of the term." She avidly read accounts of meetings, invariably working herself up "to quite a pitch of enthusiasm," and she believed in "the general depravity of men" with one *"noble exception"*— her husband.[1]

It was without Southern support, however, that Northern women launched their anti-slavery and woman's rights crusades, many more participating in the former than in the latter. Under Maria Weston Chapman's leadership the Boston Female Anti-Slavery Society was founded in the thirties, and similar organizations soon sprang into being throughout the North and West. Lucretia Mott, Abby Kelley Foster, the Grimké sisters, Lydia Maria Child, Martha Wright, and Laura Haviland were only a few of the prominent leaders. Other important crusaders were Negroes, among them Sojourner Truth, Frances Watkins Harper, Sarah Remond, and Harriet Tubman. When John Quincy Adams presented to Congress an abolition petition signed by 148 Massachusetts women, Mary Livermore was an eyewitness to Viriginians' reaction to women petitioners. "The men raved incoherently . . . pounded the table with their fists . . . cursed Massachusetts," she reported, and they "wished that the women of the state . . . might swing . . . from a lamp-post." The mistress, usually indifferent to political affairs, was irritated that Northern women presumed to interfere with slavery in Virginia, and she made it quite clear that she did not approve of women mixing in politics.[2] This was certainly a more typical reaction for a Southern woman than Mrs. Thomas's, but a great many Northern

[1] Ella Gertrude Clanton Thomas Diary, MS.
[2] Livermore: *The Story of My Life*, pp. 273, 275.

women concurred that the sex had no business petitioning Congress or any other legislative body.

After 1840, when the World Anti-Slavery Convention in London refused to seat women delegates, including Lucretia Mott and Elizabeth Stanton, a few men, among them William Lloyd Garrison, joined them in launching a woman's rights movement. The crusade dates from the Seneca Falls Conference in 1848, but not until two years later was there a national organization. From 1850 until the outbreak of the war, annual meetings were held except in 1857, and state, local, and regional groups came into being during the decade. In this period stress was placed primarily on obtaining state laws guaranteeing women's right to control their property and wages, to be legal guardians of their children, and to be paid salaries commensurate with their labors, while a few women advocated more liberal divorce laws so that they could rid themselves of alcoholic, insane, criminal, or brutal husbands. States did enact laws giving married women control of their property, the first being Mississippi in 1839, but women had very little to do with this legislation. Among exceptions, however, was Mary Upton Ferris who submitted annual petitions for six years to the Massachusetts legislature before a property law was passed in 1854. By 1861 most states had either granted property rights to women or were following the community property principle; and some states had given women a voice in educational matters, custody rights and control of their children, the right to sue and be sued, and control over their earnings.

Little was done to obtain equal pay for women, although the matter was often discussed, but when the leaders became more interested in obtaining the franchise they lost the support of wage earners who were more concerned about a decent standard of living than the ballot. Newspapers called public attention to the effects of wage discrimination, frequently citing cases of women masquerading as men and when arrested stating that they had disguised themselves in order to get men's wages. They were said to be usually "calm, stout, good-natured, rather illiterate damsels . . . whose only excuse is that they can't get along" financially on women's pay.[3]

The press frequently denounced and ridiculed the "strong-

[3] *Frank Leslie's Illustrated Newspaper*, Nov. 24, 1860.

minded" women, while reserving its bitterest satire for advocates of dress reform. This, however, was long overdue. Women's hoopskirts monopolized entire sidewalks, their trains were dragged through dust and mud, and they were so tightly corseted that fainting was a common occurrence. They needed simpler and more comfortable clothing; but the Bloomer costume was, in the eyes of most people, a ridiculous or indecent answer to the problem. The baggy trousers and shortened, full-cut overdress were unbecoming to most women, and those appearing in this garb, including the plump Elizabeth Stanton, were jeered off the streets. Yet one thing can be said for the style: it brought more humor to the nation than any other feminist cause. Although most Southerners were shocked, a few girls were intrigued by Bloomers, and one wrote her fiancé in Boston that she thought them "very pretty." An editor's views were more in keeping with the South's reactions, however. He was pleased to note that the style "did not thrive" in the region and was proud that Southern "ladies blush that their sisters *anywhere* descend to such things."[4]

Temperance was one antebellum reform with nationwide appeal. The Sons of Temperance, organized in the forties in the North, soon had chapters in the South. But when Northern women banded together in the Daughters of Temperance, Southern women generally remained aloof although many endorsed the idea. Everything moved along peacefully until the "Sons" denied Susan Anthony the privilege of speaking before a New York state convention, whereupon she and her followers stalked from the hall and formed the Woman's State Temperance Society. In 1853 delegates from various temperance groups met in New York City to formulate plans for a World Christian Temperance Convention to be held the following fall, but when Miss Anthony was refused a seat on the council her champions created such a disturbance that the meeting was adjourned. When the international group met, Antoinette Brown started to speak and pandemonium again broke loose, and this session was also adjourned. The audience was composed primarily of ministers,

[4] Ellen Thompson to Benjamin Hedrick, Sept. 1, 1861; Benjamin Hedrick to Ellen Thompson, Aug. 6, 1861, Benjamin S. Hedrick Papers; *Southern Literary Messenger*, XX (1854), 300.

among them John Hartwell Cocke, a Virginia liberal on most issues but an opponent of woman's rights. Writing William H. McGuffey about the riotous session, he expressed pleasure at the men's "rebuke to this most impudent clique of unsexed females," and McGuffey replied, "I most heartily rejoice with you in the defeat of the shameless Amazons. . . . I trust and believe that it will be final."[5] McGuffey and others were destined for disappointment; it was only beginning.

The growing interest in unfortunates—the insane, blind, deaf and dumb—was one movement in which "quiet" ladies might participate without risking public disapprobation. This crusade often began in the churches, and women's support of religious institutions and programs was readily acknowledged as one of her proper spheres. The movement also offered no threat to any group's economy or way of life, and since women were endowed with an abnormal amount of compassion, it was natural that they would be stirred by the afflictions of others. Dorothea Dix stands out as a dedicated humanitarian who, for more than twenty years before the war, urged the establishment of mental institutions. She spoke before state legislatures and helped to found state-supported asylums in all sections, yet she emerged from her battles a respected lady. In the fifties Miss Dix visited Florence Nightingale, toured European hospitals in the Crimea and elsewhere, and returned to the United States probably the best prepared woman in the country for the duties soon to be thrust upon her. Miss Bremer said, "The activity and influence of this lady is one of the most beautiful traits of female citizenship in the New World."[6]

During the thirty years prior to the Civil War American women could claim specific economic, social, and intellectual gains. Yet even more important was the development of their talents for organization, cooperation, leadership, and self-expression. It was a time of beginnings and not fulfillment, a time when most women realized and accepted the fact that they lived in a man's world, a time when a few dedicated but belligerent visionaries were frustrated in their attempt to remake the social order

[5] Clement Eaton: *The Growth of Southern Civilization* (New York, 1961), p. 322.
[6] Bremer: *The Homes of America*, I, 443.

"overnight." Women shared their men's principles and prejudices and most refused to align themselves with causes which the male disapproved. The majority of Northern and Western women and virtually all in the South viewed feminist crusaders with indifference, curiosity, derision, disgust, or apathy, and it was this lack of enthusiasm on the part of their own sex rather than male hostility that most chilled the leaders of woman's rights. They were, however, reluctant to admit this publicly, preferring to blame men for all their woes. Most women simply lacked the inclination and time to join female organizations, attend conventions, listen to harangues on the social injustices, or fight for vague principles.

If the majority of American women were to be awakened they must be given an incentive and they must gain greater self-confidence. This might be accomplished by long, slow indoctrination, or more rapidly by creating a situation which would inspire women by making them feel needed, not by other women but by their men and their nation. If a movement should develop which would arouse their emotions, permit them to work with and not against their men, remove them mentally and physically from their narrow domestic world, and challenge them to perform great new tasks and assume new responsibilities, this movement might do wonders. Just such a "movement" did get under way in 1861, giving all women an opportunity to prove themselves by developing theretofore latent talents.

2

"A Woman's War"

GEORGE AUGUSTUS SALA, a British journalist who observed the American people at war, concluded that there was probably no conflict in history which was as much "a woman's war" as that of 1861–65. He found the women in both camps to be "the bitterest, most vengeful of politicians," "unanimous" in their "exasperation and implacability."[1] Although conditioned in contrasting environments and schooled in opposing philosophies, women stepped forward as defenders of their respective causes. Emotions, energies, and talents that even they did not realize they possessed were unleashed. Here was a crusade in which they were needed and one in which they enthusiastically participated.

For months before the outbreak of hostilities women were watching the gathering storm clouds. Although not privileged to vote in the election of 1860, they were interested in the candidates and issues and disturbed by the ominous threats emanating from the South. Most Northern women were more confused than excited, and to many this election seemed far less colorful than

[1] George Augustus Sala: *My Diary in America in the Midst of the War* (London, 1865), I, 359.

the one in '56 when Jessie Benton Frémont had dominated the scene. None of the candidates in 1860 offered so attractive, effervescent a wife to the public. Things were different in the South where the "fire-eaters" harangued on the dire consequences of electing a "Black Republican" and threatened secession should Abraham Lincoln become President. Never before had Southern ladies been as interested in any campaign or entered as zealously into the fight, for it had been considered "extremely unladylike to meddle in politics." But in 1860 Southern women were avidly reading the newspapers and leaving their homes "to attend a speech or procession," and by November they were convinced that Lincoln's election would mean the complete destruction of their way of life.[2]

When the outcome became known, women everywhere asked, "What now?" Very few in either section had taken seriously the secession threats, for surely the differences would be reconciled as so often in the past. If they were not, many Northern women thought it would do no great damage if the South broke away, and some said but probably few believed that it would be good riddance. Southern women expressed mixed emotions, some urging withdrawal without thinking of the possible repercussions, yet as the states seceded one by one, many became apprehensive. Mary Boykin Chesnut was shocked by her husband's resignation from the Senate, saying that had she been in Washington she would have tried, probably without success, to dissuade him, but now that he had resigned, she was "ready and willing" to go along despite her "nervous dread and horror."[3] Wives of other officials mentioned similar sensations, but most tried to conceal their misgivings with an outward display of self-confidence and arrogance. These were proud women, and not all who haughtily flounced out of Washington with their heads held high were as sure of the future as they appeared to be.

It was much easier for women to abandon the Federal capital for the Confederate if their families resided in the South, but for those who would be separated from loved ones by battle lines

[2] Kate Cumming: *Gleanings From the Southland* (Birmingham, Ala., 1895), p. 19.

[3] Mary Boykin Chesnut: *A Diary From Dixie,* ed. Ben Ames Williams (Boston, 1950), p. 3.

the decision was heart-rending. Many like Margaret Sumner Mc-
Lean spent anguished months between the secession of South
Carolina and the firing on Fort Sumter, waiting for their husbands to make a decision. Captain Eugene McLean was one of
the many Southerners serving in the United States Army; his wife
was the daughter of General Edwin Vose Sumner of Massachusetts and she had two brothers in the Federal Army. Confiding
her anguish to her diary, Mrs. McLean never doubted that her
place would be with her husband, and when the Captain resigned his commission she obediently left Washington "to follow
the stream without asking whither it cometh or whither it goeth."
She was very sure, however, that the country had become one
giant "insane asylum for the exclusive benefit of two classes of
monomaniacs,—abolitionists and secessionists," and if she could
have her way, she would place her "platform on Mason and
Dixon's line."[4]

Whatever objectivity women in the Deep South might have
possessed in the fall of 1860 they lost that winter as their states
withdrew. While it must not be assumed that all believed secession the answer, the majority were caught up in a movement
which gained momentum in a carnival-like atmosphere created
by emotions, not reason. For the first time they could participate
in riotous celebrations, express their opinions on political matters, and be noisy spectators without losing their position as
"ladies." They were to be found in the galleries of secession conventions, in the throngs observing torchlight parades, and waving their handkerchiefs when it was announced that another
state had left the Union. Amid this wild jubilation those who dis-
agreed were shouted down, and before the first shot was fired
some of these opponents had already accepted the fact that it
was to their best interest to say nothing. In this period the people
were being assured that secession did not mean war, but should
the North instigate one, it would be brief and the South the
victor. This most women believed.

Northern women were disgusted, angered, and dazed as they
read of these proceedings, and many made known their impa-
tience with President Buchanan. A Kentuckian who had never

[4] Mrs. Eugene McLean: "When the States Seceded," *Harper's Monthly
Magazine,* CXXVIII (1914), 282–88.

met Robert J. Breckinridge wrote this staunch Unionist, criticizing the lame-duck administration and pleading with him to do what he could to keep Kentucky in the Union. She reported that the very thought of its being swept into the Confederacy sent "terror through the community" in which she lived, and it was these fears that "impelled" her to write a stranger. A Minnesotan raised a question others were asking, "Are these Free States going to sit down quietly and let those Southern lunatics have their own way?"[5] If Northern women had earlier been phlegmatic about verbal threats of disunion, secession aroused them from their lethargy.

The die was cast and the air cleared with the firing on Fort Sumter and Lincoln's call for troops. The country was now at war. If the secession of seven states and the birth of the Confederacy had served to awaken Northern women, the firing on their flag set them in motion as they joined in patriotic demonstrations, wore red, white, and blue cockades, and flew the Stars and Stripes from their windows. Southern women were overconfident and exuberant, and now that there was a war to be fought many anti-secessionists joined Confederate ranks while Unionists hastened to leave the Confederacy for a more favorable climate or kept their thoughts to themselves. Southern women welcomed 2,000,000 of their sisters when North Carolina, Virginia, Tennessee, and Arkansas cast lots with the Confederacy, bringing their number to approximately 4,400,000, less than one-half as many as could be rallied in the North and West. But in none of these areas were all loyal or active. The outbreak of hostilities shocked a great many women, but none more than those living in Southern states which had earlier held conventions and voted to remain in the Union. Mrs. William C. Rives of Virginia, whose husband had served in the Senate and as minister to France, thought the state would "stand still, being conservative, rather lazy, and more disposed to keep old fashions than set new ones," but when proved wrong she was separated from two of her children and their families in the North. The "impassable gulf" left her a "childless mother with living children," and like others in

[5] ——— to Robert J. Breckinridge, Jan. 18, 1861, Breckinridge Family Papers; Ann Loomis North to George S. and Mary Loomis, Jan. 28, 1861, John Wesley North Papers.

similar circumstances she would have preferred to remain in the Union.[6]

One of the surest indications that Southern women did not expect secession to lead to war was their failure to withdraw their daughters from Northern schools before the firing started. They then moved quickly. Julia Tutwiler, later an Alabama reformer, was hastily withdrawn from Mme. Maroteau's school in Philadelphia, and Mrs. Louis Trezevant Wigfall, whose husband had resigned his Senate seat to take a similar position in the Confederate Congress, recalled her two teen-aged daughters from Boston. Virginia Moon of Memphis got herself expelled from an Ohio school after shooting down the United States flag as it floated above the campus. And a young Southerner enrolled in Miss Sedgwick's school in Massachusetts who was compelled to remain for several weeks after the outbreak of war spent the time crying. "The little goose," wrote one of her classmates, "why don't she toddle home to her beloved South . . . she has no business here. It wouldn't be so hard on her if she wasn't such a dunce—but she says she hates the North, while she is under its protection."[7]

Among those leaving the South were hundreds of Northern teachers who departed through choice or under pressure, while other women were sent to their families in the North, often at their husbands' insistence. Frequently, however, entire families, including the men, moved out of the region. Southerners also came home, and the experience of Fannie Beers, later a Confederate nurse, is typical of thousands caught in enemy lines. She was visiting her mother in New York State and when war started her friends of many years' standing suddenly stopped calling on or receiving her. Realizing that this complicated her mother's life and wishing to be with her husband, who had enlisted in the Confederate Army, she left home. Sometimes one who kept quiet was permitted to remain undisturbed, but if she expounded un-

---

[6] Mrs. William C. Rives to Judith Walker Rives, n.d., Rives Papers, Alderman Library, University of Virginia.

[7] Anne Gary Pannell and Dorothea E. Wyatt: *Julia S. Tutwiler and Social Progress in Alabama* (Tuscaloosa, 1961), p. 12; Francis Butler Simkins and James Welch Patton: *The Women of the Confederacy* (Richmond, 1936), p. 12; Ellen Wright to Martha Wright, May 27, 1861, Garrison Family Papers.

popular ideas she was sure to be harassed. A woman aroused her New Orleans neighbors when she flew the United States flag from her window during the celebration of Louisiana's secession.[8] In this "woman's war" many a "battle" was fought over the teacups and backyard fences.

When war came women everywhere asked the same question: what can we do? Their first task was to encourage men to enlist, and while the older ones were usually less enthusiastic than the younger, all had been led to believe that it would be a short war. In the beginning the Southern women approached the task with greater fervor than did those in the North, and Northern journalists, foreign observers, and others stressed the part played by Confederate women in getting their men into uniform. A Chicago paper explained the way in which this was done: they promised to favor them when they returned, "to watch over them on the field and in the camp," to reserve their charms "for those who go forth to battle" while denying them to men "who stay at home." Men who held back were "snubbed" into the army and both Northern and Southern journals reported girls volunteering when men were hesitant.[9] Sarah Emma Edmonds, the Federal nurse and spy, reported that Southern women were "the best recruiting officers," absolutely refusing "to tolerate, or admit to their society any young man who refuses to enlist." Catherine Cooper Hopley, an English subject teaching in the South, was appalled by the lighthearted manner in which southern women pressured their men into service.[1] Yet throughout the war some wives and mothers, their numbers increasing late in the conflict, believed the men were more needed by the families, and this was especially true among the poorer classes.

The younger women in the North also exercised the greatest pressure on men to enlist, but they did not as often make it a prerequisite to social acceptance. In the fall of 1861 the twenty-one-year-old Ellen Wright patriotically exclaimed, "I wouldn't look at a nonresistant," but in less than a year, after hearing that

[8] Frank Leslie: *Heroic Incidents, Personal Adventures and Anecdotes on the Civil War in America* (New York, 1862), pp. 74–75. Hereafter cited as *Heroic Incidents*.

[9] Chicago *Tribune*, Mar. 31, 1862; New York *Herald*, Apr. 7, 1862.

[1] Sarah Emma Edmonds: *Nurse and Spy in the Union Army: Comprising the Adventures and Experiences of a Woman in Hospitals, Camps, Battle-Fields* (Hartford, 1865), pp. 331–32; Catherine Cooper Hopley: *Life in the South From the Commencement of the War* (London, 1863), I, 283.

Philadelphia girls were ignoring men not in service, she confessed to feeling sorry for boys goaded into the army by women who could stay "at home amid luxuries." By 1863, Miss Wright had nothing to say about "nonresistants" in general, but she had quite a bit to say about one in particular, her fiancé William Lloyd Garrison II.[2]

The adoption of conscription, first in the Confederacy and later in the Union, lessened women's recruiting activities but officials sometimes called on them to use their influence in getting men to volunteer. Those with men in the service bitterly resented draft evasion and often hurled invectives at all males who stayed at home except the obviously infirm and superannuated. A dodger's wife was variously pitied, embarrassed, or maligned by her husband's critics.

Most women helped to provision the soldiers, and many worked countless hours without receiving any recognition other than that accorded the group, but the personal satisfaction they derived from assisting the cause was its own reward. Because neither the Union nor the Confederacy was ready for war, women were reminded in the very beginning that this was their war as well as the men's. They set to work immediately sewing, cooking, and knitting, but being overeager and lacking guidance they sometimes made blunders. Imagine the soldiers' reaction when a pair of elaborately embroidered velvet slippers arrived in camp or a shipment of mittens from Quaker ladies who had refused to knit them with a trigger finger. No less amusing was the arrival of trousers which "lapped the wrong way," making it necessary for the recipient to "stand on his head to button them."[3]

The havelock mania which swept the country at the beginning of the war was the most ridiculous blunder. This headgear was named for General Henry Havelock whose soldiers in India had adopted the covering to protect their head and neck from the sun. Although a few Confederates were known to wear havelocks, Federal troops were deluged with them as Northern women determined to protect their men from the "tropical" heat in the South. During the first month of the war one sewing circle

[2] Ellen Wright to Lucy McKim, Nov. 16, 1861; Ellen Wright to Annie McKim, Aug. 21, 1862, Garrison Family Papers.
[3] Eliza McHatton Ripley: *From Flag to Flag: A Woman's Adventures and Experiences in the South During the War, in Mexico, and in Cuba* (Boston, 1889), p. 14.

in New York presented to the 69th regiment more than 1200 havelocks, and even schoolgirls were entangled, the students in a Massachusetts academy having completed 138 before the end of June. An observer concluded that the luckiest man in the Union Army was the one with fewest women relatives and friends, for he would be less encumbered with havelocks. Few soldiers ever used them for the purpose intended, although they enjoyed devising new and unusual uses for this strange headgear.[4] Women soon learned from their mistakes, however, and many received a practical education the like of which they might never have enjoyed in time of peace.

Within two weeks after the outbreak of war there were more than 20,000 aid societies hard at work in the Union and Confederacy, but not all were able to continue throughout the conflict, and many in the South were compelled to disband because of invasion, civilian displacement, and scarcity of supplies. Early in the war these local societies supplied only men from the community or the state, and in the Confederacy this generally continued to be the situation, although there were exceptions, as when a North Carolinian conducted a one-woman campaign to raise supplies for a Texas regiment.[5] In the North many local groups were soon brought together under the supervision of the Sanitary Commission, which informed the women of what was needed and systematized their efforts. After the war Henry W. Bellows paid a glowing tribute to those on the home front who, he said, were responsible for "by far the largest part" of the $15,000,000 in supplies collected by the commission. Not only did women contribute food, clothing, and hospital necessities, and give freely of their time to fairs and benefits, but they were eminently successful in obtaining donations from businessmen. It was in their local societies, said Bellows, "that women . . . rendered their immense service to the national struggle."[6] The commission's drive for fresh fruits and vegetables to fight scurvy was successful primarily because farm women answered the appeal, many cultivat-

[4] New York *Herald,* May 21, 1861; Ellen Wright to Martha Wright, June 20, 1861, Garrison Family Papers; Septima Collis: *A Woman's War Record, 1861–1865* (New York, 1889), pp. 12–13.

[5] "To the Ladies of Chapel Hill," typescript, Cornelia Phillips Spencer Papers.

[6] "Letter of the Reverend Henry Bellows to Henry Dunant," *The American Association for the Relief of the Misery on Battlefields* (New York, 1866), *passim.*

ing a "Sanitary potato patch" or "onion patch" for the commission.

It was unfortunate that the Confederacy did not have a similar agency, but even had one been established early in the war it probably could not have functioned efficiently after widespread areas were overrun and transportation facilities destroyed. It is amazing that local groups were so successful; much that they did accomplish represented a real sacrifice on the part of individuals. That their efforts were not coordinated was not so much the fault of the women as of the state and Confederate officials who often refused to cooperate for the common good. Primary loyalty to the state rather than to the Confederacy was clear in the women's war work as in other aspects of the struggle.

From the very beginning of the war a few Northern women recognized the need for efficient organization, and in late April 1861, 3,000 New Yorkers attended a meeting in Cooper Union to discuss the question. Here the New York Central Association of Relief was formed with a 25-member board, twelve of whom were women. Dr. Elizabeth Blackwell, one of the instigators of the meeting, was elected to the board and Louisa Lee Schuyler was chosen president. Among other projects, the association was interested in training nurses.

Local aid societies were organized in much the same way in all areas. They met in private homes, churches, or public rooms where sewing machines, tables, and other essentials were collected. The fashionable Girard House in Philadelphia was converted, as one young lady said, into one "vast workshop," and another commented that "so many sewing machines are running . . . that it sounds like a factory."[7] Everywhere churches took an active part in these projects and women of a specific congregation often organized their own society. Although it is women's nature to prefer working with a group, many unable to attend regular meetings performed the same type of service in their homes. Men sometimes jested about the aid societies, convinced that the ladies met to gossip rather than work. Ezra Cornell, the financier, thought more would be accomplished if there was less talk at these affairs and promised to contribute fifty dollars to the aid society in Ithaca if twelve members could be found who

[7] Collis: *A Woman's War Record,* p. 12; Marianna Mott to Ellen Wright, May 20, 1861, Garrison Family Papers.

could sew all day without saying a word. Fifteen volunteered and all but one remained silent despite the attempts of hecklers to get them into conversation. Some men were of the opinion that these groups did more harm than good when the members fell out and spread idle rumors. A Confederate officer wrote his fiancée that she must not affiliate with the local soldiers' aid society, for he had never seen any woman's organization "where controversies did not arise." If she wished to dispense charity, let her do it in private.[8]

Had critics examined the productivity of these wartime societies they would have realized that the women did far more than talk. Typical of the Northern aid groups was that in Weldon, Pennsylvania, organized in 1862 with fifty charter members, some of whom did resign because of personal disagreements. It was efficiently organized with officers and committees, each assigned a special task such as cutting the cloth, sewing, or purchasing necessary materials. This society contributed clothing, bandages, and a variety of food to a miltary hospital, funds being raised through donations and benefits, which included a fair, musical program, and a lecture on "The Chemistry of Agriculture." In one year the Weldon Society dispensed $1,731.04 worth of supplies.[9] Of approximately the same size was the Society of Center Ridge, Alabama, which in one month of 1862 contributed "422 shirts, 551 pairs of drawers, 80 pairs of socks, 3 pairs of gloves, 6 boxes and a bale of hospital stores, 128 pounds of tapioca and $18 for hospital use." Later in the war similar societies were still making impressive contributions under adverse circumstances. While Charleston, South Carolina, was threatened with seizure near the end of the conflict, an aid society in that city sent soldiers a total of 519 shirts, 267 pairs of drawers, 189 pairs of socks, 179 pairs of pants, 23 pairs of shoes, 37 blankets and comforters, handkerchiefs and scarves.[1]

[8] *Frank Leslie's Illustrated Newspaper*, Feb. 20, 1864; Nathaniel Henry Rhodes Dawson to Elodie Todd, Nov. 12, 1861, Nathaniel Henry Rhodes Dawson Papers, Southern Historical Collection, University of North Carolina.
[9] *First Annual Report of the Ladies Aid Society of Weldon, 1862–63* (n.p., 1863), Henry E. Huntington Library.
[1] E. Merton Coulter: *The Confederate States of America, 1861–1865* (Baton Rouge, 1950), p. 417; Mrs. Thomas Taylor *et al.* (ed): *South Carolina Women in the Confederacy* (Columbia, S. C., 1903, 1907), II, 90.

Not all assistance came from groups, for individuals did much on their own. Wealthy women were known to outfit an entire company of soldiers and endow institutions for their care, but nobody did more proportionately than the poor women who deprived themselves for the men. Accounts are legion of farm women who traveled miles to aid society headquarters to get cloth from which they made clothing, or yarn from which they knit socks or caps. When these articles had been finished they returned them, collected another batch of material, and repeated the process many times. The busiest of women somehow found time to spin, weave, sew, and knit so that they might contribute. Many an impoverished woman shared her scant supply of food with passing troops or an individual soldier, perhaps not knowing where she could get more. Occasionally one of these selfless women would be mentioned in the press or in some personal record, but the majority remained anonymous.

Men in both armies should have been well supplied with knitted articles, for this was the handwork with which most women were occupied. Contemporary accounts abound with mention of the "everlasting sock" or "everlasting mitten" dangling from knitting needles. The experienced knitter could talk, read, and travel while plying the needles, and the necessary materials were less bulky to carry than most other handwork. Women were seen knitting furiously while riding in carriages, walking along the streets, attending social functions, and even conducting classes. A New England teacher, reported one of her pupils, be- came "so rabid on the sock subject" that she tried to knit as she taught, but she dropped stitches every time she looked at her book and had to pause to pick them up, much to the amusement of her class.[2]

Early in the war ladies were enthusiastically stitching flags and regimental emblems, always partial to those which would be carried to the front. This pursuit was confined to neither side but in the beginning the Confederacy had few flags or emblems on hand and during its existence four different flags were adopted, one of which was the battle flag designed after First Manassas. This situation kept the flag-makers busy, but the demand for

[2] Ellen Wright to Martha Wright, June 20, 1961, Garrison Family Papers.

emblems in both the Union and Confederacy continued throughout the struggle. A New York woman, hoping that there would be a Federal flag "on every inch of American soil," offered to make all needed provided material was furnished, for she described herself as a poor lady who was as "moved to patriotic deeds" as had been her grandmothers in '76. Constance, Hetty, and Jennie Cary were accredited with making the first Confederate battle flags, which they presented to Generals Earl Van Dorn, Joseph Eggleston Johnston, and Pierre Gustave Toussaint Beauregard respectively. It is known that Van Dorn carried his in every campaign, and after his murder in 1863 it was returned to Constance.[3] Whether women enjoyed the making of a flag as much as its presentation is doubtful, for long after the war they continued to tell of the formal ceremonies. Some of them received full press coverage, like that in New York City at which Mrs. John Jacob Astor presented the regimental emblem to Colonel Elmer Ellsworth and his New York Zouaves. Coming in the first month of the war, it was an exceptionally colorful affair to which the *Herald* devoted two columns in its April 30th issue.

Women devised ways to aid soldiers passing through the community, the Northerners operating "refreshment saloons" and the Southerners "wayside homes." Here the men might rest, obtain food and drink, and care if sick, all services donated by patriots in the area. Refreshments, sometimes prepared in a community kitchen but often in the home, were served either in suitable quarters, at the railroad station, or along the line of march. This could make heavy demands on the volunteer workers, for often they had little if any notice of the men's arrival and had to rush to prepare the food and drink. "Two rivals in good work" in Philadelphia, the Union Volunteer Refreshment Saloon and the Cooper Shop Refreshment Saloon, by early 1864 had dispensed more than $80,000 worth of supplies and served more than 600,000 meals.[4] South Carolinians opened the first wayside

[3] New York *Herald*, Apr. 19, 1861; Mrs. Burton Harrison: *Recollections Grave and Gay* (New York, 1911), pp. 61–65. See also Mrs. Burton Harrison's notebooks, Burton Harrison Papers.
[4] Linus Pierpont Brockett: *The Philanthropic Results of the War in America* (New York, 1864), pp. 29–31. See also James Moore: *History of the Cooper Shop Volunteer Refreshment Saloon* (Philadelphia, 1866), *passim*.

home in Columbia and similar institutions sprang into being elsewhere in the Confederacy, but in both North and South much of what was done came from individuals or small unorganized groups. Although there were women in both sections who felt no compulsion to feed the soldiers, many were generous to a fault.

In the wake of war came other demands on women's time and energy, including assistance to thousands of displaced whites and Negroes. Meanwhile indigent families of soldiers and their widows and orphans had to be sustained. Aid programs established by local and state governments, and in the North by the Federal Government, were inadequate and so enmeshed in red tape as to be painfully slow. Therefore these unfortunates had to be aided by the communities. Church women and other groups shared the responsibilities, but most of what they did was on a person-to-person basis. It is impossible to know how many, moved by compassion for poor families, kept them supplied with food and clothing or assisted them to get work, but private records indicate that the number quietly dispensing assistance was exceedingly large.

Confederate women were especially active in conducting fund-raising drives for the construction of gunboats and providing other material of war. "There was," said one woman, "a perfect *furore* throughout the Confederacy for 'Ladies Gun-boat Funds'," and during the winter of 1861–62, women were busily engaged in these projects in Charleston, Savannah, New Orleans, Mobile, Richmond, and other communities. The Georgians christened a floating battery in the summer of 1862 and the South Carolinians launched a gunboat the following fall, both events accompanied by colorful ceremonies.[5] Newspapers encouraged these drives, always listing persons making contributions, but a perusal of the lists indicates that a great many women preferred to remain anonymous and often only identified themselves as "a woman from Charleston," or another community. Yet as the war continued an increasing percentage became less reluctant to see their names in print.

Although men's moral and financial support was sought in most fund-raising fairs, bazaars, raffles, and entertainments, many were planned and managed entirely by women. They

[5] Hopley: *Life in the South*, I, 257.

sparked the movement, provided the initiative, gave freely of their time, energy, and talents, and contributed material possessions ranging from a priceless family heirloom to a jar of pickles. Demands of this kind were made throughout the war, for no sooner was one call answered than another was issued.

In 1863, when Mary Livermore, Jane Hoge, Eliza Porter, and other imaginative women outlined plans for the Northwestern Sanitary Commission Fair to be held in Chicago, the men on the board "barely tolerated" the idea and the city's business leaders were indifferent, but this did not deter the ladies. They carefully planned every step, traveled hundreds of miles to arouse the interest of Midwestern women, and dispatched "seventeen bushels" of letters and circulars advertising the affair and urging donations. Women contributed thousands of articles, some costly and elaborate, others inexpensive but expressive of true patriotism. A contraband whose nine children were slaves in Alabama sent a homespun sheet, and another who had just lost her son in battle gave a pair of socks originally intended for him. Six girls in southern Illinois "planted, hoed, and dug" five bushels of potatoes which they sent for the fair. The mountains of contributions enabled the event to continue for two weeks, netting $100,000 for the commission's war work and winning such recognition for its sponsors that women elsewhere were inspired to emulate them. Similar fairs were held in Northern cities from Boston to St. Louis, and while New York's was brilliant, none was more successful than the first held in Chicago. The Californians did not forget the commission, and so generous were the residents of the Far West that Henry Bellows later singled them out for tribute.[6]

Southern fairs were of necessity smaller but along with benefit performances, tableaux, raffles, and bazaars were amazingly successful. Less than a month before Sherman marched into Columbia, the local women held a bazaar which had taken weeks of planning. The state capitol was given over to the affair, and booths representing each of the Confederate states were laden with contributions from generous persons. "To go there," wrote

[6] Mary Ashton Livermore: *My Story of the War* (Hartford, 1889), pp. 414–15, 456–58; Mrs. Sarah Edwards Henshaw: *Our Branch and Its Tributaries: Being a History of the Work of the Northwestern Sanitary Commission and its Auxiliaries During the War of the Rebellion* (Chicago, 1868), pp. 210–19.

young Emma LeConte, "one would scarce believe it was war times, [for] the tables were loaded with fancy articles—brought through the blockade, or manufactured by the ladies." The prices were indicative of the inflation of the period, and Miss LeConte wondered that anyone but speculators could afford to pay from $500 to $2,000 for dolls or $75 for a small cake. The sponsors had planned for a bazaar of two weeks, but because the Federals were nearing the city it closed after two days.[7]

Women realized that the time might come when they would need to face the enemy, and some young women took lessons in the art of self-defense and banded together in drill teams. In April 1861 a woman's drill group was organized in New York City, and a member of the city's police force instructed the ladies in "sword and club exercises" so that they would "be ready to defend themselves in case of emergency." The public was assured that this was perfectly proper under the circumstances and that the "nice little uniform" worn by the students was both "chaste and proper." Elizabeth Cooper Vernon of Philadelphia did not have to take lessons in self-defense, for she had studied the manual of arms and been taught to shoot by her father. Early in the war she instructed a company of men in the basic elements as outlined in the manual. Women's drill groups were formed in the Confederacy, some in girls' schools, and so many suddenly became interested in learning to use firearms that Catherine Hopley watched with amazement as they took lessons and threatened "to kill the first 'Yankee' who came within sight of their homes." This sort of training, she said, was going on "throughout the country."[8] Both sections had ladies' home guard units, although most evaporated after the initial enthusiasm had died down.

As women fought the war from their own firesides they were challenged in innumerable ways. In addition to philanthropic work with their own soldiers and unfortunates, some extended aid to prisoners of war. They nursed in their homes and local hospitals, an impressive number took time to keep diaries, and most wrote regularly to their men in the service, some of the

[7] Earl Schenck Miers (ed.): *When the World Ended: The Diary of Emma LeConte* (New York, 1957), pp. 12–13, 15, 17.

[8] New York *Herald*, Apr. 29, 1861; Gertrude Biddle and Sarah Dickinson Lowrie (eds.): *Notable Women of Pennsylvania* (Philadelphia, 1942), pp. 185–86; Hopley: 285.

uneducated penning a greater number of letters during the war than in all previous years combined. Many performed exceptionally heavy domestic chores and labored at tasks normally assumed by men, while thousands were compelled for the first time to take remunerative jobs outside the home. Educated mothers, whose days were already filled to overflowing, sometimes undertook to teach their children when there was no one else to shoulder this responsibility. Women did not have to go to the front or serve in distant hospitals to support their cause; they encountered battles aplenty at home.

Many tributes were paid women in both camps even as the war was being fought, and most men were impressed with their accomplishments though at times baffled by their conduct. Late in the war the attorney James T. Brady told a New York audience that "nothing" during the conflict had interested him more than "the conduct of the women in the two sections . . ." Those in the Confederacy reminded him of Spartan women, while those in the North were more like the Romans, and he warned that "the greatest difficulty" the North would face "in putting down this rebellion" would be the "women of the South" who had been so intimately involved in the struggle.[9] If, as one journalist noted, the Confederate women's patriotism at first "burst forth in a beautiful flame" but failed to "hold out like the slow, deep fire" of Northern women, this can be explained by the fact that Southerners worked hard, sacrificed much, and were frustrated when invasion and economic circumstances prevented them from doing more for their men and their families.[1] If their enthusiasm turned to despondency it was because the overoptimistic, unrealistic outlook which nourished the flame in 1861 could not be sustained.

Although women in both camps shared many of the same problems and experiences, one very important distinction existed. This "woman's war" was being fought by Southerners on their own doorsteps and the women had to battle the enemy as best they could. Northern soldiers and other observers frequently commented on their vehemence, vindictiveness, and unladylike

[9] New York *Herald*, February 19, 1865.
[1] John Townsend Trowbridge: *The South: A Tour of Its Battle-Fields and Ruined Cities* (Hartford, 1866), p. 189.

behavior. The Northern press assigned them unflattering epi-thets, including "screaming furies," "depraved females," "brutal secessionists," and "venomous she-creatures." Northern women who came South were shocked at their conduct. A Sanitary Commission worker told of those in Memphis who pushed the Northerners against the wall and off the sidewalks, butted them in the stomach, flounced from the room when they entered, or "held their handkerchiefs to their nostrils" when one approached. And the friendly George Sala, commenting on their rudeness to Federal soldiers, was convinced that many of the most diabolical acts of these men resulted from the women's influence. Sala went so far as to attribute General Benjamin Butler's retaliations in New Orleans to his wounded pride, for until he encountered these spitfires he had considered himself a "ladies' man."[2]

A great many Southern women admitted fighting back, using insults and indignities. One of the wartime cartoons shows two secessionists in Federal-held territory who, lacking other enter-tainment, planned to "go out spitting" that evening. Mothers often taught their children to hate the enemy, one threatening to buy her little daughter no more dolls if she ever let a "Yankee" kiss her. This same woman's letters are filled with deep-seated hatred for the Federals, and she once wrote her husband, "God forgive me if I hate too much." A Confederate nurse, who was more tolerant than most, wrote her sister, "The feeling here [Richmond] against the Yankees exceeds anything I could imagine, particularly among good Christians."[3] These "battles" consumed energy that might have been expended on more worthwhile pursuits, but even more damaging were the scars they left. Yet the conduct of these Southerners—and not all were included in this group—was similar to that of women in other wars who have been compelled to endure an enemy invasion.

Examples of the Southern women's zeal and determination were used by Northern journalists to arouse their women to

[2] New York *Herald*, July 31, 1862; *Frank Leslie's Illustrated Newspaper*, Sept. 7, 1861, June 21, 1862; Livermore: *My Story of the War*, pp. 290–91; Sala: *My Diary in America*, I, 351–52.

[3] Issa Desha Breckinridge to Mary C. Desha, Aug. 7, 1864; Issa Breck-inridge to William Campbell Preston Breckinridge, Feb. 6, 1865, Breckin-ridge Family Papers; Phoebe Yates Pember to Eugenia Phillips, Sept. 13, 1863, Philip Phillips Family Papers.

greater activity. The press often urged them to emulate their Southern sisters, who supposedly showed far greater devotion and sacrifice. Naturally Northern women were infuriated by these comparisons, and one wrote a lengthy pamphlet refuting such allegations. Northern women, she said, were "tender and true," while Southerners were "bright and fierce and fickle"; and as for Northerners' lacking "passion," they simply did not see "any occasion for it" but were always ready to do their duty. The writer found it difficult to make this a personal war against her Southern friends, yet she staunchly supported the Union cause. Although she recognized that Southern women had made far greater sacrifices than Northerners, this was the price they had to pay for "starting the rebellion."[4] Whether intentionally or unintentionally, the women did make this their war.

[4] "A Few Words in Behalf of the Loyal Women in the United States," *Tract of the Loyal Publication Society* (New York, 1863), *passim.*

3

All Our Women Are
Florence Nightingales

B Y 1861 thousands of American women were familiar with the outstanding achievements of Florence Nightingale, and many hoped that if the nation were ever plunged into war they might follow in the footsteps of this pioneer army nurse. They did not realize how soon the opportunity would present itself, yet when war came hundreds immediately offered their services to the governments. The press soon dubbed them the "Florence Nightingales" of the Union or the Confederacy, and one editor, impressed by the number rushing into hospitals, proclaimed, "All our women are Florence Nightingales."[1] This unexpected development was significant not only because of the numbers involved but also because it represented a radical departure from American tradition.

No one denied that most women had an aptitude for nursing, that many had gained experience from tending their families and friends, and that necessity had required those in rural areas to be amateur pharmacists, yet public opinion doubted the pro-

---

[1] New York *Herald*, Apr. 5, 1864.

priety of their nursing in army hospitals. Refined, modest ladies, said the critics, had no business caring for strange men and certainly not rough, crude soldiers from all walks of life. They would be exposing themselves to embarrassing situations, and the mere thought of what could happen was appalling. While impropriety was the most compelling argument, opponents also stressed that the work was too demanding and exhausting and its pressures too great for delicate women to undertake. The nurses acknowledged that hospital duties were grueling but refused to concede that there was anything improper about the work. They argued that if some were of questionable character and others inefficient, the majority fell in neither category. By 1865 nurses had done so much for their respective causes that they had won over some, but not all, of their earlier opponents. Yet this victory had not been easily attained.

Why, if threatened with public disapprobation, did women want to be nurses? The overwhelming majority were motivated by patriotism, compassion, and the realization that they were needed, but there were other reasons. Some were looking for excitement and a short cut to fame. Others wanted to be near their loved ones in the service, and some who followed their men to camp turned to nursing after seeing the need. A great many single women were dissatisfied with seemingly useless, parasitic lives spent in someone else's home, and the war gave them an opportunity to become independent, useful persons. Widows often found nursing appealing, for as Emily Elizabeth Parsons suggested, each hoped "that fifty men . . . [would] console her for one." Also on Miss Parsons' staff were women whose marriages had failed, and one admitted that when her husband left her for another woman she turned to serving others, hoping it would make her forget her heartbreak. Some nursed because they needed the money, one confessing that "the choice of such a life would naturally be an absurdity. . . . I had no means and it was a necessity."[2] A few women, among them Dorothea Dix, were called to a specific position, and others, including Clara Barton, had reached a crossroads in their lives and were search-

[2] Emily Elizabeth Parsons: *Memoir of Emily Elizabeth Parsons* (Boston, 1881), pp. 88, 119; Phoebe Yates Pember to Eugenia Phillips, Sept. 13, 1863, Philip Phillips Family Papers.

ing for a new challenge. But whatever their reasons, only the most dedicated nurses could withstand the physical, mental, and social pressures of the work for an appreciable length of time.

As women came forward the press praised their patriotism, zeal, and selflessness. Within a few days after the firing on Fort Sumter a New York newspaper reported that scores of women had already volunteered as nurses, one then trying to rent her house so as to be free for hospital duty.[3] Southern women were slower to enlist but one of the first, Catherine Gibbon of North Carolina, had entered on her duties by summer. Many eager young women in both sections were restrained from volunteering by their parents, and one in Auburn, New York, was told that she could nurse only if the elderly family physician enrolled as a surgeon and agreed to take and keep her with him, an arrangement never consummated. The girl indignantly wrote a friend that if she was ever to be a nurse it would have to be in an "Old Maid's Hospital."[4] Southern girls usually encountered even greater opposition, for prejudice against the nursing of soldiers by young unmarried women was especially deep-seated in the South. A South Carolinian confided to her diary, "I want to go and . . . put forth my energies in doing for the sick and wounded," but because she was only twenty-two and unmarried she was not permitted to make a life for herself.[5] When Julia Tutwiler's father withheld his permission, she addressed a poetic appeal to him:

> Shall I be a baseborn coward
> Harder hearted than the foe?
> See, my country, Duty calls me:
> Dearest Father, let me go![6]

Much to her disappointment, he was unmoved by the plea.

Julia Tutwiler's friend and neighbor, Kate Cumming, encountered opposition from her brother-in-law, who said that no "refined lady" would consider nursing soldiers. This, thought Miss Cumming, was a strange argument from a man whose mother

[3] New York *Herald*, Apr. 19, 22, 30, 1861.
[4] Ellen Wright to Lucy McKim, Sept. 2, 12, 1862, Garrison Family Papers.
[5] Grace B. Elmore Diary, MS.
[6] Anne Gary Pannell and Dorothea E. Wyatt: *Julia S. Tutwiler and Social Progress in Alabama* (Tuscaloosa, 1961), p. 13.

and sister had been with Florence Nightingale at Scutari, but he responded that they were supported by a stronger, wealthier government than the Confederacy. The logical Kate replied that this was all the more reason why she should offer assistance. During the three years she served as a nurse, Miss Cumming had to defend her position many times, but she maintained that "a woman's respectability must be at low ebb if it can be endangered by going into a hospital."[7]

Many middle-aged women also encountered protests, and most who did not had been self-supporting for years. At sixty Dorothea Dix had to ask no one's permission, and at forty Clara Barton had long ceased to take orders from anyone; but others within the same age brackets met with determined opposition. If they overcame this obstacle and offered their services, they next encountered the hostility of most men in the medical departments. Few were enthusiastic about having women nurses on their staffs and many vehemently opposed the innovation. Some of the army doctors who in the beginning had been reluctant about women nurses eventually became their champions, but others held to their prejudices throughout the war.

Realizing that women might render valuable service as army nurses, Dr. Elizabeth Blackwell had her training program approved by the Woman's Central Relief Association and before the end of April 1861 was interviewing and assigning promising applicants to New York hospitals. Not all who applied were accepted, and some admitted to training were later dropped. When it was known that an efficient, qualified woman would be needed to supervise the army nurses, Dr. Blackwell was considered for the position; but because most medical men were suspicious, hypercritical, or jealous of her, Dorothea Dix was appointed Superintendent of Women Nurses. Thus on June 10, 1861, began four years which Miss Dix referred to as only "an episode" in her life. She immediately set to work outlining the qualifications and rules for nurses. Although both were clear cut, Miss Dix occasionally made an exception and was then accused of being inconsistent or playing favorites. Many young women were disap-

[7] Kate Cumming: *Gleanings From the Southland* (Birmingham, Ala., 1895), pp. 38, 127; Kate Cumming: *Kate: The Journal of a Confederate War Nurse,* ed. Richard Harwell (Baton Rouge, 1959), pp. 65, 178.

pointed on hearing that the minimum age was thirty and only those who were "plain in appearance" need apply. One young miss exploded that the "Dragon Dix . . . won't accept the services of any *pretty* nurses. . . . Just think of putting such an old thing over everyone else. . . . Some fool man did it," she continued, "so now . . . his sex must suffer from it."[8] Many nurses at first resented being required to wear somber, unadorned, hoopless dresses, but after entering on their duties the sensible ones realized the wisdom of Miss Dix's rule. No salary was promised these first volunteers, but Congress soon provided forty cents a day plus subsistence and transportation to and from their posts.

Miss Dix was an enigma to many with whom she worked. Soft-spoken and at times gentle and sympathetic, she also could be brusque, recalcitrant, and opinionated—traits which her male colleagues especially disliked. When it was seen that many surgeons intended to boycott women, Surgeon General William A. Hammond ordered that at least one-third of all hospital nursing posts be given to them; whereupon some doctors requested permission to appoint Sisters of Charity to these places. These nuns were respected for their efficiency, calm demeanor, lack of prejudice, and probably most important, their obedience to authority. Hammond granted the surgeons' request but Miss Dix indignantly objected to this discrimination against her nurses. This determined lady's exceedingly difficult job was made all the harder because she had constantly to defend her "Florence Nightingales." It is not always clear whether the men resented Miss Dix because she was dictatorial or because she was more efficient than many of them. The nurses' opinions of their superintendent were mixed; the new ones almost invariably were afraid or awed, but after a time most came to respect her and many were sincerely devoted.

The Confederate Medical Department was slow to work out a coordinated system and at first depended on state and local groups and on individuals to maintain hospitals. Sally Tompkins was one of the first Southern women to support a hospital. She

[8] Ellen Wright to Laura Stratton, Jan. 31, 1863, Garrison Family Papers; Sophronia E. Bucklin: *In Hospital and Camp: A Woman's Record of Thrilling Incidents Among the Wounded in the Late War* (Philadelphia, 1869), pp. 39–40.

rented a private home in Richmond, which was used for her twenty-two-bed infirmary, and because of her early services she was commissioned a captain by Jefferson Davis and continued in "command" of her institution throughout the war. Late in 1861 the government took over the hospital system, but not until September 1862 did the Confederate Congress grant official status to women nurses. They were then classified as chief, assistant, or ward matrons with a monthly salary of forty, thirty-five, and thirty dollars respectively. As prices soared, this wage was so inadequate that nurses sometimes worked at a second job to supplement their incomes. One, Phoebe Yates Pember, was soon writing for one of the government departments at night, and by 1863 the cost of living in Richmond had risen so high that she appealed to Senator Henry Stuart Foote to try to get a pay increase for nurses. Mrs. Pember felt sure he would welcome "any opportunity to hear himself talk." Several months later her wages were raised to $3,000 a year, scarcely more in purchasing power than the original $480 had been in 1862.[9] Although Mrs. Pember had accepted the position because she needed the money, neither she nor any other nurse became wealthy from hospital work.

The Confederate Government had no standard qualifications for nurses and made no provision for their formal training. Most women depended on their past experience and natural talents, but Mrs. Ella King Newsom trained briefly in a Memphis institution before joining an army hospital at Bowling Green, Kentucky. She was soon appointed superintendent and when the army retreated she followed it to Nashville, later serving elsewhere in Tennessee, Mississippi, and Georgia. This widow had rare administrative ability. A wealthy woman in 1861, she expended a large part of her fortune on her patients and lost the remainder in the war. Because of her social position, gentility, and selflessness Mrs. Newsom's entry into nursing helped make it more respectable in the eyes of many conservatives.

Some of the Union's most remarkable women served with the Sanitary Commission as nurses, agents, or both. Their motto seems to have been to find the need and promptly supply it no matter what it was or where. The most colorful and dynamic of these women was the widowed Mary Ann Bickerdyke, an experi-

[9] Phoebe Yates Pember to Eugenia Phillips, Jan. 30, 1864; Phoebe Yates Pember to Mrs. Jeremy Gilmer, Feb. 19, 1864, Phillips-Myers Papers.

enced nurse in her middle forties when she first attracted attention by bringing order out of chaos in the Cairo, Illinois, military hospitals. Moving like a tornado through the filthy, inefficient institutions, she ordered the buildings cleaned, bathtubs made from barrels, diet kitchens established, and lazy, dishonest employees dismissed or punished. It was here that she got the reputation for ordering around high-ranking military officials as if they were lackeys. Months later, when she accused an army surgeon of misconduct and the officer appealed to Grant, he replied, "My God, man, Mother Bickerdyke outranks everybody, even Lincoln. If you have run amuck of her I advise you to get out quickly before she has you under arrest." This simply dressed woman, in her Quaker bonnet and shawl, was familiar to thousands who saw her scurry over nineteen battlefields in four years, administering aid to all in need. Few women were more beloved and respected by those with whom they worked. An officer once said that Mother Bickerdyke meant more to the "army than the Madonna to Catholics," and a colleague, dumbfounded by what she accomplished, wrote, "She talks bad grammer, jaws at us all . . . and is not afraid of anybody . . . but Lord, how she works!" Nothing mattered to Mrs. Bickerdyke but getting the job done; and no one was going to stop her, not even the generals.[1]

Much of the Sanitary Commission's success may be attributed to its utilization of individual talents. Women with entirely different backgrounds, temperaments, and abilities often worked together as efficient teams; and paired with the brusque, fiery, unpolished Mrs. Bickerdyke was the gentle, quiet, refined Mrs. Eliza Porter, who was equally dedicated to the task. Mrs. Jane Hoge and Mrs. Mary Ashton Livermore traveled so widely and accomplished so much that a contemporary said their names became "household words." It was while appealing to scores of ladies' aid societies for hospital supplies that Mrs. Hoge first realized her potentialities as a public speaker, for her stories of the pitiful plight of sick and wounded soldiers invariably stimulated her audiences to greater efforts. Mrs. Livermore, former teacher,

---

[1] Mrs. John A. Logan: *The Part Taken By Women in American History* (Wilmington, Del., 1912), pp. 326–29; Mary Ashton Livermore: *My Story of the War* (Hartford, 1889), p. 477; Nina Brown Baker: *Cyclone in Calico: The Story of Mary Ann Bickerdyke* (Boston, 1952), *passim;* James Phinney Munroe: *Adventures of an Army Nurse in Two Wars* (Boston, 1904), pp. 193–94.

editor, and the only woman reporter to cover the 1860 Republican convention, poured all of her "magnetism, sparkle and imagination" into writing and speaking in behalf of the commission.[2] Among the many wartime services of Mrs. Annie Wittenmyer was the establishment of army diet kitchens, which eventually brought her an appointment as superintendent of all army diet kitchens and led her to write a widely used manual on the feeding of the sick. For a time Mary Shelton worked with her, but Miss Shelton's greatest service was her defense of the Sanitary Commission in 1863, when it was under attack from the public.

Cordelia Harvey, widow of Governor Louis Harvey of Wisconsin, who was drowned in Tennessee in 1862, was the author of many good deeds. Until her husband's death she had been interested in the provisioning and employment of indigent families of soldiers, but then she devoted herself to nursing in field hospitals, establishing convalescent hospitals in the North, and working with war orphans. She twice conferred with Lincoln about bringing men away from the battle areas to recuperate, and although he at first opposed the idea, believing that it would encourage desertion, she eventually won him over.

Some of the best-qualified Union nurses were to be found in the Sanitary Commission transport service, which evacuated sick and wounded soldiers by ship from the battle areas to hospitals behind the lines. In this group were Mrs. Eliza Howland and her sister, Georgeanna Woolsey, from an amazing family of seven sisters, all of whom with their mother rendered valuable wartime service. Also nursing on the "floating hospitals" was Katherine Prescott Wormeley, born in England and reared in wealth in Rhode Island. Before the war she was recognized as a philanthropist and humanitarian, and after its outbreak she offered her services as a nurse and was later appointed director of Portsmouth Grove Hospital. Her most difficult assignment was on the transports, yet she found it a "thorough enjoyment," for as she noted, *"it is life."* Of her colleagues she wrote, "They are as efficient, wise, active as cats, merry, light-hearted, thoroughbred, and without the fearful tone of self-devotion which sad experience makes one expect in benevolent women."[3] Helen Gilson, a

[2] Livermore: *My Story of the War*, p. 160; Mrs. Sarah Edwards Henshaw: *Our Branch and Its Tributaries* (Chicago, 1868), pp. 208–9.

[3] Katherine Prescott Wormeley: *The Other Side of the War with the Army of the Potomac* (Boston, 1889), p. 44.

wartime nurse and later a teacher of freedmen, saw her first service on hospital ships and moved from there to hospitals attached to the Army of the Potomac. She labored harmoniously with all groups, including officers, hospital staffs, patients, and other women, and few nurses seem to have been as popular. Overwork in wartime was blamed for her untimely death.

Hospitals were mainly supplied by state and local groups from all parts of the Union, but some individuals crusaded for contributions and decided where and how they would be used. Such a person was Clara Barton, whose first service was to aid the men in the Sixth Massachusetts who lost their baggage in the Baltimore melee on April 19, 1861. After she turned to nursing Miss Barton made personal appeals to New England friends to provide her with food, medicine, and clothing needed on the battlefield. Always believing that she could be most useful in the thick of battle, Miss Barton was often the first nurse to arrive on the scene. "I did not wait for reporters and journalists to tell us that a battle had been fought," she later said, but "I went in while the battle raged." Arriving at Antietam, she saw "no trace of Woman Kind" but was indifferent to a surgeon who showed surprise at seeing her suddenly appear in an oxcart laden with medical supplies. This battle she always remembered because here for the first time she removed a bullet and saw a wounded soldier shot in her arms as she gave him water. When discussing her experiences after the war she told audiences that if her work in battle appeared to be "rough and unseemly for a *woman*," they should remember that fighting was equally "rough and unseemly for *men*." Although she gave an appearance of limitless stamina, she was very ill twice during the war, and in South Carolina a friend feared for her life. Ten years later she had reason to recall these illnesses as the beginning of a more serious health problem.[4]

Clara Barton worked as independently as a nurse could in wartime and never was associated with Dorothea Dix, but it is interesting to speculate what might have happened had these two strong-willed women been brought together with one as boss of the other. Chances are that the nation would have lost the

[4] "Work and Incidents of Army Life," MS, Clara Barton Papers, Smith College Archives; Leander Poor to Samuel Richard Barton, Aug. 23, 1863; Clara Barton Papers, Henry E. Huntington Library.

services of one of them. Because she was independent, Clara Barton was often irritated by rules and red tape, but she would appeal directly to her friend Henry Wilson, chairman of the Senate Military Affairs Committee. Wilson befriended her during the war and after, and it was shortly after his death in 1875 that Miss Barton suffered a breakdown which incapacitated her for more than a year. All women actively engaged in the war made a great many new friends and their lives were affected in a variety of ways, but a whole new world opened to Clara Barton.

Figures vary as to the number of women who made a career of nursing during the Civil War, but it is safe to say that at least 3,200 held paying positions in the Union and Confederacy. Not all served for four years and some who nursed had been employed to fill other positions, but excluded from this figure were thousands on both home fronts who gave some time to hospital work but were uncompensated. Included, however, are both whites and Negroes, slave and free. Contraband women often worked as nurses although employed by the Federal Government as laundresses or cooks, and there were many slaves and free Negro women on hospital payrolls in the Confederacy although the slaves' pay went to their owners. Midway in the war four Negro matrons and two female Negro nurses were employed at General Hospital Number Ten in Richmond, while nineteen male slaves and six free Negro men were also listed there as nurses. Hospital officials often placed their slaves on the payroll, and other owners welcomed the chance to have theirs fed in return for services whether or not they were given a monthly wage. Sally Tompkins of Robertson Hospital and Mrs. Jane Gaines of General Hospital Number Twelve, both in Richmond, were among the matrons whose slaves were employed in their hospitals.[5]

The journalist who commented that "all our women are Florence Nightingales" included those who donated part of their time to hospital work. Their duties varied, but most staffs preferred them to confine their activities to writing letters for the patients, reading to them, comforting or cheering them, or just listening to them. Some of the capable were permitted to give

[5] Confederate Hospital Rolls, War Department Collection of Confederate Records, Record Group 109, National Archives.

medication, serve food and drink, or sponge patients' faces, but many well-meaning women were more of a nuisance than a help, and some who disregarded hospital rules were a positive danger. A great many ladies brought much-appreciated flowers, delicacies, reading materials, and clothing to the men, some doing so at great sacrifice, but others slipped them forbidden food and drink, making it necessary for attendants to be on guard at all times. Public opinion and most parents questioned the propriety of young unmarried women and girls visiting hospitals unless chaperoned, and even when they were accompanied by older women the practice was frowned upon by many. The regular nurses often opposed their coming, most being convinced they came to meet and flirt with men and have a good time, and giddy girls often created problems. In the South many parents who forbade their daughters to go into hospitals took sick and wounded soldiers into their homes and gave their girls permission to tend them. Many a romance begun in this way culminated in marriage.

Union and Confederate nurses encountered many identical problems, not the least of which was the opposition of most army doctors. Mary Safford found surgeons and officers everywhere resentful of her presence and prejudiced against her program, while Sophronia Bucklin believed they "were determined by a systematic course of ill treatment . . . to drive women from the service." Kate Cumming, reporting the antipathy of Confederate medics, indignantly proclaimed, "The war is certainly ours as well as that of men." Military officers were equally vehement, among them General Grant who threatened to send his wife home if she persisted in visiting camp hospitals. Early in the war John A. Logan wrote Mrs. Logan that his command was not as yet plagued with "female nurses" and assured her that there never would be "one in this department," but a few months later Mother Bickerdyke and her contingent of "females" stormed into Logan's camp, set up shop, and remained. Most men explained their attitude by saying they felt an army hospital was no place for women, but one young surgeon admitted he was not sure. Some with whom he had worked were very capable, but he found also that "many women abuse their privilege of nursing." An officer told Mary Livermore that if he must tolerate women, he preferred Sisters of Charity because they "never write for newspapers . . . nor see or hear anything they shouldn't" and were never responsible for bringing government investigators to the scene.[6] For various reasons many men opposed their wives' visiting hospitals; and while Lincoln offered no opposition, Jefferson Davis preferred Mrs. Davis to devote her time to other war work.

Offsetting the critics were men who paid glowing tribute to the nurses, among them Frederick Law Olmsted. He often referred to the "glorious women" in the Sanitary Commission transport service and once commented, "God knows what we should have done without them, they have worked like heroes night and day, and though the duty is frequently most disagreeable . . . I have never seen one of them flinch for a moment." Samuel Hollingsworth Stout, Director of Hospitals of the Army of Tennessee, at first opposed women nurses but after observing them care for the Shiloh casualties praised their efficiency and ability. He thought they had rendered a real service to the Confederacy but confessed that it was the "refined, intellectual, self-denying ladies" like Mrs. William Gilmer, Mrs. Ella King Newsom, and Kate Cumming who convinced him it was entirely proper for women to serve in this capacity.[7] Unfortunately, much of the praise accorded nurses came after, not during the war when they desperately needed it.

The supply problem was constant in hospitals near the front, and nurses often had to be expert foragers. Records of Confederate women stress the never-ending scarcity of many essential items and the countless hours spent scouring the countryside for foods and especially milk. But some of their most discouraging experiences were amusing in retrospect. Fannie Beers delighted in telling about the time she spotted several stray cows and needing

[6] Livermore: *My Story of the War*, pp. 206, 224; Bucklin: *In Hospital and Camp*, pp. 124–25; Cumming: *Kate*, pp. 38–39, 65, 178; John A. Logan to Mary Logan, Sept. 17, 1861, Mrs. John A. Logan Papers; Ellen Wright to William Lloyd Garrison II, June 13, 1863, Garrison Family Papers.
[7] Frederick Law Olmsted: *Hospital Transports: A Memoir of the Embarkation of the Sick and Wounded From the Peninsula of Virginia in the Summer of 1862* (Boston, 1863), pp. 33, 36, 69; Samuel Hollingsworth Stout: "Some Facts of the History of the Organization of the Medical Service of the Confederate Armies and Hospitals," *Southern Practitioner*, XXV (1903), 156.

milk for her patients tried for the first time in her life to milk the animals. She found that the task was not as simple as it seemed and returned with empty pails. Union nurses had a smaller supply problem but were not entirely unfamiliar with it. Mrs. Bickerdyke, irritated that "her boys" lacked milk and eggs, left camp for the Midwest where she "recruited" more than a hundred cows and a thousand chickens. Commandeering transportation over the protests of several officers, she returned to Tennessee at the head of her "army." To show their appreciation, the men groomed the cows and honored their "leader" with what was to be forever remembered as "Mother Bickerdyke's Cows Review." When Northern admirers sent this practical woman inappropriate finery, she took the articles into rural areas and exchanged them for produce. Nor did she have trouble disposing of the items, for poor country women in the South were happy to give her food in return for clothing.

The requisition system was another source of irritation, and many nurses complained bitterly about being denied necessities which were in stock at the commissary. Their requests were not always honored and were often rejected because of a technicality or prejudice. A nurse at Gettysburg was infuriated when denied sheets she desperately needed because they were being saved for a hospital not yet opened. Anna Holstein, working under serious handicaps in Virginia, later noted, "Army life taught . . . *all* who were in it many useful lessons." One which she learned was to prepare food for several hundred men with no equipment except a small camp stove, "a coffee pot, a half-gallon tin cup and one small iron boiler."[8] The requisition system, like many other hospital practices, was often hopelessly enmeshed in red tape.

Most women expected to be inconvenienced and were good sports, but their patience was sorely tried by the makeshift quarters in which they had to work. All kinds of structures were commandeered for hospitals—private residences, stores, offices, courthouses, churches, factories, warehouses, schools, and outbuildings. Many nurses also cared for the sick and wounded in tents, caves, under trees and in the open fields. It was difficult to

[8] Charlotte Elizabeth McKay: *Stories of Hospitals and Camp* (Philadelphia, 1876), pp. 55–56; Anna Morris Holstein: *Three Years in Field Hospitals of the Army of the Potomac* (Philadelphia, 1867), p. 26.

maintain any efficient system under these conditions. Nor were their living quarters much better. In base hospitals which were not moved with the armies they usually managed to get comfortable accommodations, but in the field they often lived in miserable quarters. Some found rooms in private homes with physical comforts, but the atmosphere was not always pleasant; and others were billeted in cabins, outhouses, and occasionally in a wing of the hospital, but propriety as well as lack of space and privacy dictated that they should have sleeping quarters apart from the patients. In many instances these poor accommodations were unavoidable, but women who moved with their hospital into a new community discovered that local citizens who could were often reluctant to rent rooms to nurses. And if they were so fortunate as to find comfortable lodgings these might be a great distance from the hospital. Nurses worked long hours under sad and strenuous conditions and if they were denied rest and relaxation during off-duty hours their physical and nervous systems soon showed the effects.

Another problem which confronted some nurses many times during the war, and especially those in Confederate field hospitals, was having to move patients and equipment when a retreat was sounded. It was a harrowing experience under pressure of time and fear, when transportation facilities and roads were congested with refugees and retreating soldiers. The most frequently uprooted nurses were those attached to the Army of Tennessee, and Kate Cumming tells of "chasing" her hospital through four states, while Fannie Beers followed three hospitals through two states. When it was necessary to evacuate Newnan, Georgia, within a few hours, Mrs. Beers chose to remain with the men who could not be moved. Women displayed amazing courage and stamina during a retreat as they helped to transfer men to ambulances, boxcars, or any other available conveyance, packed hospital supplies, and directed the procedure—often with greater efficiency and composure than their male colleagues.

Nurses everywhere complained about incompetent, immoral, and demoralizing laundresses, orderlies and cooks. Mrs. Bickerdyke had no patience with these people and upon her arrival in Beaufort, North Carolina, reported the hospital "in bad shape and honored by . . . the greatest lot of pimps it has ever been . . . my fortune to meet," her most scathing attack being reserved for the "swearing" laundresses.[9] Others complained that employees would not work and that some invariably drank on the job, usually stealing whiskey from the hospital supply. Nurses were compelled to keep the liquor under lock and key, some actually having to guard it themselves, and it had a mysterious way of disappearing after being poured in a glass but before reaching the patient. Phoebe Pember was one of many nurses who caught assistants drinking dosages, and Kate Cumming believed that her drunken cooks obtained their liquor from hospital stores. Workers also had a way of abandoning their posts without warning and failing to report when expected, and the tendency of contrabands to do both drove Northern nurses to distraction. Katherine Wormeley rarely complained about anything but admitted that her "hardest work . . . was to keep two colored ladies . . . steady to the work of scrubbing the lower deck" of their transport. They left their duties so often "on the pretext of getting fresh water" that Miss Wormeley decided it would be easier to fetch the water than to run after them.[1]

It is understandable that thousands of women, on hearing that loved ones were sick or wounded, rushed to their bedsides, yet they often created problems for the hospital staffs. Entire families descended on crowded hospitals and some stayed for weeks or months expecting to be housed, fed, or permitted to cook food brought from home. One of Phoebe Pember's unusual experiences involved a patient's wife who remained at the hospital for weeks and, during Mrs. Pember's overnight absence, gave birth to a daughter on her husband's cot in the ward. For a month thereafter Mrs. Pember cared for mother and infant, bought and begged clothes for the baby, and finally got them a ticket home to western Virginia. Thankful to be rid of this "sore annoyance," she then heard that the baby had been abandoned at the station. Rousing the father from his bed, she sent him home with his daughter, who incidentally had been named for Phoebe Pember. Like other nurses she had her share of patients' thoughtless relatives who stayed for extended periods, lounging on beds, embarrassing the men, laughing merrily while some in the ward were dying, and disregarding patients' diets by overfeeding

---

[9] Mrs. Mary Bickerdyke to Julia Smith Clark, May 1, 1865, Lincoln Clark Papers.
[1] Wormeley, *The Other Side of the War*, p. 84.

them, often with the very food they were forbidden to have. But the women visitors most offensive to Mrs. Pember were those who persisted in using pipes and filling the wards with smoke.[2]

A few of these visiting women were assets rather than liabilities, however, and Mary Livermore told of one who scrubbed floors, walls, and windows and who brought a trunk filled with clean clothes and bedding. She worked quietly, obeyed hospital rules, and asked no special privileges. Sometimes a mother or wife arrived too late to see her loved one alive, and this was always a heart-rending experience for the staff. An Illinois mother arrived just minutes after her son had passed away. Seeing where he had died, she exclaimed, "Oh my son! my son! That *you* should die *so! On the floor and in the corner!*"[3] When parents and wives were dissatisfied with hospital conditions, they sometimes removed their sons or husbands to private houses in the community or took them home to recuperate. Some understood the situation in hospitals but many were carping troublemakers with whom all nurses grew familiar.

Poor women often had little if any money left after reaching the bedside of relatives and were entirely dependent on others for food and lodging. The problem was especially serious in Northern communities where there was a concentration of large military hospitals, but once the citizens were made aware of it they came to the aid of destitute travelers. The need was soon apparent in Washington, and individuals like Dr. Mary Walker, and organized bodies including Congress, eventually assisted in establishing homes for the "friendless." The general public was sometimes critical of the impractical women who rushed to loved ones without thinking about their lack of adequate funds, but on June 21, 1864, the editor of the Washington *Chronicle* reminded readers that "affection is often stronger than reason."

Even affluent visitors often had problems getting to a hospital and felt they merited consideration for coming. Marianna Mott of Philadelphia endured hardships en route to Gettysburg to nurse her wounded half-brother. From Baltimore to her destination she had great difficulty staying on the flatcar which she was compelled to ride, and among the passengers were the dirti-

[2] Phoebe Yates Pember: *A Southern Woman's Story,* ed. Bell I. Wiley (Jackson, Miss., 1959), pp. 90–96.
[3] Livermore: *My Story of the War,* p. 203; Henshaw: *Our Branch and Its Tributaries,* p. 45.

est, dowdiest, most uncouth women she had ever seen. They professed to be nurses, although not in the pay of the government, but she thought they were following a less honorable calling, having seen them "attach themselves to . . . smiling doctors" in Baltimore. After arriving in Gettysburg, Mrs. Mott encountered lodging problems the like of which she had never before experienced, nor were conditions improved when she moved into a field hospital where she shared a room with four uncongenial women. In addition to the women there were, she said, "many *other* insects, no sheets or pillow cases . . . one family towel and a little water brought once a day in a small basin." On arising the first morning she found in her bed "a woman, a grasshopper, a spider, many smaller creatures which 'graze upon the human body,' and a moving canopy of flies." She was one of the privileged few who ate at the surgeons' mess, but she didn't enjoy having to drink from tin cups or eat with iron spoons, and as soon as she was assured her brother would recover, Mrs. Mott beat a hasty retreat to Philadelphia.[4]

Most hospitalized soldiers were courteous and grateful for the attention given them; some fell in love with their nurses and many became their lifelong friends. But there were also the rude, boorish, and vulgar who delighted in making suggestive remarks to the women; and into all nurses' lives came the practical jokers who raided the pantries, hid animals and insects in their beds, and faked a sudden turn for the worse. There was also the ever-present malingerer. The men generally enjoyed having women around but some were embarrassed to have them as nurses and usually preferred that men attend to their physical needs. But the women who most embarrassed them were the visitors who insisted on washing their faces, straightening their beds, asking personal questions, and "killing them with kindness."

Prisoners presented unique problems for hospital staffs, who had to stay on the alert to prevent their mistreatment by hostile visitors or conspiracy with friendly ones. Regular nurses usually cared for them as they would their own men, but visiting women were known to abuse them and even endanger their lives. For this reason the staff often did not reveal their identity, knowing that many women would react as did the South Carolinian who

[4] Marianna Mott to Agnes Hopper, July 10, 1863; Marianna Mott to Martha Wright, July 12, 1863, Garrison Family Papers.

"couldn't bear to see Yankees there with Confederates" and who, "through ignorance," administered to them as though they were on her side, confessing she would not have done so had she known the truth.[5] Federal surgeons captured with their wounded men were sometimes permitted to care for them but invariably requested medicines and drugs which were scarce or nonexistent in most Confederate hospitals. When they were not provided, the doctors assumed this to be malicious, though most medical attendants were humane and regretted their inability to ease pain.

Despite their long hours, overwork, and innumerable pressures and problems, many nurses took time to acknowledge contributions from individuals and home-front groups; not that rules required them to do so, but some thoughtless donors made them feel that they must. The supplies often had no more than reached their destination before letters began to arrive asking if the shipment had been lost. Sanitary Commission workers usually had secretaries with them, but if a contribution was addressed to a specific person she was expected to acknowledge it personally. Mrs. Bickerdyke had a secretary, but this busy woman nevertheless wrote letters of appreciation to women she had never met, realizing that cordial public relations demanded it. Because Clara Barton personally solicited supplies, she was bombarded with indignant queries which she usually courteously and apologetically answered at the first opportunity. Typical of hundreds of her acknowledgments was that written to the New York women who several times demanded to know why they had heard nothing from her. "I am sorry that the uncertainties of war should have compelled me to cause you so much trouble," she wrote, and telling of her recent field assignments which included service at Harper's Ferry, Falmouth, and Fredericksburg, she assured the ladies their supplies had arrived safely and been used at Fredericksburg.[6] Had women behind the lines understood the situation at the front, they might have been less demanding.

There were in both North and South many young women whose hospital work consisted primarily of entertaining patients

[5] Grace B. Elmore Diary, MS.
[6] Clara Barton to "The Ladies of the Soldier's Relief Society in Watkins, New York," Dec. 3, 1863, Clara Barton Papers, Smith College Archives.

with songs, tableaux, musical programs, and readings. One of the most remarkable was Elida Rumsey Fowle, who wanted to be a nurse but was rejected by Miss Dix because she was only nineteen. She turned to singing and storytelling and in one year gave more than two hundred performances for hospitalized soldiers. Wanting to do something more, she established a soldiers' library in Washington for which she collected thousands of books, tracts, and newspapers; and before she was done, this institution resembled the later USO clubs, for refreshments were served, entertainment was provided, and writing supplies were furnished the servicemen. Mrs. Fowle and her husband, riding in a wagon filled with medical supplies and food, were the first nurses to arrive on the battlefield at Second Manassas and had been caring for the troops several hours when Miss Dix and her nurses appeared. Many soldiers long remembered Mrs. Fowle, who created opportunities for service when denied the one she most wanted.[7]

Others discovered new wartime challenges. Mary Morris Husband of Philadelphia became interested in court-martialed soldiers condemned to die. Mrs. Husband interceded in their behalf, taking her appeals from the company commanders to the Commander in Chief; and while usually failing with the former, she was amazingly successful when pleading with Lincoln. Sadie Curry of Georgia was not permitted to nurse in hospitals but did care for several wounded soldiers in her father's home. She taught one, Elijah Ballard, to read and write, and her assistance later enabled him to study bookkeeping and make a career. Amy Bradley of Maine nursed first on a hospital transport and later in Alexandria and Washington, but her unique contribution was founding and editing the *Soldier's Journal,* in which were published stories and information of special interest to servicemen. Most important were instructions to be followed in applying for back pay, and she personally assisted a great many in securing theirs.

A few women were assigned the responsibility for investigating hospital conditions, among them Mrs. Charlotte Dailey, who was appointed by Governor William Sprague to report on institutions in which Rhode Island soldiers were patients. Sixty-one hospitals were included in her tour of inspection and the names

[7] Mary Gardner Holland: *Our Army Nurses* (Boston, 1895), pp. 71–76.

of 408 men with the rank, regiment, and nature of illness of each were listed in her well-organized, informative report, which was generally favorable to the hospitals and staffs. Mrs. Mary H. Johnstone of Georgia made a similar but more informal report to Alexander H. Stephens after he had requested her to investigate hospitals attached to the Army of Northern Virginia. She was caustically critical of the surgeons' inefficiency, which she attributed primarily to heavy drinking, a vice often mentioned by nurses on both sides. Mrs. Johnstone suggested that they be more carefully screened before being assigned to duty, that disabled soldiers be brought from camp and placed in permanent hospitals, and that something be done to increase medical supplies.[8]

There were no women physicians in Confederate service, but several claimed appointments in the Union, including Dr. Mary Walker, who was commissioned a contract surgeon in 1864, three years after first making an application which left the Medical Department stunned but not speechless. This was an unexpected turn of events, for no other woman had dared suggest such a thing, and the Surgeon General, rejecting the application, implied that it had never occurred to him that one would. Dr. Walker remained in Washington to hound officials, nurse in the Indiana Hospital and nearby camps, and organize the relief society for needy women visitors. When in early 1864 she at last received an appointment she left for the Chattanooga front, where her spying soon resulted in her capture by the Confederates. A Confederate captain, as surprised as his fellow soldiers to see "a female doctor" among the prisoners, wrote his wife that they "were all amused and disgusted . . . at the sight of a *thing* that nothing but the debased and depraved Yankee nation could produce." He noted that "she was dressed in the full uniform of a Federal Surgeon . . . not good looking and of course had tongue enough for a regiment of men," and he supposed the general was right in having her sent to Richmond, although he thought she would be more at home in "a lunatic asylum."[9] Dr. Walker was accustomed to stares and innuendoes, but she was not prepared

[8] Mrs. Charlotte Dailey: *Report Upon the Disabled Rhode Island Soldiers* (Providence, 1863), *passim;* Mary H. Johnstone to Alexander H. Stephens, Feb. 3, 1862, Alexander H. Stephens Papers, Library of Congress.

[9] Benedict Joseph Semmes to Jorantha Semmes, Apr. 12, 1864, Benedict Joseph Semmes Papers.

for the Southerners' reactions. Crowds gawked as she was led through Richmond to Castle Thunder, where she was incarcerated, and newspapers had a picnic at her expense, but she remained in prison only four months and was then exchanged for a Confederate surgeon. Appointed superintendent of the Female Military Prison in Louisville and discharged from service in 1865, she was awarded a medal by President Johnson and until her death in 1919 never let the politicians forget her war service although her medal was withdrawn.

As might be expected, nurses sometimes broke under the strain and had to resign, among them Louisa May Alcott, who after a few months returned to Massachusetts and devoted her time to writing. Practically all had to take periodic furloughs and at least one in ten suffered physical breakdowns while in the service. A great many later reported their health impaired by their wartime nursing, several known to have been deafened when shells burst near or as a result of camp disease. Some were crippled or scarred, Elida Fowle going through life with facial scars caused by an infection contracted while she was nursing in the field. A score or more died while on duty or furlough, including Margaret Breckinridge, Mrs. Mary Brady, and Mrs. Arabella Barlow, wife of General Francis Barlow.

The prejudice against women in medicine did not disappear during the war years, but the barriers erected against them were beginning to crack. The Chicago Hospital for Women and Children was opened in 1863 with a Sanitary Commission worker, Dr. Mary H. Thompson, as director. In the same year the New York Medical College for Women was chartered, and its first class of fifteen was graduated a few weeks before Appomattox. Yet the question whether women should train for a career in medicine was debated throughout the struggle. In the last winter of the war the New York *Times* published an interesting series of letters on the subject, but only the defenders of women doctors offered a new argument—and a valid one—woman's invaluable service in military hospitals.

Discussed later will be the effects of the war on the lives of specific nurses, but it should be noted here that immediately following the cessation of hostilities most of the "Florence Nightingales" were discouraged by public indifference. Although sometimes praised for their work, they were more often criticized, ridiculed, ignored, or "damned with faint praise." When Henry Bellows was asked what women had contributed, he enthusiastically outlined what those on the home front had accomplished but said little that was complimentary about those who had worked so hard in hospitals. "Women are rarely in place at the front," he said, "or even at the bases of the armies." *The Medical and Surgical History of the War of Rebellion* states that their "best service was rendered in connection with extra diets, the linen-room and the laundry," rather than as nurses. Jane Stuart Woolsey, writing three years after the war, was as aware as others that she and her colleagues were being criticized but attributed their failures to the lack of organization and system rather than to the women themselves.[1]

Many complex factors explain why the Civil War nurses did not immediately receive the acclaim they merited, but basic to all others was their inability to overcome in only four years the long-standing, deep-seated prejudice of the general public and the military officials. Most army doctors were not yet ready to admit they had been wrong in trying to halt woman's invasion of the male's world, and many were too proud to bestow credit. The patients were much more inclined to praise the nurses than were their medical colleagues. The home-front population, especially those far removed from the battlefields, had no conception of the nurses' problems or the extent of their sacrifices. They were all too willing to retain preconceived ideas, to accept as fact malicious rumor, and to draw unjustified conclusions. Because some nurses were untrained, inefficient, careless, and uninspired and a few were of doubtful reputation, although these were often impostors, the dedicated, efficient, innocent ones suffered. The war had its most obvious and immediate impact on the individual nurse rather than on the profession as a whole.

[1] "Letter of the Reverend Henry Bellows to Henry Dunant," *The American Association for the Relief of the Misery on Battlefields* (New York, 1866), *passim; Medical and Surgical History of the War of Rebellion* (Washington. 1881), Part III, I, 958; Jane Stuart Woolsey: *Hospital Days* (New York, 1868), p. 41.

4

Teeming with Women

THOUSANDS OF WOMEN were attracted to military encampments, and their motives were as varied as the individuals. A Southern journalist discovered three distinct groups in Confederate camps—the officers' families, the cooks and laundresses, and the prostitutes. He omitted not only the nurses but also women who served as soldiers, spies, scouts, and couriers. Not all of these traveled with the armies or lived in camp, however, and some could be subsumed within one of the correspondent's three broad classifications. A similar situation existed in the Union armies, none of which was as well known for its numbers of women as the Army of the Potomac. During its first three winter encampments women's presence greatly enlivened the social scene, and during one Princess Agnes Salm-Salm noted that the place was "teeming with women."[1] Although many civilians and military personnel looked with suspicion on any woman who stayed in camp, the wives of officers usually came away with their reputations intact. The motives and conduct of most others were questioned, and while some were unjustly accused of misbehavior, there is reason to believe that guilty ones may have

[1] New Orleans *Daily Crescent*, Jan. 8, 1862; Agnes Salm-Salm: *Ten Years of My Life* (London, 1875), I, 37.

escaped public censure. Any unmarried, unchaperoned woman who followed the armies subjected herself to criticism.

Officers' relatives, and especially their wives, wanted to be near their men, and if facilities were not provided in camp often lived as near the installation as possible. While affection was usually their primary motive for leaving comfortable homes to endure the inconveniences of camp, some were looking for gaiety and excitement. Many simply wanted to share their men's experiences or to keep an eye on them, for the press kept the public informed of the prevalence of drinking, gambling, and immorality. Some wanted to escape lonely or unhappy surroundings, especially those compelled to live with uncongenial relatives. Others wanted to be near if needed, and thousands rushed to camp on hearing their men were sick or wounded, some remaining long after they recuperated. But most wives were in camp because that was where they wanted to be, and no amount of dissuasion would keep them away.

Women were told that under the best of circumstances they must expect to be inconvenienced, if not endangered, and would be left behind if the army changed its base and military conveyances and personnel could not be spared for their evacuation. This last problem was especially serious for the retreating Confederates, who were naturally reluctant to abandon their women to the enemy but needed all their vehicles and men to move the army. When women refused to leave an endangered area, they were often caught in the line of fire or in such a siege as those of Vicksburg and Petersburg, where they endured countless hardships. They also contributed to supply problems, and Confederate food shortages were especially serious. Even women who tried to make themselves useful in emergencies seldom compensated for the trouble they caused, and many could not or would not render assistance.

Husbands advanced every argument when they thought it inadvisable for their wives to come to camp, but the women were often more persuasive in pointing out reasons why they should. General Logan was among the men who thought it improper for "nice ladies" to be with the army; but Mary Logan, wanting the experience of living "in the barracks," assured him that "no man shall ever see anything that would be unpleasant or mortifying." This was not what the general feared most. He argued that if she came, other officers would expect to send for their wives, and in his opinion this would be catastrophic. Mrs. Logan reminded him that her living expenses would be less, she would be there if he needed her, he would know what she was doing, and, the most popular of all feminine arguments, other husbands let their wives accompany them. But not until Logan was wounded at Fort Donelson did she set foot in camp. Again in the winter of 1862–63 she was permitted to join him in Memphis. Sending her home before the spring campaign, he later wrote, "Don't come any more to camp. I will meet you in Cairo or come home when I can." He did not want her a "nuisance" like some other wives, nor did he want her "talked about" like the "Sanitary women," who he said "almost all turn out badly."[2]

Some officers encouraged their wives to visit, and General Benjamin Butler was quoted as saying that he insisted that his accompany him on "every expedition." He considered himself more fortunate than "his brother commanding generals" in having his "faithful, true, and cool-headed, conscientious and conservative" Sarah with him. Not only did she make him a home, but as an adviser she "could always be trusted."[3] Many of his "brothers" did at times have their families in camp, including Generals Grant, Garfield, and Lew Wallace. General William T. Sherman not only let his wife and the children visit on occasion but offered no protest when other officers had theirs. After the fall of Memphis so many families came down the Mississippi to be with the men that Sherman thought it necessary to protect them from guerrilla shore batteries. After warning Confederate authorities that the attacks must cease, he ordered that whenever a vessel carrying "the wives and families" of Union officers was fired upon, he would banish ten wives of Confederate sympathizers from Memphis. And this he did, sending scores of women into the refugee ranks.[4]

[2] Mary Logan to John A. Logan, n.d., 1861, Feb. 16, 1862; John A. Logan to Mary Logan, March 10, 1862, Mrs. John A. Logan Papers; Mrs. John A. Logan: *Reminiscences of a Soldier's Wife: An Autobiography* (New York, 1913), pp. 125–43.

[3] Mrs. John A. Logan: *The Part Taken by Women in American History* (Wilmington, 1912), pp. 286–87.

[4] *The War of Rebellion: A Compilation of the Official Records of the Union and Confederate Armies* (Washington, 1902), XVII, Part 2, 98–99. Hereafter cited as O. R. See also William Tecumseh Sherman: *Memoirs of General William T. Sherman* (Bloomington, 1957), I, 268.

Confederate wives were no less determined than Union women to be with their husbands, and apparently a larger percentage located themselves in the environs of camp and remained near their men for a longer period of time. This was partly because so many were refugees, who when displaced often went directly to their husbands, some living in camp and others within visiting distance. Mrs. Joseph E. Johnston, Mrs. Roger Pryor, and Mrs. Edward P. Alexander were among those who managed to be in or near camp most of the war years. The ubiquitous Mrs. John B. Gordon irritated several of her husband's fellow officers, including General Richard Ewell, who became tolerant of her only after he left the bachelor ranks to marry his nurse. But General Jubal Early, a confirmed bachelor, never changed his opinion of Mrs. Gordon or any of the other wives "who insisted on following the armies in order to be with their husbands." Once when watching army wagons being brought up for the night, Early spotted Mrs. Gordon's carriage in the line. "Well, I'll be damned!" he exclaimed. "If my men would keep up the way she does, I'd never issue another order against straggling." General Gordon later reported Early as saying, "I wish the Yankees would capture Mrs. Gordon and hold her until the war is over." But Gordon praised her bravery, nursing ability, and good influence on him and others.[5] Many men in both armies were sensitive about the criticism their wives received, but apparently it did not bother the women and certainly did not drive them out of camp.

Many Union and Confederate women who yearned to be with their husbands were never permitted to visit them. The men had to reassure them in every letter that they were not being rejected but that circumstances made it impractical for them to come for even a brief visit. And there was often a very personal reason for the women's not going. Although many couples were reluctant to have children, hundreds of women became pregnant during their sojourn in camp. Between April 1861 and her husband's death in July 1863, Mrs. Dorsey Pender visited the general three times, and each time she left pregnant. One pregnancy resulted in a miscarriage, after which she stated positively that

[5] John Brown Gordon: *Reminiscences of the Civil War* (New York, 1903), pp. 91, 157–58, 316–19.

6 8

while she wanted to be with him she did not want any more children during the war. Pender replied, "Surely if you do not want children you will have to remain away from me, and hereafter when you come to me I shall know that you want another baby."[6]

Some army wives figured prominently in the war, among them Belle Reynolds, whose husband served in the Seventeenth Illinois. Except for a brief visit home in 1862, she remained with him throughout his enlistment, and at Shiloh she was caught in the crossfire. Taking refuge on a hospital ship, she so distinguished herself as a nurse that Governor Richard Yates of Illinois commissioned her a major. While her husband was aide-de-camp to General John A. McClernand, she, Mrs. McClernand, and Mrs. Grant became close friends, and Belle was among the wives of Federal officers who enjoyed the gay winter season in Vicksburg during 1863–64.[7] Princess Salm-Salm, wife of the Prussian Prince Felix who served with the Union Army, shared with Mrs. Reynolds the honor of being commissioned by Governor Yates for hospital work in Tennessee. This rather mysterious woman was an actress and circus performer at the time of her marriage in Cuba in 1862. During the war she spent most of the time with her husband in camp and later accompanied him to Mexico and to Europe, where she nursed and he was killed during the Franco-Prussian War.

Madame John Turchin, as colorful as she was controversial, accompanied her husband on his campaigns, once led his regiment in a skirmish, and both nursed the soldiers and served as their confidante. When Turchin was court-martialed for the "rape" of Athens, Alabama, she personally appealed to Lincoln in his behalf and has been credited with helping to win him a promotion before he was removed from command.[8] Kady Brownell went to war with her husband's Rhode Island regiment and became a legend as she marched with the men and endured all the hardships of army life. Most army wives did not choose to fight,

[6] Mrs. Dorsey Pender to General Dorsey Pender, Feb. 25, 1862; Dorsey Pender to Mrs. Pender, Mar. 6, 1862, Dorsey Pender Papers, Southern Historical Collection, University of North Carolina.

[7] Frank Moore: *Women of the War* (Hartford, 1867), pp. 254–57.

[8] Mary Ashton Livermore: *My Story of the War* (Hartford, 1889), pp. 115–16; New York *Herald,* Aug. 4, 1862.

but those who, like Mrs. Brownell and Mme. Turchin, did participate in battle must not be confused with women who disguised themselves as men and were billeted with the soldiers.

There is some doubt whether or not Annie Etheridge of Michigan accompanied her husband to the front. She marched off as a vivandière but was soon recognized as an efficient nurse, and this was the only service she claimed when later applying for a pension. Also from Michigan was Bridget Deaver, better known as "Irish Biddy," who enrolled as a laundress in her husband's company but nursed when needed. Mary Livermore praised her work at the front, and after the war as an army laundress in the West.[9] Among other army wives who turned nurse were Mrs. William Penn Lyon of Wisconsin, Mrs. Jane Hinsdale of Michigan, and many wives of surgeons, including Mrs. William T. McAllister, Mrs. Francis Thornton and Mrs. W. S. Lee, all married to Confederate physicians attached to the Army of Tennessee. Paradoxically, these selfless women and countless others were on the scene only because they had determined to stay with their husbands.

For obvious reasons it was almost impossible for the wives of "Galvanized Yankees" to be with their men, for these former Confederates who were prisoners of war usually went from prison directly to the frontier after taking the oath of allegiance to the United States and enlisting in the Union Army. At least one wife did accompany her husband, however, for when Private Patrick Cardwell of Virginia left with the First U.S. Volunteer Regiment, his bride Elizabeth was with him. She was the only woman sailing from Virginia on the government transport, and she exhibited soldierly qualities despite the hardships. On July 9, 1865, less than a year after leaving Virginia, she and her newborn baby died at Fort Rich, Dakota Territory, where they were interred with full military honors.[1]

Women who participated in the gay winter encampments of the Army of the Potomac long remembered the festivities. A

[9] Livermore: *My Story of the War*, pp. 118–19; Moore: *Women of the War*, pp. 109-12; Charlotte Elizabeth McKay: *Stories of Hospitals and Camps* (Philadelphia, 1876), p. 124; Linus Pierpont Brockett and Mrs. Mary Vaughn: *Woman's Work in the Civil War* (Philadelphia, 1867), p. 773.

[1] D. Alexander Brown: *The Galvanized Yankees* (Urbana, 1963), pp. 71–72, 78–80, 90–91, 99–101.

Charlestonian, Septima Levy Collis, who defied her Confederate friends to marry a Pennsylvania Zouave, Captain Charles Henry Collis, recalled that the winter of 1863–64 in camp was "an unthinking time" when extravagant balls and feasts were the order of the day. The Philadelphia bride, Laura Stratton Birney, was so enthusiastic that she opened her letters by exclaiming, "There Cheers for Camp Life!" Although surprised to find so many women in camp, she gaily reported that none lacked attention, for the officers outnumbered them four to one. Her "peep behind the military curtain" included balls, dinners, sight-seeing trips, horseback riding, and concerts, but equally enjoyable for Mrs. Birney were "all the gossip and jealousies" she daily encountered. Although aware that the situation could change at any moment, she thought this all the more reason "to take pleasure" whenever she could. When the Salm-Salms wintered in camp, the Princess found pleasure in the large carpeted hospital tent in which they lived. It was furnished with a damask-upholstered sofa and a "large bedstead" with a red and white silk canopy, and a smaller tent sheltered their kitchen and accommodations for her maid. She long remembered the supper prepared by Delmonico and his staff, for better food was never served her even "in Paris." Such extravagance, she said, would have "created . . . a bad feeling" in wartime Germany, but she erroneously assumed that American soldiers "did not begrudge Generals their luxury." Not only did most in fact resent this, they were also indignant that officers could have their wives in camp when they could not. George Sala was shocked at the epicurean atmosphere, but what interested him most were the Virginia girls who took part in the festivities, their fathers "having made peace with the Government."[2]

Most army wives did not live amid such elegance and if anxious to win favor accepted whatever accommodations were provided and complained as little as possible. Yet many made nuisances of themselves and some had the reputation of dictating to their husbands even on military matters. Mrs. Robert H. Mil-

[2] Septima Collis: *A Woman's War Record, 1861–1865* (New York, 1889), pp. 11–12, 28–36; Laura Stratton Birney to Ellen Wright, Feb. 1, 18, March 3, 8, 1864, Garrison Family Papers; Salm-Salm: *Ten Years of My Life*, I, 36–40; George Augusta Sala: *My Diary in America* (London, 1865), I, 302–9.

roy was accused of making her husband commandeer the most beautiful mansion in Winchester as his headquarters so that she might live there, but the eviction of the women who owned it aroused a storm of protest across the state. It was not unusual, however, for wives of officers to persuade their husbands to take over enemy homes. General John A. Logan became rabid on the subject of a colonel's wife who moved with the army and made her husband "play the fool." Another Federal colonel was said to be so dominated by a "petticoat," and the regiment so demoralized by her interference, that she ruined his career.[3] So many officers and enlisted men mentioned these dictatorial wives that it must have seemed at times that the army was led by matriarchs.

The question whether young, unmarried women should visit camps was debated throughout the war. Many parents forbade it under any circumstances and others ordained rules of conduct to be enforced by a chaperone. Girls were inclined to resent strict supervision, and a group of teen-aged Bostonians slipped away from the spinster aunt who was to have accompanied them, but she pursued them in a second carriage and arrived at the destination just as they were alighting from theirs. The young women were often a bother, and as a soldier said, those living near his camp scarcely gave the officers "time to change their clothes."[4] Richmond belles, accompanied by chaperones, attended social functions in nearby encampments, and like their Northern sisters, entertained the men with musical programs and tableaux. The three Cary cousins were favorites of officers in the Army of Northern Virginia, and in September 1861, Jennie and Constance sang "Maryland, My Maryland" for a group encamped at Manassas, this being the first time most of the men had heard the wartime favorite. So popular were these girls that General Beauregard dubbed them the "Cary Invincibles."

While wives and relatives of officers were on the top rung of the camps' social ladder, on the bottom rung were those whom a journalist described as lacking "that great and only voucher of respectability for females in camp—the marriage tie."[5] Both armies had camp followers who were periodically ordered out

[3] Junius Henri Browne: *Four Years in Secessia* (Hartford, 1865), p. 31
[4] Florence Howe Hall: *Memories Grave and Gay* (New York, 1918), pp. 145–49.
[5] New Orleans *Daily Crescent*, Jan. 8, 1862.

only to establish themselves nearby and return at the first opportunity. Wherever the armies went they found prostitutes who capitalized on the men's presence and then often trailed in their wake. If the soldiers were in the area for an appreciable period the number of bawdy houses invariably increased, though some communities were already well supplied with these establishments. An Illinois private reported four in Pulaski, Tennessee, all with a price schedule which he thought reasonable. He told of one which permitted a man to spend the night for only five dollars "in tennessee monney." After discussing the matter at some length he added, "You may think i am a hard case but i am as pious as you can find in the army."[6]

The armies sometimes moved out of an area so rapidly that the prostitutes were left behind, but those traveling with the Federals usually caught up and those with the retreating Confederates often awaited the foe. After the Confederate evacuation of Island Number Ten, the Union soldiers arrived to find "a bevy of nymphs . . . disheveled and rumpled . . . but as much at home as though they had campaigned all their lives." The hour was early and the women were preparing breakfast, their hair tousled and bodices "unlaced," while the camp "bore all the marks of femininity," with hoop skirts and "abbreviated pantaloons" hung on trees and the baggage of Confederate officers "mingled in admirable confusion with crumpled dimity and calico." The observer erred in saying that this was "a new feature of war," for it was not among the innovations which the Civil War could claim. Another correspondent traveling with the Federal Army came upon a similar scene in Tennessee. Here twenty prostitutes abandoned by retreating Confederates were biding their time until Union forces arrived, "as willing to extend their gentle favors to the National officers as to their late Rebel protectors."[7]

Many of these Cyprians gained notoriety at the time but none received more widespread publicity than "Major" Annie Jones, the rank supposedly having been conferred on this twenty-

[6] Henry Shelling to William F. Hertzog, Nov. 21, 1863, MS, Chicago Historical Society, copy in possession of Bell I. Wiley, Atlanta.
[7] Frank Leslie: *Heroic Incidents* (New York, 1862), pp. 57–58; Browne: *Four Years in Secessia*, pp. 133–34; New York *Herald*, Sept. 16, 21, 1863, Mar. 19, Aug. 15, 1864.

year-old Massachusetts girl by General Julius Stahel. Slipping away from her uncle's home, she went to Washington and according to her account applied for a nursing appointment but was rejected by Miss Dix because of her youth. Her next move was to the camps in the environs of the capital, to which she was attracted, she said, "more out of curiosity" than for any other reason. For a time she was the "guest" of General Sigel's "staff officers" and according to the New York *Herald* was favored first by Stahel. After his removal from command Annie attached herself to "the young and gallant Custer with whom she remained" until he was ordered to send her away. According to her later statement, she was involved with General Hugh Judson Kilpatrick, as were many other camp followers before the end of the war, and he was jealous when she "went to the front, as a friend and companion of General Custer." It was then, said Annie, that Kilpatrick accused her of espionage, a charge which led to her incarceration in Old Capitol Prison. She confessed to spending the first two years of the war as "a guest of different officers who kept her supplied with her own tent, horses, orderlies, escorts, sentinels . . . rations, etc.," and during this period she had "always worn major's stripes." She vehemently denied ever serving as a "guide, scout, spy or hospital nurse," although officers testified she served in one or all of these capacities. "I was never anything but a companion to various commanding officers," she said.

Because several high-ranking officials were implicated, the case was investigated and Lincoln asked Annie to give him her side of the story. She was at the time imprisoned in the House of Correction in Barnstable, Massachusetts, where she had been sent after twice being committed to Old Capitol. She told the President her story, assuring him that she was loyal to the United States, and that those who accused her of spying had "blighted . . . [her] whole future life." She also stated that she had illicit relations with John L. Lockwood, the guard at Old Capitol, and that he had been dismissed by the superintendent, William P. Wood, who humiliated her by forcing her to travel to Barnstable in the company of "a common prostitute." She asked Lincoln to see that she was given a trial so that her name might be cleared, or permit her to leave the country. When Custer was questioned, he said Annie had arrived in his camp with a nurse's pass issued by the War Department but when a week later orders arrived "prohibiting all females from accompanying the war" he sent her out of camp and told her never "to visit . . . [his] command again." Custer said that a few weeks afterward she returned, riding "in an army ambulance with escort," and it being late in the day he gave her permission to spend the night provided she left the following morning. This he presumed she did since he never saw her again. In his statement Superintendent Wood admitted calling Annie a liar, thief, and prostitute; and as for making her travel with another prostitute, Mary Johnson, he said the latter was "a much better looking young lady . . . and just as decorous."

After she was sent to Barnstable, the press forgot Annie, but her story did not end. In May 1864 she wrote Fernando Wood, the controversial former mayor of New York who was then a Congressman, and introduced herself as a stranger, told her story, and asked for money, clothes, or books, but preferably all three, saying she was penniless and down to her "last copy of Shakespeare." Wood sent her fifty dollars, forty of which had been donated by his friends, and then requested that Secretary of War Stanton release her in his custody. On July 3, 1864, Stanton granted the request and wrote Wood, "I hope you may be able to exercise sufficient influence to keep her away from the Army." Thinking the matter settled, Stanton was surprised the following March to receive a bill for her upkeep from the Judge Advocate General of Massachusetts, who asked why she had not been released the previous July. Stanton was told that Governor Andrew had thought it "politically" unwise to turn her over to the disgruntled politician. He feared that Wood would use her "to the disadvantage" of the Republican party during the 1864 campaign.

Annie was paroled shortly thereafter on condition that she not go "south of the Susquehanna," but the war was nearly over. She wrote Stanton that she wanted to go to New Orleans to teach contrabands and asked that he rescind the condition, pleading with him: "Mr. Stanton, will you let me go? Give me passage to New Orleans and I will never trouble officials again." What happened to the "major" is uncertain, but in early 1866 there was an Annie Jones on the payroll of the Freedmen's Bureau first in

Meridian and then Vicksburg, Mississippi. However, the name is not unusual and this may not have been the same woman. Apparently not everyone lost interest in her after the war, for in 1879 John D. Sabine of the Adjutant General's Office requested a copy of her papers for "a friend in Boston." He did not explain what use was to be made of them and the request was denied for the reason that it was "not deemed advisable or conducive to the public interest."[8] It is highly improbable that the complete story will ever be told, but as it stands, none of those involved was ever cleared of the charges.

If camp followers left records, most have been destroyed or remain closeted with other family skeletons. However, government records testify to the presence of thousands in and near the military encampments. They created innumerable problems for the command; they demoralized the troops, spread venereal disease, bootlegged liquor, created disturbances, acted as spies, and received stolen government property as payment for their services. Records also show that some brazenly claimed pensions, although they usually tried to conceal their real wartime activities. Forty years after the war a pension applicant from the hills of Tennessee, who had served briefly in the Union Army, identified himself as the son of a camp follower. He implied that she had been better known in camp than he, and letters from those with whom he had served confirmed the fact. All remembered that his mother had been run out of camp repeatedly, and one wrote that "she was notorious for following the regiment and had a reputation for being a common prostitute." He recalled that she usually "bunked in some shanty, crib, or stable" but sometimes occupied "a tent and stayed as long as officers would permit. It would not be long until some row was raised over her and she would be driven out"—not always by officers but by soldiers who, according to another veteran, "couldn't stand her ways."[9]

Cities serving as army headquarters or frequented by soldiers always abounded in houses of prostitution, but Nashville affords an example of how the military authorities were frustrated in trying to solve the problem. In July 1863, General Wil-

[8] Annie E. Jones File, Record Group 19, Adjutant General's Papers, National Archives; New York *Herald*, Sept. 16, 1863.
[9] Pension File Number 1,070,204, Veterans Administration Records, National Archives.

liam Rosecrans ordered the provost marshal "without loss of time to seize and transport to Louisville *all prostitutes* found in the city or known to be here," giving as his reason the "prevalence of venereal disease." John M. Newcomb's luxurious new pleasure boat, the *Idahoe,* was immediately commandeered for the trip despite the owner's protests, and approximately one-third of the city's registered prostitutes, all suffering from venereal disease, were placed aboard. In addition to Newcomb and the 111 women was a crew of three, but there was no military escort and the four men were unable to keep others from coming aboard even when the vessel was anchored in midstream. Newcomb reported that they became violent when he tried "to drive them away," and once on board they and the "bad women" wrecked the furniture and damaged the boat. Before leaving Nashville, Newcomb had been issued 180 rations, enough to get them to Louisville unless an emergency arose.

A week after leaving Nashville, the *Idahoe* arrived in Louisville and Newcomb was told he must take his passengers on to Cincinnati; but arriving there the women were not permitted to go ashore and he was ordered to anchor across the river at Newport, Kentucky, and to keep the prostitutes on board. For thirteen days the ship remained, and during this time fourteen of the women were taken off by men who served Newcomb with writs of habeas corpus. On July 28 he was ordered to go to Louisville and upon arrival was told to take the ninety-seven remaining passengers back to Nashville. On August 4, 1863, the badly damaged *Idahoe* docked and Newcomb immediately demanded that it be inspected by a military official. Four days later Rosecrans's appointee, Captain James Hughes, made his report. He found the "stateroom furniture badly broken, the mattresses badly soiled . . . the boat badly damaged"; and because the vessel had been new when commandeered, Hughes recommended that $1,000 in damages be paid. Newcomb also billed the government for his purchases of food and "medicine peculiar to the diseases of women in this class," in the amount of $4,300. He was reimbursed for the damages and provisions three years later, but not until he had gone to Washington, waded through endless red tape, and finally appealed to Stanton. He told the secretary that he had been forced to sell his boat because after its bizarre wartime voyage its reputation was ruined and it came to be known as the "Floating Whore House." The women who had taken the twenty-eight-day pleasure cruise were turned loose in Nashville and probably returned to their profession. Military officials tried to stop the spread of venereal disease by ordering that prostitutes have periodic examinations, but not all complied.[1]

The army camps' female population included many women who were not authorized nurses, wives of officers, or professional prostitutes, and the respect which they commanded depended on the individual. Any laundress, cook, emergency nurse, or woman soldier not accompanied by a male relative, preferably her husband, was vulnerable to unflattering criticism. Even the most altruistic was being indiscreet, for a society as yet not ready to endorse wholeheartedly the idea of supervised women nurses would certainly question the motives of an unmarried woman or girl who insisted on going to the front. Some who did win the men's respect were not necessarily accepted as quite proper by the general public, but the common soldier was often devoted to the older, more motherly souls who looked upon them as they would their sons, and this was later borne out when these kindly women were honored guests at army reunions. As long as she lived "Mother" Bickerdyke was affectionately received by the veterans at the Grand Army of the Republic encampments; and so beloved was Mrs. Rose Rooney of New Orleans, who spent four years sewing, cooking, nursing, and counseling the men in the Fifteenth Louisiana that she was appointed matron of the Louisiana Soldiers' Home. The GAR also honored Bridget Deaver and other humble women, and the Confederate Veterans never forgot Mrs. Betsy Sullivan, known as the "Mother of the First Tennessee Regiment," or Mrs. Bettie Taylor Philips who cared for the men in Kentucky's "Orphan Brigade." Others also served in camps without having their character or motives questioned, but most were not so fortunate.

Many a romantic girl dreamed of being a second Joan of Arc, but those who actually entered the ranks by posing as men

[1] The Idahoe File, Record Group 217, United States General Accounting Office, National Archives. The Nashville *Dispatch*, July 8, 10, 26, 28, 1863, refers to 150 prostitutes, but this is an exaggeration. There would have been no reason for Newcomb to report a smaller number since he was filing for reimbursement.

were usually viewed by contemporaries as mentally unbalanced or immoral. Some were looking for excitement and adventure, but others unquestionably had baser motives. It has been generally agreed that approximately 400 women posed as soldiers, but Mary Livermore was convinced there were more who at some time fought as men, and the fact that a number were not unmasked until they had served two or more years would seem to indicate that some were never detected. Mrs. Livermore noted that "startling histories of these military women were current in the gossip of Army life; and extravagant and unreal as were many of their narrations, one always felt that they had an element of fact." But like most of her generation, Mrs. Livermore believed that "such service was not the noblest that women rendered" during the war.[2]

The press was in part to blame for girls' trying to emulate Joan of Arc, for early in the war journalists lauded those who dashed to the recruiting offices. While most became less commendatory, the New York *Herald,* on June 7, 1864, continued to praise their "spunk and pluck." In this instance the writer was referring to a girl who had written to ask that he help her find a physician willing to certify she was a man so that she could enlist, but judging from the number who ostensibly passed medical examinations she had no cause for worry.

Fragmentary accounts of unidentified women soldiers evidence their determination, pathetically illustrate the effects of their unconventional behavior, and raise doubts about the individual. After having enlisted with her brother and fought "right up to Ringgold," a girl known only as Nellie A. K. had been discharged when her sex became known. She pleaded with the spy Pauline Cushman to assist her in re-enlisting, saying that she "laid awake all night" thinking of war and cursing "the fate" that made her a girl. Widely circulated at the time was the story of the mysterious "Emily" from Brooklyn who had become obsessed with the idea that she was the second Joan of Arc. Her distraught parents, on the advice of a physician, sent her to an aunt's farm in Michigan, thinking that she would have less of an opportunity to enlist, but a few weeks after her arrival she slipped away, enrolled as a drummer, and was sent to the Army of the Cumber-

[2] Livermore: *My Story of the War,* p. 120.

land. Her sex was detected when she was mortally wounded at Lookout Mountain, but before she died she requested that a message be sent her father asking his forgiveness and explaining that she had "expected to deliver her country, but the fates would not have it so." When a New Jersey girl who had enlisted with her lover was later sent home she tried to commit suicide. Ellen Goodridge of Wisconsin was disowned by her father when she announced her intention to accompany her fiancé to war, but for three years she fought by his side, nursed him, and said they were married during his last illness. Mary Owens returned from the war and reported that she had been secretly wed to the man with whom she had enlisted eighteen months earlier. He was killed and she was wounded in the same battle, and upon her return the press noted that she was "the heroine of the neighborhood," which may or may not have been the case.[3]

Women soldiers were almost certain to be found out if they required hospital treatment. When Lizzie Compton was wounded and her sex detected she claimed to have enlisted at fourteen and served eighteen months in seven different regiments, leaving one and enrolling in another when fearing detection. Fanny Wilson of New Jersey had also served eighteen months before her sex was discovered during the Vicksburg Campaign. She was sent to Cairo where she danced in a local ballet before re-enlisting in the Third Illinois Cavalry, only to be discharged a second time. An unidentified Minnesota girl claimed two years' service before being wounded, as did Mary Wise, who was paid for this period before being mustered out of an Indiana regiment. Not all who enlisted, however, made it to the front, for Sarah Collins of Wisconsin was "detected by the way she put on her shoes and stockings" and sent home before the regiment left town, and Mary Burns, attired in uniform, was arrested in Detroit before her company departed.[4]

[3] Ferdinand Sarmiento: *Life of Pauline Cushman* (Philadelphia, 1865), pp. 368–70; Brooklyn *Daily Times*, Feb. 20, 1864; Washington *Chronicle*, Feb. 22, 1864; Frank Moore: *Women of the War*, pp. 529–32, 532–33; New York *Herald*, Oct. 14, 1861; *Frank Leslie's Illustrated Newspaper*, Mar. 7, 1863.

[4] *Frank Leslie's Illustrated Newspaper*, Dec. 19, 1863; New York *Herald*, Dec. 28, 1863, Aug. 12, 14, 1864; Ethel Alice Hurn: *Wisconsin Women in the War* (Madison, 1911), p. 103; Detroit *Advertiser and Tribune*, Feb. 25, 1863.

The most famous Federal female soldier was Sarah Emma Edmonds who, under the name of Franklin Thompson, enrolled as a male nurse in the Second Michigan Cavalry and served for two years in this capacity without being detected. Rather than be hospitalized after contracting malaria, she requested a furlough, and when it was denied she deserted and later went to the Virginia front. Her book published in 1865 and her later pension claims state that she was a nurse, spy, mail carrier, and soldier, all the while having the Union soldiers believing she was a man. Marrying after the war, she was eventually able to prove to the Federal Government's satisfaction that she had served during the conflict and in 1884 was given a pension of twelve dollars a month. More incredible than "Franklin Thompson's" record was that of Jennie Hodgers, who posed as "Albert Cashier," fought undetected for four years, and continued the masquerade after the war. Apparently no one's suspicions were aroused, not even the physicians who examined "Albert" when "he" applied for a pension in 1899. Not until an automobile accident in 1911 sent her to a veteran's hospital was it known that "Albert Cashier" was a woman. An investigation indicated that none of the veterans questioned knew or admitted they knew that their fellow soldier was a woman, but they did recall that "Cashier" had been rather introverted and "hard to know."[5]

Among the Confederate soldiers was Mrs. Amy Clarke, who enlisted with her husband and continued in the service after he was killed at Shiloh. Not until she was wounded a second time and captured by the Federals was her sex detected, and as soon as she had recovered they gave her a dress and sent her into Confederate lines; but a short time later she was seen in Mississippi making plans to re-enlist. Mrs. Malinda Blalock of North Carolina, posing as her husband's brother, enlisted as Sam Blalock, but in this instance the recruiting officer was said to have been in on the secret. Newspapers mentioned Southern women who were arrested in uniform, and less than two weeks before the end of the war Mary Wright and Margaret Henry,

[5] Linus Pierpont Brockett: *The Camp, the Battle Field and the Hospital* (Philadelphia, 1866), pp. 70–72; Bell Irvin Wiley: *The Life of Billy Yank* (Indianapolis, 1951), p. 337; Pension File Number 1,001,132, Veterans Administration Records, National Archives.

described as "dashing young creatures," were captured by the Federals and imprisoned in Nashville.[6]

The most famous Confederate woman soldier was Mme. Loreta Janeta Velasquez, but it should be noted that her fame rests entirely on her fantastic account published more than a decade after the war. Nor has it been definitely established that the author might conceivably have had any of the experiences described. It seems impossible that any one woman could have done all she claimed—traveling from one end of the Confederacy to the other as a soldier, spy, and railroad conductor, and to Washington and Canada as a secret agent, while managing to work for a time in an Indiana arsenal and run the blockade. It is possible that she did some of these things, but her story has the earmarks of a composite picture of several women's experiences, publicized or rumored at the time and later enlivened by the author's vivid imagination. The controversy created by the book's publication will be discussed elsewhere, but as Mrs. Livermore noted, since there is "an element of fact" in the account, Mme. Velasquez' claims merit consideration.

She told of raising a battalion of Arkansans in 1861, serving first in Florida and then at First Manassas, Ball's Bluff, Fort Pillow, and Shiloh. While in Washington as a secret agent she claimed that she duped several officials, including Lincoln and Lafayette Baker, and at other times she bested the generals, among them Butler and Rosecrans. While masquerading as Lieutenant Henry T. Buford she romanced the ladies in nearly every Confederate state, leaving a trail of broken hearts while acquiring "an idea or two" which were, she said, "subsequently . . . useful." While courting a Florida widow she learned more about "the fine points of feminine human nature" than she had in the preceding twenty years, and living in camp taught her that the men's conversation was "revolting and utterly vile" and their references to women "thoroughly despicable." Lecturing her sex, she said if they could hear the "masculine viciousness" applied to women, they might be more careful of their conduct, although

[6] Jackson *Mississippian*, Dec. 30, 1862; Henry W. R. Jackson: *The Southern Women of the Second American Revolution* (Atlanta, 1863), p. 7; Fayetteville (North Carolina) *Observer*, Oct. 9, 1923; Walter Clark (ed.): *Histories of the Several Regiments and Battalions from North Carolina in the Great War* (Raleigh, 1901), II, 330–31; Washington *Chronicle*, Mar. 30, 1865.

she doubted that "those disposed to sin" would heed her warning. Admitting that life in camp was rough, she nevertheless thought nice women safer there than among the scandalmongers in "city, village, and country," and she placed herself among those whose reputation was "unblemished."

Whether she raised a battalion and whether there was a Henry T. Buford are questionable; there was a story told of a Mrs. Laura J. Williams from Arkansas who, disguised as Lieutenant Henry Benford, raised and commanded a company of Texans early in the war and fought at Shiloh and elsewhere in the Western area. Madame Velasquez said that one of the names she used while a secret agent was Mrs. Alice Williams, and such a person was arrested in Richmond, imprisoned in Castle Thunder, and released as soon as her identity was established. Richmond papers lauded Mrs. Williams's work as a soldier and nurse but naturally refrained from mentioning her espionage activities. At the time of her incarceration Henry Birch, the New York *Herald* correspondent, was also a prisoner, and much of what he wrote about Mrs. Williams is included in Mme. Velasquez' later account. Birch said the woman was released when it was proved she was a Confederate agent, that she told him she was going to Washington on a mission, and that three weeks after her discharge a guard had a letter from her written in that city. One interesting comment made by Birch was not included in Mme. Velasquez' book: he mentioned that after Mrs. Williams was released she remained at the prison for several days "boarding, drinking, gambling, and carousing with Captain Alexander and the other officers."[7]

Mme. Velasquez said that she was married four times, her first two husbands being killed in the war, the third dying soon thereafter and the fourth in the seventies. Immediately after the war she traveled in Europe, Latin America, and the Far West, and she became involved in the Confederate colony in Venezuela. She wrote her book because she was in desperate financial straits, and as might be expected, her editor lauded her beauty, bravery, vitality, and business ability; but it was his statement that Mme.

[7] C. J. Worthington (ed.): *The Woman in Battle* (Hartford, 1876), *passim;* Matthew Page Andrews: *The Women of the South in War-Times* (Baltimore, 1927), pp. 112–15; Richmond *Daily Examiner,* July 2, 1863; Richmond *Daily Whig,* June 19, 1863; New York *Herald,* Oct. 19, 1863.

Velasquez was "a typical Southern woman of the period" which stirred up a hornet's nest.

Nurses and Sanitary Commission workers often came in contact with "female soldiers" once they were unmasked, and they generally concluded that these women were something less than virtuous. A "stout and muscular" woman in her late twenties was wounded in battle, captured by the Confederates, and returned to Federal lines with this note: "As Confederates do not use women in war, this woman, wounded in battle, is returned to you." While she was recuperating, Annie Wittenmyer talked with her several times and once asked her why she had enlisted. The woman replied that she "wanted camp life" and added that she planned to re-enlist, but Mrs. Wittenmyer urged her to go home and forget the army, cautioning her that "officers had been warned" to be on the lookout for her. Military officials as well as Mrs. Wittenmyer interrogated the men with whom she had tented, and not one admitted knowing that she was a woman.[8] This was not unusual, however, for in instances where they were aware of the sex, they usually did not—for obvious reasons— report it.

There is no question that many and probably most of the women soldiers were prostitutes or concubines. That archenemy of women in camp, General Rosecrans, raved about the "flagrant outrage" when one of the sergeants *was delivered of a baby, which,*" he irately noted, "is in violation of all military law and of the army regulations." He continued, "No such case has been known since the days of Jupiter." And in December 1864 it was reported that a "bouncing baby boy" had been born to a Confederate officer imprisoned on Johnson Island. The reporter facetiously concluded that "he was undoubtedly a woman." With the complete lack of objectivity so common in war, he further stated that Northern women who went into the service "disguised as men" were prompted only by "patriotism or love" but this Confederate mother had probably enlisted for "profit."[9] In the fall of 1864, General Early sent to Richmond two women soldiers, Mary and Molly Bell, who for two years had served as Tom Parker and Bob Martin. Until recently they had not, said Early, excited "the

[8] Mrs. Annie Wittenmyer: *Under the Guns* (Boston, 1895), pp. 17–20.
[9] Brockett: *The Camp, the Battle Field and the Hospital*, p. 303; San-dusky *Register*, Dec. 12, 1864.

suspicions of their Captain or their comrades," yet the captain earlier had reported them to be "common camp followers and . . . the means of demoralizing several hundred men" in his command. They had, he said, "adopted the disguise of soldiers better to follow the army and hide their iniquity." The reporter confidently stated that there were "more of the same . . . left in the ranks, masked by a Confederate uniform," and concluded that this explained "the utter worthlessness and inefficiency of some of the commands in the Valley." The Misses Bell spent three weeks in Castle Thunder and were then sent to their home in Pulaski County, still dressed in their uniforms and "perfectly disconsolate at being separated from their male companions in arms."[1]

The vivandières, or daughters of the regiment, did not disguise their sex and they were usually accompanied by a chaperone or a male relative, but it was primarily in the early days of the war that they marched off with the troops. Most returned home when they realized that war was something more than a dress parade, but some stayed to nurse. Kady Brownell, Annie Etheridge, and Bridget Deaver were all said to have been vivandières; and Eliza Wilson, the daughter of a wealthy mill owner, accompanied the Fifth Wisconsin and carried with her the prayers of a host of well-wishers. She was said to have been "worshipped by the rough soldiers . . . and held in high esteem by all the officers," and as a vivandière she was expected "to head the regiment when in parade, and to assuage the thirst of the wounded and dying on the battlefield." Sarah Taylor was the "daughter" of the First Tennessee, who looked on her as a "guardian angel"; and Lucy Ann Cox was the vivandière of the Thirteenth Virginia but soon turned to nursing. These women did not lose their respectability, but some others who later in the war attached themselves to the troops and assumed the title of "daughter of the regiment" were of dubious character. A Georgia private told of one he had seen who was "too free and easy . . . and somewhat under the influence of liquor. A drunken man is bad enough," he said, "but a drunken woman is an awful sight."[2]

[1] Richmond *Examiner*, Oct. 31, Nov. 25, 1864.
[2] *Frank Leslie's Illustrated Newspaper*, Aug. 17, 1862; Hurn: *Wisconsin Women in the War*, pp. 100–102; Frank Leslie: *Heroic Incidents*, pp. 4–6; Logan, *The Part Taken by Women in American History*, p. 492; Theodore T. Fogle to his parents, Sept. 11, 1861, typescript in possession of Frances Harrold, Atlanta.

Some officers maintained that Annie Jones's first appearance in camp was as a viandière attached to a New York regiment, but if this is true, she was added to the ranks after the regiment reached Washington.

Mrs. Ella Hobart seems to have been the only woman who served as a chaplain, although others occasionally preached in camp. Mrs. Hobart was elected to this position by the First Wisconsin Artillery in 1864 and served in this capacity for nine months. After the war she lectured in the North and in September 1865 addressed a large audience in Cooper Union, but according to the New York *Herald* of the eighteenth she did not discuss her war experiences although "spicey ideas" were inserted among her more serious comments.

The army camps were not only "teeming with women"; they were teeming with all kinds of women who came from all walks of life and had different reasons for being there. Some recalled camp life with nostalgia; some remembered the hardships, frustrations, and deaths; and some could look back on their experience as a turning point in their lives—for better or worse. Many officers did not welcome them to camp and others thought they enlivened the scene, while some found them a source of amusement. General Ewell once said that they "would make a grand brigade—if it were not for snakes and spiders."[3] Although most women eventually settled back into routine after their camp experiences, many adventuresses had tragic later lives. But it was the war which had afforded all of them, as Laura Stratton Birney said, "a peep behind the military curtain."

[3] Gordon, *Reminiscences of the Civil War*, pp. 41–42.

5

Risked Everything

WOMEN WHO SERVED as spies, couriers, guides, scouts, saboteurs, smugglers, or informers remembered the war years as the most exciting of their lives. There was always an element of risk in any of these activities, but many spirited girls and imaginative women were challenged by the opportunity to perform daring deeds for their cause. The most succinct statement of the dangers encountered is inscribed on the marker at the grave of the Union spy Elizabeth Van Lew, in Richmond's Shockhoe Cemetery. It reads, "She risked everything that is dear to man—friends, fortune, comfort, health, life itself . . ."

Anyone engaged in espionage did indeed stand to lose "everything," for spies were not publicly identified by those they represented, and their eccentric, unconventional conduct often aroused suspicion, damaged the reputation, and made them a target for abuse and ridicule. A woman's morals were questioned if she lived in camp, met with soldiers, or received men callers at strange hours, and if arrested she would likely spend the rest of her life under a cloud, for some would always doubt her integrity. Women engaged in espionage eventually learned that few people completely trusted or respected a spy, not even a "friend." This Sarah Emma Edmonds suggested when she asked that her other war services be remembered and her spy activities forgotten because "so much mean deception" was implied in the latter. "It may do in war time," she noted, but "it is not pleasant to think about in time of peace."[1]

Some of the most effective espionage was conducted by women in their own neighborhoods, and once the public became aware of this, any person was likely to be suspected and falsely accused. A Kentuckian saw a *"pretty woman in black"* in the hotel in which she lived, and not knowing her, concluded she was *"the devious resort* of the Yanks *to find out something."* Although Phoebe Pember discounted much of the gossip about Richmond women suspected of espionage, she wrote her family about what was being said. Mrs. Pember reported that Margaret Sumner Mc-Lean was suspected of spying, although the charges were being whispered because "her husband stands high in the army."She might have added as another possible reason that Mrs. McLean was an intimate friend of the Davis family. Having been born in the North and having a father and brothers in the Federal Army, Mrs. McLean needed nothing more to make her suspect. Mrs. Pember quoted others as saying, "Lincoln pays Mrs. McLane [*sic*] for her information . . . Jeff Davis pays Mrs. Greenhow for watching her, and Mrs. G. is also paid by the Federals for not seeing too much, and lastly the two ladies are in collusion and divide the spoils." Complicated as this facetious comment was, it was no more so than most webs spun by the wartime rumor-mongers. The cool, logical Mrs. McLean may have been suspected because she delighted in asking irrational women to prove their accusations and generalizations, yet she did have many friends in Richmond.[2]

Contemporary accounts indicate that at some time during the war a large percentage of citizens were suspected by someone, and while the newspapers in both sections cited rumors, those in the North called names with reckless abandon. On

[1] Pension File Number 282,136, Veterans Administration Records, National Archives.

[2] Issa Desha Breckinridge to Mary C. Desha, Aug. 16, 1864, Breckinridge Family Papers; Phoebe Yates Pember to Eugenia Phillips, June 25, 1863, Phillips-Myers Papers; Mary Boykin Chesnut: *A Diary From Dixie*, ed. Ben Ames Williams (Boston, 1950), pp. 49, 67, 83, 85, 86, 89, 90, 91, 427. Both Mrs. Pember and Mrs. Chesnut spell the name McLane, which is the way it was pronounced, but the correct spelling is McLean.

August 23, 1861, the New York *Herald* reported that Mrs. William McKendree Gwin, wife of the Tennessee-born Confederate sympathizer and former Senator from California, was under house arrest in Washington, but five days later it printed a retraction after Mrs. Gwin assured the editor that she was at West Point, New York, "residing very quietly" with her family and "occupied in domestic concerns." This same paper on January 7, 1862, retracted an earlier report that General Lorenzo Thomas's family had been arrested, explaining that it was a neighbor who had been taken into custody for "communicating with the enemy." The correspondent noted the number of women who had been imprisoned for espionage and concluded, "There has been a great abridgement of the privileges heretofore accorded the sex."

Women spies made excellent newspaper copy and even those from prominent families received no mercy from the press. If not referred to outright as prostitutes, they were accused of having clandestine relations with specific officials, of being a "Cleopatra," "seductress," "courtesan," or insane. The respect ordinarily accorded upper-class women was cast aside when they were suspected, arrested, imprisoned, or banished. The Federal Government was generally more successful in dealing with enemy agents and Northern newspapers were more outspoken than those in the Confederacy, where women spies were usually ignored until it was too late. Richmond papers implied that Elizabeth Van Lew, her mother, and others were secret agents but their names were seldom used; and since Miss Van Lew posed as an eccentric, she was thought by officials to be "crazy" but harmless, which was just what she desired. She was one of the war's most effective spies because she was let alone.

After the outbreak of war Washington officials realized that the city was threatened from within by secessionists, and severe measures were taken to rid the capital of dangerous enemies. Men were the first to be arrested, however, and women considered themselves immune from such treatment. Nor did officials think them dangerous until it was learned that they had transmitted secret military information to the Confederates before First Manassas. No sooner had this Federal rout taken place than newspapers circulated stories of young women crossing into Confederate lines with secret messages pinned in their hair, and only then did the government begin its investigation. Two weeks before the battle Mary Chesnut confided to her diary that "women from Washington come riding into our camp, beautiful women. They bring letters done up in their back hair, or in their garments." A week later when her husband failed to meet her as expected, Mrs. Chesnut concluded it was because he "had too many spies to receive from Washington, galloping in with the exact number of enemy done up in their hair."[3]

After being under surveillance for nearly a month, Mrs. Rose O'Neal Greenhow, Mrs. Philip Phillips, and other known Southern sympathizers were placed under house arrest on August 23. By this time Washington had become a hotbed of suspicion and rumor. Mrs. John A. Kasson, a newcomer to official circles, her husband having been appointed First Assistant Postmaster General, found when trying to make calls in the early autumn that the homes of many Southern sympathizers were under guard and was told she might leave her card but could not enter. She sadly concluded that she "may as well look upon that acquaintance as ended," for any sign of friendship on her part could make her suspect. Mrs. Kasson had already observed "how expert in tongue-guidance many women" had become since everyone found it necessary "to give an account of words inadvisedly uttered."[4]

Rose Greenhow's arrest was the first to attract widespread attention. This poised widow of forty-four was one of Washington's most popular hostesses and had many influential Republican friends, including William H. Seward, Henry Wilson, and Charles Francis Adams, all of whom she entertained after the outbreak of hostilities. She had moved in official circles during the Buchanan administration, knew prominent Democrats, and was the aunt of Mrs. Stephen A. Douglas. Not trying to conceal her Southern sympathies, she assumed that her political connections would enable her to assist the Confederacy without jeopardizing her position. This charmingly mysterious woman could attract, repel, or frighten men as she chose and was adept at

---

[3] Chesnut: *A Diary*, pp. 77, 81.
[4] Caroline Eliot Kasson: "An Iowa Woman in Washington, D.C., 1861–1865," *Iowa Journal of History*, LII (1954), 62; Des Moines *Iowa State Register*, Nov. 13, 1861.

tricking them into disclosing state secrets. She had all the attributes of a successful spy, and when Captain Thomas Jordan of the United States Army, soon to be Colonel Jordan of the Confederacy, suggested that she transmit military information in secret code to the Confederate Army, she enthusiastically agreed. Prior to First Manassas Mrs. Greenhow sent two messages, one conveyed by Bettie Duvall and the other by a former Federal employee, and this information helped the Confederates to plan their strategy and bring up necessary reinforcements, thus contributing to the Southern victory.

After the battle Mrs. Greenhow continued to supply the Confederates with information extracted from friends and prisoners of war, realizing all the while that she was being watched. Not until August 23, however, did the secret police search her home and place her and her eight-year-old daughter under house arrest. A week later the house, thereafter known as "Fort Greenhow," became a prison for other women suspects, including Mrs. Philip Phillips, her daughters and sister. Also confined at the "Fort" were Mrs. Betty A. Hassler, whose husband was a Confederate officer; the aged mother of James T. Jackson who had killed Ellsworth in Alexandria; and Ellie Poole, who had been imprisoned by the Federals in Wheeling only to escape and be recaptured, after which she was brought to Washington for "safe-keeping." Ellie was a hotheaded Confederate sympathizer who had been a correspondent for the Richmond *Enquirer* and Baltimore *Exchange*. Also imprisoned in "Fort Greenhow" were a Mrs. Baxley and a Mrs. Onderdunk, the latter being especially offensive to Mrs. Greenhow, who said she was "a woman of bad repute and recognized by . . . the guard as such, having been seen . . . in the exercises of her vocation." She was probably planted there to spy on Mrs. Greenhow, for they were compelled to eat together for a time.

Mrs. Greenhow was not permitted to read newspapers, her mail was censored, and only her sister, Mrs. James Madison Cutts and niece, Mrs. Douglas, could visit her. For the first week guards watched her every hour of the day and night, much to her embarrassment and indignation. Mrs. Chesnut read a "most bravely indelicate letter" in which Mrs. Greenhow described this first week spent in the "full sight of men, her rooms open . . . sleepless sentinels watching . . . and looking at her by way of amusement." Mrs. Chesnut noted that beautiful as Mrs Greenhow was, "few women like all the mysteries of their toilette laid bare to the public eye."[5] Despite the guard and rigid censorship the prisoner somehow managed to send messages outside, and in January 1862 she, her daughter, and Mrs. Baxley were removed to Old Capitol Prison. Here Mrs. Greenhow stayed until the following May, during which time she remained aloof from the guards, Mrs. Baxley, and the other inmates. One of the guards said that of all the women prisoners she was "the most ladylike in her manner and conversation . . . and although rather severe at times in her denunciations of the North," showed herself to be "possessed of a woman's heart in her sad moments."[6]

In May, Mrs. Greenhow, her daughter, and others were sent into Confederate lines, and on June 4 she was received by Confederate officials in Richmond, among them Jefferson Davis, who was quoted as saying, "But for you there would have been no Battle of Bull Run." Mrs. Greenhow later wrote that this one statement had repaid her for all her suffering, and the moment at which it was spoken was "the proudest of . . . [her] whole life." For approximately a year thereafter she traveled through the Confederacy and in August 1863 took a blockade runner out of Wilmington, transferred to a British vessel in Bermuda, and landed in France, where she placed her daughter in a convent. After being presented to Napoleon III she went to England, where she was received at the court of Queen Victoria, visited with Confederate representatives, and met British leaders. While she was abroad, her book, *My Imprisonment and the First Year of Abolition Rule at Washington,* was published in London and fairly well received.

She was said to have carried to Europe official papers from Jefferson Davis and to have had on her person other papers and a money belt filled with gold when she embarked on the voyage home. As the ship approached Wilmington it was spotted by the

[5] Rose O'Neal Greenhow: *My Imprisonment and the First Year of Abolition Rule at Washington* (London, 1863), pp. 102–68; Margaret Leech: *Reveille in Washington, 1861–1865* (New York, 1941), pp. 19–20, 94–96, 135–41; Chesnut: *A Diary,* p. 169. See also Ishbel Ross: *Rebel Rose* (New York, 1954), *passim.*
[6] New York *Herald,* Jan. 22, 1862.

Federal patrol, and Mrs. Greenhow and two Confederate agents, fearing capture, asked to be rowed ashore. The boat capsized and she was drowned, the legend being that she was weighted down by the gold. When her body was brought to Wilmington, "hundreds of ladies lined the wharf," and all funeral arrangements were taken care of by the local soldiers' aid society. Mrs. Greenhow had given her life for the Confederacy, although most of her contemporaries did not realize it at the time. After the war Burton Harrison, private secretary to Jefferson Davis, lauded this woman of "beauty and charm" who, in helping to win First Manassas, enabled the Confederacy "to muster men and resources . . . that might never have been available" had this first major battle resulted in defeat.[7] Her daughter was in the French convent when she received word of her mother's death and after leaving the school several years later tried her hand at acting before marrying and settling in California.

The Philip Phillips' home in Washington was searched the same day as Mrs. Greenhow's. Mr. Phillips, a former Congressman from Alabama, had a lucrative law practice in the capital and hoped to remain there despite his family's Southern background. He many times warned Mrs. Phillips to guard her tongue and control her fiery temper, but she continued to express her opinions, associate with known secessionists, and show more than a casual interest in imprisoned Southern sympathizers and soldiers, for neither discretion nor humility was among her virtues. When the police descended on her home and placed her under house arrest, she wrote in her journal, "this day has ushered in a new era . . . one which marks the arrest and imprisonment of women for political opinions." A week later she and the other women in the family were taken to "Fort Greenhow," where they spent a miserable three weeks. Nothing was in plentiful supply, said Mrs. Phillips, except mosquitoes, and no friend sent her "a message of kind inquiry," although many were within "speaking distance." Her twenty-fifth wedding anniversary passed without incident other than her daughter Caroline going outside the prison to a dentist and the women debating what type of clothes

---

[7] Wilmington *Journal,* Oct. 3, 1864; Richmond *Sentinel,* Oct. 3, 1864; New York *Herald,* Oct. 15, 1864; Memo on Rose O'Neal Greenhow, MS, Burton Harrison Papers.

a "prisoner of war" should wear into the outside world. While at "Fort Greenhow" Mrs. Phillips mused, "What will come from this Rebellion we know not, but women always act first and think later," seeming to imply that she regretted her foolhardy indiscretions, but later events prove that such was not the case. Mr. Phillips's influence and lack of evidence brought the release of the women in September, and they left Washington for the Confederacy.[8]

During the late summer of 1861, Mrs. Greenhow and Mrs. Phillips were discussed in the newspapers and over the teacups; but even before her arrest Mrs. Phillips was a topic for gossip, her name having been linked with those of several Southerners, including Stephen Mallory, the Confederate Secretary of Navy. One prominent social leader thought her a "beautiful, clever Jewess" but a very "mad, bad woman," yet some ladies in Richmond spoke of both prisoners as "saints and martyrs," and one facetiously quipped, "Think of ladies of their age being confined!"[9] That Mrs. Greenhow was under suspicion both North and South was not unusual in the case of spies, but not until after the war were her morals openly questioned and her name linked with that of Henry Wilson and other political officials.

Whether or not Mrs. Phillips was a spy in Washington, she left the city as a courier, carrying official papers to Jefferson Davis. After a brief stopover in Richmond the family moved on to New Orleans where Mr. Phillips opened a law office. The fall of that city brought the couple within Federal lines for the second time and Mrs. Phillips into conflict with General Butler, who accused her of laughing when the body of a Union officer was borne under her balcony. She explained that the laughter had come from a children's party and was not intended as disrespect, but the general was not convinced and ordered her imprisoned on Ship Island. Her accommodations must have made those at "Fort Greenhow" seem palatial, for she was compelled to live in a cell which was nothing more than "a huge box on a pile of sand." Throughout the summer of 1862 she was sick, uncomfortable, and daily humiliated by the guards and navy wives who stared at her as if she were a caged animal. When released in the

---

[8] Journal of Mrs. Eugenia Phillips, MS, Philip Phillips Family Papers.
[9] Chesnut: A *Diary*, pp. 10, 23, 124, 266.

fall, she and her family were banished into Confederate lines and joined a colony of New Orleans refugees in La Grange, Georgia, where they lived for the duration of the war. They then returned to Washington where Mr. Phillips resumed the practice of law, but for the rest of her life Eugenia Phillips remained embittered by her wartime experiences. Writing in 1889, she maintained her innocence, positively stated that she had not been a spy, and indignantly protested against the "shameful" way in which "many histories" had condemned her.[1]

The other women imprisoned at "Fort Greenhow" met with varied treatment. Ellie Poole was soon released, it being said that she took the oath of allegiance to the United States and left the house with fifty dollars in gold, which Mrs. Greenhow called a gift of the Federal Government. Mrs. Baxley, a divorcee, had appealed to Seward in the hope that he would order her release, but the evidence against her was overwhelming. She would probably never have been arrested had she not told fellow passengers on a truce boat en route to Baltimore that she was carrying secret papers out of the Confederacy. Taken into custody as soon as the boat docked, she was found to be carrying nearly a hundred letters and documents on her person, fifty in her bonnet alone. These were addressed to Southern sympathizers in Maryland; but the most incriminating evidence, found in her corset, was a surgeon's commission from Jefferson Davis addressed to Dr. Septimus Brown of Baltimore, complete with passes and route of travel to Richmond. Brown was imprisoned in Fort McHenry and Mrs. Baxley was held for a time in a Baltimore hotel before being sent to "Fort Greenhow" and later to Old Capitol. She proved to be a problem, high-strung, given to tantrums, fainting, and according to Mrs. Greenhow, "vehement language." She fought and clawed her guard at Old Capitol, once giving him a bloody nose, yet she might have been released had she been willing to take the oath or agree to an honor parole. She would

[1] "A Southern Woman's Story of Her Imprisonment During the War," typescript, Philip Phillips Family Papers; New York *Herald*, July 14, 1862. A *Herald* correspondent described Mrs. Phillips when she confronted Butler as "remarkable . . . She was so cool that I found it quite refreshing to sit in her shade. Occasionally she . . . would break into a broad smile of amused contempt, and affect to hide it behind her fan. . . . A notice on the door especially attracted her . . . It reads 'There is no difference between a he and she adder, in their venom.' "

do neither but made it quite clear that she did not want to return to the Confederacy. However, she was in the group sent South with Mrs. Greenhow.[2]

Sent into Confederate lines at the same time was Mrs. Augusta Morris, a gay, sprightly, gentle little woman who had been arrested in February 1862 on charges of being in communication with the Confederates. She was a suspect after trying to sell the Federals the Confederate signal system and was sentenced to Old Capitol and then to banishment on refusing to take the oath. Another inmate of Old Capitol, Mrs. L. A. McCarty, was arrested for wearing men's clothing, but a search of her baggage turned up a projectile invented by her husband, a large quantity of contraband drugs, and a pistol. En route to the Confederacy when apprehended, she swore allegiance to the United States and was permitted to return to Philadelphia. Mrs. McCarty was the only one of her fellow prisoners whom Mrs. Greenhow liked and respected.[3]

Any mention of Confederate spies invariably brings to mind the colorful teen-aged Belle Boyd, who helped create this image of herself in her account, *Belle Boyd in Camp and Prison*. Yet it is no more exaggerated than similar autobiographical works and more reliable than many. After nursing for a brief time early in the war, Belle gained fame as a spy and courier by eavesdropping on Federal councils of war, gleaning military secrets from enchanted admirers, and conveying the information to General Jackson and others. Dashing on horseback through the Valley of Virginia became a favorite pastime for this young lady, who once rode thirty miles in a single night to report on General James Shields's plans, returning to Front Royal before daylight so that Shields and other Federal officers at her uncle's hotel would not note her absence. In July 1862 she was betrayed, arrested, and imprisoned for a month in Old Capitol.

By this time she was widely known and the news of her capture was gleefully noted in the Northern press. *Leslie's* gloated, "The Secesh Cleopatra is caged at last," and the Philadelphia *Inquirer* was jubilant because her imprisonment would remove her from command of a teen-aged spy ring in Virginia.

[2] Frank Leslie: *Heroic Incidents* (New York, 1862), pp. 34–35; Leech: *Reveille in Washington*, p. 140.
[3] New York *Herald*, Feb. 11, 1862.

The *Inquirer* writer said the other girls had too much sense to make themselves as "conspicuous" as Belle, who had gone beyond "the boundary of her sex's modesty," but were capable of doing great damage when properly directed. While accusing Belle of being indiscreet and immodest, the *Inquirer* lashed out at journalists who charged her with being immoral. The New York *Herald* handled her brutally, as it did all Confederate spies, and stated that if she was not the "village courtesan" in her home town of Martinsburg, she was "something not far removed." Although older women who had been so interested in Rose Greenhow and Eugenia Phillips apparently paid little heed to Belle, the younger women were fascinated. One young lady who met her in East Tennessee was enchanted by this dynamic spy, and a Georgian applauded her daring until Belle left the Confederacy and married a Yankee.[4]

Released from Old Capitol and sent into Confederate lines, Belle was soon arrested a second time when she went to Martinsburg, then in Union territory. Confined this time in Carroll Prison, where she suffered a severe attack of typhoid, she was again released, sent back to the Confederacy, and told never to enter Federal lines again. She wrote that she then decided to go abroad for reasons of health, carrying on her person Confederate dispatches. Her vessel was captured by the Federals and placed under the command of a naval officer, Ensign Samuel Hardinge, soon to be her husband. When the ship docked in Boston, Belle made her escape, went to Canada, and booked passage for England. Meanwhile Hardinge was held responsible for her escape, arrested, tried, and dismissed from the service. He joined Belle in London, where they were married in 1864. Shortly thereafter he returned to the United States, where he was imprisoned but then released when he became ill. His reason for coming back has never been satisfactorily explained. He returned to England, and according to Belle's biographer, died "no later than July, 1866, and probably before the end of 1865."[5]

Left with an infant daughter and no income, having sold her

[4] *Frank Leslie's Illustrated Newspaper*, Aug. 23, 1862; Philadelphia *Inquirer*, July 28, 1862; New York *Herald*, Aug. 3, 1862; Myrta Lockett Avary: *A Virginia Girl in the Civil War* (New York, 1903), pp. 51–58; Ella Gertrude Clanton Thomas Diary, MS.

[5] Louis A. Sigaud: *Belle Boyd, Confederate Spy* (Richmond, 1941), pp. 90–190.

personal possessions, Belle turned to the stage and made her debut in Manchester in 1866. She returned to the United States the same year and continued her stage career until 1869, when she married John Hammond, a businessman and former Union officer. Two daughters and a son were born of this marriage, and for a few years Belle quietly occupied herself with maternal and domestic duties; but in 1884 this marriage ended in divorce, and shortly thereafter Belle married Nathaniel Rice High, eighteen years her junior. When financial problems again necessitated Belle's earning a living, she turned to lecturing on her war experiences, melodramatically concluding every address with a plea for national unity. Her most enthusiastic audiences were Union veterans. In June 1900 she went to Kilbourne, Wisconsin, to speak to the local GAR post, where she died of a heart attack. Buried here, she was carried to her grave by four Union veterans and two sons of veterans. Although as a reckless, enthusiastic teenager she had risked her life for the Confederacy, whatever hatred she may have felt for the North was short-lived. As two of her husbands were Northerners and the third, a Britisher, had served in the Union Army, after the war Belle belonged as much to the North as to the South. Late in the century several women claimed to be Belle Boyd and tried to capitalize on her name, and her obituary in the Philadelphia *Telegraph* took note of this when it referred to her as a "semi-myth" whose identity had not always been positively established.

A great many other Southern women engaged in espionage, including Belle Jamieson, who was imprisoned for making drawings of Federal fortifications in Florida, and Belle Faulkner, wife of a former Congressman and minister to France, who was considered even "more dangerous" than Belle Boyd because of her social influence and adroitness. *Leslie's* referred to all three Belles as the "feminine desperadoes of the Confederacy." It was said that Antonia Ford of Virginia supplied Colonel John Mosby with information which enabled him to capture General Edwin Henry Stoughton, but this Mosby later denied. However, the Federals considered her dangerous enough to imprison in Old Capitol, her captives finding on her $1,000 in gold and an aide-de-camp's commission dated October 7, 1863, and signed by General "Jeb" Stuart. The appointment stated that at all times Miss Ford was to be "obeyed, respected and *admired* by all lovers of a noble nature . . ." Laura Radcliffe of Fairfax County, Virginia, gave information to Mosby, who addressed impassioned poems to her, and to Stuart, who credited her with having saved his life, but she managed to escape imprisonment and notoriety. The war left her impoverished, but a wealthy friend, Milton Hannah, came to her aid, built her a home, and later married her. She lived quietly, and unlike many others, never capitalized on her espionage activities. North Carolina's most famous spy and smuggler was Emeline Piggot, who had engaged in these activities for several years before she was arrested in New Bern. Swallowing the evidence, she was detained for a time on charges of blockade running before being dismissed and sent home.[6]

Many women, whether guilty or innocent, were given unwanted publicity when their arrests were made known. Among these were Mrs. Rachel Mayer of Charleston, apprehended upon her arrival in New York; Mrs. William Morris of Baltimore, accused of furnishing clothing to Confederate soldiers; and Susan Archer Talley of Virginia, imprisoned for two months in Fort McHenry on spy charges. For weeks the press kept alive the case of Mrs. Isabella Brinsmade of New Orleans, first arrested in Washington and later in New York, where she was held incommunicado for forty days without formal charges. Police Commissioner John Kennedy had her case investigated, despite criticism for exceeding his authority, and obtained her release because of insufficient evidence. Three young girls, Jennie Hart, Mary Jane Green, and Maria Murphey, were imprisoned for several months in Fort McHenry on suspicion of espionage.[7] The Federal authorities respected neither age nor sex if suspecting an individual of working with the Confederates; and while falsely accusing many, they failed to apprehend countless others who gave information and aid to the enemy.

During the last year of the war the trial of two prominent

---

[6] *Frank Leslie's Illustrated Newspaper*, Aug. 9, 1862; LaFayette Baker: *History of the United States Secret Service* (Philadelphia, 1867), pp. 170–73; John J. Williamson: *Mosby's Rangers* (New York, 1896), p. 46; Henry W. R. Jackson: *The Southern Women of the Second American Revolution* (Atlanta, 1863), p. 9; Jean Rust: "Portrait of Laura," *Virginia Cavalcade* (Winter 1962–63), pp. 34–39; John A. Hedrick to Benjamin Hedrick, Mar. 10, 1865, Benjamin S. Hedrick Papers.

[7] New York *Herald*, Nov. 21, 25, 29, Dec. 3, 1862, May 9, 1863.

Baltimore women received widespread newspaper coverage. Mrs. Sarah Hutchings was convicted of sending arms to the Confederate guerrilla Harry Gilmore and sentenced to from two to five years' imprisonment in the Fitchburg (Massachusetts) House of Correction but after a few weeks was pardoned by Lincoln after promising "to conduct herself in a loyal manner." Mrs. Bessie Perrine was arrested for aiding the Confederates but her trial did not take place until May 1865. The prosecutor realized that because the war had ended and she was a woman it would be difficult to get a verdict of guilty and therefore stressed that her sex should not make her immune to punishment, citing as precedent many women who had received sentences for treasonable activities.[8] The stern punishment meted out to women jolted them into realizing that they were no longer necessarily accorded special treatment, yet none was executed for wartime espionage.

The Union also had its spies and informers, but they more successfully evaded capture. The *Official Records* and other sources reveal that thousands of Southern women gave valuable information to the Federals, and this was especially true of Union sympathizers who came into Federal lines as the armies advanced. In other areas also information was transmitted, especially in communities where prisoners were held. While much of the "spy-talk" in Richmond was rumor, some spies were undetected or ignored. Two years after the war, Sallie Ann Putnam confessed to having heard many rumors of espionage, and Mrs. Chesnut heard that "a regiment of spies" had been sent South "by the wily Seward," but she doubted this since they were not needed when "newspapers tell every word that there is to be told."[9] The papers often warned of a spy ring in the city, and on May 4, 1864, the disgusted *Enquirer* editor, who had frequently reported two women as spies, informed his readers that these same two had gone into Federal lines, never having been questioned by the Richmond authorities although it was generally known that they harbored "Yankee deserters . . . and escaped prisoners" through whom they transmitted information to the enemy.

[8] New York *Herald*, Nov. 26, 30, 1864, Jan. 8, 1865; Washington *Chronicle*, May 16, 1865.
[9] Sallie Ann Putnam: *Richmond During the War* (Richmond, 1867), p. 212; Chesnut: *A Diary*, p. 47.

The most sensational arrest in Richmond was that of Mrs. Mary Caroline Allan, the Cincinnati-born wife of Patterson Allan of Goochland County. The story broke while she was a guest in the home of Mrs. Moses Drury Hoge in 1863, during the Rev. Dr. Hoge's absence in Europe. Mrs. Allan was accused of sending information and expressing Union sentiments to friends and relatives in the North, among them the statement that Dr. Hoge should be arrested before he could return to the Confederacy. She was also accused of having sent to the Rev. Morgan Dix, father of the general, a list of Southern sympathizers in the North, recommending their arrest; and she was believed to have forwarded maps which showed "commanding locations" on the James River where Federal guns should be placed. Mrs. Allan confessed writing letters to the persons named, but pleading ill health she was sent to the Hospital of St. Francis de Sales rather than to Castle Thunder. A Richmond lady later noted that this mild punishment irritated Southern women who "remembered the treatment to which Mrs. Greenhow, Mrs. Baxley, Mrs. Phillips . . . and numerous other females had been subjected," and she went on to say that "the Confederate government did very little in the way of arresting and punishing spies." In December 1863, Mrs. Allan was freed on $100,000 bail, and despite the damaging evidence her lawyer, former Secretary of War George Randolph, managed to get the trial delayed several times so that the war ended before Mrs. Allan could be declared guilty or innocent.[1]

As previously noted, Elizabeth Van Lew was unmolested in her espionage activities, although her neighbors and the press became increasingly suspicious. It was known that she was abnormally interested in the Federal prisoners in Libby while steadfastly refusing to assist the Confederates. What was not positively known was that she helped prisoners to escape, and that in addition to her mother's cooperation she had the assistance of at least two other Richmond women. Miss Van Lew, a lifelong resident of the city, was the daughter of a wealthy, respected merchant who died before the war. After Grant moved his forces to the Petersburg area, "Crazy Bet," as she was known, supplied

[1] Richmond *Enquirer*, July 20, Dec. 21, 30, 1863; Richmond *Examiner*, July 23, 1863, February 22, September 13, October 28, December 19, 1864; Putnam: *Richmond During the War*, pp. 249–50; Clifford Dowdey: *Experiment in Rebellion* (Garden City, 1946), pp. 302–3, 336.

him with a steady stream of information, and when Richmond fell he returned the favor by stationing guards outside her home. She mentioned in her journal that during Richmond's evacuation many of her harshest critics begged her to keep their valuables, presuming they would be safer in her home. When Grant was President, he did not forget Elizabeth Van Lew but appointed her postmistress of Richmond, a position she held during his two terms.[2]

Pauline Cushman, the most colorful Federal spy, was in many ways like Belle Boyd although ten years her senior. Born in New Orleans and an actress in that city in 1861, she had lived briefly in the North, but not until 1863 did she enter into espionage activities. They consumed scarcely a year of her life—a year, however, of wild adventure, even if many experiences described in books published in 1864 and 1865 are discounted. She was already a secret agent when she toasted Jefferson Davis and the Confederacy from a Louisville stage. Following the Confederates out of Kentucky and into Tennessee, Pauline collected military information which she successfully sent to the Federals until caught in possession of drawings she had stolen from a Confederate army engineer. She was arrested, escaped, was recaptured and sentenced to be executed but because of illness was permitted to recuperate in the home of a physician. When the Confederates retreated she was rescued by the Federals and taken to Nashville. By this time her activities were too well known to permit her to continue spying and she returned to the stage under the name of Pauline Cushman, or the "Little Major," a title said to have been conferred by Lincoln. She was enthusiastically received throughout the North for her war exploits and played the role of spy with a flair, always dressed in a military jacket, skirt, and plumed hat.[3]

Like so many young women who won fame and notoriety, Pauline Cushman had a turbulent and pathetic later life, but not until she applied for a pension in 1892 was the full tragedy revealed. At the time of her wartime exploits, it was not known that

[2] Elizabeth Van Lew Journal, Archives Division, Virginia State Library, Richmond; Elizabeth Van Lew Papers, Manuscript Division, New York Public Library.
[3] Ferdinand L. Sarmiento: *Life of Pauline Cushman* (Philadelphia, 1865), p. 371; anon., *The Thrilling Adventures of Pauline Cushman* (Cincinnati, 1864), pp. 5–47.

she had been married, widowed, and was the mother of two children, both of whom she had given up for adoption. She claimed a pension not for her war service but as the widow of a soldier, but she could not recall the dates of their marriage, of his death, or the birth and death dates of her children. Some who were questioned maintained that she and the man had never been married, but a woman in Louisiana and another in Mississippi stated positively that they had attended the wedding in 1853 in a New Orleans hotel. It was eventually established that her husband had died in December 1862; and the government, satisfied that she was his widow, granted her a pension of eight dollars a month from that date until she remarried in 1872. After the war Pauline Cushman Dickinson acted in the Far West but soon lost her following and after seven difficult years married August Fitchner of San Francisco, who died in 1879. Shortly thereafter she married Jerry Fryer, with whom she lived for only a few years, and when she applied for a pension she was living in El Paso. One of her references stated that she was "doing a little sewing . . . as a return for what she eats" and was sleeping "on a cot in . . . the kitchen of a dressmaker's humble abode." In 1894 the "Little Major" died penniless in El Paso.[4]

Rebecca Wright, a young Quaker schoolteacher in Winchester, Virginia, was not so glamorous, but the rewards for her wartime service were more substantial. General Philip Sheridan did not forget that her information enabled him to defeat General Early's forces, and two years after the war he sent her a watch as a token of his appreciation. The Wrights suffered great privation after the war. It was known that they had been loyal to the Union; and Rebecca lost her teaching position, her mother's boarding house was boycotted, and both were ostracized. When Pennsylvania friends heard of Rebecca's destitution, they requested Senator Simon Cameron to use his influence to get her a pension for war services. But Cameron, like many of his colleagues, opposed pensions for civilians because, he said, there were "numberless loyal Southern sympathizers" who had done as much as Miss Wright for the Union cause, and not all could be pensioned. He offered two suggestions, that Sheridan should marry her or get her a clerkship in Washington. Phil Sheridan

[4] Pension File Number 326,644, Veterans Administration Records, National Archives.

decided on the latter, and in 1868 she received an appointment in a government office, remaining there for the rest of her days.[5]

Among the young women who engaged in dangerous activities to further their cause was Emma Sansom of Alabama. She was only fifteen when she led Nathan Bedford Forrest and his men to a ford in Black Creek after the Federals had burned a bridge. In recognition of her deed, the Alabama legislature in 1864 awarded her a medal and promised her a section of land, a promise not honored by the reconstruction legislature but eventually made good in 1899. At this time Emma was living in Texas, a widow with seven children. But she was not forgotten, and in the same year John Trotwood Moore recalled her wartime service in "The Ballad of Emma Sansom," while later a marble statue was erected to her in Gadsden. Antoinette Polk was long remembered for having made possible the escape of Confederate soldiers from her father's home near Columbia, Tennessee. She later married the Baron de Charette, who had fought for the Federals during the war, and the couple lived on the family estate in Brittany. Ella Herbert won local fame as a mail carrier, making the run from her home in Missouri to Confederate troops in Mississippi and in the process winning a husband.

One scout and courier for the Federals in Missouri was Alvira Smith, who later applied for a pension on the basis of these services. Mrs. Anna Campbell, a Unionist in northern Alabama, once rode seventy miles in thirty-six hours to carry information to General Streight; and an unidentified Unionist girl in East Tennessee, who was also popular with Confederate soldiers, helped Junius Henri Browne and his imprisoned newspaper colleagues escape from the Confederates and guided them to safety. Countless other women similarly aided one or the other army, for there were thousands who by a single deed rendered valuable service.[6]

[5] Anon., "The Loyal Girl of Winchester," Scrapbook, John Page Nicholson Military Collection, Henry E. Huntington Library; Philadelphia *Times*, Feb. 26, Apr. 5, 1884.

[6] Malcolm C. McMillan: *The Alabama Confederate Reader* (Tuscaloosa, 1963), pp. 201–3; Bromfield L. Ridley: *Battles and Sketches of the Army of Tennessee* (Mexico, Mo., 1906), pp. 490–95; Mrs. Burton Harrison: *Recollections Grave and Gay* (New York, 1911), pp. 163–64; James Bradley: *The Confederate Mail Carrier* (Mexico Mo., 1894), pp. 87–229; New York *Herald*, Aug. 4, 1862; Junius Henri Browne: *Four Years in Secessia* (Hartford, 1865), pp. 421–26; Linus Pierpont Brockett: *The Camp, the Battle Field and the Hospital* (Philadelphia, 1866), p. 366; Leslie: *Heroic Incidents*, pp. 18–19.

Risked Everything

One wartime development which shocked many Americans was the increasing use of violence by women. Southern women were among the most successful saboteurs, and when caught many willingly and haughtily admitted their guilt. A Mrs. Hunter and her daughter not only confessed the destruction of several bridges in Tennessee to block the Federal advance but told Union officials they would do it again if given the chance. To prevent them from making good the threat, Rosecrans banished the women into Confederate lines. When in 1864 Sarah Jane Smith was arrested after two years at sabotage and smuggling in Missouri, she admitted that she had begun her exploits at the age of fourteen. Cited by a journalist as one of the "most aggravating" nuisances of the war, Sarah Jane committed her most serious offense when she cut four miles of telegraph wires in the southeastern part of the state. She was sentenced to be hanged, but General Rosecrans commuted the sentence to imprisonment for the duration of the war. Equally noted as a saboteur, smuggler, and spy was the Confederate sympathizer Katie Beattie, who was charged with helping prisoners escape and with burning Federal boats and warehouses in Missouri. She was said to be highly esteemed by rebel generals and to have "a dash and abandon of manner well calculated to see her through," but she and her landlady were nevertheless imprisoned.[7]

A constant problem for the Federals were women who tried to smuggle contraband goods and messages into the Confederacy, and the early reluctance of officers to order a search of a lady's baggage and person soon disappeared. This wartime necessity, however, did give employment to Unionist women. A Confederate wrote, "False hair . . . is searched for papers. Pistols are sought for with crinoline reversed, bustles are suspect. All manner of things . . . come over the border under the large hoops now worn. . . . Not legs but arms are looked for under hoops, and sad to say are found."[8] One of the most sensational arrests of the war was that of Louisa Buckner, niece of Federal Postmaster General Montgomery Blair, who had loaned the young lady money with which to buy supplies in Washington to take back to Virginia. When stopped and searched on the way home, Miss Buckner was found to have more than a hundred ounces of quinine sewed in

[7] O.R., XXX, Part 3, 223; New York *Herald*, Nov. 25, 28, 1864.
[8] Chesnut: *A Diary*, pp. 124–25.

her skirt. She was sent to Old Capitol but soon released. This gave her uncle's enemies additional ammunition—although Blair maintained that she had said the money would be spent on groceries.

Along the Mississippi and Ohio, in northern Virginia and in coastal areas, officials had to keep a sharp lookout for smugglers. As early as the summer of 1861, a Northern journalist warned that "crinoline often contains many contraband articles" and estimated that "hundreds if not thousands of pistols" had already been taken South. If the modest lady protested being searched, he continued, "let her blush. Better that the blood should mount to her face than that the blood of our countrymen should be shed through her crime." Women were ingenious and many slipped through with valuable cargoes, but a great many did not make it. Three were stopped in Vicksburg after passing inspection in New Orleans, and a large quantity of quinine was found concealed under false bottoms in their trunks. Parasols provided one of the best hiding places and were seldom searched. Items of apparel were often difficult to get through the lines; women were arrested for trying to take Confederate uniforms to men in service, while thousands of pairs of shoes were confiscated at inspection points. Some tried to bring luxury items into the Confederacy. Constance Cary, for example, went on a buying spree in Washington midway in the war. Her experiences getting through the lines were exciting, but once her presence in the city was known she was ordered out before she had completed her shopping. Because she was escorted from the city by the authorities, her luggage was not searched at the check stations and she arrived in Richmond with a part of her finery. Being every inch a typical young lady, her proudest possession was a new spring bonnet which made her the envy of her "clothes-starved" friends.[9]

Mary Louisa Walker of Philadelphia, who had been persuaded by her school friends in Baltimore to cast her lot with the Confederacy, nursed for a time in Richmond and watched men die because of inadequate medical supplies. In 1864 she went to

[9] New York *Herald*, July 12, 1861; Vicksburg *Herald*, Aug. 20, 1864; *Frank Leslie's Illustrated Newspaper*, Apr. 4, 1863; Washington *Republican*, Mar. 20, 1863; Mrs. Fairfax Cary to Clarence Cary, Mar. 29, 1863, Burton Harrison Papers; Harrison: *Recollections Grave and Gay*, pp. 97–115.

Canada, where she appealed for contributions of money or medicine. Meeting with remarkable success, she loaded her hospital supplies on sleds, took them down the frozen St. Lawrence, had them transferred to a ship which took her and the cargo to Havana, and saw them placed on a blockade runner and brought into Galveston. Although the supplies arrived too late to be of great value, hers was one of the most imaginative and daring exploits. Escorted to Pennslyvania after the war by one of General Gordon's staff, she later married a genuine Kentucky colonel and moved to Texas.[1]

By April 1865 it was less difficult than four years earlier for Americans to accept the fact that a woman could be involved in diabolical schemes. Yet none of the women secret agents had been executed although there was no question of the guilt of many. When Mrs. Mary Surratt was charged with helping to plot President Lincoln's assassination, the public was all too ready to believe her guilty. Wartime hatreds were too deep-seated and the crime too infamous to be viewed objectively; and the people, goaded by Stanton, screamed for vengeance against all those responsible, whether men or women. Mary Surratt was caught in the fury, tried by a military court, condemned on circumstantial evidence, and sent to the gallows while she and others maintained her innocence. Although declaring her guilty, the court had recommended that she be imprisoned because of her age and because no woman had ever been executed by the United States Government, but President Johnson signed the death warrant. Thus she was the first of her sex to die for a crime against the United States government. It is interesting to speculate whether the women whose espionage activities had been widely publicized did not help condition the public mind to believe Mrs. Surratt guilty. Whether she was guilty or innocent is still argued, but there are two certainties: the trial was a mockery and Mrs. Surratt was the victim of circumstances.

[1] Gertrude Biddle and Sarah Dickinson Lowrie (eds.): *Notable Women of Pennsylvania* (Philadelphia, 1942), pp. 189–91.

6

A Female Teacher Will Do

FOR THE FIRST TWO YEARS of the war the citizens of Bellville, Texas had seen men teachers come to the one-room school, stay a few weeks, and then move on to the army or more lucrative positions, and often months elapsed before another teacher was found. Parents were concerned about the disruption of their children's schooling, yet no one seemed to think of employing a woman. The education-conscious German editor of the town's newspaper did not entertain this possibility until July 1863, when he grudgingly admitted that perhaps "a female teacher will do" if no man could be found; but a man did apply for the place shortly thereafter, only to be followed by a succession of others. When Bellville was again without a teacher in February 1865, the editor reiterated with no greater enthusiasm his earlier remarks about appointing "a female teacher," and this time one was given the job. Three months later the journalist conceded that "the best teachers are women," not because they performed their duties more satisfactorily, however, but because they demanded less pay and considered teaching a "prime vocation" and not merely a stepping stone to a better job like most men.[1]

[1] Bellville (Tex.) *Countryman*, July 4, 1863, Oct. 14, 1864, Feb. 21, May 16, June 10, 1865.

A similar situation existed in other communities in all parts of the country, for there was still prejudice against employing women if men could be found to teach. Although the war cannot be credited with opening the profession to women, since thousands were already teaching in 1861, it did greatly enhance their opportunities when male teachers enlisted or took more remunerative jobs in industry and business. While some men did try their hand at teaching during the war, many did so in the hope of avoiding conscription and most were neither academically qualified nor personally suited to instruct the young. Although the same may be said of many women, some at least proved to be so determined, efficient, and reliable that the public could not but be impressed by their performance. The most convincing argument in their favor was nevertheless their willingness to assume greater responsibilities for less money than would most men. It was primarily because of this and the increased openings in the educational field that women advanced more rapidly in the profession than in others.

In no area was there a greater change in attitude toward women teachers than in the South, where necessity forced many proud, once affluent ladies into the classroom. Although the vocation was already recognized as respectable, prewar society had pitied the woman driven to teach. As the number of women teachers increased during the war, young ladies were seldom bothered by the false pride which so disturbed their elders, many of whom felt as did Mrs. John Berkley Grimball that they preferred to forego necessities rather than have their daughters teach. Although the Grimballs' plantations had fallen within Federal lines and the family had fled to Spartanburg, where they lived without regular income, Mrs. Grimball opposed her daughter's assisting in a private girl's school in the neighboring village of Union. While Mr. Grimball confessed that he was "much disturbed" by this "economic necessity," his wife was humiliated that Elizabeth must follow "the treadmill life of a teacher." No sooner had the war ended than she demanded that her daughter resign and return to her family, where tradition dictated that she live. It was still in dire financial straits and Elizabeth tactfully tried to explain that she preferred to teach; but when her mother persisted, the irritated daughter wrote, "I have received your ultimatum . . . and have made up my mind to one thing. I will hereafter act upon my own judgment . . . I will not be a dependent old maid at home with an allowance doled out to me while I could be made comfortable by my own exertions." This outburst was followed by a tirade on the injustices done unmarried women by demanding that they live under the parental roof, and she assured her mother that her friends approved her teaching and that "many noble women" had entered the profession during the war.[2]

Public opinion gradually rallied to the support of women who, like Elizabeth Grimball, replaced false pride with accomplishment. While there was less prejudice against women teachers in the North and West, many communities there would have preferred men. But the way in which Southern women battled local feeling was especially remarkable. If Southern children were to be educated, women must replace not only the men who had gone to war but also the Northern "schoolmarms" who had held teaching positions, and this meant they must fill vacancies in the public schools as well as private institutions. One of the most revolutionary changes during and after the war was society's gradual acceptance of "high-bred" ladies in the public schools. North Carolina had made greater progress in public education than any other Southern state, yet in 1859 only 7 ½ per cent of the state's public school teachers were women, while by 1863 the figure had increased to 40 per cent.[3]

With secession, the Southern press let it be known that the region had erred in permitting Northern women to educate the Southern youth, and the war made editors even more outspoken. On July 11, 1861, the Nashville *Banner of Peace* launched a crusade against the Northern "monarchs of the mind" and insisted that Southerners *"demand southern teachers!"* On August 9 the Savannah *Daily Morning News* printed what was soon to become a typical advertisement for teachers: "All must be natives of the South, or some European country . . . at peace with the Southern

[2] John Berkley Grimball Diaries; Meta Morris to John Grimball, Aug. 23, 1866; Elizabeth Grimball to Meta Morris Grimball, Sept. 11, Dec. 8, 1866; Elizabeth Grimball to John Berkley Grimball, Aug. 6, 1867, John Berkley Grimball Papers.

[3] M. C. S. Noble: *A History of the Public Schools of North Carolina* (Chapel Hill, 1930), p. 245.

Confederacy." Hostility toward Northern teachers increased, and when in 1863 a Richmond editor heard that two in North Carolina had requested to be paid in tobacco rather than depreciating Confederate scrip, he asked, "What business have Yankee teachers in North Carolina?" He suggested that they be paid in neither money nor tobacco but "in hemp."[4]

The Northern press protested that women were "sent off without their pay," but one editor was relieved that they made "their escape when they did." These teachers had an adjustment to make, though most seem to have found jobs and some turned to nursing. Yet one who had gone South for her health and taught for thirteen years before being forced out was unable to get a school in Kentucky despite credentials proving that she had been a "useful and successful teacher."[5] Teachers who had been in the South often found on their return North that they were suspected of disloyalty. George Sala exaggerated when he stated that "the majority" reflected an "anti-Union feeling and . . . did their best politically to demoralize their friends and relations," but some did try to explain the Southern position and pointed out those things they may have admired about the region. This was readily misinterpreted by many. They baffled "the most resolute men," said Sala, and confused the government, which did not know what to do with them.[6] Northern teachers who remained in the South were likely to be accused of disloyalty to the Confederacy no matter how long they had lived in the region or how much they did for the cause, but this was true of other Northern-born people in the area.

Teachers in both sections were expected to support the government and indoctrinate students in its principles, and failure to do so could result in immediate dismissal, often without the privilege of facing accusers or defending themselves. This was always a potential danger in divided communities, and while it most often existed in border areas and in the South, it was also to be found in the North. In a Wisconsin village where the school

[4] Richmond *Enquirer*, Nov. 21, 1863.
[5] New York *Herald*, Sept. 1, 1861; Louisville *Journal*, Aug. 9, 1861; L. L. Ruggles to Robert J. Breckinridge, June 18, 1864, Breckinridge Family Papers.
[6] George Augustus Sala: *My Diary in America in the Midst of the War* (London, 1865), II, 354.

board had Confederate sympathies, a teacher was fired because she taught her students Union songs, and the school was closed. When the board refused to pay her salary she took the case to court and won.[7] Several New Orleans teachers and principals were dismissed when they were accused of criticizing Federal authorities or when a search of their classrooms revealed Confederate flags, books, or pictures of Southern leaders. General Milroy banished Helen Duncan from Winchester, Virginia, because she expressed anti-Union sentiments, although there was no proof that she did so in the presence of students. In this case the school was closed and all the teachers lost their jobs.[8] In areas which changed hands often, it took a diplomatic, cautious teacher to retain her position under both armies.

Teachers in the Far West were not immune to these problems, for there were both Confederates and Unionists in many communities, and the children naturally reflected their parents' views. It took great tact for a teacher to keep peace and answer the perplexing questions of her pupils. A little boy in Santa Clara, California, asked why the "Union would win over the rebels" if the Confederates "were as strong as the Union," and he was told that the North would win because it was in the right and "God was on the side of the Union." The puzzled youngster then suggested that if God was on the Northern side it seemed He "never would have made the rebels at all," and the teacher explained that "God had made them upright and they had made themselves rebels," but she realized the answer did not satisfy the inquisitive youngster.[9] Others acknowledged their inability to handle similar situations, and many were distressed to see academic freedom, objectivity, and toleration disappear from the classrooms.

Few women felt that they were "called" into the teaching profession, and while this was to some extent true earlier it became more apparent during the war when much larger numbers taught only for the salary. A Michigan woman told of having

[7] Ethel Alice Hurn: *Wisconsin Women in the War* (Madison, 1911), p. 87.

[8] Jefferson Davis Bragg: *Louisiana in the Confederacy* (Baton Rouge, 1941), pp. 277–78; Cornelia McDonald: *A Diary with Reminiscences of the War and Refugee Life in the Shenandoah Valley* (Nashville, 1935), p. 153.

[9] Clarissa North to Ann Loomis North, Aug. 18, 1864, John Wesley North Papers.

"three or four chances to take schools" but deciding on the one paying the highest wage, "four dollars a week." A Louisianian impoverished by the war was not prepared to support herself but presumed she could teach, although she "would rather die" than instruct children. "Teaching before dependence," she declared, and "death before teaching." Shortly after making this statement she did accept a teaching position rather than be supported by others but was not happy in her work. Mrs. Cornelia McDonald, a war widow with five children, was just as unenthusiastic about taking private pupils, but she was her family's sole support, and like many others she found that neither her responsibilities nor her teaching career ended with Appomattox.[1]

A young Vermonter, who started teaching during the war and had been unable to find other employment four years later, confessed that she "despised" the work but explained that there were "only two occupations open to women" in her town. They could teach school for five months a year at three dollars a week or hire out to a farmer's wife and work from "dawn till nine P.M." for two dollars. She had chosen the lesser of two evils but believed she merited a higher calling. Their lack of enthusiasm for the work explains why many teachers were criticized by parents, the general public, and the press. An editor once asked, "How many really *good teachers* do we have? How many eminently successful? How many devoted to the business . . . and really in love with it?" He estimated that not more than one in a hundred teachers met these standards.[2] Had such critics taken the time to analyze why this was true, they would have discovered among contributing factors the low salaries, innumerable demands made by the community, and lack of public appreciation and encouragement.

New teachers did not always realize the restrictions placed upon them. While they would be expected to adjust to community mores at any time, during the war they had to be on vigilant

[1] Virginia Everham (ed.): "Letters From Home," *Michigan Women in the Civil War* (Lansing, 1963), p. 57; Sarah Morgan Dawson: *A Confederate Girl's Diary,* ed. James I. Robertson, Jr. (Bloomington, 1960), pp. 104–5; McDonald: *A Diary,* pp. 199, 233, 246–47, 254, 261.

[2] Emily Shaw to Anna Dickinson, Apr. 10, 1869; Libbie Throop to Anna Dickinson, Apr. 30, 1869, Anna E. Dickinson Papers; Bellville *Countryman,* Apr. 18, 1865.

guard lest their words and actions be misinterpreted. Nor did the teachers always understand that unreasonably heavy burdens might be imposed on them, for women were often assigned more school and community responsibilities than men and were always paid less. One young lady was so overburdened that she concluded the principal must have thought her "made of india rubber," able to "stretch to any number of duties." Many young women resented denial of the normal social outlets accorded others their age, and those new to the job were often made miserable by strict regulations. Only desperation could have driven a fun-loving girl of sixteen to teach after being told she must not be "too lazy . . . strict or lenient" with the students, that she must remain in the schoolhouse "during the daylight" hours, go directly to her living quarters at dusk, never loiter on the way to or from the school, and "do nothing to create talk."[3] A great many of the new wartime teachers were in their mid-teens. Yet most stuck with the job through the term and many continued to teach because they had no other choice.

The demand far exceeded the supply of qualified teachers, and some were teaching students who had as much formal schooling as themselves. Lack of preparation undoubtedly contributed to their frustration and helped to explain their dislike for the work. While found in all areas, unqualified, inexperienced teachers were especially numerous on the frontier and in the South, where the need was great and training facilities inadequate. The crusade in the Confederacy for employing only Southern-born teachers made it clear that something must be done to train the South's women, but as the war spread more schools were closed than opened. The obvious answer was to start the training program in existing institutions; and while this would take time, if begun immediately it would provide a nucleus of trained women teachers for the postwar schools. The press clamored for such preparation as the surest way to keep education in the hands of Southerners, and farsighted academicians realized that the challenge could not be ignored. One was Edward Joynes, who had joined the faculty of Hollins Female Institute after William and Mary closed. He first published his ideas in the 1863–64 Hollins catalogue, urging that existing

[3] Richmond *Enquirer*, Dec. 22, 1863; Thomas Conn Bryant: *Confederate Georgia* (Athens, 1953), p. 226; Bellville *Countryman*, July 4, 1863.

academies stress the training of "Southern Female Teachers" so that girls "of a pre-mature age" could be educated in their home communities and not have to be sent away to boarding schools. Such a teacher-training program would make it unnecessary to "import ready-made school marms and governesses from Yankee land," many of whom, said Joynes, had been "adventurers, unfit even for associates, much less for models" for Southern girls. He suggested that scholarships be established to assist those who had qualifications for teaching regardless of their economic or social class; and from this time until his death, he was an exponent of training programs for women teachers.

In December 1864 the North Carolina General Assembly enacted a bill embodying Calvin Wiley's ideas on teacher education, including among those eligible for training "all white females under 27 who wished to prepare to teach." Although Wiley himself staunchly supported a broad acceptance of prospective women teachers, this bill provided that only women loyal to the Confederacy and North Carolina would be eligible for the program. Not all Southern educators were as enthusiastic as Joynes and Wiley about women competitors, and many thought of them as only another temporary expedient to which the stricken Confederacy had to resort but which would disappear with peace. They did not look upon women colleagues as equals and did not invite them to serve as delegates to educational conferences during the war, though Northern women had long been attending similar meetings. It therefore came as a shock to educators convened at Petersburg when the president of Davidson College suggested that women be permitted to teach "college entrance branches for boys and all branches in the most advanced seminaries for girls." But they were no less startled by his defense of the much maligned "Yankee school marms," who he said had "never accomplished anything to our detriment," for his experience had shown that their students were no "less loyal" to Southern principles.[4]

Confederate teachers had innumerable problems not generally encountered by those in the North. The invasion and blockade made it necessary for many girls' schools and public institutions to cease operation, not because they lacked students, but because of economic problems and wartime dangers. Both armies at times

---

[4] Noble: *A History of the Public Schools of North Carolina*, pp. 239–47.

commandeered buildings for military use, and as in the case of Mount Lebanon Female College in Louisiana, states sometimes purchased them—in this instance for laboratory use. Students had to be moved when buildings were endangered by enemy fire, and during the bombardment of Charleston all the city schools but one were brought together in the relatively safe Morris Street School. Boarding students were the responsibility of teachers and principals, and when possible they were sent home if invasion seemed imminent; but if they could not get to their homes and had nowhere else to go, the staff had to care for them.

Salem Academy in North Carolina furnishes an example of a girls' school which stayed open throughout the war and actually increased in enrollment, having approximately 300 students in 1865. Some had remained for the entire four years without going home, for in 1861 girls were enrolled from as far away as Louisiana, Texas, and California. Teachers and principal had to assume a great many responsibilities not normally required of them and made all the more difficult because of the war. In order to feed the students, the principal had to forage for supplies and call on interested persons to contribute food. Among those responding was Governor Vance, who sent two barrels of sugar. The 1862 catalogue stated that the school could no longer furnish students with clothing because of the blockade, and women teachers assisted in darning, patching, and renovating that which the girls had brought with them. Living as they did in the same building with the students, the teachers were subjected to more than the usual annoyances and inconveniences and found it especially disturbing to hear students clomp around in wooden shoes, one of the noisier wartime expedients. When the Federals approached Salem in April 1865, the girls were told to stay in the building, be orderly, and do nothing to provoke enemy wrath, but this was a lot to ask of zealous young Confederates. As the troops passed the school a hotheaded Alabamian opened the window waved the Confederate flag, and gave the rebel yell. Fortunately nothing came of the incident, perhaps because the commander was an old friend of the principal.[5]

[5] Mary Elizabeth Massey: "The Civil War Comes to the Campus," *Education in the South: Institute of Southern Culture Lectures* (Farmville, Va., 1959), pp. 23–24; Salem (N.C.) *People's Press*, June 9, 1864.

The war conjured other problems for teachers. Madame Ascélie Togno was said to have "raised an awful shindy" when she heard that her students in Columbia, South Carolina, had been waving to Federal soldiers imprisoned across the street from her fashionable finishing school. And Mme. Sosnowski of Barhamville Institute on the outskirts of that city had the responsibility for evacuating her girls before Sherman's army arrived. The thought of what could happen to young ladies caught in an invasion weighed heavily on those responsible for their safety; and even after Mme. Sosnowski had sent the girls on their way, she could not sleep for worrying about them. In both the North and South teachers in boarding schools realized that they must be careful not to permit their students to associate with soldiers not approved by the girls' families. Most schools had never let them correspond with young men without the written consent of parents or guardian, but those in the South who were cut off from their families could not always obtain permission. A Mississippian asked her brother's consent to her corresponding with a soldier she had somehow managed to meet, but he refused because he did not want her writing to any man.[6] The presence of soldiers in the community always placed the faculty under a strain, for their charges were invariably attracted by men in uniform and devised ingenious ways of circumventing regulations.

Teachers everywhere complained that the excitement of the time interfered with the girls' studies, and the students admitted they had difficulty concentrating on their books, but when an instructor tried to calm them she was often accused of lacking patriotism. The excited girls in Catherine Sedgwick's school detected no change in her manner with secession, and a little abolitionist wrote her mother that the headmistress was nothing more than "a milk and water reformer." This attitude, said the student, only served to make her more radical, and to make sure that her teacher knew where she stood she hung over her bed a picture of her "saint, John Brown." After the war started, Mrs.

[6] Mary Boykin Chesnut, *A Diary From Dixie,* ed. Ben Ames Williams (Boston, 1950), p. 189; Sophia Sosnowski: "Burning of Columbia," *Georgia Historical Quarterly,* VIII (1924), 195–214; Willis K. Sively to Jane Sively, Feb. 25, 1864, Jane Sively Letters, Southern Historical Collection, University of North Carolina.

Sedgwick worked so ardently for the Union cause that the girl decided she was not "a traitor after all."[7]

Schoolgirls were encouraged by their instructors to assist the war effort by organizing knitting and sewing circles and performing in recitals, tableaux, and other benefits. Some were permitted to form drill groups while their elders "looked the other way." But their impulsive, impractical ideas often had to be vetoed by those in authority. In both sections girls wanted to feed the passing troops and their generosity was lauded in the press, yet the scarcity of commodities in the Confederacy made this inadvisable. When General Early's men were encamped near Hollins, the president of the school was beset with innumerable problems, one of which was to keep the students from emptying the institution's larder into the laps of the soldiers. It is a matter of speculation whether the Wesleyan, Georgia, girls had their teachers' approval when they stripped their beds of blankets for the Confederates, but those in the Lucy Cobb Institute probably received an amused endorsement when they collected $120 to endow the Confederate Government.[8]

All Southern teachers were plagued by a scarcity of the educational supplies generally taken for granted in the North. In addition to shortages of paper, chalk, slates, pencils, and ink they felt the lack of books, for the South had depended on Northern and European texts; with the outbreak of war the former became unpopular, and both were difficult to obtain through the blockade. A movement was begun to produce Confederate texts, and editors urged teachers to prepare them, but educational conventions were not in agreement as to what should be done. Not only did the shortage of essentials, dearth of publishing houses, and destruction of printing establishments hinder the movement, but because most Confederate texts were poorly prepared and propagandistic, scholarly academicians preferred to use the old reliable books when they were available.

[7] Ellen Wright to Lucy McKim, Jan. 1, 1861, Garrison Family Papers.
[8] Judith Brockenbrough McGuire: *Diary of a Refugee* (New York, 1867), p. 103; Mrs. D. Giraud Wright: *A Southern Girl in '61: the War Time Memories of a Confederate Senator's Daughter* (New York, 1905), p. 118; Macon *Telegraph*, Mar. 5, 1862; Dorothy Scovil Vickery: *Hollins College* (Hollins, Va., 1942), p. 14; E. Merton Coulter: *College Life in the Old South* (New York, 1928), p. 318.

Women compiled some of the readers and spellers for the lower grades, but they were not responsible for any texts on the upper levels. Mrs. S. A. Poindexter, Mrs. Adelaide de Vendel Chaudron, and Mrs. S. A. Vaughan published their readers and spellers in Nashville, Mobile, and Atlanta respectively, but Mrs. Marinda Branson Moore of North Carolina was probably the most effective propagandizer. Her *Dixie Primer for Little Folks* went through three printings, and also widely used was her *Dixie Speller,* which was "revised from Webster and adopted for Southern schools . . . leaving out all Yankee phrases and allusions." She was the only woman to write a geography text, which frequently strayed from the subject to justify slavery and secession and to blame the war on the Union. Its little readers were told, among other things, that Lincoln was "a mean man" elected by abolitionists and "so enraged" by secession that "he declared war, and . . . exhausted nearly all the strength of the nation in a vain attempt to whip the South back into the Union." Of the South, Mrs. Moore wrote, "It is a great country! The Yankees sought to starve us out . . . but we have learned to make many things." She assured the students that the Confederacy would win because God was on its side, "Jefferson Davis is a good, wise man, and many of its generals . . . are pious."[9] The full effect of such statements on the impressionable youngsters cannot be determined, but they show how indoctrination replaced education in some schools.

In many areas schools were closed for extended periods by the war, and if children were to be taught the responsibility rested with the family, usually with the mothers or other women relatives. Some were not qualified to teach and many lacked the time, but a number of inexperienced women tried to tutor their young, many of the uneducated being determined that their sons and daughters should have advantages which they had been denied. Letters to husbands evidenced concern which many semi-

[9] Stephen Beauregard Weeks: "Confederate Textbooks: A Preliminary Bibliography," *Report of the U.S. Commissioner of Education, 1898–99* (Washington, 1900), II, 1139–55; Marinda Branson Moore: *The Geographical Reader for the Dixie Children* (Raleigh, 1863), *passim;* see also Lawrence F. London: "Confederate Literature and Its Publishers," *Studies in Southern History* (Chapel Hill, 1957), XXXIX, 89–91; James W. Albright: "Books Made in Dixie," *Southern Historical Society Papers,* XLI (1916), 57–60.

literate mothers conveyed with misspelled words and strange or archaic expressions laboriously penciled on rough paper. A Virginian many times wrote her husband that their daughter was "needing learning bad" and that she wanted "a school the worst I ever saw a person." When a teacher came to the neighboring village, the impoverished mother somehow managed to pay a half-bushel of corn a week to board the child and another seventy-five cents in commodities, usually homespun cloth, to pay the teacher. Although the young instructor came from "very sorry people" and was herself "poor," the mother refused to believe the malicious rumors about her, because her daughter appeared to be "learning nothing only that she ought to learn." Whether the town gossips caused the teacher to leave or she found a better place, she taught only six weeks; but she did so well that the mother proudly reported her child "has learned the fastest for the time I ever saw." Records show that during the four years of the war this eager little girl had less than six months' schooling and that after early 1864 there was no school anywhere in the area for her to attend. Similar situations existed elsewhere in the South and in remote areas of the North and West.[1]

Women who desired to teach were not bothered by a lack of accreditation or certification, for anyone who announced her intention to educate the youth of a community might conduct classes in her home or elsewhere provided she could enroll the necessary students. When Hortensia Boggs decided to teach she posted a notice on the saloon door in Murray, Kentucky, letting it be known that classes would be held in an abandoned seminary building. She warned prospective patrons that she could not "boast of much experience" but assured them that her "mind was stored with such elementary knowledge . . . as will amply justify" parents' sending their children to her; and several months later a newspaperman reported that she was "meeting with desired success." Many women conducted classes in their homes, and this was a major source of income for proud Southern ladies who found it necessary to support themselves. When they announced the opening of their select schools for young ladies, they often

[1] Jestin Hampton to Thomas Hampton, n.d.., 1862, Jan. 28, Feb 19, Apr. 3, 10, 13, May 1, 1864, Thomas Hampton Letters, Eugene Barker Library, University of Texas.

stressed their ancestry rather than their educational qualifications. For example, the Misses Clopton of Richmond were identified only as the "daughters of the late Judge Clopton" of that city. Few of these schools endured beyond the war years and some struggled along for only a few months. Women who sought to replace tutors were often shocked to find that instead of teaching the children in only one family they often had to instruct a dozen or more of all ages whom their employer had brought together as a school, charging them room, board, and tuition. Newspapers frequently published announcements like that of a Virginian who stated that he had employed a "competent governess" for his daughters and would welcome other young ladies into his home for $800 a session.[2]

Teachers' salaries were deplorably low in all areas, and those in the Confederacy were usually paid in rapidly depreciating paper money, yet many women felt themselves fortunate to be guaranteed room and board in these uncertain times. In 1864 a Virginian advertised for "an experienced female teacher" to conduct classes in "English, French and Music" for $600 a year, and about the same time a North Carolinian sought one to teach the same subjects at $400. Both promised lodging and board in addition to the salary, which if paid in gold would have amounted to approximately thirty and twenty dollars a year respectively. Public school teachers were even worse off, although they usually were boarded by the families of students, for the average monthly salary for women teachers in North Carolina was only twenty-five dollars in Confederate scrip, which by 1865 amounted to about sixty-four cents in gold.[3] It is understandable that most teachers preferred their salaries to be paid in commodities, for even if not used they could be bartered for other items at a favorable rate of exchange.

Northern teachers generally fared better, but they also battled inflation and were paid approximately half as much as men. In February 1865 the average public school teacher in New York City received an annual salary of $500 in greenbacks or $200 in

<hr>

[2] New York *Herald,* Jan. 19, 1862; Richmond *Enquirer,* Sept. 13, 1861, Sept. 2, Oct. 2, 1863.

[3] Richmond *Enquirer,* Jan. 15, 1864; Richmond *Examiner,* Feb. 6, 1864; Noble: *A History of the Public Schools of North Carolina,* p. 245.

gold, which was "less than the average wages of unskilled labor." This figure included both men and women's salaries, and according to a report published at this time, "hundreds of women" were making only $240 a year; and while the average male principal's salary was $1,800, that of women was $960. Teachers' wages rose approximately 20 per cent during the war years, but the cost of living rose 100 per cent in the same period. In villages and rural areas, women teachers were paid from twelve to twenty dollars per month; men made much more except in a few instances, as in Wisconsin, where the women averaged $22.24 to the men's $24.50 a month.[4] The low salaries gave teachers little incentive to excel and unquestionably contributed to their frustration, yet it was in part these low wages that drove men into other work and increased the opportunities for women.

The emancipation of slaves made evident the Negroes' need for education and thereby opened up the most significant new field for teachers. Hundreds of selfless, determined women volunteered to teach Negroes during and after the war. No group of teachers was more inspired and well-meaning, yet few at first understood the ignorance and confusion of the Negroes or the mores of Southern white society. Many impractical visionaries were soon discouraged and returned North after a few months or years, but usually much the wiser for their experiences. What they set out to do had to be done, however, for not more than 5 per cent of the liberated slaves knew how to read and write. It had been contrary to state laws to educate slaves, and although some Southerners had defied the statutes, the vast majority of Negroes were unprepared to assume the responsibilities of free people. They needed to be taught not only the rudimentary subjects but the rules of behavior, their obligations to society, and the importance of self-discipline and work. Northerners were not alone in recognizing their educational needs, for as soon as it was clear that slavery was doomed, many Southerners determined to teach their Negroes even while the war continued. Unfortunately, many whites were as easily discouraged as Kate Cumming, who after trying to instruct those working in her hospital concluded the race would never be able to master anything more

[4] *Report of the Male Principals Association,* New York *Herald,* Feb. 15. 1865; Hurn: *Wisconsin Women in the War,* p. 86.

than simple reading and writing. A great many northern teachers eventually came to the same conclusion.[5]

As thousands of contrabands flocked to Washington early in the war, it was apparent that something must be done about their education. By this time Myrtilla Miner's school had been closed and she had gone to California, but Emma Brown, a Negro, opened a school in 1861; and when Congress abolished slavery in the District, public schools were established for freedmen. Even before they were put into operation more than a dozen Northern groups set to work educating contrabands. By May 1864 the District had thirteen schools employing twenty-three teachers and enrolling 1,200 Negroes, and within three years more it boasted sixty-two schools with eighty colored and white teachers and 4,800 pupils. "Gail Hamilton" (Mary Abigail Dodge), recalling Miss Miner's academy in the fifties as a "rock of offense" to many people, was pleased to find that in 1867 schools for colored children were "springing up in various directions, unconcerned and unnoticed . . . and in no respect essentially different from any common country district school."[6] A similar development took place in other Northern areas possessing an appreciable number of Negroes, and teachers of both races engaged in the work of educating colored girls and boys.

During the winter of 1861–62, abolitionist and religious groups recruited Northern teachers to go South to set up schools in Federally occupied areas. In March the first large contingent, approximately one-fourth of them women, arrived off the South Carolina coast. They were correctly referred to by one newspaperman as "missionaries." This journalist was obviously amused by the idealism and naïveté of most, including one woman who rushed down the gangplank, threw her arms around a startled Negro, and enthusiastically exclaimed, "You are my sister! You are no longer a slave; you are . . . as free as I am!" He noted that the eyes of the dazed Negro "protruded from mingled fear and pleasure."[7] Very few of the Northern teachers had ever seen Ne-

[5] Kate Cumming: *Kate: The Journal of a Confederate Nurse,* ed. Richard Harwell (Baton Rouge, 1959), p. 270.

[6] Edward Ingle: *The Negro in the District of Columbia* (Baltimore, 1893), pp. 8–30; "Gail Hamilton" (Mary Abigail Dodge): *Wool Gathering* (Boston, 1865), p. 311.

[7] New York *Herald,* Mar. 22, 1862.

groes en masse and they did not always understand them or their needs, but they came South with the best of motives and often at great personal sacrifice. While their salary of twenty-five dollars a month plus living expenses was as high or higher than they would have received in the North, some accepted no compensation and many who did were soon spending it on their pupils. The sponsoring organizations preferred that they accept pay, however, for this made it easier to supervise their activities and gave greater assurance they would stay with the job for at least their term of contract.

The large number of organizations sponsoring schools created confusion as they overlapped and competed, for by late 1865 approximately 300 such groups were operating schools in the South. Early in 1867 most institutions had been brought under one of two organizations which received financial assistance from the Freedmen's Bureau; but many teachers opposed consolidation, preferring to retain more personal relations with their sponsors and greater independence. By 1869 there were 9,000 teachers in the colored schools, approximately one-third of whom were Southerners, seven times as many Southerners as were teaching Negroes in 1865, for until after the war almost all had come from the North. Southern white women usually had to contend with local criticism when they taught Negroes, and most of them did it only because they needed the money, but some were convinced of the necessity for educating the colored people and thought it better for all concerned if they were trained by Southerners. Many people were distressed that so many of the "freedmen's schools" were staffed by Northerners and believed with one North Carolinian that Southerners were obligated to offer their services since they were the Negroes' "best friends." Hundreds of Southern women were reluctant to teach in these schools but conducted Sunday school classes for the race, and this was more generally condoned by the community.[8]

Northern teachers who went South during the war encountered problems which only the most dedicated could have endured for an appreciable length of time. They were grossly over-

[8] Charles Phillips to J. B. K., Mar. 2, 1866, **Cornelia Phillips Spencer Papers.**

worked, often holding classes for youngsters during the day and adults at night. They walked miles to take assignments to absentees or to entice dropouts back to the fold, and they were expected to teach Sunday school and assist in innumerable projects besides, leaving little time for diversion. Their teaching was made more difficult because of inadequate equipment. Elizabeth Breck pleaded with her Northampton, Massachusetts, sponsors to send textbooks, suggesting that the local teachers urge their students to collect them for the Negroes. This they did, and in many Northern communities boys and girls had as one of their wartime projects supplying freedmen's schools with educational necessities. The drive for these essentials as well as for food, medicine, and clothing occupied much of the teachers' time, and as soon as a shipment arrived they were expected to express their gratitude and inform the donors how it was used.[9] Teachers were also expected to report regularly on the progress made, and dared not hint that they were pessimistic about their ultimate success lest they be looked upon as failures.

Classes had to be held in any makeshift quarters available, and fortunate was the teacher who had access to a school building or church. One room sometimes had to be shared by two or more teachers who conducted their classes simultaneously. Even more deplorable were the living quarters of many teachers, some of whom found hovels or shared cabins with the Negroes, not because they preferred to do so as many Southerners thought, but because no other accommodations were offered. They were often more resented by the whites than were Federal soldiers. Shortly after the war a reporter in Richmond noted that the residents "were glad enough to board army officers for their money; but few were prepared to receive and treat decently 'nigger teachers' at any price."[1] Faring better were those assigned quarters in the confiscated homes of Confederates, and a few bought abandoned houses for a pittance. Miss Breck was one of twelve women occupying a Charleston mansion vacated by the owners during the war, but it was without furniture until agents

[9] E. P. Breck to M. A. Cochran, Dec. 23, 1864, June 5, 1865, E. P. Breck Letters, Smith College Archives.

[1] John Townsend Trowbridge: *The South: A Tour of Its Battle-Fields and Ruined Cities* (Hartford, 1866), p. 188.

of the Freedmen's Bureau made the rounds of the city to select items from other homes. No sooner had Miss Breck reported herself "quite comfortable" than she was told to expect a transfer to Orangeburg—but this did not materialize because no one in the town was willing to accommodate "a teacher of colored children." She was sent instead to Sumter, where one man finally agreed to rent her and a companion a small house, but while it was being readied for occupancy the women had to live in a Negro's cabin.[2]

On first arriving in a community the teachers could expect to be ostracized, and many met with rudeness, intimidation, and even physical violence. Mrs. Laura Haviland visited Negro schools from Virginia to the Mississippi Valley and talked with a great many frightened teachers who actually feared for their lives, some having been stoned, spat upon, and threatened. When she tried to obtain lodging in Harper's Ferry, Mrs. Haviland was told, "We don't have nothing to do with Bureau teachers," and another resident warned, "No one in town would disgrace himself by walking on the street with a nigger teacher." Horace Mann's sister was teaching there and was completely ostracized by the white citizenry because she "kept herself exclusively with colored people . . . and boarded with them."[3] This was more than most Southerners could accept, and even those who did not object to their teaching colored children were opposed to their social relations with Negroes. Some had no choice, for they were often denied accommodations in the whites' homes because the owners feared they would entertain their colored friends there.

The Negroes baffled and dismayed many Northern teachers. The newcomers were confused by their obedient, respectful attitude toward their white teachers and their sadistically cruel treatment of one another, and they could not explain why so many children and adults enthusiastically enrolled, attended classes for a short time, and then dropped out. Enrollment often declined by one-half within a few weeks after school opened; and if the teachers reported this to Northern headquarters, they were

[2] E. P. Breck to M. A. Cochran, Nov. 8, 1866, E. P. Breck Letters, Smith College Archives.

[3] Laura Haviland: *A Woman's Life Work* (Grand Rapids, 1881), pp. 300, 383–84, 408, 425–27.

usually reminded that many students had to work and others were warned by whites not to attend classes. There were many other contributing factors, including the type of curriculum offered and the failure of teachers at first to comprehend the Negroes' needs. The prompt, efficient New Englanders were driven to distraction by their pupils' failure to adhere to schedule and recognize the necessity for being punctual, for they came to school when they chose and might arrive at any hour of the day. How could they be so docile and yet so irresponsible? asked many a confused teacher.[4]

Records indicate that most women engaged in teaching freedmen took both their work and themselves very seriously, and many lacked one characteristic they desperately needed: a sense of humor. They were inclined to be crusaders who pitied rather than appreciated these people so recently lifted out of bondage. But their most grievous error was their failure to realize in the beginning that the Negroes could not be expected to react to a literary education as would a typical Northerner. Helen Gilson, an experienced teacher and nurse, was one of the few who immediately saw that they did not need political sermons or lectures on the joys of freedom; they needed a practical education. Addressing them in simple terms, Miss Gilson impressed on them that freedom brought responsibilities, that they could no longer expect to be fed, housed, and clothed unless they worked, and that they must prepare themselves for jobs they were suited to do. Mary Peake, the free mulatto, recognized this and incorporated her ideas in the school she founded in 1861 at Fortress Monroe. Susan Walker, after spending several months trying to teach the South Carolina freedmen, decided she could not devote her life to the work as it was organized and returned North to open a school in abandoned army barracks near Washington. Here she taught Negro women to sew and was making progress when cavalrymen stationed near broke into the building and destroyed its property and records. Charlotte McKay and her friend

---

[4] E. P. Breck to M. A. Cochran, Dec. 23, 1864, E. P. Breck Letters, Smith College Archives. See also Katherine Smedley: "The Northern Teacher on the South Carolina Islands," Master's Thesis, University of North Carolina Library; Bell Irvin Wiley: *Southern Negroes, 1861–1865* (New York, 1938), pp. 26–94; Willie Lee Rose: *Rehearsal for Reconstruction* (Indianapolis, 1963), *passim*.

Jane Stuart Woolsey, after several years with the Sanitary Commission, remained in Virginia teaching the freedmen, and Miss McKay also conducted classes in sewing. Other Sanitary Commission workers were attracted to teaching during and after the war, including Catherine Lincoln Clark of Illinois, who accompanied her mother on commission business and started teaching the Negroes in northern Alabama. As she wrote her sister, she would never have come South to teach contrabands, but seeing the need she was soon so devoted to her students that when she had to leave she worried for fear no one would replace her.[5]

Mrs. Frances Gage of Ohio spent thirteen exhausting months with freedmen in South Carolina and Florida and was so enthusiastic about the work that she toured the North lecturing on the schools, the teachers' accomplishments, and the need for financial support. Probably no woman did more to awaken the Northern people to what was taking place, and she stressed the dedication of the teachers who worked against overwhelming odds. She confirmed what one young instructor in Virginia wrote, "I want to stay here as long as I live and teach these people. . . . I am happy only here with them." Another who had been discouraged when she first arrived in North Carolina reported after four years that she was at last happy in her work and the local citizens no longer "set their dogs on nigger teachers." Those who could endure the first year or two often found themselves tolerated if not accepted.[6]

If they could cling to the job over the first difficult months or years the teachers sometimes made it their lifework. Among the more remarkable was Laura Towne of Philadelphia, who arrived on the South Carolina coast in April 1862, and while not sent as a teacher soon made it her chosen work. Founding her school on St. Helena Island and working with the equally dedicated Ellen Murray, Laura Towne spent her remaining thirty-eight years teaching Negroes, many of whom themselves became teachers. Martha Schofield, also a Pennsylvanian, did not arrive in South Carolina until late 1865, but she gave the last fifty years of her

[5] William Howell Reed: *Hospital Life in the Army of the Potomac* (Boston, 1866), pp. 50–53; Charles William Dabney: *Universal Education in the South* (Chapel Hill, 1936), I, 447; *Special Report of the Commissioner of Education, 1871* (Washington, 1872), p. 242; Catherine Clark to Julia Clark, Apr. 24, May 17, 1864, Lincoln Clark Papers.

[6] *The American Freedmen* (April, 1869), pp. 7–10.

life to the industrial school she founded for Negro girls near Aiken. When she arrived and announced her intention, after three years on the South Carolina coast, the residents protested vehemently and threatened both the school and the teacher, but she was determined to win and did. Other women were as devoted, and some had their health permanently impaired by the heat or by diseases contracted while living in the South. *Harper's Weekly* bestowed one of its warmest wartime tributes on Mary Sheffield, who died while teaching Memphis freedmen. Lauding her work "among the poorest and most friendless of her fellow creatures," the writer contrasted her modesty with the vanity of wartime adventuresses who sought "the applause of spectators."[7]

The author of the tribute to Mary Sheffield noted that the teachers were "little heeded," and he might have added that they were often little appreciated. They were distrusted if not despised by most Southerners, ignored or criticized by many Northerners, ridiculed by the press, and pushed around by military authorities. Unlike the nurses who had at least their patients' gratitude, the teachers were working with a people who at the time had little opportunity to express their appreciation except in a simple direct way or who were unable to appreciate what was being done for them. The teachers had reason enough to feel insecure and in the years following the war feared their work would be terminated at any time, but their concern was not so much for their jobs as for the Negroes. In 1866, Martha Schofield was afraid that the Freedmen's Bureau would be abolished though convinced that its educational program was too valuable to scuttle. She thought the Northern people did not understand the work and were too impatient for results but if given a generation would see miracles accomplished. She resented the slurs of a visiting committee from Washington and of journalists, one of whom told a group of South Carolinians that "Northern teachers were the scum of society," and if they remained in the South, the Southerners should "make it hot for them." Miss Schofield feared the effect such statements would have on the impressionable Negroes, theretofore cooperative and respectful.[8]

[7] Rupert Sargent Holland (ed.): *Letters and Diary of Laura Towne* (Cambridge, Mass., 1912), *passim; Harper's Weekly*, July 2, 1864; Gertrude Biddle and Sarah Dickinson Lowrie: *Notable Women of Pennsylvania* (Philadelphia, 1942), pp. 200–201.

[8] Martha Schofield to William Lloyd Garrison, May 23, 1866, Garrison Family Papers.

Primarily for health reasons, teachers were offered a furlough at regular intervals, and upon their return home sponsoring organizations entertained them at "freedmen festivals." Here they were welcomed with speeches, musical programs, and refreshments, which served to frighten and embarrass many. These affairs were held annually in Boston through 1869, and one resident who attended them regularly became increasingly critical of the returning teachers, who when asked to say something about their work, "persisted in having nothing to communicate. If they do venture to say a word they make a horrid mess of it." She wondered what manner of woman was being sent South and what kind of teachers they must be.[9]

Women got a firm hold on the teaching profession during the war and continued to enter the field by the thousands. In 1860 they composed approximately 25 per cent of the nation's elementary and secondary teachers; by 1880 the figure had risen to 60 per cent and by 1910 to 80 per cent. On September 21, 1865, a New York *Times* editorial praised the advances made by women educators during the preceding four years, noting that more than half of the institutions announcing fall terms in the paper were administered and staffed by women. He noted that by no means all were finishing schools, nor were they open only to girls. "It is pleasing to see women assuming such great prominence among us as educators of youth," wrote the editor. "It is a duty in which many more ought to be engaged . . . It is work to which intelligent women are preeminently adapted" and a "mission for which so many seek and sigh in vain through life."

Writing thirty-five years after Appomattox, an educator stated that it was the Civil War which gave American women their first real opportunity to teach. In no other country has this ever been the case, he said, for their wartime achievements had not been temporary but were permanent. The American people must accept the fact that teaching was placed "increasingly in the hands of women."[1]

[9] Ellen Wright Garrison to Martha Wright, July 3, 1869, Garrison Family Papers.
[1] Nicholas Murray Butler (ed.): *Education in the United States* (Albany, 1900), p. 5.

7

Competitors for Bread

Uring the war Jane Grey Swisshelm descended on Washington to deliver a scathing attack on the government's Indian policy in Minnesota and then settled down to assisting in hospitals and a War Department office. True to her nature, she found much to condemn in the capital, but as an ardent feminist she was favorably impressed with the number of clerical positions which the war had opened to women. Delighted to see members of her sex as "competitors for bread in the world's labor market," she stated that only necessity had forced these women to work outside the home.[1] Although this was one of Mrs. Swisshelm's many inaccurate generalizations, it is true that these women gave little indication of expecting to build a career. Like most people, they assumed the job was temporary and would be given to a man when the war was over. Yet the "government girls" were to become a permanent part of the Washington scene, and many women employed in business and industry elsewhere would be able to hold their jobs after peace was restored. Although these wartime "competitors" helped immeasurably to broaden woman's employment opportunities, they also contrib-

[1] Arthur J. Larson: *Crusader and Feminist: Letters of Jane Grey Swisshelm* (New York, 1934), p. 308.

uted to the loss of many privileges, courtesies and immunities theretofore accorded the sex.

Clara Barton and her colleagues in the Interior Department had been dismissed before the outbreak of war, and women's employment in the Washington offices dates officially from the appointment of Francis Spinner as Treasurer of the United States in 1861. It was Spinner who appointed the first "government girls," defended them against critics, praised their efficiency, and stressed the economy of hiring women. After the war Spinner fought to retain them in the Treasury Department, and when he retired in 1875 women's position in government offices had been secured. Wartime changes in fiscal policies increased the work of this department and made it necessary to employ hundreds of additional clerks, copyists, and currency counters. Their numbers increased steadily throughout the war until, in 1865, 447 were employed in the department, 107 of whom worked in Spinner's office. Those who held full-time jobs received the standard salary of $600 a year until late in the war it was raised to $720.[2] This was an exceptionally high wage for women and must have seemed like a small fortune to teachers, nurses and factory operatives, but the high cost of living in overcrowded Washington made it almost impossible for those paying rent to provide themselves with essentials.

The number of women employed by the Treasury Department elsewhere in the Union also increased, their salaries varying according to the job and location; but as was generally true in all lines of work, wages were higher in the Far West. In 1865 women working in the Philadelphia Mint were making only $500 a year, while the lone woman on the payroll of the San Francisco Mint received $1,872; the top wage paid women in the New York Customs House was two dollars a day, but those performing the same services in San Francisco made $1,200 a year. Matrons' salaries in marine hospitals ranged from $150 a year in Pittsburgh to $450 in San Francisco, and the pay of lighthouse keep-

---

[2] *Register of Officers and Agents, Civil, Military and Naval in the Service of the United States . . . 1861, 1863, 1865, 1867, 1869* (Washington, 1862, 1864, 1866, 1868, 1870). The *Register*, published biennially, is the principle source used for the number of women employed, salaries paid, and other statistical information unless otherwise stated, and it will not be cited in instances when the year is referred to in the text.

ers from $100 on the Atlantic coast to $1,000 on the Pacific. However the higher wages in the West were somewhat offset by the higher cost of living, especially in San Francisco.

Other departments eventually followed the Treasury's lead in their Washington offices, and the Post Office continued to appoint postmistresses, a policy endorsed by Lincoln especially in the case of soldiers' widows having "claims and qualifications" equal to those of male applicants. When a man and a woman applied for the position in Rockford, Illinois, Lincoln supported the latter because she was a war widow and therefore had "the better right" to the job.[3] Sometimes facetiously contemporaries expressed doubt as to the wisdom of letting women come in contact with the mail lest curiosity tempt them to pry. It was during the war that the Post Office Department first employed women in the Dead Letter Office, but in 1865 they were being paid $120 a year less than those in the Treasury. The War Department also came around to hiring women copyists, the first being assigned to the Office of the Quartermaster General, and after the war they were given jobs in the Freedmen's Bureau offices. The Interior Department appointed a few women clerks and copyists as an economy measure; and though in 1865 Secretary James Harlan dismissed most of them, when he retired shortly thereafter they were reinstated. In the postwar period the increasingly heavy work load in the Pension Office placed hundreds of women on the Interior Department's payroll.

Male reaction to the "government girls" ran the gamut from staunch support by a few to vehement opposition by many. Foes questioned whether or not they were really an economy if they were as inefficient as was often alleged, and critics questioned their manners and morals. Unless they refrained from "carrying the drawing-room to the office," warned a Washington observer, "the experiment must fail, [for] ball gowns . . . coqueteries" [sic] and women bent on "corrupting public morals" were out of place in an office. Like many other men this critic condemned the "fair sex" for distracting their male colleagues. But occasionally some man spoke in behalf of the ladies, among them a Washington correspondent who maintained that they made "the very best clerks." When he praised the Republican party for "lifting

[3] New York *Tribune,* July 29, 1863.

up and benefiting humanity regardless of the class or condition of life," he was referring specifically to the elevation of white women and Negroes, a common allusion of the war years.[4]

Among the most caustic critics of government workers were their women colleagues. Jane Swisshelm divided her co-workers into five categories. She was convinced that the majority were Southern sympathizers, mostly old women who tried to give the impression of being "a miss of sixteen" by smoothing their wrinkles with "pipe clay," penciling their eyebrows with "lamp-black," dyeing their crisp dry hair, and being coy. There were others "as pure as the New England frost, bright as a button, active as a bee," who did as much work "in a month" as any man and for half the pay, but because they had no influential friends they might be fired for a single error. There were also the habitual tardies who wasted time, distracted everyone in the office, and departed early in the day but managed to retain their positions because they claimed to be aristocrats. In all offices were the silly, love-starved women who always had a crush on some man and spent most of the time devising ways to see him. If successful, they assumed "the St. Agnes attitude," said Mrs. Swisshelm, maneuvering their eyes "like a duck in a thunderstorm." And the fifth group was composed of dull, decorous drones whose work was done promptly and properly but whose pay envelope was no heavier and chances for promotion no better than their laziest, most inefficient colleagues. Although Mrs. Swisshelm's classification is too narrow and rigid, some women fitted into these categories, and as she said, there were those holding jobs through influence who should have been dismissed.[5]

Rumors were repeatedly circulated that the women employees in one or another of the departments were to be fired, but there was no wholesale dismissal during the war. Congress discussed the matter during the winter of 1865–66. It was the opinion of many that they should be replaced with returning soldiers, but public sentiment was divided. The New York *Herald* tried to

[4] New York *Times*, Nov. 10, 1865; Washington *Chronicle*, Nov. 8, 1865; New York *Herald*, Nov. 13, Dec. 10, 1865; St. Louis *Missouri Democrat*, Jan. 25, 1864.

[5] Larsen: *Crusader and Feminist*, pp. 309–13; St. Cloud *Democrat*, Dec. 21, 1865. See also Lester Butler Shippee: "Jane Grey Swisshelm: Agitator," *Mississippi Valley Historical Review*, VII (1920), 206–7.

put the women's minds at ease by suggesting that any legislation probably would call for their removal to New York where living was less expensive than in Washington, for this had often been considered during the war.[6] But the daring Treasury workers, petitioned Congress in December, 1865, for a pay raise, although they were then making more than those in other departments. The women in the Bureau of Printing had struck for an increase during the war, and with peace they and their co-workers demanded and received an increase of $180 a year to the $900 level. This was to be the last raise given most "government girls" for more than twenty years and it represented approximately one-half that paid men performing comparable tasks.

As previously noted, Rebecca Wright, General Sheridan's "heroine of Winchester," received an appointment in the Treasury Department where she was to work for forty-seven years, twenty-five of them at $900. In 1892 her salary was raised to $1,000, and after she passed a competitive examination in 1902 it was increased to $1,200, the amount she received until her retirement in 1914. Only once in all these years was her job threatened, that being in 1882 when she wrote Sheridan that a man was trying to get the position and begged his assistance. The general immediately reminded Secretary Charles James Folger that she had made possible his Winchester victory shortly before the 1864 election and this, said Sheridan, had helped to re-elect Lincoln. He told Folger that in his opinion she should have been pensioned, but since Congress opposed this the Republican party certainly could not afford to dismiss her. At this time her husband, William Bonsal, was living on the Kansas farm which she was helping him buy, but after crop failures for two years Rebecca feared he would lose the place. Her prediction came true and soon thereafter Bonsal returned to Washington working at first one job and then another while Rebecca continued as the family's financial mainstay.[7]

Other women obtained appointments because of influential friends and relatives. In 1863, General George Meade's sister Margaret sought a position in the War Department because, as

---

[6] New York *Herald*, Dec. 10, 11, 1865.

[7] Rebecca Wright Bonsal Papers, Record Group 56, Ser. 343, Correspondence of the Treasurer, National Archives.

she stated in her application, "the sad condition of the country has . . . confused my small means." Among her sponsors were the superintendent of the U. S. Coast Survey, Alexander Dallas Bache, the former Secretary of War Robert J. Walker and her cousin John Courtlandt Parker, an influential New Jersey Republican. Receiving an appointment during the war, she was working in the seed room of the Bureau of Agriculture in 1867, at a salary of $600, and some time thereafter was transferred to the Pension Office where she remained until dismissed "because of age and inefficiency." Records show Miss Meade unsuited for clerical work, yet after her dismissal from the Pension Office Parker succeeded in getting her another place in the Quartermaster Depot. No sooner had she assumed her duties than she demanded that her desk be moved to the ground floor so that she would not have to climb stairs, and not long after, Parker asked General Montgomery Meigs to have her assignments sent to her home so that she might work in bed. The irate Meigs not only refused but stated, "This is not the sort of work needed . . . if Miss Meade is confined to her bed and too ill to work in a room on the ground floor, I fear she will be found physically unable to earn her salary." He informed Parker, "Public money which is appropriated for the Army cannot be used for a mere charity."[8]

Other women from prominent families were given wartime appointments in the Treasury, including the daughters of Robert J. Walker and Roger B. Taney. After the war numerous Southerners came, some of them widows and daughters of Confederate officers and public officials. Many continued in government work for extended periods although none topped Rebecca Wright Bonsal's record of forty-seven years. Mrs. Angelina Ware worked twenty-five years in the Patent Office; and Helen McLean Kimball, widowed by the war, held a Treasury post for twenty; while another war widow, Mrs. Willard Leonard, worked for an even longer period as the "chief counterfeit detector"; and Sarah Hoey spent forty-five years as a currency counter.[9]

One of the most sensational wartime scandals involved the "government girls" in the Treasury Department, and after the

[8] Margaret G. Mead Papers, Record Group 92, Quartermaster General's Office, Consolidated File, National Archives.
[9] Mrs. John A. Logan: *The Part Taken by Women in American History* (Wilmington, 1912), pp. 889–92.

press and the Congressional investigating committee had completed their exposé the innocent as well as the guilty lived under a shadow. In April 1864, Congressman James Brooks of New York demanded an investigation of the department, which he said had become "a house for orgies and bacchanals," and a House committee headed by James A. Garfield was immediately appointed to look into this and other Treasury conditions. Lafayette Baker, the notorious provost marshal of the War Department, gathered information for Brooks, whose primary purpose was to discredit Spencer Clark, a Treasury official, but who hurt many young women while doing little damage to his intended victim. In the most ruthless, underhanded manner Baker gathered what he alleged to be evidence of Clark's illicit relations with three girls in his office, all teen-agers. The three girls had roomed in the same boardinghouse where the questionable Ada Thompson lived, and it was this burlesquer who conspired with Baker to obtain damaging information about their relations with Clark. The couple broke into the young women's rooms while they were at work and rummaged through and abstracted their private papers, including diaries. Baker then arrested the girls individually and confronted each with what he had found, telling her that the others had confessed to being immoral and threatening her with imprisonment in Old Capitol unless she admitted her guilt. When each one appeared, Baker presented her with a prepared confession and the frightened girls foolishly signed the paper.

All three girls were most certainly indiscreet and two may have been as immoral as Baker claimed, but the death of one, Laura Duvall, the opening week of committee hearings brought her exoneration. This aid not take place, however, before the newspapers quoted Baker as stating that he had irrefutable proof that she had died from the effects of an abortion, and Ada Thompson told the committee that Laura had been "in a family way." Expecting to prove his story, Baker ordered the girl's casket removed from the hearse as it was en route to the cemetery and demanded that three physicians perform an autopsy, but to his disappointment the examiners unanimously agreed that they had found "incontestable evidence of unsullied virtue" and that the cause of death had been pneumonia. Laura Duvall was cleared, but the shocked committee lost no time in informing Baker that his ruthless act was "a barbarity rarely surpassed."

The reputations of many other girls were ruined by the widely publicized accusations of immorality and promiscuity made by Baker, Brooks, Ada Thompson, and others. Miss Thompson gave especially damaging testimony when she quoted one young woman as saying that her job was to interview women applicants for Treasury posts and make sure they "could be improperly used" by Clark and others before recommending their appointment, but Miss Thompson's statements were discounted by the committeemen who thought she was in no position to "throw stones." Many witnesses came before the investigators to tell of the drinking that went on in the offices of the department, and a fourteen-year-old employee described the clandestine meetings she had witnessed in the ladies' "bonnet room." The committee tore most of the stories to shreds and not only cleared Spencer Clark of any misconduct but commended his "great energy and skill" in conducting the "affairs in his department." Brooks's and Baker's allegations were condemned as "exceedingly unjust and cruel" because they had "compromised the reputation of three hundred females . . . a majority of whom [were] . . . wives or sisters of soldiers fallen in the field." In an effort to right this wrong, the committee stated that nowhere could there be found "a larger proportion of noble and reputable women than . . . in the Treasury Department," and Brook's charges of "orgies and bacchanals" was "wholly unwarranted in facts and in the highest degree unjust and injurious."[1] But some public doubts about the "government girls" persisted.[2]

The hundreds of women employed in Confederate offices saw their jobs evaporate with the government's collapse, but for nearly four years they shared many of the same problems and experiences as their Northern sisters. In the Confederacy as in the Union, the Treasury Department was the first to offer them employment, and the Post Office and War Department eventu-

[1] *U.S. House Reports 140, 38th Congress, 1st Session, Select Committee To Investigate Charges Against the Treasury Department* (Washington, 1864), pp. 1–29, 44–71, 148–49; 209–21; 264, 405–10. See also New York *Herald*, May 2, 3, 4, 6, 7, 8, 1864; Washington *Intelligencer*, Apr. 30, May 2, 4, 6, 7, 8, 1864.
[2] Isaac S. Bonsal to Congressman S. M. Randall, May 9, 1868, Rebecca Wright Bonsal Papers, National Archives.

ally followed suit. The competition for jobs was especially keen in the South, and in December 1862, Secretary of the Treasury Christopher Memminger was quoted as saying that "each vacancy" in his department "brought a hundred applications" from women in desperate need. One was the middle-aged Judith McGuire, an Alexandria refugee and wife of the eminent minister and educator, John P. McGuire, who was himself a civil servant. Before the war it had never occurred to Mrs. McGuire that she would need to seek remunerative work, and then it was a year after the need arose before she was called to take an examination "in simple arithmetic" to determine her qualifications for a place in the War Department. Irritated by this requirement and indignant that she had to prove her indigence, Mrs. McGuire exclaimed, "No lady would ever bind herself to keep accounts for six hours a day without dire necessity." She received the appointment and found the work "not very onerous" but confining, yet the Confederate employees worked fewer hours and had greater freedom while on duty than did those in Washington.[3] According to the supervisors' monthly reports days and often weeks passed when there was little or nothing for the women to do.

As in the North, influential friends were an asset when one sought work with the government, and character references were required of all applicants, but the individual's need was also a major consideration. The war's effect on once affluent women and their humiliation at having to ask for a job are pathetically revealed in their letters of application and reference. Typical of hundreds was one written "to bespeak the need of Margaret Fisher," a refugee with no immediate family, no property, and no income but too much pride to ask favors. She had managed to get along for two years by selling her personal possessions but was now reduced to the clothing she wore. "Many a poor girl remembers with gratitude the kindly encouragement . . . of officials," wrote a Richmond lady after the war, and she recalled that "the most high-born ladies . . . filled these places as well as the humble poor."[4] Records support her statement, and the payrolls of the Treasury offices in Columbia show that among the note signers

[3] Judith Brockenbrough McGuire: *Diary of a Refugee* (New York, 1867), pp. 174, 238–39, 244, 250, 298.
[4] M. Wise to George Trenholm, n.d., Confederate Records Group 56, National Archives; Sallie Brock Putnam: *Richmond During the War* (New York, 1867), p. 175.

were women from the DeSaussure, Huger, Rhett, Izard, and other prominent South Carolina families. In this group also was twenty-year-old Malvina Black Gist, widow of Major William Gist whose father had been governor of the state just before the war. An exceptionally effervescent, energetic young woman, she was cited by her supervisor for her efficiency, but like most of her colleagues she complained bitterly about the high cost of living. While annual salaries rose rapidly from $500 in 1862 to $3,000 in 1864, they were paid in depreciating Confederate scrip and by 1864 were equal to approximately $150 in gold. In the last months of the war yearly salaries were not quoted but monthly wages were $325, and women who at first were paid one-half as much as men were now receiving equal compensation.[5]

Primarily because of the congestion, scarcity of provisions, high living costs, and defense problems in Richmond, it was suggested that most government employees be transferred to other communities, but relatively few were sent out of the capital. It was feared that such a move would be construed as an evacuation, bringing satisfaction to the enemy and further weakening Confederate morale. But in 1864 more than a hundred Treasury Department note signers were ordered to Columbia, and those who protested the move were told they could either follow orders or lose their jobs. Because no provision was made for mothers to take their children, many needy women were compelled to remain in Richmond with scant hope of finding other employment. The public decried the government's action as arbitrary and ruthless, and as the workers traveled South sympathetic citizens met them at the stops with food and drink, treating them like martyrs. Many were shocked that ladies would be ordered by their government to move into a strange community, for Southerners were slow to realize that all civilians must relinquish certain privileges and preferences in time of war. When it was known that the note signers were being sent South, workers in other departments worried lest they also be transferred; among them was Mrs. McGuire, who said that if her office was ordered away from Richmond she "would be obliged to resign."[6]

[5] Treasury Note Signing Department Payrolls, Confederate Records Group 56, National Archives.
[6] McGuire: *Diary*, p. 259.

As Sherman's forces neared Columbia in February 1865, the "government girls" were ordered to return to Richmond. The early morning departure of ten cars of "sleepy-eyed" women in the "most unattractive *disabille*" made excellent newspaper copy. True to feminine nature they arrived at the station with tons of baggage, some containing friends' possessions entrusted for safe-keeping. Most was somehow crammed aboard, but a tremendous pile of hoop skirts was left behind. Malvina Gist was one of the reluctant participants in this hegira, for she was tired of being "tucked away in a safe place" just because she was a woman and thought it "high time" she got in on some of the "excitement of war." Realizing that this may have been foolish, she admitted finding "a certain satisfaction in being young and foolish rather than old and wise." When boarding the train Mrs. Gist was weighted down with a sufficient stock of watches and other items "to fill a small jewelry shop," and although heavy laden and uncomfortable, she and her colleagues eventually arrived in Richmond where they were assigned rooms in the Ballard Hotel. Judging from Malvina's account, the remaining weeks of the war were gay ones in the doomed capital.[7]

Although the Confederate employees were not involved in a scandal like their Union counterparts, they nevertheless had their critics who questioned their morals, manners, efficiency and seriousness of purpose. A Virginia girl among those transferred to Columbia wrote a friend that she and her co-workers were thought by the residents to be "fast," one of the many disparagements she heard on "every side." But she assumed that jealous Columbia ladies resented the "very pretty" government girls who were popular with the local men. Mrs. Chesnut said she "did not wonder" that their names were in "everybody's mouth," for however broad-minded, she was shocked by their "familiarity and intimacy . . . [with] noted Legislators."[8] Most references in Congress to the Confederate workers were complimentary and

[7] Richmond *Whig*, Mar. 7, 1865; Richmond *Dispatch*, Feb. 23, 1865; New York *Herald*, Feb. 26, 1865; Mrs. Thomas Taylor *et al.*: *South Carolina Women in the Confederacy* (Columbia, 1903, 1907), I, 244–49.

[8] Bettie J. Clark to Lizzie ———, August 27, 1864, Bettie Clark Letter, South Caroliniana Library, University of South Carolina; Mary Boykin Chesnut: *A Diary From Dixie*, ed. Ben Ames Williams (Boston, 1950), p. 464.

deferential, but one Congressman went a bit too far when, late in the war, he proposed that government vehicles be used "in conveying female clerks to and from their offices when . . . their lives and health . . . are jeopardized by the weather." Undismayed by his colleagues' guffaws, he suggested that the matter be considered by a special committee, and "such excessive and long continued laughter" broke loose "on the floor and in the galleries" that the session was adjourned.[9] This extremely protective attitude toward self-supporting women was slowly disappearing during the war, but there were men who refused to recognize that necessity had compelled most women to be more self-reliant and that many were enjoying their greater independence.

Male civil servants rarely if ever mentioned their feminine colleagues in their personal records, although some were obviously amused by them. One unusually articulate clerk in the Confederate War Department commented once about their noise overhead, and he occasionally referred to some in other departments, but he never indicated hostility toward the women or the practice of employing them in government offices. Bartholomew Fuller, whose job was to interview applicants for the Post Office Department, was unenthusiastic about them but reported only one woman whose appointment caused "a sensation," not because she was a woman, however, but because she was assigned a private office opening into that of her boss. If women were to be employed, reasoned Fuller, then he intended to appoint refugees rather than Richmond citizens, for the former were usually in greater need since they had to pay high rents while the residents usually owned their homes or lived with relatives.[1]

The female industrial wage earners attracted less attention in the North than did the civil servants, primarily because woman's employment in industry was an extension of antebellum practice rather than a wartime innovation. Yet more than 100,-000 new jobs in factories, sewing rooms, and arsenals were opened to women during the war years. While many of the operatives replaced men called into service, the expansion of industry to

[9] Richmond *Examiner*, Nov. 22, 1864.

[1] John Beauchamp Jones: *A Rebel War Clerk's Diary* (Philadelphia, 1866), II, 179, 189, 191, 192, 377, 426, 234; Bartholomew Fuller to Mrs. Fuller, Mar. 9, 24, 1864, Bartholomew Fuller Papers, Southern Historical Collection, University of North Carolina.

meet wartime demands was also responsible for the increase. But many women in industry were unable to retain their positions when cotton mills closed during the struggle and when men returned from the battlefields and war industries cut back or ceased operations in 1865. Southern workers had all of these problems and were also left without work when factories were destroyed by the invading army.

Sewing was a vocation in which women did not compete with men and which was thought quite proper for a lady. The need for seamstresses increased during the war as the armies called for clothing, bedding, and tents and as the prosperous Northern citizenry also made greater demands for clothing. Although sewing machines were used increasingly, tens of thousands of women earned a livelihood with their needles while thousands of others wished they might, and this oversupply of labor kept wages depressed to a disgracefully low level. But blame also rested upon both governments' contract system, which pitted the women against unscrupulous contractors bent only on making profits. When possible, the men ignored suggested government wage scales, knowing that if a woman was dissatisfied she could easily be replaced with one willing to work for any amount; and while this was an old industrial practice, it worked a hardship on the victims who had to battle the ever-rising cost of living during the war.

Prominent community leaders and the press sought to educate the public on the desperate plight of the "sewing women," but it always takes time to stimulate widespread interest in any such prosaic movement and little was accomplished in the war years. Public-spirited individuals established sewing rooms, the purpose being to give soldiers' indigent womenfolk employment making clothing for the army; but because they were determined to pay the seamstresses a decent wage, these citizens were unable to underbid government contractors and large industries. Mrs. Caroline Kirkland, who organized a sewing room in New York, begged for funds and pleaded with influential friends to help her obtain government contracts so that the project might be continued. In the summer of 1862 she wrote a patron that she was completely discouraged, for while she paid the women nine cents for making "a shirt or pair of drawers," the contractors paid half as much. Her seamstresses received four cents for stitching a pillowcase, but a man who the year before had paid ten cents a dozen now lowered his price to eight cents, saying, "There's competition." She could not compete with these exploiters, and unless the government gave her work, she said, she would have to close the room. She warned that if this became necessary, "nothing short of starvation awaits the poor wretches," for while those using sewing machines might "make their bread," the ones sewing by hand would go hungry.[2]

Under the circumstances, it is not surprising that the sewing women, guided by sympathetic citizens, instigated a protest movement. In August 1863 those making clothing for the army at Schuykill Arsenal in Philadelphia met to oppose Colonel George Crossman's order that all who were not soldiers' relatives were to be discharged; but he was at the time being pressured to help indigent women whose men were fighting for their country. The needy seamstresses without kin in the service denounced the order as "oppressive and prejudicial," as did many of their colleagues, and they reminded Crossman that no such ultimatum had been issued women in other Philadelphia sewing rooms. They forwarded their protest to Secretary of War Stanton and begged him to see that "justice was done."[3] Stanton and other officials received many such requests and were bombarded with grievances from other women workers, but none were more articulate than the sewing women who were at the mercy of army contractors.

A few weeks after this protest, strikes occurred in many Northern communities but those in New York were especially numerous and serious. In industries where there was a labor shortage the women generally were granted their moderate demands; but while workers in the Miller Shoe Company received their requested 12½ per cent increase, "several hundred sewing girls" were denied a fifty-cent weekly raise to three dollars. One employer fired all seamstresses who had participated in the strike and replaced them with others willing to sew for $2.50. The

[2] Caroline Stansbury Kirkland to Alexander Dallas Bache, June 9, 29, 1862, Rhees Collection, Henry E. Huntington Library.

[3] Philadelphia *Ledger*, Aug. 5, 1863; Philadelphia *Inquirer*, Oct. 5, 1863; New York *Herald*, Aug. 7, 1863.

widespread labor unrest in November caused the New York *Herald,* on the thirteenth, to devote more than half of its front page to strikes then in progress in the city. The writer stated that "no class in the community has greater claim to the sympathies than our sewing girls who work for inadequate wages," and he criticized all employers who had lengthened hours while reducing wages of women workers. An editorial the following day exposed the disgraceful situation which made it impossible for the fastest sewer working twelve hours a day, six days a week, to earn more than two to four dollars; and it was also noted that wages for seamstresses were 25 to 50 per cent lower than in 1860, although living costs had increased by more than 50 per cent in the same period.

On November 18, 1863, fifty-three representatives of New York's sewing women met in a closed session presided over by a "gentleman who did not want to be identified," but it was later revealed that he was Judge Charles Patrick Daly. Not only did he help to organize the Workingwomen's Protective Union which developed out of this meeting, but for more than thirty years thereafter he and Mrs. Daly devoted their energies to improving women's working conditions. This organization included others besides seamstresses, and while not accomplishing as much as hoped for during the war, it later became a powerful force in assisting women workers. The second meeting on November 24 was open to the public, and the following day the *Herald* reported that "the workingwomen of the city are fairly on the move." And indeed meetings were held regularly thereafter and the one in Cooper Union on March 22, 1864, attracted widespread attention when several sewing women presented their case most effectively, informing the audience about their long hours and low wages and exhibiting their handiwork. With each article they related the time consumed in its making and compensation received, and included were shirts which netted twelve cents and took an entire workday to stitch by hand. Reports of this meeting so aroused the editor of the Washington *Chronicle* that on the twenty-eighth he delivered a tirade against these conditions which he said should make every citizen blush with shame. In an editorial entitled "Woman and Her Work" he appraised the war's effect on women whom he said "we profess to honor so chivalrously and love so tenderly." While not mincing words in condemning those responsible for the wrongs done the sex, he suggested that one reason for women's economic plight was society's refusal to permit women then to follow any but the most "limited range of occupations." Society must also be held accountable, he said, for their "utter want of business education" and for their being made to believe that only "teaching and the ill-paid needle" were respectable, genteel pursuits.

Little was done to improve conditions, but women were becoming increasingly articulate. In the fall of 1864 the Workingwomen's Protective Union reported to Stanton that they were being paid starvation wages by government contractors and as their compensation was being reduced there was "an unprecedented increase in all necessities of life." In January 1865 a committee representing more than 10,000 sewing women in Philadelphia called on Lincoln "to inform him of the relation that existed between themselves and the contractors of the Government," and for two hours they spoke of their unhappy situation and answered the President's questions. Lincoln then asked the Quartermaster General to investigate conditions and obtain for women "the wages ordinarily paid." In all their organized protests the women had support from journalists like Frank Leslie, who noted, "Surely even in a great war we cannot become parties to such crushing down of our workingwomen."[4] But as comforting as these words may have been, unfortunately they could not buy bread.

The Confederacy's sewing women were similarly plagued by the contract system, but they were also handicapped by long periods of unemployment caused by the scarcity of cloth. In 1864 there were approximately 4,000 Confederate women making clothing for soldiers, most working in the Eastern states, for others earlier employed by the government had either fallen within Federal lines or could not obtain the necessary materials or ship the finished product to the army. The typical procedure was described by a Virginia lady whose sisters and daughters helped her. They procured cloth and other essentials from the government depot and taking these home organized as a team

[4] New York *Herald*, Sept. 4, 1864; Washington *Chronicle*, Jan. 27, 1865; *Frank Leslie's Illustrated Newspaper*, Sept. 24, 1864.

and worked on routine. They arose "before day . . . breakfasted . . . attended to chores and then," she said, "begins the day's work." One girl did all of the machine sewing, substituting this for the "pianna," and the others cut, basted, finished, and pressed while the youngest daughter attended to the cooking and house-keeping. Every Thursday they took the finished garments to the depot, were paid for their week's work, and if material was available took home another batch and repeated the process. At the time of writing, the family had been employed for about six months and had made "81 large overcoats, 53 jackets, 38 pairs of drawers and six pairs of pants" and could have turned out more "except for the scarcity of cloth." The total pay for the five women averaged ten dollars a week, not as much as New York sewing women made, but this particular family had the advantage of living on their farm and raising most of their food.[5]

The Southern sewing women had no protest organizations nor did they strike, but they complained individually about low wages and aired their grievances in letters to officials. Yet not all women in the government's pay shunned protest movements. Those in the Confederate States Laboratory, an arsenal near Richmond, struck for higher wages in December 1863, and as a result an arrangement was worked out whereby single women were to be paid five dollars a day while married ones with a family were to receive seven. The following fall 300 of the girls demanded seven dollars for all and when refused they again struck, only to be greeted the next day by a newspaper notice of a work stoppage and a call for 300 replacements. Although press and public were usually shocked when Southern women participated in public demonstrations, the Richmond *Examiner* reminded its readers that these girls "engaged in a perilous and hazardous occupation" were paid far less than the "pets" in government offices. The writer noted that while the "pets" rarely worked a full six-hour day and could be seen strolling along Richmond streets when they were supposed to be on duty, they nevertheless received full salaries; yet those in the arsenal were paid only for a full day's work. When Congress convened in No-

[5] Jones: *A Rebel War Clerk's Diary*, II, 357; Marinda Cochran to Mary Newby, December n.d., 1863, Larkin Newby Papers, Southern Historical Collection, University of North Carolina.

vember a special committee was appointed to study complaints of both the laboratory workers and the sewing women, and the greater sympathy seemed to be with the latter whose compensation was said to be so inadequate that they could not buy bread for their families. Also discussed were the malpractices of contractors which were responsible for further depressing their wages, but by the time Congress got around to giving serious consideration to the matter the war had almost run its course.[6]

The Richmond editor was justified in calling attention to the dangers involved in working in arsenals, for a greater number of women lost their lives there than were reported killed in battle areas. Some died in explosions, but most were probably burned to death in the resultant fires. They became hysterical and dashed to windows and doors; and as they crowded together trying to escape, the flaming clothing of one ignited that of others. Dressed as they were in long, full skirts, and many in hoop skirts, it is a wonder that not more were burned to death. The explosion in the Confederate States Laboratory in Richmond took the lives of forty and that in the Washington Arsenal nineteen, while scores died in similar mishaps in other munitions plants including the Jackson (Mississippi) and Allegheny (Pennsylvania) Arsenals and the Waterbury (Connecticut) Flask and Cask Company.

In the investigation of the Allegheny explosion many things other than the cause were uncovered, including the questionable activities of both male and female workers. Two men were dismissed after it was disclosed that they had made improper advances to women workers, and new "rules relating to female employees" were adopted. Included were specific instructions to the girls to go directly to their work tables upon arrival, await the distribution of materials, proceed with tasks assigned without communicating with co-workers, and remain seated unless given permission by their superior to move about or leave the room. Work areas would be policed to make sure that the women were "decorous" and that there was no "turbulence and disorder." And they would be notified when the time came to leave; then they must go to their homes by way of "the roads and pathways already established." It was also announced that any openings would henceforth be filled with "unprotected girls, widows or children

[6] Richmond *Examiner*, Dec. 7, 1863, Oct. 13, 15, 18, Nov. 26, 1864.

of widows" who gave proof of "good character," and should an employee fail to complete work assigned on any given day she "would not be retained."[7]

Thousands in the South lost their jobs when mills were burned during an invasion. When the burning of the cotton factories in Saluda, South Carolina, left approximately 400 women unemployed, one witness of the "sad scene" reported the "female operatives weeping and wringing their hands in agony as they saw . . . their only means of support in flames."[8] Another 400 working in the Roswell, Georgia, mills were ordered by Sherman "to foot it to Marietta" nine miles distant where they would be put on cars, taken North, and released to get along as best they could. They had been making cloth for the Confederate Government, and Sherman did not want them sent South lest they resume their occupation. It is known that they reached Louisville but, as one commentator noted, "What became of them is nobody's business." Some may have crossed the Ohio but many remained in Louisville where local papers announced their need and availability for work. A sympathetic contemporary trusted that all found "friends and shelter" but feared many starved and some had been forced "to seek bitter, shameful bread" in a redlight district.[9] Wartime records indicate that hundreds and perhaps thousands of unemployed or underpaid women did turn to prostitution; and while not a new problem by any means, it was more serious and widely publicized during the war.

As new business opportunities were made available to women they proved their varied aptitudes, often to the astonishment of men, one of whom said they "knew all about business." He was surprised that any woman would understand money transactions but after observing them noted, "You must get up early in the morning if you want to delude her on the question of dollars and cents." Although he thought they might succeed in banking, very few engaged in high finance, yet a sufficient number became brokers and speculators to cause a New Yorker to exclaim that the "crinoline" had invaded Wall Street and "caught

[7] Allegheny Arsenal Investigation Papers, Record Group 94, Adjutant General's Office, National Archives.

[8] New York *Herald*, Mar. 20, 1865.

[9] *O.R.*, XXXVIII, Part 5, 822, 837–38; George Augustus Sala: *My Diary in America in the Midst of the War* (London, 1865), II, 226.

the gambling fever." These women, he noted, were "dividing their time between the latest fashions and the market reports," conversing with intelligence on stocks and for the first time becoming "alive to per cent," much to the dismay of men who held "an old fashioned view of women's sphere." Another reported women who suffered from "cotton on the brain," referring specifically to those who obtained permits to go to Savannah early in 1865 for speculative purposes. He reported that one had joined with a group of Bostonians to speculate in cotton, and convinced that she was being cheated, had brought suit against her partners for $30,000.[1]

Southern women had less opportunity to engage in business, for nearly all trade was disrupted during the war except that related to blockade running. But there were women who defied tradition to manage or clerk in mercantile establishments, although this was as yet frowned upon by most people. Many Southern women were even more conscious of "dollars and cents" than their Northern sisters when wartime hardships compelled them to budget, barter, and balance accounts. As they swapped personal possessions for necessities, their talent for bargaining rivaled that of the proverbial Yankee trader. But the mistress left with the management of a plantation also exhibited unusual business ability, for not only did she have to keep the enterprise as productive as possible, but she was also responsible for feeding, clothing, and disciplining the slaves. Plantation management did not usually bring women into contact with the general public, but it should be noted that there were Southern women who personally arranged for the storage and sale of cotton. In their negotiations with stewards, overseers, factors, and bankers, it was necessary for these women to show "a head for business." Among the South's "business women" were speculators who competed with men on a small scale. They were frequently haled into court for buying large quantities of food and other essentials and accused of holding them for a rise in price, but this was difficult to prove since many were obviously hoarding and not speculating. In less than a week three were brought before the Richmond court for buying a large supply of apples and chickens, and two

[1] Sala: *My Diary*, I, 225–27; New York *Herald*, March 24, 1864; Washington *Chronicle*, Jan. 31, 1865.

were declared to be speculating, fined, and lost their produce. But the third managed to convince the court that she had bought twenty chickens for family use.[2]

In the North it became increasingly commonplace to find women behind counters, this being work which ladies knew they could do as efficiently as their brothers. Often mentioned were groups of women who tried to goad salesmen to enlist by offering to replace them, and who indicated their contempt for men who stayed home to "sell thread and measure ribbon." The press usually supported the idea of their replacing "the yard-stick gentlemen" and the "hated exempts"; and aided by conscription and the expansion of business, thousands of women became clerks and were so successful that many retained their positions after the war.[3] The census of 1870 reported nearly 10,000 salesladies and 3,000 "female traders and dealers" in the country.

Although the 1860 and 1870 census reports are not entirely reliable and the figures for the war years are spotty and varied, it is safe to conclude that women wage earners increased by more than 60 per cent during the decade, the figure being somewhat higher for the war years than later. The greatest increase of women workers was in "personal services," which included 867,354 domestics in 1870, many of them former slaves or recently arrived immigrants not listed in 1860. Also included in this category were the government workers, teachers, and nurses, many of whom got their opportunity during the war years. While the women employed in "personal services" increased by 33.4 per cent in the sixties, those in industry rose by only 16.5 per cent, there being approximately 53,000 more operatives in 1870 than in 1860. Their numbers decreased in New Hampshire, Vermont, New Jersey, Alabama, Georgia, Kentucky, Mississippi, North Carolina and Virginia, yet only North Carolina and Virginia showed a decrease in manufacturing establishments. Increased mechanization, women's replacement by men, the lack of women's jobs in the new, heavier industries, the return of their breadwinners from war, and the westward migration of thousands serve to explain the decrease of women workers in these

[2] Richmond *Examiner*, Oct. 5, 7, 18, 1864.
[3] *Harper's Weekly*, Aug. 30, 1862; *Southern Illustrated News*, Aug. 8, 1863.

states. It is also significant that in the same decade male industrial workers increased by 30 per cent, or nearly twice that percentage of women.

The greatest increase in the number of women employed was in industries producing ladies' apparel, tobacco, canned goods, jewelry, and woolens, while the most noticeable decrease was in those turning out men's clothing, shoes, thread, and cotton textiles. In the "trades and transportation" category there was a 7.3 per cent increase in women employed, with only 18,698 engaged in all occupations, 10,000 of these being the salesladies mentioned above. Scattered around the country were female teamsters, steamboat captains, pawnbrokers, bankers, brokers, morticians, and the long familiar keepers of saloons and boarding establishments.

The war did increase appreciably the number of women breadwinners, but just as significant as the numbers were the new opportunities afforded by the conflict. Once the door of a vocation was opened to the ladies, it was difficult to evict them. If they proved capable no attempt might be made to get rid of the feminine newcomers, for they had one powerful argument in their favor: they would always work for less pay than men. This wage discrimination was widely condemned by women's groups in the postwar years, but little was done to remedy it. Martha Wright was one of the feminists who had long been irritated, and when a friend asked her what she would do if oil were discovered on her property, Mrs. Wright replied that she would set aside the "first million to pay the *women*" she employed "precisely what the men received for the same amount of work."[4]

4 Martha Wright to William Lloyd Garrison II, Apr. 1, 1865, Garrison Family Papers.

8

This Change in Woman's Tactics

M OST PEOPLE PITIED rather than scorned the poor woman who had to earn a living in a man's world, and admired rather than rebuked the one who defied tradition to serve humanity, but the general public was more disturbed by those who delivered political tirades, denounced officials, gave advice on military strategy from the lecture platform, or participated in violent public demonstrations. What purpose could possibly be served by these brazen acts, asked their critics, and what did "this change in woman's tactics mean?" queried a bewildered editor.[1]

Although it was apparent that an alarming number of women were throwing convention to the wind during the war, those who boldly addressed mixed audiences on affairs of state were especially disconcerting. Most people were as yet unwilling to surrender the rostrum to articulate feminists, but the situation was rapidly getting out of hand. Some critics advocated the caustic methods of a Geneva, New York, journalist who editorialized on "Gynaekokracy . . . a disease which manifests itself in absurd endeavors of women to usurp the places and execute the func-

[1] *Frank Leslie's Illustrated Newspaper*, Oct. 10, 1863.

tions of the male sex." Although those afflicted with the malady were "by no means destitute of sense or genius," they were too "ambitious to mingle in the discussions of men, and direct the affairs of state." The writer included in this group the lecturers, whom he described as "free thinkers . . . radicals . . . women of doubtful morals . . . bold, unblushing, flippant, unfeminine . . . and bad imitators of men." Others no less concerned were inclined to be more indulgent and to heed the women as little as possible. "Leave the girls alone [to] . . . emancipate themselves," suggested another journalist, although he was unsure as to what they wanted "to be emancipated from." He was positive, however, that ladies were "an unknown quantity," and that men who claimed to understand them or be able to analyze their actions invariably talked "nonsense." He attributed the women's confusion to man's having encouraged them to assist in the war effort and enter new lines of work while at the same time demanding that they be "graceful . . . feminine . . . self-asserting, self-denying, obedient, independent and correct in all accounts—moral and arithmetical." The American woman, he said, "is trying to be everything at once" and should be let alone to adjust to the situation.[2]

Although Anna Elizabeth Dickinson was not the first woman to speak to mixed audiences, she was the first to deliver political diatribes in every major Northern city and was unquestionably the most unconventional feminine orator yet heard. Her meteoric rise to fame during the war was a popular topic of conversation, for wherever this "Female Demosthenes" went and whatever she said or did interested the public. Whether praised, condemned, ridiculed, or envied, Anna Dickinson loved the limelight, and the greater the attention the more outspoken, daring, and unconventional she became. Capitalizing on the war, she won fame and fortune during the conflict. No one quite like this magnetic, attractive, young lady had ever appeared on the American scene, for by comparison the antebellum feminists seemed colorless. No other woman had ever made a fortune from oratory, yet Anna's prosperity was to be as short-lived as her popularity, for her emotional instability, lack of business ability, extravagance, and

[2] Geneva (N.Y.) *Gazette*, Mar. 1, 1864; *Frank Leslie's Illustrated Newspaper*, Sept. 22, 1862.

demanding family left her impoverished before middle age. Impractical and unpredictable, Anna Dickinson was driven by her egotism and excessive ambition to heights never before achieved by a woman, and after a few years to extremes that made her one of the most tragic figures of the war generation.

Anna's Quaker background accustomed her to hearing women speak in religious meetings and converted her to the abolition cause. At fourteen she published an anti-slavery article in the *Liberator*, at sixteen she taught school but detested the job, at seventeen she went to work in the Philadelphia Mint but was fired at eighteen for accusing General McClellan of treason. Anna was only eighteen when Martha Wright, hearing her address an antislavery meeting for the first time, was impressed by her sweet simplicity, inspired delivery, and the way "she stood her ground amid rude and ungentlemanly interruptions." Two lears later, in the spring of 1862, Anna wrote William Lloyd Garrrison that she was out of work and in desperate need of money and asked that he arrange speaking engagements for her in Boston on either "The Woman Question" or "The National Crisis." Garrison suggested that since she was not "publicly known" she should confine her talks to anti-slavery topics and planned for her to lecture in Boston and other New England communities, promising "satisfactory remuneration" and inviting her to be his guest.[3]

While staying with the Garrisons, Anna wrote her sister Susan of their many kindnesses, but her letters centered around one member of the household, William Lloyd Garrison II, whom she described as "the most splendid specimen of simple, natural, dignified,—attractive manhood" she had ever met. Susan was "decid-ed-ly suspicious" when bombarded with "such a conglomeration of adjectives" and concluded that a romance was in the making, but if Anna was seriously interested in "Willie" it is not revealed in her letters. However, those written by Garrison's wife, whom he married two years after meeting Anna, indicate that something may have happened at this time which later caused them to "blush beautifully at being forced to shake hands

[3] Martha Wright to Ellen Wright, Nov. 16, 1860, Garrison Family Papers; Anna Dickinson to William Lloyd Garrison, Mar. 16, 27, 1862; William Lloyd Garrison to Anna Dickinson, Mar. 22, 30, 1862, Anna E. Dickinson Papers.

in a most cordial manner" and to be obviously embarrassed whenever they chanced to meet. Mrs. Garrison once asked her sister-in-law, Frances Garrison Villard, if she did not wish that William had married Anna, implying it had at some previous time been considered.[4]

Anna Dickinson lectured on abolition in the spring of 1862, but by fall she was speaking on political and military affairs, topics which women had ignored or touched on superficially. In the spring of 1863 she attracted widespread attention by campaigning for the Republicans in New Hampshire and Connecticut, and fresh from this success she spoke in May before her largest audience at New York's Cooper Union. Excepting Greeley's *Tribune*, the city's newspapers were brutally sarcastic, one referring to her as "a crowing hen on the rostrum" who was trying to drive military men "from their power at the point of a broomstick." On May 3 the *Herald* devoted five columns to her speech in which she praised Frémont and Butler while condemning Halleck, Seward, and her "pet peeve," McClellan; and on the fourth the *World* declared that she was more scandalous than the spiritualists who were much less dangerous because they dealt only with "trivial matters" while this "political sister" tried to "corrupt and inflame the heart." The following day the *Herald* referred to Anna as "the sweet mouthpiece through which abolition politicians . . . address the President and public." But she was on her way to fame and undeterred by the criticism. In the fall she journeyed to Chicago, where she spoke in behalf of the Sanitary Commission and was denounced for accepting a fee when others were donating their services. Although the Chicago *Tribune* was kinder than most Eastern journals, referring to her as a "born orator and a remarkable woman," the writer nevertheless regretted that the time had come when "good but mistaken women were induced to make these unwomanly exhibitions, much to the scandal of the sex."[5]

Anna Dickinson's greatest moment came on January 16,

[4] Anna Dickinson to Susan Dickinson, Apr. 18, 1862; Susan Dickinson to Anna Dickinson, May 5, 1862, Anna E. Dickinson Papers; Ellen Wright Garrison to Martha Wright, Oct. 31, 1864, October n.d., 1869; Ellen Wright Garrison to Frances Garrison Villard, Jan. 22, 1867, Garrison Family Papers.

[5] Chicago *Tribune*, Nov. 11, 1863.

1864, when high-ranking military and political officials gathered in the hall of the House of Representatives to hear her speak in behalf of the Freedmen's Aid Society. After a glowing introduction by Vice President Hannibal Hamlin, she launched forth on a two-hour tirade against government policies and leaders, one of whom was the President seated directly in front of her, but in her closing statements she confused the audience by urging his re-election. Various theories have been advanced as to why she so abruptly changed her tune, but the most credible explanation lies in Anna's lack of emotional control, for she became so aroused when she spoke that her statements often became inconsistent and irrational. She had never liked Lincoln, having referred to him two years earlier as an "ass," and during the spring and summer of 1864 she stumped the country berating him and admitting she had erred in urging his re-election. She lost the support of many old friends when she stooped to ridiculing his manners and dress, for as "Willie" Garrison said, her comments were "in the worst possible taste." He regretted "that Anna with her great gifts should be so wanting in her perception of true dignity and fitness," and he noted that her Boston audience was more "pained" than stimulated "by her dark impressions." Yet after Lincoln's assassination Anna Dickinson delivered impassioned eulogies of the man she had so recently denounced, much to the disgust of many people who, as Clara Barton said, recalled "how she had scolded him a year and a half ago." Miss Barton, so "vexed and ashamed of her" that she had wanted to reply "in his vindication," doubted that Anna's views had "changed since then" despite her eulogies.[6]

When "Willie" Garrison heard her speak in Boston during the 1864 campaign, he reported that she "looked as pretty as a picture," and by this time she had long since discarded her simple Quaker dress for elegant silks, satins, and jewels. Older people regretted the transformation, but the younger set enjoyed reading about her extravagant wardrobe and seeing her pace

[6] Anna Dickinson to Susan Dickinson, May 27, 1862, Anna E. Dickinson Papers; James Harvey Young: "Anna Elizabeth Dickinson and the Civil War: For and Against Lincoln," *Mississippi Valley Historical Review,* XXI (1944), 69–70; William Lloyd Garrison II to Ellen Wright Garrison, Apr. 29, 1864, Garrison Family Papers; Clara Barton Diary (1865), Clara Barton Papers, Manuscript Division, Library of Congress.

back and forth across the stage in elaborate gowns. Anna had many teen-aged fans, some of whom, dreaming that they might some day emulate her, asked that she help them escape from their dreary life in the factory, schoolroom, or on the farm and from under the watchful eye of "old-fashioned" parents. Most of these she never met, but years after she had passed her prime, women wrote Anna that they had never forgotten how, as wide-eyed girls, they had thrilled to her performances and hoped to follow in her footsteps. A young Quakeress, who wished she "had talents . . . for public speaking," wrote Anna, "I marvel at the . . . determination that carried thee through to thy well-earned success. . . . I don't believe any man could ever comprehend how hard it was for woman to do as thee have done." Feminists of all ages admired her audacity, but her most grateful admirers were the women who ascended the lecture platform with greater ease because she had blazed the trail. Mary Livermore, one of the most successful postwar lecturers, said of Anna, "She made it possible for any woman who had anything to say and knew how to say it, to follow her on the platform."[7]

After the war Anna lectured on a variety of subjects but emphasized primarily the political, social, and economic injustices done women. She wrote two books, neither of which was generally well received, and when she realized that her popularity was waning tried her hand at acting but failed to make the grade. By the mid-seventies she was capitalizing on her past fame, already more legendary than real. Her increasingly erratic behavior worried her family and friends, many of whom she ignored or offended, and in the nineties she was declared insane and committed to a mental institution. After her release she was placed in the care of friends, and the last thirty years of her life were spent in seclusion. Three days before her ninetieth birthday, in 1932, Anna Dickinson died, a recluse.

During the war several young women competed with Anna on the lecture platform, but none was able to depose the "Queen of the Rostrum." Emma Webb, the spirited defender of the Democratic party, more than once took issue with Anna; and Terese

[7] Lillie B. Chace to Anna Dickinson, Mar. 30, Apr. 17, 1863, July 9, 1868, Anna E. Dickinson Papers; Mary Ashton Livermore: *The Story of My Life* (Hartford, 1899), pp. 489–90.

Esmonde, the Irish girl, literally "talked" hundreds of men into military service. Terese, an ardent Democrat, opposed Anna's "rampant abolitionism and abuse of McClellan" and in the spring of 1863 and challenged her to debate on political issues but was rebuffed, probably because Anna realized that while she could speak to an audience she would probably fail dismally in a discussion requiring supportable assertions and logical rebuttals. Late in the war Emma Hardinge emerged as a speaker, and while her Cooper Union speech in March 1865 was fairly well received one critic was decidedly unhappy to note "female lecturers . . . on the increase." Undoubtedly Mrs. Charles Daly was referring to Miss Hardinge when she wrote, "Another Joan of Arc inspired by self-conceit versus patriotism" was to deliver a lecture. "I suppose," said Mrs. Daly, that "fired by Miss Dickinson's success, [she] wishes to make a nice little sum by giving advice. . . . What fools people are to go and listen." When Cordelia Phillips, another "female debutante and candidate for lecture honors," was campaigning for "Abe and Andy" in the fall of 1864, her speeches were said to have been "fairly well written and pretty effectively delivered," but the young lady lacked the magnetism of Miss Dickinson.[8]

Before Anna Dickinson was born Jane Grey Swisshelm had delivered lectures on a variety of subjects but was better known for her journalistic tirades. During the war the Indian outbreaks in Minnesota provided her with a fresh lecture topic which she exploited to the hilt in cities of the Midwest and Northeast. Like Anna Dickinson she had the ability to hold an audience spellbound for two hours and relied heavily on sarcasm and negative criticism. Mrs. Swisshelm sharply attacked the government's preoccupation with the Civil War, which she said was being fought at the expense of frontier people, but her most vituperative remarks were reserved for ex-Governor Henry Sibley whom she accused of failing to protect Minnesotans from the Indians, repeatedly referring to him as the "Minnesota State Undertaker."[9]

[8] *Frank Leslie's Illustrated Newspaper*, Mar. 18, 1865; New York *Herald*, May 21, 1863, Oct. 28, 1864; Harold Earl Hammond (ed.): *Diary of a Union Lady, 1861–1865* (New York, 1962), p. 399.

[9] Arthur J. Larsen: *Crusader and Feminist* (New York, 1934), pp. 159–60, 180–96, 225–28; *National Intelligencer*, Feb. 28, 1863; *Frank Leslie's Illustrated Newspaper*, Feb. 7, Apr. 4, 1863.

Several women spoke before groups of soldiers on political issues. "Grace Greenwood" (Mrs. Sara Clarke Lippincott) often addressed hospitalized soldiers as well as the general public and gave lectures in behalf of the Sanitary Commission and other philanthropic organizations. She advocated abolition, condemned the Copperheads, and staunchly supported Lincoln. After hearing her speak several times to hospitalized soldiers, a Sanitary Commission worker referred to her visits as "oases in the desert." Other lecturers selected topics peculiar to the war, and many told of their personal experiences in battle areas or with freedmen, often for the purpose of winning home-front support for various groups. As previously mentioned, Mrs. Frances Gage lectured on her months spent with freed Negroes in South Carolina and Florida and appealed for funds needed in the expansion of education. Mrs. Burger Stearns of Michigan championed many causes, lectures being her contribution to the war effort while her husband was at the front; and like most women motivated by interest in others, she was respectfully received by the public. An editor noted that she had proved it "possible for a lady to speak effectively to a promiscuous audience . . . without stepping out of her true sphere, or compromising her dignity and modesty as a woman."[1]

During the war women more frequently spoke on subjects considered by most to be too indelicate for discussion before mixed audiences; and while many refused to attend, curiosity-seekers and rowdies jammed the hall. When it was announced that Sarah Wright would speak on love, New Yorkers flocked to hear what she had to say and many were disappointed that she slighted the sexual aspects of the topic. Because she advocated neither free love nor miscegenation, the press twitted rather than derided her presentation, noting that she "could scarcely be heard at all" over the shouts of the hecklers. Losing her temper, Mrs. Wright became so hysterical that she "succumbed to the confusion!"[2] A fiasco such as this delighted the opponents of articulate feminists, for most critics obviously believed that with

[1] *Frank Leslie's Illustrated Newspaper*, Feb. 6, May 28, 1864; Julia S. Wheelock: *The Boys in White* (New York, 1870), p. 178; Frank Moore: *Women of the War* (Hartford, 1867), pp. 382–86.
[2] New York *Herald*, Mar. 11, 1864.

the restoration of peace they could sweep the women from the rostrums of the land. Because so many had gained access to the public platform by airing anti-slavery views, it was assumed that emancipation would silence them forever; and because most of the woman's rights advocates were preoccupied with war work, it was presumed that this movement had been killed, but the wishful thinkers were doomed to disappointment. As the cause of the freedman replaced that of the slave, as woman's rights leaders became more belligerent, as old subjects were resurrected and new ones discovered, women speakers were even more numerous and noisy in the decade following the war. Now more secure on the platform, they held forth on woman suffrage, prostitution, free love, birth control, various other reforms, and as their critics should have predicted, on their war experiences.

Contemporaries did not fail to recognize their increasing interest in politics, but the public could not know that thousands who would not dare address an audience were expressing their political views in letters, diaries, and conversations. As the war touched them personally, women did not hesitate to criticize politicians whom they often blamed for their woes, and as home-front problems increased and worsened, and loved ones were lost, they became increasingly critical of their leaders. In both North and South the criticism tended to be negative and personal, and much of it was petty, but ignorant as well as intelligent women voiced their political opinions as never before.

The election of 1864 stimulated discussion among Northern ladies who manifested unusual interest in campaign issues and personalities. The Democratic sentiments of Mrs. Charles Daly not only caused her to champion McClellan but also to "record all of the bad things" she heard about Lincoln, hoping that these would be published. Some stories of "Uncle Ape," as she called him, were hearsay and others were based on personal prejudice, but she summarized her opinion of Lincoln when she wrote, "He is a clever hypocrite under the mask of boorishness, else he could not stay in a position for which he is so eminently disqualified." Some Republican women also distrusted him, like Martha Wright whose views on slavery did not coincide with his. Although disgusted that he was nominated in 1864 instead of an abolitionist, Mrs. Wright refused to join Elizabeth Cady Stanton and Susan Anthony in supporting Frémont as a third-party candidate, and she could not support McClellan whom she had intensely disliked since early in the war. For two years her daughter Ellen was enthusiastic about Frémont, though her letters fail to show whether it was the romantic "Pathfinder" or his spirited wife who most attracted her. By 1864, however, Ellen Wright Garrison had either changed or buried her pro-Frémont sentiment.[3]

Northern women evinced distrust and vindictiveness in their comments on politics, often stressing the need for "keeping an eye on officials" lest they be too lenient with the "Rebs" or make a compromise peace. Many attacks on Lincoln originated with those who distrusted his views on slavery and conciliatory attitude toward the South, and it was the latter which prompted some to consider his death providential. A poorly educated Michigan woman wrote: "God intended Andrew Johnson should have the handling of the rebels[.] He is a man of sterner temperment [sic] and one that has suffered [sic] in person and property and I think will more likely do them justice."[4] And Mrs. Daly resented rather than mourned his assassination because she feared that as a martyr his faults would be soon forgotten. Some Southern women who had hated Lincoln during the war rejoiced at his death, but the more discerning realized that in him lay the South's only hope for a mild restoration program.

The political situation in the Confederacy differed from that in the Union. There was no two-party system, no presidential election after the installation of the permanent government in 1862, and Confederate politics were affected by the military invasion, yet Southern leaders like those in the North had their feminine critics. Jefferson Davis later became a hero to thousands of Southern women, but this was because he became a martyr and symbol of the Lost Cause, not because he was an astute political leader, and during the war women no less than men

[3] Hammond: *Diary of a Union Lady*, pp. 213, 300–301, 305, 353–56; Martha Wright to Marianna Mott, June 20, 1864; Martha Wright to Ellen Wright Garrison, Oct. 6, 13, 15, 1864; Ellen Wright to Martha Wright, Mar. 6, 1861; Ellen Wright Garrison to William Lloyd Garrison II, July 1, 1864, Garrison Family Papers.
[4] Virginia Everham (ed.): "Letters from Home," *Michigan Women in the Civil War* (Lansing, 1963), p. 62.

berated the man and were all too ready to blame him for their problems. Typical of the feminine carpers was the North Carolinian who declared that "a noble cause and free people are being sacrificed on the altars of *bad government* . . ." But Davis also had friends like Mrs. Chesnut who, when hearing him criticized, invariably rushed to his defense. "In battering down our administration," she wrote, "these people are destroying our last hope of success."

Confederate, state, and local officials were deluged with letters of complaint from bold, discontented women who criticized and advised leaders on economic, military, and political matters, but their most frequent grievances related to conscription and wartime hardships. In 1864 a Mississippian included a cross section of complaints in a letter to Davis as she described in detail the innumerable problems encountered by the average citizen, including "speculation and extortion" which she said were "more injurious to civilians than the war." She wrote, "men who pretend to be in your army are spending more time making money than fighting," but she reserved her most caustic remarks for the exemption policy. "Let the Petitions for men to stay at home come from the Ladies," she said, "and they will be fewer in number."[5] The South produced no Anna Dickinsons during the war, nor did the people look any more favorably on women lecturers than in the antebellum period, yet ladies were becoming more articulate as the conflict was brought home to them. If their assistance was as desperately needed as they were led to believe, then surely their opinions must be of some value.

Contrary to general appearances, the woman's rights advocates did not bury their movement during the war; rather they set it aside for a couple of years, after which they disguised it by changing their tactics. In 1861 most crusaders turned their attention to the soldiers' needs despite Susan Anthony's declaration, "I have not yet seen *one good* reason for the abandonment of all our meetings, and am . . . more and more ashamed and sad . . . that the means must be sacrificed to the end." As she continued to

[5] Catherine Ann Edmonston Diary, MS, North Carolina Historical Commission; Mary Boykin Chesnut: *A Diary From Dixie*, ed. Ben Ames Williams (Boston, 1950), p. 411; Mrs. S. M. Hunt to Jefferson Davis, July 14, 1864, Confederate Record Group 56, National Archives.

pressure the feminists to keep up their fight, Martha Wright told her it was foolish to call a meeting "when the nation's whole heart and soul are engrossed with this momentous crisis and . . . when nobody will listen." As for herself, Mrs. Wright said, "I am too busy watching the politicians, calculating the effect of [their] every action . . . and reading with anxiety the account of battles, in which many of us have a personal interest." She reminded Susan that most women agreed with her views and Miss Anthony was compelled to bide her time.[6]

This moratorium on woman's rights conventions especially delighted New York opponents who had long dreaded the annual spring invasion of the city, and in May 1861 the *Herald* rejoiced that the feminists had "beat a hasty retreat until further notice" since no one now had "time for such nonsense and tomfoolery."[7] Many feminists who favored emancipation channeled their energies in this direction, and most anti-slavery societies continued to meet during the war. In the spring of 1863, Susan Anthony, Elizabeth Cady Stanton, Lucy Stone Blackwell, and other "strong-minded" women found a way to bring their "sisters" together in an honorable, patriotic endeavor. Emancipation having been declared by Lincoln, they organized the National Woman's Loyal League dedicated to pressuring Congress to enact the Thirteenth Amendment, and the same women who had led the prewar woman's rights movement were elected to offices in the league. Although most were sincerely dedicated to the cause of the Negro, Susan Anthony and others were even then hitching their woman suffrage wagon to his star.

When it was known that the women were to convene in New York to organize the league, all newspapers except the *Tribune* groaned at the prospect, and the *Herald* suggested that they might "call on Lincoln to dismiss his Cabinet" and fill the vacancies with women, perhaps making Anna Dickinson Secretary of War since she knew "all about generals and their plans." Satirizing "the great uprising of the women of the North" and facetiously noting that the country might as well rely on women since it "couldn't be any worse off," the reporter found the first session

[6] Susan Anthony to Martha Wright, May 28, 1861; Martha Wright to Susan Anthony, Mar. 31, 1862, Garrison Family Papers.
[7] New York *Herald,* May 7, 1863.

so much like "the funny woman's rights conventions of former days" that he could not resist describing it. Mrs. Stanton's remarks brought loud laughter from the women whom he found more amusing than her jokes, especially when she told them that she wished Lincoln "had as much skill in cutting down rebels as he did cutting down trees" and when she advocated sending Southern planters to Liberia. Even more entertaining was Susan Anthony's interruption of the loquacious Mrs. Stanton to announce a meeting of the business committee; but this was not unusual since the impatient Susan had always preferred talking to listening. The reporter was also intrigued by an unidentified Wisconsin delegate who announced that if the league favored woman's rights, temperance, or citizenship for the Negro it would lose the support of "thousands of earnest, loyal and able women" who opposed these ideas. She warned that the group should do only what it was called together to do—that is, discuss "the best practical way of advancing the interests of the government in the struggle." As others became suspicious of the leaders' real purpose a heated debate followed, for this meeting which was, as one reporter said, "originally designed for the most patriotic and praiseworthy motive had been distorted into . . . a revolutionary woman's rights movement."[8]

Instead of voting to give the government its unconditional backing, the league agreed to support it for only as long as the Union fought a war for freedom, meaning of course the Negro's freedom. The members pledged themselves to secure a million signatures on the petition advocating Congressional enactment of the Thirteenth Amendment, and this was to be their major work during the remainder of the year. The ladies did obtain more than 400,000 names, and credit for this impressive number goes more to Susan Anthony than any other, for she devoted most of her time and energy to the task. She had the help of hundreds of women, however, one of whom wrote her daughter that she had just received "a half an acre of petitions" from Susan which she was supposed to circulate, collecting a penny from each signer to help defray expenses. The petition was presented to Charles Sumner who introduced it in the Senate, and from this moment until after the war the ladies presumed that their cause was

[8] New York *Herald,* May 10, 12, 13, 15, 16, 1863.

linked with that of the Negroes and that Senator Sumner could be relied upon to support their suffrage demands. They should have had doubts, however, when Sumner addressed the Loyal League in the fall of 1864, and after expressing his appreciation for their petition, went on to say that he thought women should not engage "in the strife of politics." They should, he said, be available when needed but their immediate task was to help "crush out the wicked rebellion."[9]

The league members were dead serious in all they did and their earnestness and inconsistent behavior was a source of amusement for onlookers who delighted in satirizing their meetings. The women applauded Susan Anthony's tirade against the Copperheads and the government's handling of the Vallandigham case and gave her a standing ovation when she opposed freedom of speech in time of war, yet a few days later they announced their support of "free speech, free schools, free suffrage and free government." There were other incidents in which the ladies found nothing humorous but which entertained observers, as when in June 1863 they did not receive a printed report as promised because the printer had exhausted his supply of the letter "W," having used it so often to spell "women" in the report.

As the woman's rightists were planning their postwar crusade, hundreds of women who had long enjoyed anti-slavery meetings realized that with emancipation the societies' days were numbered. These organizations had first enabled many of the "strong-minded" to air their views and train for leadership, and sentimentalists hoped to delay their dissolution as long as possible. One nostalgically recalled the "dear excellent meetings" of early days when they had to convene in "dark holes" where nothing could be seen shining in the darkness except "Lydia White's ear trumpet." When in January 1866 the Philadelphia society was scheduled to vote on whether or not to disband, Lucretia Mott, now seventy-three, pressured for its continuance "awhile longer." On the momentous evening the weather was so inclement that many women stayed home, but not Lucretia who ac-

---

[9] Martha Wright to Ellen Wright, June 22, 1863, Garrison Family Papers; New York *Herald*, Nov. 5, 6, 1864; New York *Tribune*, Nov. 6, 1864; New York *Times*, Nov. 6, 1864.

cording to her sister would have gone "in Pompeii, with half the streets filled with ashes." Mrs. Mott's will prevailed and the society "stuck together" for several months more.[1] Those who, like Lucretia Mott, had devoted a lifetime to crusading for abolition naturally experienced a letdown when their mission was accomplished; and while some took up the cause of the freedmen, it was never quite the same. The Civil War marked the end of an era for these dedicated reformers.

The war afforded many unusual opportunities for women to assume responsibilities which brought them into contact with military and political officials. Thousands interceded to get their men exempted or released from military duty or prison; boldly demanded favors, privileges, or immunities; and vehemently protested injustices done them and their families as well as damages to their property. This was so commonplace both North and South that it was seldom considered newsworthy, but occasionally someone went on an unconventional mission of interest to all. When Jessie Frémont carried a dispatch from her husband in St. Louis to Lincoln, it was not the first time she had taken over her husband's responsibilities or interceded in his behalf. Many, however, construed it as her most unbecoming act. Lincoln had asked Frémont to modify his policies in Missouri and it was his refusal that Jessie carried to Washington. After traveling for more than forty-eight hours on a hot uncomfortable train, the weary, dirty, short-tempered Mrs. Frémont notified the President that she had a message for him which she wished to deliver personally, but she had no idea that he would expect her to call immediately. Having no time to bathe or rest, she was scarcely serene when she arrived at the White House, and in her conversation with Lincoln she was disrespectful and rude. The story was soon published in newspapers across the land, and many people thought, with Francis P. Blair, Sr., that she had no business meddling in "affairs of state" and should have stayed in St. Louis to attend to her domestic duties. Apparently Lincoln concurred, for she was not permitted to carry his reply.[2]

[1] Martha Wright to Marianna Mott, June 23, 1865; Martha Wright to Ellen Wright Garrison, June 14, 1866, Garrison Family Papers.

[2] Catherine Coffin Phillips: *Jessie Benton Frémont, a Woman Who Made History* (San Francisco, 1937), pp. 239–40, 248–51; New York *Herald*, Jan. 21, 1862; *Frank Leslie's Illustrated Newspaper*, Nov. 6, 1861.

When Frémont was relieved of his command two months later, Jessie proved that she did not intend to sit idly by while politicians pushed her husband around. During those two anxious months her hair had turned white, and when she arrived in Washington in the fall, friends were shocked at the change in her appearance and feared she was on the verge of a nervous breakdown. Believing her husband in the right and anxious to win supporters for him, she called on officials, entertained people of influence, and tried to put her best foot forward. Women who met her for the first time in this period were generally favorably impressed. A New York matron exclaimed, "I like her very much," and while emphasizing her brilliance, originality, unaffected manner, and sincerity also noted that Jessie was "too positive and truthful" to be "popular in New York." The wife of a Congressman especially admired her devotion to her husband and determination to see him vindicated, while others were impressed by her interest in worth-while causes, as when she converted her New York drawing room into a Sanitary Commission sewing center. In *The Story of the Guard: A Chronicle of the War*, published in 1863, she gave her version of affairs in Missouri and paid tribute to the Zagonyi Guard which had supported her husband, the proceeds from the book going to the families of those killed. This work, translated into German, sold well and brought the author many new friends and admirers, among them John Greenleaf Whittier.[3]

Although controversy still rages as to Anna Ella Carroll's role in the war, one fact is indisputable: she was not a typical nineteenth-century woman. This daughter of Thomas King Carroll, former governor of Maryland, was interested in political theory and practice and was a profound logical thinker as well as an effective propagandist for the Union. Although a friend of many Southern sympathizers, Miss Carroll was among the Marylanders who warned Governor Thomas Hicks against calling the legislature in the spring of 1861 lest the secessionists gain control, and when Hicks left office he expressed his appreciation to

[3] *Frank Leslie's Illustrated Newspaper*, Nov. 9, 1861; Hammond: *Diary of a Union Lady*, p. 321; Phillips: *Jessie Benton Frémont*, 252–56; Caroline Eliot Kasson: "An Iowa Woman in Washington, D.C., 1861–1865," *Iowa Journal of History*, LII (1954), 65; Des Moines *Iowa State Register*, Jan. 29, 1862.

① SOUTHERN WOMEN HOUNDING THEIR MEN ON TO REBELLION

RUBBING IT IN—SCENE IN THE PARK BARRACKS.

Dramatis Personæ—A sick and wounded, but good-looking soldier, and an anxious lady nurse in search of a subject:
LADY NURSE—" *My poor fellow, can I do anything for you?*"
SOLDIER—(emphatically)—" *No, ma'am! Nothin'!*"
LADY NURSE—" *I should like to do something for you. Shall I not sponge your face and brow for you?*"
SOLDIER (despairingly)—" *You may if you want to very bad; but you'll be the fourteenth lady as has done it this blessed mornin'.*"

⑤

THE FAIR THING.

NORTHERN LADY *who "sympathizes" with the Rebels to Grocer's Boy*. "Why, gracious! HANS. Your Master has charged me *awful prices!* Three Dollars per pound for Tea— Soap a Dollar per Bar—Butter Two Dollars per Pound—"

HANS. "Yes, Ma'am. The Boss says as you like to *talk* Secesh, perhaps you would'nt mind *paying* Secesh prices."

⑥

(PHOTOGRAPHED AND ENGRAVED BY PENFIELD FROM A STATUETTE BY JOHN ROGERS)

⑤ THE FAIR THING

⑥ TAKING THE OATH AND
DRAWING RATIONS
*One of John Roger's most famous statuettes, which depicts
the pathos of Southern women having to swear allegiance to
the United States in order that their children might be fed.*

⑦ LADY LOBBYISTS AT THE WHITE HOUSE IN FALL 1866
*Contemporaries often mentioned the increase of women lobbyists, pardon and pensio
agents, and a great many Southern women sought President Johnson's pardon for
their husbands and for themselves if their property exceeded $20,000 in value.*

(Drawing by A. R. Waud)

(8) The Wedding of a Colored Soldier and a Vicksburg Ex-Slave Being Performed by a U. S. Army Chaplain in 1866

(Drawing by A. R. Waud)

⑨ THE LOST FOUND
The search for the graves of soldiers was a heartbreaking ordeal
for thousands of women after the war.

⑩ The Mercer "Girls" aboard the Continental en route
for the Washington Territory, January 1866

*The artist and journalist erred in saying there were four hundred making the trip.
There were only one hundred passengers, and all of these were not women.*

⑪ WOMEN EMPLOYEES LEAVING THE TREASURY BUILDING IN WASHINGTON

⑫ A NORTHERN ARTIST'S VERSION OF RICHMOND WOMEN ON THEIR WAY TO RECEIVE
RATIONS DISTRIBUTED BY THE UNION ARMY AFTER THE FALL OF THE CITY

⑬

⑬ WOMEN WAIT FOR PENSIONS AT THE U. S. PENSION OFFICE
IN THE NEW YORK CUSTOM HOUSE
*The inefficiency and delay in handling registration and disbursements
were condemned generally in the press.*

⑭ Nurses Destined for Service with the Army Visiting
the New York City Hospital in August 1861

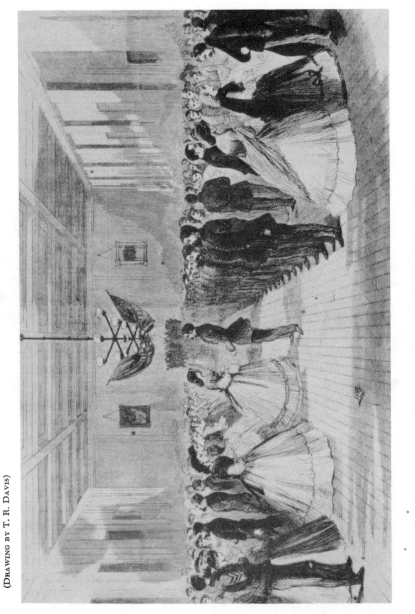

⑮ Union Soldiers Entertain the Ladies with a Military Ball at Huntsville, Alabama, in Spring 1864

(Drawing by A. R. Waud)

⑯ Negro Families Coming into Camp after the Emancipation Proclamation Was Announced

(Drawing by A. R. Waud)

⑰ THE ARTIST'S TRIBUTE TO THE SELFLESS, PATRIOTIC WOMEN
WHO CONTRIBUTED TO THE WAR EFFORT

⑱ AN ELEMENTARY SCHOOL FOR FREEDOM IN VICKSBURG, 1866

⑲ THE MEETING OF NEW YORK WOMEN AT COOPER UNION, APRIL 1861
*Here the New York Central Association of Relief was organized with
Louisa Lee Schuyler as president.*

(DRAWING BY WINSLOW HOMER)

20 BELL-TIME
Operatives leaving the textile mills in Lawrence, Massachusetts.

her for having helped uphold the Union cause in the state. When she defended Lincoln's suspension of habeas corpus in Maryland, he called her to the White House and ordered her treatise distributed among government officials; and when she wrote a response to John C. Breckinridge's speech of resignation from the Senate it was printed and circulated by the War Department. She wielded a powerful pen in behalf of the Union and the Chief Executive, for as she wrote her longtime Unionist friend, Robert J. Breckinridge, "I am writing to aid my country." No woman of the age surpassed Anna Ella Carroll as a political pamphleteer.[4]

It is not Miss Carroll the propagandist but Miss Carroll the military strategist who has been controversial. After the war several political leaders supported the claim that she had suggested the plan followed in the Tennessee River Campaign, explaining that this had not been made public at the time because she was a civilian and a woman. It was said that had Lincoln lived she would have received due credit, and there are too many supporting documents to disregard her claim completely. Ben Wade, Henry Wilson, and others acknowledged that she submitted plans for military campaigns, but most statements only imply they were used. Three weeks after the capture of Forts Henry and Donelson, Henry Miller quoted Lincoln as saying, "When the history of this war is written, she will stand a good deal taller than old Charles Carroll ever did," but it is not clear to which of her deeds he referred. However, in 1869, Ben Wade positively stated in a letter to Anna, "I know that some of the most successful expeditions of the war were suggested by you, among which I might instance the expedition up the Tennessee River." Her most recent biographer concludes that Miss Carroll was a "tragic victim of reconstruction," for if a military strategist, she was not given due credit. As long as Thomas King Carroll lived his daughter honored his request that she not file a claim for wartime services, and it was March 1870 before she memorialized Congress for recognition and compensation, this document meeting with strange "accidents" as it was misplaced at opportune moments and tossed about for years by evasive legislators. In the

---

[4] Anna Ella Carroll to Robert J. Breckinridge, Nov. 29, 1864, Breckinridge Family Papers; Sarah Ellen Blackwell: *A Military Genius: Life of Anna Ella Carroll of Maryland* (Washington, 1891), *passim*.

mid-eighties, woman's rights advocates seized upon her story, and while attracting attention to Miss Carroll and their suffrage crusade they did nothing to help her cause in Congress. Matilda Joselyn Gage, Mary Livermore, Cornelia Hussey, the Blackwells, and others maintained that had women been voting this injustice would not have been perpetrated. After a quarter-century of controversy, the embittered invalid died in 1894, having been supported for twenty years by her sister who held a government job in Washington.[5]

Women protested and petitioned in the antebellum period but never before had so many participated in mob violence, tactics deplored by critics who could scarcely believe women would resort to such extremes. In most instances the agitators were ignorant, desperate, destitute people who knew no other way to publicize their plight, but some were bent on looting and destroying, and in either case they followed the leader who assured them that they had nothing to lose since authorities would not fire on or imprison women. Protest demonstrations occurred in Northern and Southern cities where conditions among the poor were so deplorable that it took only a spark to convert hungry, disillusioned, disgruntled women into a mob of rowdies, many of whom were rancorous relatives of soldiers who were not being cared for as promised at the time of the men's enlistment.

In July 1861 a demonstration of "half-starved . . . wives, mothers and relatives of volunteers" took place in New York City as the women swept through the streets demanding "bread, bread, bread" and shouting "maldelictions" on those who had sent "their male providers" to war. The city council immediately appropriated funds for their relief and when it was announced that supplies were available for distribution, bedlam broke loose as the women clawed and fought their way into the building. Despite their thinking themselves immune to punishment, scores

[5] Lucinda B. Chandler: "Anna Ella Carroll: The Great Unrecognized Military Genius of the War of Rebellion," *Godey's Magazine*, LXI (1896), 249–67; Mary C. Francis: "More About Anna Ella Carroll," *Godey's Magazine*, LXI (1896), 378–83; Marjorie Latta Barstow Greenbie: *My Dear Lady: The Story of Anna Ella Carroll, the Great Unrecognized Member of Lincoln's Cabinet* (New York, 1940), pp. 267–76; Mary Ashton Livermore: *My Story of the War* (Hartford, 1889), pp. 174–75.

were arrested for misconduct or because they tried to obtain supplies under false pretenses. The following May a similar outbreak occurred when relief funds were again exhausted, and thousands of shouting women appeared at the offices of Mayor George Opdike, screaming "fierce threats" and refusing "to listen to reason." A sympathetic observer commented that as a mob they were "prompted to say and do many things they would doubtlessly regret in their sober senses," but many New Yorkers were more shocked than sympathetic. A similar demonstration occurred in New Orleans in July 1861, when 10,000 relatives of volunteers besieged the offices of Mayor John T. Monroe demanding food and rent money. He explained that the Volunteer Relief Committee's funds were exhausted, but the women ignored his words, knowing that in the past he had given money from his own pocket to help a needy individual. The hastily convened city council appropriated funds for immediate relief and established the New Orleans Free Market to be supported by city funds and private contributions. The Free Market proved so successful that other Confederate cities modeled their charitable agencies on it.[6]

As economic conditions worsened in the Confederacy and the war-weary people grappled with scarcities, high prices, and speculation, a number of communities were shaken by riots which spread like a chain reaction through the South. In March and April 1863, so-called "bread riots" occurred in Atlanta, Salisbury, Raleigh, and Petersburg. The most violent was in Richmond, where the population had more than doubled since 1861 and where necessities were in scant supply. Hundreds of indigent women were among the rioters, but their leader and others were interested only in looting clothing and jewelry stores. While most of the former dropped out when promised food, the latter continued to pillage and destroy. Mrs. Mary Jackson, a known speculator, extortioner, and rabble-rouser, led the mob in sacking busi-

---

[6] New York *Herald*, July 16, 21, 1861; New York *Times*, July 16, 17, 21, 1861; New Orleans *Daily Picayune*, July 31, Aug. 2, 7, 29, 1861; New Orleans Daily *Crescent*, July 31, Aug. 2, 1861; Adelaide Frances Elliott: "Feeding New Orleans During the Civil War," unpublished master's thesis, Tulane University; Mary Elizabeth Massey: "The New Orleans Free Market, 1861–1862," *Louisiana History*, III (1962), 203–5; New York *Herald*, May 13, 1862.

ness houses while ignoring bakeries and refused to heed the pleas of the mayor, governor, president of the Young Men's Christian Association, and Jefferson Davis to cease the pillage. Not until she and others were arrested and an order given to fire on women refusing to disperse was the riot brought under control.

Local newspapers were asked to refrain from printing the story, but the anti-administration *Examiner* reported the riot the following day, April 4, describing the participants as "prostitutes, professional thieves, Irish and Yankee hags, [and] gallow birds." The *Sentinel*, on the seventh, said that the mob was for the most part composed of "misguided women" accustomed to be treated with tenderness, who presumed that nothing would be done to stop them. This reporter characterized the leaders as "thieves in pantaloons." Richmond residents were shocked that the legendary image of Southern women had received a deadly blow at the hands of shrieking, plundering females. Those who recorded their reactions usually spoke of the incident as sad or disgusting; but Judith McGuire, who often told of regretting women's changing attitudes and uninhibited behavior, was appalled by the riot, the first such incident that "ever darkened the annals of Richmond." She defended the city's feminine population by saying that only "the worst sort" had participated in the demonstration. Local Unionists naturally interpreted the incident differently, one stating that in the mob were "some of the most respectable women" in the city, while another later recalled that the rioters had "looked like a flock of old buzzards, picked geese, and cranes . . . armed with hatchets, knives and axes."[7] Later in the year and during 1864, similar outbreaks occurred in Savannah, Mobile, and other communities, but none was as destructive and violent as that in Richmond. In resorting to these tactics, the women were not only calling attention to economic privations, but were also evidencing their disrespect for the city, state, and Confederate governments.

[7] Mrs. Roger Pryor: *Reminiscences of War and Peace* (New York, 1905), p. 238; Judith Brockenbrough McGuire: *Diary of a Refugee* (New York, 1867), pp. 202–4; Sallie Brock Putnam: *Richmond During the War* (New York, 1867), pp. 208–11; Mrs. E. C. Kent: *Four Years in Secessia* (n.p., 1864), pp. 24–25; John Townsend Trowbridge: *The South: A Tour of Battle-Fields and Ruined Cities* (Hartford, 1866), p. 167; William J. Kimball: "The Bread Riot in Richmond, 1863," *Civil War History*, VII (1961), 149–54.

Women opposed to conscription also participated in riots. When Lincoln called on states to draft additional men in the fall of 1862, several hundred citizens in Ozaukee County, Wisconsin, marched to the office of Commissioner William Pors, ousted him, smashed the draft box, and ransacked his home and the courthouse. Mrs. Pors fled with her children to a neighbor's house. When calm was finally restored, she returned to find her home a shambles and most of her furniture, clothing, jewelry, and mementoes stolen or destroyed. In the mob which had frightened the citizenry were women who "vied with men" in committing the depredations.[8]

Women were also among the most bloodthirsty participants in the New York draft riots of 1863, which started as a protest against the provision in the Federal Conscription Act permitting the hiring of substitutes but soon developed into a race riot. Instigated primarily by Irish day laborers too poor to pay for a substitute and fearful of being replaced in their jobs with Negroes, the mob hunted down colored people, ransacked, pillaged, burned homes and a Negro orphanage, and spread terror through the city. For three days mobs roamed the streets, resisted authority, and killed hundreds. Throughout the disorder, women killed and were killed, some being seen to plunge knives into the bodies of the dead. They destroyed property, looted residences, and carried away wagonloads of plunder. Several hundred were arrested, most being charged with grand larceny, and many received prison sentences. Princess Agnes Salm-Salm was shocked to see shrieking, vindictive women committing sadistic acts, and so afraid was she to venture out in her finery that she borrowed a simple dress from her Irish maid, whom she took with her for protection. Although Mrs. Charles Daly abhorred the violence and feared for her life and property, being Irish she naturally sided with the group and hoped this would "give the Negroes a lesson."[9]

In other unprotected areas women were not only found among lawless gangs who pillaged and killed but sometimes led

[8] Milwaukee *Daily Wisconsin*, Nov. 12, 13, 1862; Milwaukee *Daily Sentinel*, Nov. 13, 17, 1862.

[9] Agnes Salm-Salm: *Ten Years of My Life* (London, 1875), I, 65–67; Hammond: *Diary of a Union Lady*, pp. 246–51.

these groups. Residents often fled from their homes to be rid of the menace, only to meet the desperadoes on the road, for they preyed on individuals, families, caravans, and even on the Cotton Bureau wagons moving across Texas toward the Mexican border. Women who could scarcely be classified as outlaws sometimes "ganged up" on one whose behavior displeased them. When a woman in New Orleans was seen to wave a small Federal flag, several ardent secessionists pounced on her, gave her a sound thrashing, and in consequence were arrested and compelled to spend the night in jail.[1] Most women preferred the more customary tactics of rumor-mongering and ostracism while reserving their most unladylike behavior for the enemy soldiers. Southerners who would never have demonstrated in public as part of a mob often used mob tactics when confronting the Federals, who did not in all cases deserve the abuse. Some cursed the invader in language that no lady would have admitted understanding, for the hatreds and frustrations of war often brought out the worst in people; and when aimed at the enemy, the worst somehow seemed patriotic and therefore justified.

During the war women appeared to be breaking out in all directions at once, and nothing said to or about them could force them back into the fold. In adopting new tactics to present their ideas and protests, the women were creating a baffling situation. Instead of talking about their rights, they were usurping them under the cloak of patriotism. They were talking politics, mapping military strategy, advising officials on affairs of state, and using violent measures to obtain their demands, and they were doing so well that anyone should have been able to see the sex barriers crumbling. The editor who asked what this change of tactics meant hastened to add that he would not dare predict the outcome, yet those less wise were certain that after the war women would once again retire to their domestic routine and happily leave the lecture platform, politics, and protests to men. But as they would eventually discover, it was going to be impossible to keep the "girls" quiet and docile after four noisy, active years.

[1] Marion Southwood: *"Beauty and Booty," the Watchword of New Orleans* (New York, 1867), p. 204.

9

Taken to Her Pen

" "WOMAN HAS NOW taken to her pen . . . and is flourishing it with a vengeance," wrote a journalist in 1863.[1] This was but another manifestation of women's self-expression which became increasingly apparent during the war. They were publishing all kinds of writing—fiction, poetry, personal experiences, propaganda, essays of opinion, and letters to editors. It was to these published works that observers referred when noting women's ever-increasing use of the pen, but contemporaries would have been amazed to know that thousands more were privately recording their experiences, reactions, and innermost thoughts in diaries, journals, and letters never intended for publication. Although scores of these intimate accounts were eventually published, many not until years after the writer's death, most remain in manuscript and some are as well written as professional works. Many in the war generation also wrote reminiscences, but these are usually less accurate, realistic, and sparkling than accounts kept at the time. No other event has challenged so many women to write and publish personal accounts as did the Civil War. Those serving at the front or living in invaded areas were especially anxious to tell their story, and Confederate

[1] *Frank Leslie's Illustrated Newspaper,* Oct. 10, 1863.

women who lived with the war at their doors were generally more articulate than those remaining on the Northern home front.

Although the Civil War has inspired writers of every generation since, the purpose here is to stress those who lived through the ordeal and published significant or representative works pertaining to the war during and after the conflict. Northerners were blessed with greater opportunities for publishing at the time, for newspapers, magazines, and publishing houses operated without the scarcities so familiar to those in the South. Yet it is surprising how many Southern women managed to get their views before the public despite the relatively small number of printing establishments. A larger percentage of Southern ladies than of Northern still hid behind pseudonyms and anonymity, but this practice had by no means disappeared in the Union although the identity of most old-timers was well known to readers.

Mary Abigail Dodge continued to use her pen name, "Gail Hamilton," while writing outspoken articles of opinion and propaganda, the most widely discussed being "A Call to My Country-Women" published in the dark days of early 1863. She reprimanded the weak, whimpering, selfish women who said they could find nothing to do to aid the Union because they lacked talent or time and scolded those who relied on prayer, saying women who did nothing more were making "as great a mistake as if they did not pray at all." To those who worked only in aid societies she said that if the needle could have won the war "it would have been finished long ago. Stitching does not crush rebellion or annihilate treason," she added. What Northern women must do was show greater enthusiasm, patriotism, and courage. They must be the consolers, not the consoled; sustainers, not the sustained; and they must cease to dwell on their own misfortunes and make an effort to be optimistic and cheerful, especially when in contact with soldiers. By proving their self-reliance, confidence, and willingness to sacrifice women could make their greatest contribution toward sustaining the men's morale which was essential to victory. Don't depend on the North's superiority in "men, money and material resources," she warned. "O women," she said," the hour has need of you."[2]

[2] "Gail Hamilton" (Mary Abigail Dodge): "A Call to My Country-Women," *Atlantic Monthly,* XI (1863), 345–49.

Few wartime appeals evinced as widespread comment from other women and from journalists, and although its exact effect cannot be measured the essay did set many to thinking. One young lady who thought it "grand" said that she was at times ashamed of her sex for being "so tearful, trembling and weak," and she hoped that the "Call" would inspire women to accept their trials more cheerfully and selflessly.[3] Had "Gail Hamilton" written nothing else, this would have secured her a place among the builders of home-front morale.

Poets also aroused patriotism, especially when their verse was set to music, and Julia Ward Howe ranked second to none with her "Battle Hymn of the Republic," the "theme song" of the Union. Although she has forever been associated with this work, and as long as she lived was bombarded with requests to transcribe the words and autograph printed copies, it was not her favorite war poem. She preferred "The Flag," which she thought her most stirring verse, but she also ranked high "Our Orders," "The Jewelers Shop in War-Time," "Left Behind," and "The Battle Eucharist." The war provided her with a constant source of inspiration, and as her daughter later noted, "everything" Mrs. Howe saw and wrote "connected itself with the great struggle."[4] Controversy raged over the authorship of another popular song, "All Quiet on the Potomac Tonight," but Mrs. Ethelinda Beers always claimed it as hers. The most famous Confederate song to come from a woman's pen was "Somebody's Darling," written by Marie Ravenel de la Coste, who was inspired to record the pathos she found in Confederate hospitals.

Newspapers and magazines published columns and articles by women whose experiences were unusual enough to be of interest to readers. Mrs. John A. Kasson, living in Washington while her husband was in government service, regularly contributed her impressions of the Washington scene to the Des Moines *Iowa State Register*. As a Congressman's wife she kept the ladies "back home" informed on social activities, personalities, styles, and various developments in the capital. In Washington at the same time was the veteran journalist Jane Grey Swisshelm, who

[3] Lillie Atkinson to Anna Dickinson, Mar. 19, 1863, Anna E. Dickinson Papers.

[4] Laura Richards and Maude Howe Elliott: *Julia Ward Howe, 1819-1910* (Boston, 1915), I, 191–92; Florence Howe Hall: *Memories Grave and Gay* (New York, 1918), I, 137–38, 186–91, 324, 264.

wrote for the St. Cloud, Minnesota, *Democrat* and the New York *Tribune*. As previously noted, many women who worked with the freedmen published their experiences in Northern papers and organs of their sponsoring organizations, and while most reports were subjective, many were well written and illuminating. In May and June 1864 the *Atlantic Monthly* published Charlotte Forten's "Life on the Sea Islands," one of the most interesting accounts to appear during the war.

The war gave Louisa May Alcott her first big opportunity to write, although she had gained limited recognition earlier. During the six months that she served in a Washington hospital until illness forced her resignation, Miss Alcott wrote her family chatty, amusing letters which were first published in the Boston *Commonwealth* and in 1863 brought out as a book entitled *Hospital Sketches*. This work was widely read and its author praised for both her style and generosity, a part of the royalties going to war orphans.[5] It seems certain that Miss Alcott was destined to follow a literary career even had there been no war, for she had talent, a charming style, and gentle humor, but the conflict brought her wide recognition and furnished material for other writings including *Little Women* and *Work: A Story of Experience*.

In their writings some women unfortunately capitalized on the hatreds of the time, but the most bitter works did not endure as significant literature. In 1864, Mrs. E. C. Kent's privately printed *Four Years in Secessia: A Narrative of a Residence at the South Previous to and During the Southern Rebellion* brought to the reading public lectures she had delivered in the North. It told of her prewar experiences as a teacher in Mississippi and her journey to Richmond after the war commenced in hopes of being able to return North. She said permission was withheld by Confederate authorities and that she could not leave until 1863, having been held until then against her will, a questionable statement in light of the extraordinarily large number of passes issued early in the war. Throughout the account Mrs. Kent maligned Southerners with whom she had come in contact and revealed a vindictiveness often seen during and after the war. Published the

[5] Louisa May Alcott: *Hospital Sketches* (Boston, 1863), pp. 26, 28.

same year was Sarah Palmer's fantastic account, *Six Months Among the Secessionists*. The author had taught in Tennessee and her sole object in writing seems to have been to paint all Southern men as sadists, but in claiming it was an autobiographical account she gave the impression of being more interested in capitalizing on wartime animosities than presenting facts.

As previously mentioned, *The Thrilling Adventures of Pauline Cushman*, ghostwritten and published in 1864, while based on fact included exaggerations sensationally presented to publicize her exploits and probably to help advertise her lecture tour. The following year Ferdinand Sarmiento published *The Life of Pauline Cushman, the Celebrated Spy*, a highly romanticized account of her espionage activities, but this and the earlier work helped to make her famous for a time. Sarah Emma Edmonds told of her experiences in *Nurse and Spy*, published in the last year of the war and later acknowledged by the author to be exaggerated. Different in content was Mrs. Emily Souder's *Leaves from the Battle-Field at Gettysburg* (1864), one of the few personal experiences published by a Sanitary Commission worker during the war, although many appeared later.

Northern women, seeing in the war innumerable plots for fictional accounts, wrote a great many stories and novels even as the battles raged, and while some were popular for the moment they are seldom read today. Popular with thousands in the United States and England was Mrs. Metta Victoria Victor's dime novel, *Maum Guinea and her Plantation Children*, a pathetic tale of slavery published in 1861. Among the many who made use of war plots were Caroline Kelly in *Andy Hall: The Mission Scholar in the Army* (1863), Mrs. Sarah Towne Smith Martyn in *Our Village in War-Time* (1864), and Mary Anne Howe in *The Rival Volunteers or, The Black Plume Rifles* (1864). In 1865 Jane Goodwin Austin used a colorful, romantic vivandière as the heroine in *Dora Darling: The Daughter of the Regiment*.

Flora Simmons was an enterprising young woman who capitalized on the war. She compiled and edited newspaper accounts of battles and raids and had them printed in paper-bound booklets measuring three by five inches and costing twenty-five cents. These she vended on trains and at the stations, the profits helping to support herself and her "aged infirm mother." They have no historical value since she made no attempt to interpret the information gleaned from a few Northern newspapers, primarily in the Midwest, but they exemplify woman's ingenuity. Typical of the booklets is *A Complete Account of the John Morgan Raid Through Kentucky, Indiana and Ohio in July, 1863*, published in the same year with no mention of the place of publication but probably somewhere in Indiana, her home state. This small volume contains 108 pages, and in the preface Miss Simmons expressed her appreciation to railroad officials for permitting her to sell copies.

Women were also responsible for scores of pamphlets, books, and tracts designed to influence public opinion or raise money for worthy causes. As previously mentioned, Jessie Frémont's *The Story of the Guard* was primarily intended as a defense of her husband but also provided assistance for the needy. *The Diary of a Lady of Gettysburg* was published anonymously in 1863, the proceeds from its sale being contributed to the Philadelphia Sanitary Commission Fair. Hoping to raise money for their aid society and explain their reasons for opposing affiliation with the Sanitary Commission, the Patriotic Daughters of Gettysburg published in 1864 a well-written report of their principles and accomplishments. This was not the only such publication. One of the most interesting pamphlets issued during the war was "A Few Words in Behalf of the Loyal Women of the United States," written anonymously by "one of them." It was an answer to "Gail Hamilton" and others who criticized Northern women for their lack of patriotism and fervor. Journalists often reprimanded Union ladies for being less willing to make sacrifices than Confederate ladies, and the author astutely analyzed the differences, emphasizing the greater need for sacrifice in the South. Numerous tracts dealing with freedmen came from women's pens, but among the more significant was Emma Willard's *Via Media: A Peaceful and Permanent Settlement to the Slavery Question*, in which the author argued that the Negroes' former masters should be made their legal guardians. She suggested also that the Negroes flocking to Northern cities be taken into the homes of whites who would assume responsibility for "domesticating" them. Neither suggestion met with widespread approval.

Frances Ann Kemble's opposition to slavery was commonly

known long before the war, but not until 1863 did she consent to the publication of her personal record, *Journal of a Residence on a Georgia Plantation.* It was published in both the United States and England with the avowed purposes of justifying the emancipation of slaves and influencing British public opinion. According to the nineteenth-century biographer-historian James Parton, this work was the "best contribution ever made by an individual on the practical working of the slave system." *Harper's Weekly,* referring to the *Journal* as "a most thrilling and remarkable picture" of slave life, suggested that it was even more valuable propaganda than *Uncle Tom's Cabin,* which was only "founded in fact" while the *Journal* was "fact itself." After its release, significantly on July 4, one reviewer noted that if anyone did not know why the war was being fought he could find the answer in this work, "one of the most timely and valuable aids" to the Union cause.[6] Miss Kemble lived in London during most of the war and contributed pro-Northern articles to several British periodicals, thus helping to counteract the writings of Confederate propagandists in England.

Despite their innumerable handicaps and the deterrents to publication, Southern women were wielding their pens as never before. Constance Cary, who would later write under her married name (Mrs. Burton Harrison), began her literary career by publishing articles, poems, and stories in Confederate periodicals. In *Recollections Grave and Gay* (1911) she credits three men she knew while a refugee in Richmond with being her "literary godfathers"—John M. Daniel of the Richmond *Examiner,* John R. Thompson of the *Southern Literary Messenger* and London *Index,* and her next-door neighbor, the Irish-born journalist John Mitchel who urged her to "work hard" at her writing.[7] The most widely read of her wartime efforts was "Blockade Correspondence," which appeared regularly in the *Southern Illustrated News,* a Richmond publication. She concealed her identity behind the pen names "Secessia" and "Refugitta," the former ostensibly being a Confederate sympathizer residing in Baltimore

---

[6] James Parton *et al.: Eminent Women of the Age* (Hartford, 1869), p. 121; *Harper's Weekly,* June 20, July 4, 18, 25, 1863.
[7] Mrs. Burton Harrison: *Recollections Grave and Gay* (New York, 1911), pp. 119–20.

and the latter a refugee in Richmond. The column consisted of mythical exchanges between the two. "Secessia" told of life within Union lines, the information being obtained from women coming into the Confederacy, letters smuggled in from the North, and Miss Cary's own clothes-buying excursion to Washington. "Refugitta" described the Richmond social scene and problems common to all Confederate women—scarcities, expedients, and recipes; and she offered suggestions for altering and renovating old clothing according to the styles being worn in Paris and the North. Miss Cary's "Correspondence" was eagerly awaited by beleaguered women who hungered for the very information she gave and who needed the morale boost of her cheerful, amusing commentary. A century later her delightful columns are still illuminating.

Constance Cary wrote her first novel, *Skirmishing*, during the last year of the war, but the only copy was burned in the Richmond fire in April 1865. Although the author was driven to tears at the time, fifteen years later she humorously commented this amateurish effort had at least "created a blaze" which it could never have done as a published work.[8] After the war she wrote a great many war articles and stories for such notable periodicals as *Scribner's*, *Century Illustrated Magazine*, and *Harper's*; and among her novels were *Flower de Hundred: The Story of a Virginia Plantation* (1890) and *The Carlyles: A Story of the Fall of the Confederacy* (1905).

Elizabeth Avery Meriwether first published during and because of the war. Banished from her home in Memphis, she and her three small sons made their home in Tuscaloosa, Alabama, where they endured the hardships common to most Confederate refugees. When everything seemed hopeless she chanced to read that the displaced Jackson *Mississippian* was sponsoring a contest for the best war story, with a first prize of $500. She entered a tale based on her own experiences, entitling it "The Refugee," and to her great delight won the prize and at the same time a request from the editor to write another story for which she was promised $800. "The Yankee Spy" was soon sent off to Selma,

[8] Harrison: *Recollections*, pp. 118–25; J. M. West to Constance Cary, Dec. 26, 1863, Apr. 12, 1865; Constance Cary Memorandum (1879), Burton Harrison Papers.

where the paper's offices were then located; but before it could be published or its author paid, the only copy was destroyed by fire. "The Refugee" had meantime won her a new friend in the person of Joseph Davis, elder brother of the Confederate President and also a refugee in Tuscaloosa. After reading the story, which he could naturally appreciate, he called on Mrs. Meriwether, and from this time and for the rest of her life she cherished her friendship with the Davis family. Her later writings always evinced her strong pro-Southern views. Her first novel, *The Master of the Red Leaf* (1872), was so prejudiced that no Northern publisher would accept it and it had to be published in London. Among her other writings were *Facts and Falsehoods About the War of the Sixties* and *Sowing of the Swords, or, The Soul of the Sixties;* the latter, written when she was nearly ninety (1910), is as unforgiving as her earlier works. Her recollections covering ninety-four years remained in manuscript until 1958, when they were edited by her son and published by the Tennessee Historical Commission.[9]

Margaret Junkin Preston furnishes an interesting example of a writer who experienced the heartache of a family divided by the war. Her father and sister left Virginia in 1861 and returned to Pennsylvania, her brother and other relatives served in the Union forces, while she remained in the South with her husband who was a staunch supporter of the Confederacy. Because Mrs. Preston lost kin on both sides and endured privations familiar to most Southern women, it is not surprising that the tone of her writing changed from cheerful optimism in the fifties to bitterness in the sixties. Pathos and suffering are reflected in *Beechenbrook, A Rhyme of the War,* which Mrs. Preston wrote in pencil on coarse brown paper late in the struggle. It was sent to her husband in Richmond who had 2,000 copies printed, only fifty of which had been distributed when fire destroyed the remainder; but it was reissued in 1866 and this edition dedicated "to every Southern woman who has been widowed by the war" in the hope that the poem would be "a faint memorial of sufferings of which there can be no forgetfulness." Mrs. Preston was another who "never forgot," but not all her later writings dwelled on the mis-

[9] Elizabeth Avery Meriwether: *Recollections of Ninety-Two Years, 1824-1916* (Nashville, 1958), pp. 127-30, 227-29, 239-42.

ery of the war and its aftermath, and among her most beautiful eulogies were those written to honor Robert E. Lee and Matthew Fontaine Maury.[1]

While living as a refugee in Mobile, Mrs. Sally Rochester Ford published her rousing Confederate novel, *Raids and Romance of Morgan and His Men.* Also in Mobile was its resident author, Augusta Jane Evans, who already had two novels to her credit when *Macaria: or, Altars of Sacrifice* was published in 1863. With this work, dedicated to "the Brave Soldiers of the Southern Army," Miss Evans emerged as the foremost feminine propagandist of the Confederacy, and so persuasively did she justify its cause and denounce the Union that her book was banned in Federal camps. A copy of *Macaria* was sent through the blockade to her New York agent, who overcame legal complications, arranged for its publication, and collected and held the royalties without the author's knowledge. After the war the money was presented to the surprised young woman when she was most in need. Miss Evans did not permit herself to become bitter at the South's defeat, but this was easier for her than for some since she had not endured the enemy invasion, been displaced, or had her property destroyed. She set to work with a positive attitude and wrote her extremely sentimental fourth novel, *St. Elmo,* in which the war was mentioned only once. This was the most widely read of all her works and also the most praised and maligned, for thousands of readers laughed or cried at her emotional story and pedantic style. After her marriage in 1868 to Colonel Lorenzo Madison Wilson she continued to write and during the decade following the war was the South's outstanding feminine novelist.

Although few Confederate women published their experiences as the war was being fought, Rose O'Neal Greenhow and Belle Boyd managed to get theirs through the presses in England. Mrs. Greenhow's *My Imprisonment and the First Year of the Abolition Rule in Washington* is an embittered account of her arrest, imprisonment, and treatment by Federal authorities; and *Belle Boyd in Camp and Prison,* while not so bitter, is in places incredible and more sensational. Both works are naturally prejudiced, lacking in perspective, defensive, and written primarily to

[1] Elizabeth Preston Allan: *The Life and Letters of Margaret Junkin Preston* (Boston, 1903), pp. 198–203, 224–40, 360.

sell, yet they give insight into the writers and for that reason are not without value. Less self-centered than either is Mrs. Mary Webster Loughborough's *My Cave Life in Vicksburg*, published anonymously in 1864. This realistic account of the author's trials during the siege is so filled with human interest that despite the fact that her husband was a Confederate officer the work received favorable comment in the North, one reviewer stating that he had not "met a more interesting book on the war." Mrs. Loughborough wrote and edited after the war and in the eighties founded the *Arkansas Ladies Journal*, dedicated to the "interests and advancement" of women. This publication was possibly the first periodical in the South, according to one authority, to be "controlled, edited and published by ladies," yet it was essentially Mrs. Loughborough's project, and when she died it ceased publication.[2]

Although the quantity and variety of women's wartime publications were impressive it was not until after the conflict that the floodgates opened. In his scholarly appraisal, *Fiction Fights the War*, Robert Lively examines 512 war novels written by 371 authors, 107 of whom are women, and he shows the number published in every decade from the 1860's, when sixty-nine appeared, to the 1950's. The peak was reached in the first ten years of the twentieth century when 110 were published, but there have been at least fifty in every decade since, and women have used the war theme as consistently as men through the years. Only three of the "best" novels, according to Professor Lively were written by women, none of them living at the time of the war. Ellen Glasgow was surrounded by legends, ghosts, and scars of the conflict, yet she was far enough removed to write realistically. In Lively's list of fifteen "representative" works, six were written by women, three of whom were born before the war. Only Augusta Jane Evans was writing at the time, however, for Mary Noailles Murfree was eleven and Molly Elliott Seawell a year old in 1861. The other three, Mary Johnston, Lydia Collins Wood, and Margaret Mitchell, belong to later generations.[3]

---

[2] *Frank Leslie's Illustrated Newspaper*, May 7, 1864; Elizabeth Cady Stanton *et al.*: *History of Woman Suffrage* (New York, 1881–1922), III, 806. See also Antoinette Elizabeth Taylor: "The Woman Suffrage Movement in Arkansas," *Arkansas Historical Quarterly* (Spring, 1956), p. 3.

[3] Robert A. Lively: *Fiction Fights the Civil War* (Chapel Hill, 1957), pp. 12–15.

It would seem natural for Southerners to use Civil War themes, for they had constant reminders of the struggle in the rundown plantations, shelled towns, crumbling walls, and lonely chimneys dotting the countryside. As children they picked up minie balls on battlefields, played on abandoned fortifications, and heard of their elders' glorious deeds. Most fiction written in these surroundings was sentimental and prejudiced, but a few women, notably Ellen Glasgow, Mary Johnston, and much later Margaret Mitchell, did careful research in available newspapers and manuscript materials. Margaret Mitchell started her research for *Gone With the Wind* in the 1920's, reading the diaries and letters of Georgians who had lived during the war. One of the most valuable documents was the 1883 testimony of Margaret Ketcham (Mrs. George R.) Ward before the Senate Committee on Capital and Labor which conducted hearings in several Southern cities. Mrs. Ward gave her views on conditions in the South before, during, and after the Civil War; and although she did not write her account, it was later published with other testimony heard by the committee. In 1936, Margaret Mitchell said that had she known of its existence earlier she "would not have had to read hundreds of memoirs, letters and diaries to get a background" for her novel; and Douglas Southall Freeman stated that Mrs. Ward's testimony was "one of the most remarkable of all women's commentaries on the war."[4]

However, the war generation's greatest literary contribution was not fiction but personal records kept during the conflict and to a lesser extent later reminiscences. More than a hundred volumes and a greater number of articles based on women's experiences were published between 1865 and 1914. Some were written specifically for publication; other more personal records were published by a writer in her lifetime or by family or friends after her death. An author usually permitted publication for one of three reasons: she thought her experiences of general interest, she needed money, or she wanted recognition. If the last was primary, she made no attempt to conceal her identity; if otherwise motivated she might or might not use a pseudonym, but Southerners publishing soon after the war almost always chose to

[4] Douglas Southall Freeman: *The South to Posterity* (New York, 1939), pp. 119–123.

do so. Yet the practice was obviously being discarded in the sixties and seventies.

Most firsthand accounts of Northerners were written by women of action—nurses, teachers of freedmen, Sanitary Commission workers, and others. So many of these were published in their lifetimes that not all can possibly be mentioned, but in 1867 Mrs. Anna Morris Ellis Holstein's *Three Years in the Field Hospitals of the Army of the Potomac* and Mrs. Jane Hoge's *The Boys in Blue* paved the way for similar accounts by other war workers. In 1868 the books rushed from the presses, but two stand out, *Our Branches and Its Tributaries* . . . , a history of the Northwestern Sanitary Commission by Mrs. Sarah Edwards Henshaw, and *In Hospital and Camp*, Sophronia Bucklin's account of her nursing experiences. In the seventies Julia Wheelock and Charlotte Elizabeth McKay told of their hospital work in two of the more informative accounts of the decade. Among those published in the eighties, *A Woman's Life Work* by Mrs. Laura Haviland of Michigan is of special interest; it reveals how this dedicated abolitionist crusaded in the classroom and community, maintained a station on the underground railroad, and when war came joined forces with various relief agencies, interested herself in the freedmen's welfare, and assisted other needy persons. Always looking for a crusade, she became active in the temperance movement during the seventies and was wrapped up in this work when her autobiography was first published in 1881. Also appearing in the eighties was Katherine Prescott Wormeley's *The Other Side of the War*, one of the finest reports of a woman's experiences with the Sanitary Commission's Transport Service. Mary Livermore publicized her war activities with tongue and pen and in the eighties published *My Story of the War* . . . , which emphasized women's work with the Sanitary Commission and in other areas, military and civilian. In 1899 her autobiography, *The Story of My Life*, appeared with the author identified on the title page as "teacher, author, wife, mother, army nurse, soldier's friend, lecturer and reformer," a capsule listing of the activities of one of the country's busiest, most articulate women. Not until 1895 did Mrs. Livermore's wartime associate and close friend Annie Wittenmyer write *Under the Guns: A Woman's Reminiscences of the Civil War;* it was delayed because the author moved directly from the battlefield to the temperance crusade and pub-lized a history of this movement before settling down to relating her war experiences. In the nineties Catherine Lawrence wrote about her hospital work and Mary Holland compiled biographical sketches of one hundred Union nurses, obtaining her information primarily from the "Florence Nightingales" themselves.

Although fewer in number, Confederate nurses did not allow their Northern "sisters" to monopolize the literary field. In the spring of 1866, Kate Cumming led the way with *A Journal of Hospital Life in the Confederate Army,* and despite the inclusion of much extraneous material this was a much more revealing account than her *Gleanings from the Southland* published in the nineties. The latter is repetitious of the first but lacks its forth-rightness and wartime "flavor," yet is of interest in showing Miss Cumming's altered opinions and her views on postwar develop-ments in the South. Mrs. S. E. D. "Grandma" Smith's nursing experiences are told in *The Soldier's Friend,* a ghostwritten work which appeared in 1867. Mrs. Smith, a poorly educated but selfless woman, devoted four years to working with Confederate soldiers whose gratitude is sincerely expressed in letters included in this volume.

More scintillating than these accounts is Phoebe Yates Pem-ber's reminiscences, *A Southern Woman's Story,* first published in 1879. Although it loses less than most retrospective writings, it is more inhibited than her war letters, seven of which Bell Wiley appended to his 1959 edition of her *Story.* Mrs. Pember gives the impression of seeing, hearing, and having opinions on everything that was taking place, and she had the ability to laugh at herself as well as others, all of which makes her account both readable and informative. It was the late eighties before Mrs. Fannie Beers's *Memories* was published, and by this time she had for-gotten many incidents and was hazy about others; but the in-clusion of postwar essays, speeches, reports on Confederate re-unions, and biographical sketches indicates that Mrs. Beers had devoted the intervening quarter-century to keeping alive the "Lost Cause,"

Septima Levy Collis was among the Union women who left interesting accounts of home-front activities. *A Woman's War Record* tells what it was like to be the wife of a Federal officer and the daughter and sister of ardent Confederates, but this vivacious young lady also wrote about the gay social activities, particularly during winter encampments, and about her work with aid societies and other groups. Although relatively few Northern women were caught in an enemy invasion, several interesting accounts were published by those living in the Gettysburg area. *At Gettysburg or What a Girl Saw and Heard of Battle* is the reminiscences of Tillie Pierce Alleman who was twelve at the time. She recalled being sent away from the village in the care of a neighbor with whom, instead of finding safety, she was caught in the thick of battle and their refuge became a temporary hospital. During the quarter-century between the battle and the writing of her book she had not forgotten the carnage, the piles of amputated limbs on the lawn, the sound of bursting shells, or how her initial excitement had changed to agonizing fear. Mrs. Fanny Buehler's *Recollections of the Rebel Invasion and One Woman's Experiences During the Battle of Gettysburg,* published in the nineties, affords an exceptionally graphic description of the mass hysteria that broke out in the village when it became known that the enemy was headed that way.

The Civil War's influence is apparent in Mrs. John A. Logan's writing. Although she did not publish *Reminiscences of a Soldier's Wife: An Autobiography* until 1913, her pen had not been idle. She had founded *Home Magazine* and edited it from 1888 to 1896; compiled a huge tome entitled *The Part Taken by Women in American History,* published in 1912; and written a number of articles. Her magazine was said to have been "very respectable except for some of its advertising,"[5] but its literary quality might have been better had her sympathy for impoverished wives of veterans not influenced her to publish their scribblings. She received hundreds of stories and articles from such women and found it difficult to reject those accompanied by pathetic letters. For instance a Maine woman wrote that her crippled husband's only certain income was a pension of six dollars a month. He could not perform physical labor and only occasionally had a job repairing watches; consequently the couple had lost their home and the wife had decided to try her hand at

[5] Frank Luther Mott: *A History of American Magazines* (Cambridge, Mass., 1957), IV, 361.

writing but admitted that she lacked talent.[6]

During the war and reconstruction Mrs. Logan had supported her husband's Unionist and radical views, but when as a widow she entered upon a literary career in order to support herself she went out of her way to express sympathy for Southern women. She urged that they write for *Home Magazine* and included as many sketches of them in *The Part Taken by Women in American History* as she could collect, but Mrs. Logan obviously was unfamiliar with most of the women and dismissed them with a brief but invariably saccharin comment. Although she was interested in the advancement of her sex, this particular volume has all the earmarks of being primarily a commercial venture. Yet she was one of the few Northerners of her generation who pointed out that Confederate women not only had been as dedicated to their cause as the Unionists to theirs but had been compelled to endure twelve difficult years of reconstruction while the horrors of war ended for most Northern women in 1865. One can only surmise how her husband would have reacted to this statement, but whether Mrs. Logan published for materialistic or esoteric reasons she did extend the olive branch to her late enemy.

It is in the personal records of Confederate women that the war's impact on civilians is most vividly described, for included here are the effects of the enemy invasion, occupation, and blockade, the scarcities, inflation, destruction, displacement, defeat, and all the other vicissitudes of war. Naturally most who wrote and preserved their records were the better-educated women, many of whom said that they kept accounts both to record the unusual incidents and to improve their style of writing. But to most women this also afforded an outlet for their frustrations and thoughts which they were reluctant to express publicly.

Judith Brockenbrough McGuire's *Diary of a Refugee* was among the first such works to be published, but she is identified on the title page only as "A Lady in Virginia," and like so many others she tactfully substituted initials or a blank space for the names of most about whom she wrote. Mrs. McGuire said that the little volume was published at her family's insistence, and

[6] Mrs. E. N. Harvey to Mrs. John A. Logan, Oct. 7, 1890, Mrs. John A. Logan Papers.

this was doubtless true, but it is reasonable to assume that she hoped to receive royalties since the war left her and her family in dire straits. It takes no imagination to understand what the war did to this middle-aged lady, driven from a comfortable, secure, pleasant way of life to one of uncertainty, despair, and impoverishment; yet she held fast to her faith in God and her fellow man, always thinking first of others rather than brooding about her own misfortunes. With the Confederacy's defeat Mrs. McGuire and her husband had to go to her brother's home until the Rev. McGuire could find a pastorate, and in the late sixties he was called to serve several small rural churches in Essex County, Virginia. In the seventies the couple operated a small school for boys and it was for these students that Mrs. McGuire wrote *Robert E. Lee, the Christian Soldier,* the royalties from which were contributed to her church. Another wartime resident of Richmond, Mrs. Sallie Ann Brock Putnam, published *Richmond During the War: Four Years of Personal Observations* in the same year Mrs. McGuire's *Diary* appeared (1867). Mrs. Putnam also concealed her identity behind "A Virginia Lady" and dedicated these reminiscences to her "Southern sisters, who, in the cause of the Confederacy . . . 'Did all that woman dares.' "

Among the hundreds of books, articles, and manuscripts in which women describe the impact of invasion, four from the pens of Louisianians show its varied effects. When Marion Southwood wrote *"Beauty and Booty," The Watchword of New Orleans* (1867) she was in Vienna but scarcely detached in her presentation of conditions in the city during Butler's regime. She had never intended to be an "authoress," she explained in her preface, but Europeans roused her anger by "praising the culprit" who had so recently "robbed" the Southern citizenry and committed unforgettable "atrocities," and she wrote to remind her readers of these. *The Journal of Julia LeGrand,* published in 1911, is a vivid record by a well-educated Victorian lady of conditions in New Orleans from December 1861 until she left the city in the spring of '63. She is also supposed to have written a novel, the manuscript of which was said by her editors to have been lost. Sarah Morgan Dawson's *A Confederate Girl's Diary* has become a classic in its field since it was first published in 1913 against the specific instructions of the writer—instructions her son fortunately chose to disregard. For some unexplained reason, however, he ignored her reconstruction diary which now reposes in its original form in the Duke University Library. The published work is an excellent account of the young lady's experiences, including her involvement in the fall of Baton Rouge, its occupation by Federal troops, the Morgans' flight and wanderings before going into Federal-held New Orleans to be protected by Sarah's Unionist brother. Not until 1955 was *Brokenburn: The Journal of Kate Stone* published, yet Miss Stone kept one of the most complete, informative, realistic records of a displaced family, in this instance Louisianians in Texas.

The Civil War was a romantic episode in the life of LaSalle Corbell, who at the age of twenty married her hero, General George Pickett, eighteen years her senior. Left a widow in 1875, she worked for a time in Washington and later turned to writing and lecturing on war topics. She wrote biographical sketches of Lincoln, Lee, Grant, Jefferson Davis, and Stonewall Jackson and in 1899 published her war reminiscences, *Pickett and His Men*. She used the war theme in her novel, *The Bugles of Gettysburg* (1913), dedicated to her only son who had lost his life in the Philippines. Mary Anna Morrison Jackson also wrote about her husband, and while her *Memories of Stonewall Jackson* offered nothing new on his military career, it gave insight into the couple's home life and Mrs. Jackson's wartime problems. Twenty-five years after the conflict Varina Davis published *Jefferson Davis . . . a Memoir by his Wife,* an explanatory defense of her husband and an account of their life in Richmond.

Mary Boykin Chesnut, the most quoted of the women diarists, left a veritable storehouse of information on Confederate officialdom and high society as seen by a discerning, outspoken, clever woman. She faithfully recorded her impressions throughout the struggle, but while a refugee in North Carolina late in the war she debated burning her record, only to be dissuaded by her intimate friend, Isabella Martin, to whom she bequeathed the manuscript. In 1904 the well-intentioned Miss Martin and Myrta Lockett Avary deleted the most revealing portions before publication and thereby converted sparkling champagne into water. Most of Mrs. Chesnut's original record appears in Ben Ames Williams's 1950 edition. One can but wonder why Mrs. Chesnut did not publish her diary, for certainly she could have used the profits. Perhaps she did not think it worthy, perhaps her husband and friends opposed the idea, or perhaps she feared it would offend old friends, but if her candid record "rings true" the last is the least likely explanation.

Many women were naturally reluctant to bare their innermost thoughts to the public, and even those who wrote professionally were sometimes hesitant to publish their diaries and reminiscences. Among those who did not get around to releasing their war experiences until late in life was the remarkable Eliza Frances Andrews of Georgia, who wrote scores of articles, stories, essays, and poems as well as three novels and one textbook before she published *The War-Time Journal of a Georgia Girl* in 1908. This spirited account of the last months of the war and the first of reconstruction was written, said Miss Andrews, to practice self-expression, for even during the war she had dreams of a literary career. Regrettably she was such a perfectionist that she destroyed her journal for the early war years because the style did not suit her. During reconstruction she used the pen name "Elzey Hay" even after Mary Tardy gave away the secret in 1872 when she included a sketch of Miss Andrews in *Living Female Writers of the South*. She published her novels, *A Family Secret*, *A Mere Adventure*, and *Prince Hal: or the Romance of a Rich Young Man*, in the seventies and eighties, and her widely used textbook, *Botany All the Year Round*, went through several editions in the early twentieth century. But she is most remembered for her delightful *Journal*, and in the prologue "Fanny" Andrews explains that the girl who kept this record was as different from the woman who published it as "Philip drunk and Philip sober"; it is to her credit that she let the "drunk Philip's" version stand with all "his" emotional outbursts intact.

In the years between the dawn of the twentieth century and the outbreak of the First World War, elderly women of the Civil War generation vied with the muckrakers to get their writings in print. The many accounts published in this period not previously mentioned include Mrs. Roger Pryor's autobiographical works, *Reminiscences of War and Peace* and *My Day: Reminiscences of a Long Life*, both emphasizing the war years and published in rapid succession. In 1905, Louise Wigfall Wright's *A Southern Girl in '61* appeared and serves as an excellent example of what forty years can do to an individual's outlook, style, and possibly her memory; for in comparing this decorous work with letters of the irrepressible teen-ager of the sixties, it is hard to believe the same person wrote both. It was also early in the century that Myrta Lockett Avary won recognition as an editor of wartime records other than Mrs. Chesnut's *Diary*. Among these were *A Virginia Girl in the Civil War, Dixie After the War* and the Alexander H. Stephens diary kept during postwar imprisonment, and she also wrote a novel, *The Rebel General's Loyal Bride: A True Picture of the Late Civil War*.

Writers were often surprised, hurt, or indignant when their literary efforts met with unfavorable criticism, but those who capitalized on sectional prejudices, as so many did in reconstruction, were frequently brutally assailed. Cornelia Phillips Spencer's *The Last Ninety Days of the War in North Carolina* was a résumé of eyewitness accounts of the Federal invasion of the state, and every page riled someone. First published serially in the *Watchman* (New York) in 1866, it was brought out in book form the following year and received caustic criticism both North and South, but this did not deter Mrs. Spencer from writing for newspapers and encouraging Southerners to record their wartime experiences. When Mary Virginia Terhune's novel *Sunnybank* appeared shortly after the war, it was also criticized for reopening sectional wounds. The rabid Confederate propagandist Cornelia Matthews Jordan had her *Corinth and Other Poems* banned by incensed military officials who commanded the Richmond occupation forces just after the war.

Northern writers also aroused ire. When Mrs. Lincoln's intimate friend and modiste, Elizabeth Keckley, tried to defend the former First Lady's strange behavior in the ghostwritten *Behind the Scenes* (1868), the neurotic Mary Lincoln was so angered by the account that she broke for all time with this kindly mulatto who was probably her most understanding friend. Newspapers also had a field day at Mrs. Keckley's expense, frequently referring to the work as *Inside President Lincoln's Kitchen* and sternly reprimanding her for taking advantage of her position of trust, which incidentally she did not do. A cruel parody of this book appeared the same year under the title *Behind the Seams: By a Nigger Woman who took in work from Mrs. Lincoln and Mrs. Davis*, author unknown but the preface signed with an "*x*" identified as the mark of "Betsey Kickley." When Anna Dickinson's first book, *What Answer?* was published in 1868, Northerners and Southerners alike were infuriated by its miscegenation theme, and even her friends were disgusted, one referring to it as "trash" and suggesting that she "stick with lecturing" and leave "the writing to Mrs. Stowe."[7] The *Chicagoan,* on October 28, 1868, taking note of this work, commented on the number of amateurs writing on topics relating to the war and concluded that "no greatness is complete until it is topped out with a book." But Miss Dickinson "took to her pen" again in the mid-seventies, this time bringing forth *A Paying Investment* which supported woman suffrage, as unpopular a subject with many as miscegenation.

Not until 1876 did *The Woman in Battle* appear over the name of Mme. Loreta Velasquez, and without exception this is the most fantastic of all accounts which claimed to be factual. She said that her need for money prompted her to write the book and she very probably thought its sales would be in direct ratio to its sensational exaggerations. It was ridiculed by the press, but its sternest critic was the crusty former Confederate General Jubal Early who minced no words in declaring it a gross fabrication. When the author (Early was not convinced that she was Mme. Velasquez) heard of his comments, she wrote asking him to be specific and accusing him of trying "to injure" the book's sales. Not wishing to become involved with her, Early addressed his reply to an intermediary who promised to forward it. In his twelve-page letter Early pointed out innumerable inconsistencies, errors, impossibilities, and falsehoods, citing the pages on which each could be found. He conceded that while she "may have been a follower of one or the other army in some capacity . . . the book that is given to the public in her name cannot be the truthful narration of the adventures of any person." For this reason and because he thought it dangerous for young people, Early opposed its sale.[8]

Although space permits only cursory reference to women's

[7] Martha Wright to Ellen Wright Garrison, Apr. 3, 1868, Garrison Family Papers.

[8] Madame Loreta Velasquez to Jubal Early, May 18, 1878; Jubal Early to W. F. ———, May 22, 1878, Turner Family Papers, Southern Historical Collection, University of North Carolina.

articles and stories in periodicals, it should be noted that with the increase in magazines from 700 in 1865 to 3,300 in the nineties the ladies had greater opportunity than ever before to publish.[9] Among the better journals which solicited war accounts and stories were *Scribner's, Century Illustrated Monthly Magazine, Harper's Monthly,* and the *Atlantic Monthly,* and publications sponsored by veterans' groups and their auxiliaries afforded an outlet for both amateurs and professionals. Compilations of women's writings have been appearing since 1867, when Linus Brockett and Mary C. Vaughan brought together sketches of more than 500 women Unionists who were active in the war in their 800-page *Woman's Work in the Civil War.* In the mid-eighties Francis W. Dawson, the Charleston editor and husband of Sarah Morgan Dawson, compiled the diaries and recollections of seventy-nine women from over the South and published these as *Our Women in the War.* Included among state compilations are *South Carolina Women in the Confederacy, Confederate Women in Arkansas,* and *Reminiscences of the Missouri Women of the Sixties,* all published early in the twentieth century when an effort was made to get the surviving women of the war generation to record their experiences. The South did much more than the North in this regard, and the Southern Historical Society in Richmond published hundreds of invaluable records in its *Papers;* but the woman's rights leaders were also urging women to write of their wartime service, expecting to use this as propaganda in their suffrage crusade.

Although only a small percentage of writers on war themes have been included here, they are representative of others. With their pens a great many influenced public opinion and entertained a larger audience than did their lecturing "sisters," while an even greater number wrote to amuse themselves, occupy lonely hours, express opinions they dared not voice publicly, and record history in the making. Nor were those of the war generation the only ones to be intrigued by the conflict, for in every generation since women have "taken to their pens" to write of its history, leaders, and legends and to weave romantic and realistic tales of the period. Present-day writers are a century later still experiencing the Civil War's impact.

[9] Mott: *A History of American Magazines,* III, 5.

10

The Harder Part of War

CIVILIANS' ROLE IN WAR is often overlooked when it comes to handing out medals or writing history, yet the home front has a direct relationship to a nation's strength on the battlefield. Women compose an important part of the civilian population, and according to Robert Selph Henry, endure "the harder part of war."[1] Although Henry's statement might be challenged, it is true that women in wartime not only carry a heavy physical and emotional burden but are expected to assume new responsibilities and at the same time to sustain morale. During the Civil War the more fortunate could render service in comparative safety, but those in battle areas were faced with insurmountable obstacles; and while life was more dangerous and complicated for the latter, neither group escaped fear, insecurity, or heartache.

One of women's major problems was economic. In all parts of the country women complained bitterly about the increasing cost of living; and as the poor became poorer, theirs was a battle for survival. Those who lived on farms generally suffered less than the city folk who had to pay high rents, buy their food, and

[1] In the Introduction to Katharine Jones (ed.): *Heroines of Dixie* (Indianapolis, 1955), p. v.

197

live in the midst of an indifferent populace. But it was also in the city that one might find a job and have access to public charities. Farm families living in remote, unprotected, or invaded areas were in danger of losing their advantage if caught in battle or victimized by foraging expeditions or lawless bands. Women left in these areas without male protection often suffered to such an extent that they fled their homes and were then compelled to wander aimlessly for months or years, dependent on charity to sustain them and their families. When they had no one to turn to they usually made their way to cities in search of jobs or hand-outs, and they found greater physical but less economic security there than on the farm.

Prices were inflated everywhere and while women in middle-income groups complained about the need for economizing, the poor were threatened with starvation. Wealthy Northerners, some richer than ever, had no financial problems, but conditions were vastly different in the embattled Confederacy where even the affluent were impoverished. Confederate money depreciated to the point of being almost worthless late in the war, prices were much higher than in the North, scarcities plagued all house-wives, and speculators, extortioners, and hoarders abounded. In addition to all their other burdens, Southern women were com-pelled to spend many precious hours devising expedients, and unlike their Northern sisters they had to contend with the block-ade, impressment, poor distribution, and destruction of property. Their simplest tasks became irksome, and as a Georgian noted, the war made all Southern women "haft to work harder than . . . ever before."[2]

As the price of food rose, many Northern women had only to adjust their budgets and sacrifice a few nonessentials, but some protested as if they were on the verge of starvation. A New Yorker of the upper middle class was indignant that the price of food doubled during the war, but the only restriction she men-tioned was a reduction in the family's butter ration.[3] While food prices were resented by most women, thousands of soldiers' fam-ilies who had been accustomed to sufficiency now went hungry,

[2] New York *Herald*, Mar. 2, 1864.
[3] Harold Earl Hammond (ed.): *Diary of a Union Lady, 1861–1865,* (New York, 1962), pp. 290, 306; Caroline Eliot Kasson: "An Iowa Woman in Washington, D. C., 1861–1865," *Iowa Journal of History* LIII (1954), 85.

and they were to be pitied as much as those who had always been poor. These hard-working, thrifty, proud women did not find it easy to accept charity, but many had no alternative. Yet the rations were often so inadequate and slow in arriving that the families suffered acutely. Many who were eligible for aid meted out to soldiers' dependents or to a part of the men's pay or to a widow's pension waited an interminable period before receiving compensation, and some did not know what they were entitled to or how to go about applying for it. Mothers of small children with no income and no job were to be found in all Northern communities, but it was those in the larger cities whose plight was least likely to attract attention.

Pride was a major deterrent to the admission of need. A Wisconsin war widow who had only twenty-five cents at the time of her husband's death refused all financial aid and somehow managed to care for her family. Another with twelve children assured neighbors that she would make out, and with the assistance of two teen-aged daughters she held the brood together and provided them with essentials.[4] Sanitary Commission workers reported conversations with proud women suddenly impoverished by the war who were humiliated at having to seek jobs or handouts. Before telling their tale of woe, many extracted the promise that their name or need would never be divulged, for this was a predicament they had never anticipated.[5] They were often women who had come to the city expecting to find work, and failing to do so and without money to return home, if they had a home, they had no choice but to appeal to agencies for assistance. Probably many more suffered in silence than ever asked for help.

A mother's concern for her children's welfare prompted many North and South to seek assistance, but a larger percentage of Southern women were haunted by the fear of starvation over a longer period. There was not only a more serious shortage of food in the South but also fewer opportunities for employment and fewer charitable agencies. This problem was especially serious for refugees who settled in strange communities, far removed

[4] Ethel Alice Hurn: *Wisconsin Women in the War* (Madison, 1911), pp. 71–72.
[5] Sarah Edwards Henshaw: *Our Branch and Its Tributaries* (Chicago, 1868), pp. 201–3.

199

from friends and from sources of supply available to indigent families of soldiers. Because such aid was generally administered by county governments, those who left their home county often had difficulty proving eligibility in another. When a family stayed home but came within Union lines the only source of assistance might be the enemy; and while many women were too proud to accept his aid, those with children seldom had a choice. If the Federals moved on, many women were left to scratch together supplies somehow; and if this was hopeless, they had finally to move elsewhere in search of food. Women of any social class might find themselves in this position at some time.

Mrs. Elizabeth Meriwether's supply problems were similar to those of thousands of Southern women. Early in her displacement she worried about the lack of a balanced diet for her children, but within a few months her primary concern was a sufficiency of any food. For three years she schemed to keep the children fed as she traded personal possessions for food, collected the corn and bacon rations to which she was entitled as an officer's wife, and on one occasion stole corn from a farmer who refused to sell. If Mrs. Meriwether was not a born trader, she developed her bargaining ability for her children's sake. Another officer's wife and mother of five small children had fewer food problems than Mrs. Meriwether until late 1864 when, in addition to garden produce, it was costing $400 a month to give her family the coarsest, simplest diet. But no woman struggled harder and worried more about feeding her brood than Cornelia McDonald, whose economic status declined from middle-class comfort to abject poverty during the war years. She devised ingenious expedients, stretched available commodities, worked a garden, taught private pupils, sold precious possessions, and went hungry herself in order to feed her children, but she was never sure that tomorrow would find food on the table. Late in the war she was "so thin, . . . emaciated and weak" that she barely had strength to perform her tasks, but when friends and relatives suggested that she scatter the youngsters among those better able to provide for them, she refused.[6]

[6] Elizabeth Avery Meriwether: *Recollections of Ninety-Two Years, 1824–1916,* (Nashville, 1958), 107–28; Jorantha Semmes to Benedict Joseph Semmes, Jan. 23, 1865, Benedict Joseph Semmes Papers; Cornelia McDonald: *A Diary and Reminiscences of Refugee Life* (Nashville, 1934), pp. 251–55.

Provisioning a family in the face of such obstacles could alone have broken women's spirit, but they had heavy emotional burdens as well. The warmhearted, sensitive Margaret Preston found it difficult to carry on her domestic duties with the constant worry of having her father and sister in Pennsylvania, her brother in the Union army, her husband in Richmond, and other relatives in each army. One of her stepsons was killed in battle, a second died at home, a third lost an arm, her beloved brother-in-law Stonewall Jackson was killed, and it seemed that almost daily she heard of the death of a former Washington College or Virginia Military Institute student she had known. Despite everything she could not give way to her grief for a moment, for she had her own small children to take care of; and when her home was pillaged in 1864 her concern was not for herself or the property but for the youngsters' safety.[7] Thousands of other Southern women endured as much.

The families of Southern yeoman farmers and poor whites did not have as far to fall economically as the affluent and upper middle classes, but the women in this group were among the hardest working and longest suffering anywhere. They had to tend the farms, make the crops, sustain their families, and defend their homes. If they fled to distant towns they were usually misfits. Unfamiliar with urban ways, unqualified for the only jobs available, having few contacts and no funds, these women increased the ranks of the hungry, bitter, war-weary carpers to be found in every community. Yet the farm women who had always known work had certain advantages, although they may not have realized it. They were accustomed to few material possessions and could adjust more easily to conditions of scarcity than the spoiled rich; but even more important, they knew *how* to do a great many tasks. Most understood how to use indigenous plants to concoct medicines, tea, coffee, dyestuffs, and other items, and they knew how to spin, weave, tan leather, and perform other chores. The typical plantation mistress was by no means lacking in practical accomplishments and some had slaves who continued to perform this work and teach others, but no woman was more pitiful than one who had always had everything done for her and now had to do it herself. Hundreds sat as if in a daze, but those

[7] Elizabeth Preston Allan: *The Life and Letters of Margaret Junkin Preston* (Boston, 1903), pp. 134–36, 143–47.

with children to care for had to bestir themselves.

Although practically all Southerners had a much lower standard of living than in the prewar period, some contemporary accounts leave the impression that women moving in official circles dined sumptuously throughout the war. Some did for a time and their feasts continued long after the majority were relegated to a spartan diet, for as Mrs. Davis confessed, the officials in Richmond suffered fewer privations "than . . . persons not holding such high positions." Mary Chesnut delighted in telling of epicurean affairs she attended in the capital, but even she was compelled to exchange her clothes for food while a refugee in North Carolina. It was February 1865 before she encountered this problem, however, and she had left home with a full hamper of food. She also took a quantity of Confederate money but by this time most mountain folk knew better than to accept it. No young lady had a gayer time in Richmond than Constance Cary, yet in the last winter of the war she never finished a meal "without wishing there were more of it." Mary Custis Lee, belonging to official circles by right of birth and wartime position, was prevented by ill health and also disinclination from joining in extravagant social events. Despite gifts from friends, she was troubled by shortages before the end of the war. In January 1865, Mrs. Lee wanted to send a gift to the newlyweds Hetty Cary and John Pegram, but all she had to offer was "a pat of butter," a well-wishing but apologetic note, and her prayers.[8] With relatively few exceptions the prominent, once affluent Southern families were impoverished by the war.

Southerners were embarrassed at having to accept charity, especially that dispensed by the Federals. It was easier for Unionists, only because the aid came from a friend, and for those without political convictions; but it was a bitter experience for ardent Confederate sympathizers. As thousands flocked into Federal lines in search of food, they created serious problems, and so many congregated in New Orleans that the commanders had to limit aid. Princess Salm-Salm, seeing embarrassed Tennesseans

[8] Varina Howell Davis: *Jefferson Davis: A Memoir* (New York, 1895), II, 529; Mary Boykin Chesnut: *A Diary From Dixie*, ed. Ben Ames Williams (Boston, 1950), pp. 366–67, 484–500; Mrs. Burton Harrison: *Recollections Grave and Gay* (New York, 1911), p. 191; Mrs. Mary Custis Lee to Hetty Cary Pegram, n.d., Burton Harrison Papers.

come into camp to obtain rations, thought they "behaved with a certain dignity," but others construed this as haughtiness. Artists and reporters traveling with the Federal armies seized upon such episodes; they invariably portrayed the Unionists as humble and pathetic and the secessionists as critical and proud. The October 10, 1863, issue of *Leslie's* included a sketch and report of Vicksburg women "full of hate to those from whom they asked favors," and Richmond residents who sought free food and transportation tickets after the city's fall were similarly depicted. Yet such women were usually trying to disguise humiliation with arrogance, although most still held anti-Union sympathies. As Judith McGuire waited impatiently for the Federals to issue free train tickets, she praised the Confederate leaders and prayed for the government's resurrection.[9]

While food was the persistent primary concern of the poor everywhere, clothing was also a problem. Women working outside the home often had difficulty dressing appropriately on a limited income, and, as previously noted in the case of the government girls in Washington, this was not always taken into account by critics. Although some women may have dressed inappropriately for the lewd reasons suggested, many wore formal attire only because their street apparel had fallen apart. Mrs. John Kasson understood this and attributed the dearth of customers in the well-stocked Washington shops to "the salaried people . . . who are so cramped in meeting their expenses that unnecessary purchases are not even thought of." Confederate workers were even more poorly clad, some not having clothing enough to keep warm. When a Treasury Department employee fainted at her desk during an exceptionally cold winter she was found to be without shoes, her feet being wrapped in lint. Judith McGuire, who could scarcely be said to have had an abundant wardrobe, worried about her thinly clad co-workers in the War Department and pitied those in mourning who were too poor to buy black clothing. Inability to afford the customary "widow's weeds" was always a source of concern. Diarists often mentioned the exorbitant cost of mourning apparel, but few could pay the prices charged Mrs. Stonewall Jackson, whose *"perfectly plain*

[9] Agnes Salm-Salm: *Ten Years of My Life* (London, 1875), I, 115; Judith McGuire: *Diary of a Refugee* (New York, 1867), pp. 351–58.

crepe bonnet" cost seventy-five dollars and simple "bombazine dress" $180.[1] When Jackson died in May 1863, prices were not nearly as high as they would be later, and long before the last blood was spilled most Confederate women did not even entertain the thought of purchasing mourning.

Women might manage to be decently clad by wearing their old clothes, and while preferring new ones they were seldom embarrassed for others were also having to wear renovated, mended, outmoded garments. It was, however, more difficult to keep growing youngsters clothed, the biggest problem being to keep them shod. Shoes were among the most costly items everywhere and among the scarcest in the Confederacy. Children could go barefoot in warm weather but shoes were essential in winter even in the Deep South because of the fuel shortage and lack of adequate floor coverings in many homes. Rugs and carpets were often contributed to soldiers for use as blankets. In many areas shoes could not be bought at any price and mothers became amateur cobblers, some learning to tan leather and others making shoes from almost any available material including cloth and wood. If there happened to be a shoemaker in the area, women went out of their way to cultivate him. The one cobbler in Lexington, Virginia, infuriated one woman by demanding a load of wood for each pair of children's shoes, but he made five pairs for Mrs. McDonald's youngsters and insisted that she not pay him until after the war. This was surprising since she was a Confederate sympathizer and he a Unionist.[2]

With the exception of those in remote areas, Northerners with money or some other medium of exchange could obtain what they needed, but this was not generally so in the blockaded Confederacy. Many Southern women had to expend time and energy devising ways to clothe their families. Many also found themselves carding, spinning, weaving, dyeing, sewing, and renovating old clothes in addition to their other duties. Spinning wheels and looms were brought down from attics, the states provided the poor with cotton cards, and irreplaceable pins and

[1] Kasson: "An Iowa Woman in Washington, D.C.," p. 85; McGuire: *Diary*, p. 251; Allan: *The Life and Letters of Margaret Junkin Preston*, p. 161.

[2] Allan: *The Life and Letters of Margaret Junkin Preston*, p. 177; McDonald: *A Diary*, p. 236.

needles were carefully guarded. To clothe one's family in the blockaded Confederacy called for patience and ingenuity, traits which thousands of women developed as they converted draperies, rugs, bedding, and other items into apparel. When the woman's efforts met with success and brought compliments from others, she experienced a kind of satisfaction that only hard work and attainment can bring; but if she failed, her spirits sank, for the busy mother had neither time nor materials to waste.

Women who assumed command of the household were responsible for maintaining the home. They had to attend to taxes, mortgage payments, and possibly rents and upkeep, and (if it became necessary to move) to find new accommodations. This was a major problem for persons displaced by the war and those seeking cheaper housing in any overcrowded area. Southerners from comfortable homes were often compelled to live in places unfit for human habitation and at best ill-equipped for housekeeping; thousands in the war-torn Confederacy moved into outbuildings, caves, tents, abandoned buildings, or camped out in forests and fields. Performing domestic duties under these primitive conditions was trying, yet some seemed to prefer it to moving in with incompatible relatives. It was common both North and South for soldiers' families to live with relatives or friends; this was usually the man's idea, for most women accustomed to their own homes did not like living in another's. Grandparents had a way of counteracting the mother's discipline, mothers-in-law were often irritating, and too many families under one roof prevented privacy and fomented friction. The letters of women living in others' homes indicate that they were seldom happy, and many were so unhappy that they defied their husbands and moved into quarters which were sometimes less spacious but afforded greater privacy. Yet in time of grief even feuding relatives were likely to be drawn together.

During the war Southern women had much in common with their sisters on the frontier. Pioneer women were used to the economy of scarcity which so many Confederate women had to cope with for the first time, and wagon trains moving westward encountered difficulties like those the caravans of war refugees met when they were moving out of the enemy's path. Frontier mothers fleeing the Indians with their children in tow resembled

Confederate mothers in flight from the foe; and just as Western women knew how necessity often scorned propriety, Southern ladies "of the old school" traveled without escort on public conveyances or in their own vehicles if necessary. Just as pioneer women were required to defend their children and property, so a great many Southerners faced this same challenge, and both groups responded to the challenge by thinking first of their children's safety. It was, however, extremely difficult for protected Southern women raised in luxury to adjust overnight to frontier conditions. A crucial difference was that while Westerners struggled to build a new life, Southerners watched a way of life destroyed.

The absence of men and the reduction or withdrawal of military garrisons were in part responsible for Indian uprisings on the frontier, and this ever-present danger accounts for much of the opposition to conscription in the area. Yet many women were left alone to care for family and homestead, and if an attack threatened they had to decide the course of action. Many reacted like the Wisconsin woman who fled through the woods to the home of friends, dragging her "half-naked" children. Finding the family gone and not knowing what else to do, they hid for a time in the woods. When they returned their cabin was in ashes and all their provisions stolen or destroyed. During this three-day nightmare they had walked thirty-six miles and eaten nothing, and the youngsters were crying from hunger and fatigue. As the mother surveyed the devastation with the children clinging to her skirts, a neighbor brought word that her husband had been killed. It seemed as if she could not go on, but like other women in similar circumstances she realized that she had no choice.[3]

The havoc wrought by the 1862 Sioux uprisings in Minnesota was similar to that created by the invasion of the Confederacy. An historian noted that "practically all of the inhabitants of 23 counties abandoned their homes and took to the roads . . . [and] a region more than 200 miles long and . . . fifty miles wide was devasted and depopulated." This description might have applied to the area over which Sherman passed in his March to the Sea. Official reports include countless references to "deserted villages" in the South, while for more than a year after the Sioux

[3] Frank Moore: *Women of the War* (Hartford, 1867), pp. 65–74.

wars none of the residents had returned to nineteen Minnesota counties and only 50 per cent had gone back to the other four. A woman caught in the uprising reported the roads so congested with refugees, "their household goods and . . . stock" that they were "blocked for miles." These words also described the refugee-clogged roads of the Confederacy when Southern sympathizers and Unionists, Negroes and whites, rich and poor, young and old sought safety in flight. Most refugees in the South were women and children, and their privations, struggle for survival, homesickness, despondency, and desperation contributed immeasurably to the economic and social instability of the Confederacy and to the breakdown of home-front morale.[4]

Women who took over the management and cultivation of plantations and farms often complained, and thousands were saddled with this extra burden. Mary Livermore was surprised to see the "great number . . . engaged in . . . planting, cultivating and harvesting" in the Midwest, and most performed these chores in addition to their usual duties. The work was hard and the days long, but some unquestionably derived satisfaction from it. A New Yorker left with the family farm was praised repeatedly by friends for her successful management; they believed she had actually increased its value during her husband's absence. When a Wisconsin woman with four small children found that she could not support them in Madison without accepting charity, she claimed a homestead in Columbia County, cleared a part of the land, and raised the family's food. When her husband returned from service she proudly presented him with the holding complete with cabin.[5]

Mrs. Mary Austin Wallace of Michigan shouldered unusually heavy responsibilities when at the age of twenty-four she sent her husband into the service and took charge of their 160-acre farm. Her diary abounds with the expression "choring around," a phrase which included supervising the completion of a new home, caring for two small children, attending to innumer-

[4] William Watts Folwell: *A History of Minnesota* (St. Paul, 1924), II, 124; Mary Jane Hill Anderson: *Autobiography of Mary Jane Hill Anderson* (Minneapolis, 1934), pp. 27–28; Mary Elizabeth Massey: *Refugee Life in the Confederacy* (Baton Rouge, 1964), *passim*.

[5] Mary Ashton Livermore: *My Story of the War* (Hartford, 1889), pp. 145–49; Hurn: *Wisconsin Women in the War* (Madison, 1911), p. 83.

able business matters, chopping and hauling wood, harvesting a variety of crops, repairing the property, caring for livestock, spinning, weaving, sewing, soap-making, washing, ironing, baking, and nursing. If depressed by the hard work, Mrs. Wallace gave no indication of it in her diary, but perhaps she was too busy to feel sorry for herself, and because her efforts were successful she had less reason than some to be bitter.[6] It was seldom hard work alone which broke a woman's spirit but rather working long hours under serious handicaps and having little to show for it.

Food shortages in the Confederacy inspired many journalists to try to put a hoe in every woman's hand, and while failing to accomplish all they hoped for, they did make gardening fashionable among ladies of leisure. However, most were content with windowboxes of radishes and chives or a few tomato plants in the back yard, although others cultivated vegetable gardens big enough to help feed their families. Some women rented a plot for this purpose and many refugees sought homes with sufficient land for a garden, but there was a sharp distinction between these amateurs and women who managed plantations and farms and tilled the fields. Under the most favorable circumstances this assignment would have been difficult, but the task was complicated by invasion, property destruction, labor problems, and innumerable wartime policies such as impressment, tax-in-kind, and cotton acreage restrictions. Poor farm women, aided only by their children in cultivating a patch of ground, rarely produced more than the family needed, and when government agents impressed the products of their labors their indignation knew no bounds. They had worked hard and had little to show for it, and they came to hate the government as they did the foe. Despite obviously little schooling or writing experience they deluged Confederate and state officials with letters of protest. Although these abounded in misspellings and colloquialisms, they nevertheless conveyed the writers' anger, disgust, and despondency. Food supplies, fodder, livestock, and wagons were impressed from planters and farmers, but proportionately heavier levies were made on the latter, and what the agents left was likely to be lost to the army or to pillagers. Few women could cope with this disheartening situation for long.

[6] Julia McCune (ed.): "Mary Austin Wallace: Her Diary," *Michigan Women in the Civil War* (Lansing, 1963), pp. 133–34.

Fredrika Bremer, who thought it strange that so few white women worked in Southern fields, would have been surprised to see the changes wrought by the war, for many women had to perform every task associated with cultivating a crop and there are scattered references to women pulling plows. If they struggled against overwhelming odds and seemed to be getting nowhere, they sometimes pleaded with the men to come home. In a typical letter a Virginian recited the family's problems and worsening condition, stressing their inadequate clothing, fuel, food, and bedding. "We have nothing in the house to eat but a little bit of meal," she wrote, warning her husband that if he did not come home long enough "to fix us up some . . . 'twant be no use to come, for we'll . . . be out there . . . in the old grave yard with your ma and pa." Governor Zebulon Vance was bombarded with letters from North Carolina farm women, one begging him "to fix preperashenes to send the poor solgers" to harvest the wheat; and another who had a "posel of little children" asked Vance to have "compashion on them." A mountain woman summarized the complaints of others when she blamed her woes on "specerlators," high prices, discrimination against the poor, and favoritism for the "slave oner"; and one proclaimed her hatred for all selfish people with "harts . . . turned to gizards."[7] Like the lecturers, authors, and rioters, these women were also voicing their opinions and protests.

Farm women were not always sure how to handle their new responsibilities, but many evidenced amazing ingenuity. The more enterprising reasoned that anything was worth a try. During the battles in the Chattanooga area Mrs. Nettie Williams's farm was stripped of livestock, implements, and all other essentials for making a crop. She wrote General William Whipple offering to let the Federal Army cultivate her land provided it furnished the livestock, labor, provisions, seed, tools, and men to guard the property. In return she would expect to retain all the produce needed by her family but would sell the remainder to the army at "a fair price." An angry and disbelieving general informed Mrs. Williams that the project was too much for him and furthermore would take the time of men "whose primary

[7] Jones: *Heroines of Dixie*, p. 348; Bell Irvin Wiley: *Plain People of the Confederacy* (Baton Rouge, 1943), pp. 44–48.

purpose is the prosecution of the war rather than the pursuit of agriculture."[8]

Although those in charge of plantations had certain advantages not shared by farm women, these were not always what they seemed, for the greater the property the heavier the responsibility. For example, most had slaves to perform manual labor and overseers or neighbors to advise them, but the situation could change without warning when slaves ran away, overseers went into the army or to other jobs, and neighbors died or were displaced. The more people on the plantation, the more food had to be grown and clothes provided. Slaves must be made to work and discipline maintained, and women could not afford to let it be known that they lacked self-confidence. Many, like the Carolinian who found herself "a planter for the first time," tried to leave the impression "of knowing more" than they really did. Mrs. Robert F. W. Allston was appalled at the idea of taking over the family's plantations and more than 600 slaves but proved to have such exceptional managerial ability that her daughter proudly proclaimed her "equal to her new position."[9]

Slaves were often more liability than asset during the war. When invasion appeared imminent the plantation mistress had to decide what to do with the Negroes, and some had to let them remain and fall into enemy hands, but when possible they arranged to remove them to places of greater safety. Yet as the war continued there were fewer safe areas, and after emancipation the arrival of Federal troops spelled the departure of some if not most of the Negroes. When the war came close to Mrs. Amanda Stone's Louisiana plantation, she sent 120 of her slaves with the overseer to Lamar County, Texas, hoping to get them out of reach of the Federals. A few weeks later she and the children fled, but very few remaining Negroes would accompany them; and after settling in Tyler, Texas, Mrs. Stone made several trips to Lamar County to check on the Negroes and once returned to

[8] William D. Whipple to Mrs. Nettie Williams, Feb. 8, 1864, Record Group 98, War Department Records, Department of the Cumberland, National Archives.

[9] Caroline Pettigrew to William Pettigrew, June 27, 1862, Pettigrew Family Papers, Southern Historical Collection, University of North Carolina; Elizabeth W. Allston Pringle: *Chronicles of Chicora Wood* (New York, 1922), p. 212.

Louisiana to look after her business affairs. Even in her displacement she had to attend to these responsibilities. As her daughter explained, one cause of the family's flight was the unruly Negroes left alone on neighboring plantations; but except in this situation or when hearing of a Negro's attack on a white woman, most women seldom evidenced undue alarm when left alone with slaves. Mrs. Chesnut said, "Nobody is afraid of their Negroes," and while this was not true in all cases, she had "never thought of being afraid" until her cousin Betsy Witherspoon was murdered by her slaves. Mrs. Chesnut then admitted that the ground had been "cut away" from under her and others in the area became "wild" with fear, her mother-in-law being so suspicious of long-trusted Negroes that she was convinced they were trying to poison her.[1]

Although the war increased Southerners' labor problems, plantation mistresses seldom complained about their household workers until the enemy appeared in the area, and even then the domestics usually gave less cause for concern than the field hands. They sometimes said they were harder to discipline or more impudent with no man around, but those serving the family had always been closer and more devoted to the whites, and this affectionate understanding was generally reciprocated by the owner. While there were exceptions, the domestics stood by their mistress during the war and often rendered valuable service. A Virginian who later moved to Kansas recalled that her cook made regular visits to the nearby Federal camp to beg or steal food for the family, and only in this way, she said, was "starvation averted." It was the women in border areas or within Federal lines who usually had the greatest problems with their domestics, and this a Maryland housewife blamed on whites who were trying "to make" the Negroes "their equals, nay their superiors." Early in the war a Kentuckian was so afraid that hers would start a "servile war" that she considered going to Canada or Europe; but after most of the trouble-makers ran away, she settled down in comparative calm with the faithful.[2]

[1] Chesnut: *A Diary*, pp. 139–40, 145–47, 151–53.
[2] Adele Elizabeth Richards Orpen: *Memories of Old Emigrant Days in Kansas* (Edinburgh, 1926), p. 23; Marie B. Handy to Robert J. Breckinridge, May 14, 1861, Breckinridge Family Papers.

Northern women often complained about both white and colored domestics, who were usually less docile than slaves and were in an excellent bargaining position during the war. Capable, efficient servants were in great demand and other jobs were now available for women with little if any formal schooling. The housewife had to handle her employees gently lest she find that they had left without notice. Women's letters were filled with complaints about inconsiderate, lazy, inefficient, dishonest, irresponsible servants who insisted on higher wages and unreasonable concessions and if not granted them did not hesitate to walk off the job. Ellen Wright Garrison lived for several years in the William Lloyd Garrison home before she and her husband moved into their own, and while there she had the responsibility for hiring and supervising the servants. Within three months she employed and lost as many colored maids, all of whom deserted in the family's hour of need; and while none was satisfactory, each was difficult to replace. The first was lazy; the second "deceitful, sweetspoken, detestable"; and the third looked like an escapee "from a lunatic asylum" and refused to perform many tasks handled by her predecessors. This "insane" creature walked out of the Garrison home on Thanksgiving morning and left Ellen with the responsibility for preparing the holiday dinner for relatives and guests. The elder Garrison was beginning to lose faith in colored domestics and when Ellen told him she had hired another mulatto he "shook his head dubiously," and well he might, for three months later she walked out when the house was again filled with guests. After that Ellen employed an Irish girl who apparently gave satisfaction and was contented with the job.[3]

In addition to all their domestic duties many women had to earn a living, and while some worked outside the home many could not do so because of family responsibilities and others would not because of pride. Nowhere was this last group found in greater numbers than in the Confederacy. There proud but impoverished ladies saved face by earning a pittance at home. Household industries sprang into being as women sewed, renovated old clothing, made hats, and when supplies were available

[3] Ellen Garrison to Martha Wright, Oct. 2, Nov. 15, 25, 1864, Apr. 2, May 1, June 29, 1865, Garrison Family Papers.

baked, made jams and jellies, and prepared other foods. They marketed a variety of products from homespun to recipes calling for expedients, but one of the most profitable enterprises was soap-making. A Virginia war widow with five small children was taught by Judith McGuire to make soap, and after working all day in a government office she made soap at night. This she sold to a Richmond merchant and by working at two jobs was able to support her family. But Northerners who may or may not have marketed their products were sometimes forced by necessity to perform these same tasks for the first time. A prominent young Philadelphia lady had to learn to make laundry soap after her supplier enlisted, and seeking her mother's assistance she eventually learned the process which she was surprised to find so complicated. After this, she told her mother, she would be careful to use only as much soap as was absolutely necessary.[4]

Woman's battle for survival was intensified by the worry, fear, doubt, suspicion, hatred, and stark tragedy common everywhere. All women lived and worked in this atmosphere, and no matter which uniform their men wore, they worried and grieved for them equally. The women not only feared for their loved ones' safety; they were also afraid that the men would pick up unacceptable habits and ideas. Stories of drinking, gambling, and immorality in camp spread like wildfire, and in their letters women begged for reassurance that the men were withstanding these temptations. Mothers, wives, and sweethearts sensed that military experiences would change them but hoped that the change would not be for the worse. Many also worried lest they abandon their religious training instilled in youth, and abolitionist mothers were afraid that when their sons came in contact with slaves they might not, as one said, "stand firm" and "hold fast to the principles" they had been taught.[5] But nothing could make those on the home front more apprehensive than not hearing from their men, and if a longer than usual period elapsed between letters the women naturally imagined the worst.

The war brought death to the doors of hundreds of thou-

---

[4] Marianna Mott to Martha Wright, Oct. 1, Nov. 1, 1863, Garrison Family Papers.
[5] Martha Wright to William C. Wright, Mar. 22, May 1, Sept. 26, 1862, Garrison Family Papers.

sands of women, and many it visited more than once. Mrs. Mary Bixby's loss of five sons was widely publicized at the time, but other mothers sacrificed as many or more. Mrs. Polly Ray of North Carolina had seven sons killed in action; Mrs. Nancy Rhodes of Maine and Mrs. Ora Palmer of North Carolina each lost four, all of Mrs. Palmer's being killed in the Battle of Gettysburg; and Mrs. Eliza Upchurch of Illinois had ten sons in the Union Army, three of whom were killed. Mrs. Enoch Hooper Cook of Alabama had her husband, sons, and other close kin fighting for the Confederacy; and many other women, including Katherine Polk Gale, had a father, husband, and brother in service. Mrs. Gale's father, General Leonidas Polk, was killed; her brother Hamilton was seriously wounded; and although her husband survived without injury she worried constantly about his safety. Yet a woman's grief cannot be measured in numbers alone, for the mother who lost her only son and the wife who gave her husband made the supreme sacrifice.

The war created countless other emotional problems. A Mrs. Garvin, identified only as "a poor, hard working woman" from Troy, New York, went to New York City and Washington in search of her mentally retarded son who she said had been "kidnapped by some substitute broker and sold into the service of the United States." The sympathetic Troy mayor, Eastern newspapers, and Washington officials assisted her search which lasted for several months. Many mothers resented and feared high-pressured recruiting tactics. Mrs. Pauline Christian of Alabama was frantic when in the last days of the war her fourteen-year-old-son disappeared while on a hunting trip. Since he carried a gun, the mother feared he may have been mistaken for a Confederate soldier and captured by the Federals or that the Confederates had pressed him into service. When she pleaded with a relative to help find the boy he had been gone a week; Mrs. Christian felt she had contributed her share when the five older boys enlisted, one of whom had been killed and another captured and imprisoned.[6]

Brides who exchanged their wedding gowns for "widow's weeds" were always objects of special pity. Four months after

[6] New York *Herald*, May 21, 1864; Mrs. Pauline Christian to Robert J. Breckinridge, May 23, 1865, Breckinridge Family Papers.

Laura Stratton Birney spent her honeymoon in the Army of the Potomac winter encampment she buried her groom, but there were many brides who could not accompany their husbands to the front and were never to see them again. Hetty Cary's transformation from bride to widow in three weeks stunned Richmond society, for she was generally acknowledged to be the most beautiful and popular of the local belles and her marriage to the handsome General John Pegram was one of the social highlights of the war. The same officials and their families who attended the wedding in December 1864 reassembled the following month in the same church to hear the same minister eulogize the young officer he had so recently married. General Lee wrote his wife that he was shocked to see the change which had come over Mrs. Pegram in these weeks, yet both she and Laura Birney accepted their losses philosophically. Mrs. Birney was consoled by the thought that she had been with her husband in his last hours and would soon bear his child, and Mrs. Pegram was later heard to say that she was thankful hers did not have to see the fall of Richmond and the Confederacy's defeat.[7]

Women often waited months before hearing of their husbands' death and some never received official confirmation. Those living near telegraph lines and railroads might make it a habit to meet the trains and scan the casualty lists posted outside the telegraph or newspaper offices, but others tucked away in isolated areas could only wait, pray, and hope. A South Carolinian recalled how "poor country women with babes in their arms" converged on the Spartanburg depot hours before a train was due to arrive so that they might hear the casualty lists read. The tense silence was broken only by the calling of names until a penetrating "shriek" informed the crowd that "some poor woman" had lost a loved one.[8] A woman's first impulse upon hearing that a man had been wounded was to rush to him, and as previously noted, thousands of mothers, wives, and sisters started out with insufficient funds and were stranded miles from home. When their man was killed, women wanted to visit the grave,

---

[7] Robert E. Lee to Mary Custis Lee, Jan. 8, 1865; Constance Cary to Burton Harrison, Apr. 6, 1865, Burton Harrison Papers; Laura Birney to Ellen Wright, July 10, 1864, Garrison Family Papers.

[8] *Report of Senate Committee on Labor and Capital* (1883), IV, 830.

sometimes to make sure he had a decent resting place but often hoping to bring the body home. Few women could make the trip during the war but their pilgrimages continued for many years after. This was always a heart-rending experience but never more so than when the remains could not be found or positively identified.

Women who were not with their family when tragic news was received had their grief compounded by loneliness, and they often wrote that it would have been easier to accept the loss had others been near. A Minnesotan in Nevada, on hearing of a relative's death, wrote her sister-in-law, "If I could only have had some friend here to talk to about him I think I could have borne it better."[9] And because of the wartime shift of population, many women were living among strangers when tragedy struck. But those who were near the scene of death might find the shock even worse. After the Battle of Prairie Grove, an Arkansan went on the field and discovered the bodies of her husband and two brothers. "So intense was her grief and rage," reported a Union soldier, that her shrieks could be heard a mile away. Too stunned at first to utter a sound, as soon as she realized the meaning of what she saw the woman let go with a barrage of curses against "them Goddamned Federals" who she wished "were in hell."[1]

Few women endured greater torment than the one viewed with suspicion by neighbors, for if she was thought to be out of sympathy with the majority or if she had men in the "wrong" army, her life could be hell on earth. She might be ostracized, threatened, intimidated, or expelled and her children taunted and their lives placed in jeopardy. As previously noted, Fannie Beers's childhood friends made her life so unpleasant that she left her mother's home, and Mrs. John A. Logan was hurt to see lifelong friends in southern Illinois change into vindictive enemies overnight. No woman was so vulnerable a target for suspicion as Mary Todd Lincoln, but her younger sister Elodie was in Alabama when the war started and was made miserable by the accusations and implications hurled at her by Selma society. Not even after she married a native son who was an officer in the

---

[9] Clarissa North to Ann Loomis North, Aug. 25, 1861, John Wesley North Papers.
[1] Robert F. Braden to his mother, Dec. 12, 1862, MS in private possession; copy in possession of Bell Irvin Wiley, Atlanta.

Confederate Army was she "accepted" by all, and several jealous local belles were indignant that she had captured one of their most eligible young men. Although many women were falsely accused of disloyalty, the known Unionists in the South and Copperheads in the North were subjected to treatment ranging from a cold rebuff to physical brutality and property destruction.

It was never pleasant to live in a divided community but it was heartbreaking to have one's own family torn apart by the war. Brothers enlisting in separate armies would be with those who shared their views, but the woman left behind had to live with the animosities. She understood as did no other the real tragedy of a civil war. When Mary Logan's brother joined the Confederates, his mother experienced that heavy, sinking sensation known to so many others, and his sister grieved for "the poor unfortunate boy" who had made himself an "exile from his home." Margaret Preston was sincerely devoted to her Southern kin and to the Confederacy, yet was hurt to hear Northerners maligned, and this, she said, was "continually . . . the case." As she thought of the mounting sectional hatreds and of her family in the North, Mrs. Preston wrote, "My heart sobs to itself." That was the kind of hurt women generally did not express except in their journals, nor could it be completely understood by those who did not experience it. How could Nellie Kinsey Gordon describe what she felt when she watched her husband retreat from Savannah with the Confederate Army and her brother march into the city a few hours later with the Federals? One can only imagine the reactions of a Northern teacher in Richmond who saw her brother being taken to a Confederate prison, but several onlookers told of the incident. A fellow teacher later exclaimed, "Oh! how many such sorrows were rending the hearts of tens of thousands, both North and South."[2]

The largest concentration of divided families was in the border areas, and nowhere was the situation more pathetic than in Kentucky. The Breckinridges were one of many families torn apart by the war, and the effect on their women is apparent in their letters. When William C. P. Breckinridge enlisted in the

[2] Mary Logan to John A. Logan, May 25, 1861, Aug. 15, 1862, Mrs. John A. Logan Papers; Allan: *The Life and Letters of Margaret Junkin Preston,* pp. 136–43; Catherine Cooper Hopley: *Life in the South From the Commencement of the War* (London, 1863), II, 58–60.

Confederate service his wife Issa moved to the home of her parents who were more understanding of her Southern views than her pro-Union father-in-law, the Rev. Robert J. Breckinridge. Whether or not he slighted her as she accused him of doing, her bitterness toward him became an obsession. The minister's daughter "Sophy" was torn between love for her father and her husband, Dr. Theophilus Steele, who joined the Confederates and was twice captured and imprisoned by the Federals. Both times Mrs. Steele pleaded with her father to intercede and get him released; the second time she was frantic because he had broken his parole and was sentenced to die. "I am in a state of anxiety and misery," she wrote her father, promising that if he would get her husband out of this scrape she would see to it that he never went to war again. A few days later she wrote, "It is almost too much to bare [sic]. All looks so dark before me, not even a small ray of light to direct my pathway." Her sister Sally and her minister-husband were staunch Unionists living among Confederate sympathizers; she and the children fled on several occasions and the family was constantly scorned and threatened by neighbors. The conditions under which she was compelled to live and the split in her own family were given as reasons for her untimely death.[3]

Mothers of young children had other problems besides keeping them clothed and fed. They worried about disrupting their children's education when they had to go to work or when schools closed and private teachers could not be employed. As previously mentioned, mothers who were themselves educated sometimes assumed the teaching responsibility, but for many reasons the arrangement was seldom satisfactory. Mothers also worried about the war's psychological effect on the young. One commented that it was "sorrowful" to watch them fight mock battles, play that they were killing and mutilating the enemy, taking prisoners, building fortifications, and performing amputations, or pretend that they had lost a leg as they hobbled about with a

[3] Issa Desha Breckinridge to Robert J. Breckinridge, March n.d., 1864; Issa Desha Breckinridge to William C. P. Breckinridge, Apr. 2, 1864; Robert J. Breckinridge to William C. P. Breckinridge, Sept. 1, 1864; Sophy Breckinridge to Robert J. Breckinridge, July 19, 1862, Aug. 23, 26, 20, 1863, Dec. 4, 1864; Robert J. Breckinridge to General Ewing, Dec. 9, 1863, Breckinridge Family Papers.

cane. "It is sad indeed," she said, "that they must learn such things in their very infancy."[4] If the family was displaced, mothers wondered what effect repeated uprootings and wanderings would have; and if for any reason they were separated from sons and daughters, worry often gave way to hysteria. It was also heart-rending for impoverished mothers everywhere not to be able to provide gifts on special occasions, especially Christmas. They could record, but only inadequately describe, what they felt upon hearing the children cry because they thought they had been forgotten.

The number and complexity of women's domestic responsibilities could have broken the spirit of the strong under the most placid conditions, but to carry them for an appreciable time under the emotional pressures created by a war was more than some could endure. It is remarkable that not more women broke under the strain, and it is understandable that so many became "sick-unto-death" of the conflict. While Southern and frontier women fought the battle for survival against overwhelming odds, those everywhere were vulnerable to the tragedy and heartbreak of war. Millions served not only by watching and waiting, they also worked, worried, and mourned.

[4] Allan: *The Life and Letters of Margaret Junkin Preston,* pp. 158–59.

11

A Necessity in Protracted Warfare

IN THE SPRING of 1862 Clara Barton urged her brother to
leave North Carolina and join her in Washington. She
assured him that in the North he would find none of the "pinch-
ings of war time" already being felt in the South, and except for
"a profusion of U.S. flags" and soldiers in uniform, there was little
indication in most areas that a war was being fought. While the
North's purpose was not subjugation of the South, she wrote, this
would become "a necessity . . . in protracted warfare" and the
people must expect to suffer as the Union forces swept over the
Confederacy, leaving death, destruction, and devastation in their
wake.[1] Miss Barton did not succeed in convincing her brother to
abandon his farm but she did predict the future course of the
war, for it was the Southern people who bore the brunt of the
conflict. Northerners experienced few military invasions and
most of these came in the form of raids and were of brief duration. Although the fear of attack should not be discounted as one
of the pressures women endured, the war had a more direct impact on Southern women.

In the early months of the conflict the North expected to be

[1] Clara Barton to Stephen Barton, Mar. 1, 1862, Clara Barton Papers,
Manuscript Division, Library of Congress.

invaded by the Confederates, often described by Northerners as reckless fanatics, while most Southerners believed their military defenses would hold and those living in the Deep South were convinced they would be perfectly safe. By the time the Confederates invaded Pennsylvania in the summer of '63, most Northerners had concluded that they had nothing more to fear than sporadic raids; but by this time Southern women were disillusioned. They were shocked to see their land being overrun, homes destroyed, cities captured and occupied, and themselves displaced, nor did the tide turn during the remainder of the war. They took refuge in wishful thinking when professing that the enemy would be stopped before reaching their doors, and when he continued to advance they became increasingly bitter and weary.

Much has been written about the reactions of Southern women to invasion, but on those rare occasions when Northerners experienced invasion their conduct was no different. In every community, North and South, were phlegmatic, dazed, and moderately disturbed persons, but most were excited and many hysterical. As some calmly went about their duties, others ran through the streets and contributed to the general panic. When the enemy appeared, some women hurled insults at him, others stood quietly at their gates, but most sought safety indoors and contented themselves with peeping from behind drawn blinds. If his arrival was preceded by a bombardment, civilians scurried to dark corners, basements, and attics; but whatever the circumstances, in all areas were foolhardy, haughty, rude, vindictive, frightened women as well as cautious, humble, compassionate, and courteous ones.

Rumors were invariably spread ahead of the invader, often by refugees who circulated tales of his barbarity and warned the citizenry to flee. This was a continuous state of affairs in the Confederacy, but during the weeks preceding the Battle of Gettysburg rumors caused panic over a widespread area in Maryland and Pennsylvania. Residents made preparations for flight in southern, eastern, and central Pennsylvania, all confident the "Graycoats" were en route to their community. Sallie Mercer, Charlotte Cushman's maid, was visiting in Philadelphia when the alarm sounded, and she wired her mistress, "The Rebels are expected here [.] What shall Sallie do?"[2] This was the usual question asked by women left alone—whether to flee or remain where they were. If the rumor proved false the refugees usually returned and settled into their customary routine; but with further rumors or the sudden appearance of the enemy, bedlam again broke loose.

Women might panic or flee, but usually they did not burn their homes to keep them out of enemy hands. Early in the war some leaders and journalists did encourage the firing of property at the invaders' advance; and when this was done in towns, the fire often spread to other houses and left many homeless. A Gettysburg woman reported that thirty-six families lost their homes in Emmitsburg because a man set the torch to his,[3] and in Hampton, Elizabeth City, and other Southern communities similar actions of men resulted in widespread destruction; but women generally deplored the burning of property. Even the most ordinarily impractical women were extremely possessive of their homes and belongings and thought that what could not be hidden, sent away, or taken along should be guarded to the limit or abandoned intact. They shuddered to see cotton bales fired, primarily because they feared a wind might fan the flames to engulf their homes, and many on the scene during a conflagration knew it did not always originate with the enemy, although it might later be attributed to him.

A resident reported that by the time the Confederate cavalry rode into Gettysburg, shouting their "horrid yells," her friends and neighbors "had all gone," but she had stayed behind to guard her home. Locking herself in the house, she watched from an upstairs window while soldiers looted the abandoned house across the street and carted away their plunder in "a large four-horse wagon." Another Gettysburg lady recalled that few people went to bed that night, and it seemed to her that they milled about the streets until dawn.[4] When Margaret Preston heard of

[2] Sallie Mercer to Charlotte Cushman, June 29, 1863, Charlotte Cushman Papers, Manuscript Division, Library of Congress.

[3] Anonymous—*The Diary of a Lady of Gettysburg, Pennsylvania from June 15 to July 15, 1863* (n.p., n.d.), pp. 6–15.

[4] Fannie J. Buehler: *Recollections of the Rebel Invasion and One Woman's Experience During the Battle of Gettysburg* (Gettysburg, 1900), pp. 6–21.

the Confederate invasion of Pennsylvania, she trusted the soldiers would "not be guilty of the outrages [which had] . . . characterized the Federal Army in Virginia," but she thought it "just as well" that Northern women should "have some short experience with what war is." Mrs. Preston doubted, however, that this episode would afford them more than a "taste" of its horrors. "The country would have to be overrun for two years," she said, "before the Pennsylvanians could know what the Virginians know of war."[5] She hit on the crux of the matter, for Northern women's contact with the enemy was brief, while Southerners were constantly threatened by the Federal Army and some were repeatedly or continuously under its jurisdiction. What Mrs. Preston could not predict was that Southern women would have nearly two years more of war and then reconstruction.

Like the Southerners, the Pennsylvanians were shaken by the inclusion of women among the casualties, including teen-aged Jennie Wade who was struck down while baking bread in her home on the edge of the Gettysburg battlefield. Most of her neighbors had fled, but Jennie and her mother stayed behind to care for an older sister and her newborn infant. Their home was under fire throughout the battle, and the day before Jennie was killed a shell had ripped through her sister's bedroom and cut off one of the bedposts. Jennie became the feminine martyr of Gettysburg, but her sister survived to be reunited with her husband and after the war moved to Tacoma, Washington, where she became active in the Woman's Relief Corps and other postwar patriotic groups.[6]

Raids terrorized Northern women just as they did Southern, and the mere mention of "Jeb" Stuart or Jubal Early sent chills down the spines of Maryland Unionists, while John Morgan's name struck terror in the hearts of those in the Ohio River area, and as far away as Iowa women armed themselves when hearing he might extend his activities to that state.[7] Nor did women living near the Canadian border feel secure, and after the Confederate raid on St. Albans, Vermont, in the fall of 1864, residents

[5] Elizabeth Preston Allan: *The Life and Letters of Margaret Junkin Preston* (Boston, 1903), p. 167.

[6] Annie Wittenmyer: *Under the Guns* (Boston, 1895), pp. 206–8.

[7] Harriet Conner Brown: *Grandmother Brown's Hundred Years, 1827–1927* (Boston, 1929), p. 148.

in distant communities were obsessed with the notion that they would be next. In Auburn, New York, the usually rational Martha Wright began to view every stranger with suspicion and to connect him with a diabolical Confederate plot. She followed the policy of "watchful care," advised her neighbors to keep a ready supply of "*dry powder*," urged them not to feed or receive anyone they did not know and to bolt their doors and windows as she did every night. For months she feared that at any time her "Southern brethren from over the border" would come wildly riding into town, and her letters written in these months indicate the extent of her alarm.[8] The Confederates were losing the war in the South by the fall of 1864, but Confederate agents in Canada were winning the war of nerves against Northern women.

When invasion first threatened or occurred in a state thousands fled from the endangered area and panic seized others miles from the scene. When New Bern on the North Carolina coast fell in early 1862, it not only sparked the flight of local residents but of others in the interior, and as far away as Raleigh the citizens made preparations to move to the mountains. It was "the sole topic of conversation" in the state capital, said one lady, but in this instance it was a false alarm and Raleigh was not occupied by Federal troops until April 1865.[9] When the Sea Islands and points along the South Carolina coast fell early in the war, Charlestonians and others in the low country fled inland; and while some stayed away for the duration of the war, many returned when Charleston was held by its defenders. In Mobile, Savannah, and countless other cities the women refugees were the most anxious to go home when the towns remained within Confederate lines. Once at home they tended to construe every order to evacuate as another false alarm; and unless menfolk forced them to leave, they stubbornly remained. Not only were they attached to their homes but they preferred the social life in the city.

Beginning in the winter of 1861–62, women were urged to leave Savannah, but most who did so returned. Joined by those

[8] Martha Wright to Ellen Wright Garrison, Oct. 30, 1864; Martha Wright to Patty Lord, Nov. 4, 1865, Garrison Family Papers.
[9] Mrs. George L'Engle to Edward L'Engle, Mar. 18, 1862, Edward L'Engle Papers, Southern Historical Collection, University of North Carolina.

displaced from other areas, they were there when Sherman's troops arrived in December 1864. Their general reaction was one of indignation that they had not been given sufficient warning to permit them to flee, but the truth was they had heard the cry of wolf until they had come to ignore it. Hundreds of women and children left Richmond when McClellan threatened the city in the spring of 1862 but returned and refused to budge when military authorities pleaded with them to do so. All unnecessary people made any city's defense more difficult, consumed scarce provisions, and contributed to a host of economic and social problems. When it became necessary to evacuate a community, civilians congested transportation lines and roads. The refusal of women to do as requested created problems for themselves and the military.

Vicksburg affords an extreme example of what could happen to women who refused to do as the authorities asked. The *Whig* on July 1, 1862, described the first predawn shelling of the city, the streets of which were soon filled with women "screaming . . . seeking a place of safety . . . and crying 'where will I go?'" Mothers carrying babies pulled along the older ones, some fainted, and mass hysteria prevailed. Many did later leave Vicksburg, but many remained only to find themselves caught in the seige and compelled to live in public buildings and caves. They endured terrible hardships, including shortages of food which made it necessary for some to eat rats and mules. All lived in constant danger; a Federal officer later estimated that at least twenty women were killed and many more wounded, but recent students do not cite so high a figure.[1] Few women endured greater hardships than those in Vicksburg, and when the city fell they had the choice of flight or submission to enemy control.

Refugee life was not always the answer to civilian problems, however, and this fact slowly dawned on women as they observed or experienced the suffering of displaced people. Rarely did they move only once. Rather they became nomads whose abandoned property was likely to be confiscated, pillaged, or destroyed, whose living conditions worsened, and whose contact with family and friends was broken. Just when many had decided

---

[1] Philadelphia *Inquirer*, Aug. 10, 1863; see also Peter Walker: *Vicksburg, a People at War, 1861–1865* (Chapel Hill, 1960), *passim*.

to stay where they were, regardless of the consequences, General Sherman ordered the mass evacuation of Atlanta, and those remaining in the city learned what thousands already knew: there is no certainty in war. With few exceptions the noncombatants were hustled out of Atlanta, including some aged, infirm women and some in the throes of childbirth. They were dumped in Macon where they lived crowded together in boxcars, tents, or camps in the open country, for the city was unable to accommodate them; and since most had no friends or relatives to render assistance, they became objects of charity. Winter was soon upon them and their suffering was acute. Many who straggled back to Atlanta after Sherman's departure in November found their homes in ashes and had to live in gutted buildings, caves, or tents.

Sherman's Atlanta policy frightened those who lived in his path through Georgia and the Carolinas, for they presumed he would exile them; and while many fled, most had nowhere to go. There were approximately 25,000 people in Savannah when he arrived. Most were women and children to whom he offered transportation to Confederate lines, but he did not order them away. This apparent inconsistency further confused the residents of Columbia, Charleston, and other Carolina communities who could not be sure he had permanently abandoned his Atlanta policy. Great was the confusion when the Columbians learned the Federals were heading in their direction, and nowhere was panic more chaotic. Trains pulled from the depot with human cargo jammed inside and hanging on the top, yet thousands unable to get a place were left behind. Roads were congested with families hauling as much portable property as they could manage, and people drove their cattle toward safer pastures. As fires broke out in the city, additional thousands were rendered homeless and women moved their families to the outskirts, where some remained for days before returning. This was the experience that hundreds of thousands of women endured during "their" war, and they would never forget it.

At some time during the four years most Southern women had contact with the enemy. Although some were treated with respect, many had reason for bitterness when cherished possessions were stolen or maliciously destroyed before their very eyes.

Thousands of women had experiences similar to that of Mrs. John Letcher, wife of the retired governor of Virginia, who complied with orders to house and feed Federal officers during General David Hunter's raid on Lexington. On the morning they were to leave, the men applied the torch to draperies and furniture and the house was soon in flames, Mrs. Letcher barely having time to remove her children. Margaret Preston tried to prevent the looting of her home by reminding soldiers that she was of Northern birth and had a brother in the Federal Army, but the pillage continued. Women were sometimes able to save their property by furnishing proof of Northern birth or Unionist sentiments, however; and when a New Yorker who had married a South Carolinian submitted letters received from her father and brothers in Federal service, her property was untouched.[2] Those with Confederate sympathies were sometimes given guards if it was known that they had influential Unionist relatives, and it was because her late father had opposed secession and one of her brothers was an avowed Unionist and judge in New Orleans that Sarah Morgan and her family were given sentries after the Federals captured Baton Rouge. When they fled from their home during a Confederate attack, the house and its contents were damaged, prize possessions stolen or destroyed, portraits slashed, clothing ripped to shreds, and as Sarah said, their valuable library "borrowed permanently." These depredations were attributed to Union soldiers and Negroes, and after viewing the scene Sarah left, never to return.[3]

Looting and destruction were especially apt to occur when property was abandoned; and if the enemy did not wreak havoc, the Confederates, Negroes, or neighbors usually did. Women often had to stand by helplessly and watch their possessions carted away or smashed even though they had been assured their property would be respected. The Mother Superior of the Ursuline Convent in Columbia had been assured by Sherman that no harm would come to the building or its occupants, but fire spread to the convent and its residents fled. When Sherman heard of their displacement, he commandeered the Preston mansion for

---

[2] New York *Herald*, Mar. 19, 1865.
[3] Sarah Morgan Dawson: *A Confederate Girl's Diary*, ed. James I. Robertson, Jr. (Bloomington, 1960), pp. 190–202.

the Mother Superior, since she had once taught his daughter; and while she later returned the property to its rightful owners, the elegant home served as temporary lodging for the nuns and their charges. Barhamville Academy, a school for girls on the outskirts of Columbia, was saved because the headmistress placed the Masonic emblem on the doors. This sign was often credited with saving both property and lives during the war. Women who wrote at the time often expressed appreciation to enemy soldiers who had not permitted them or their property to be molested, but those not so fortunate were increasingly bitter in later years as they recalled the events against the backdrop of defeat and impoverishment.

While hundreds of thousands of Southern women had a brush with Federal soldiers, tens of thousands endured prolonged contact with them. There were all kinds of men in the service, some vindictive, rude, and vulgar, others sympathetic and understanding. But there were also all kinds of women in the Confederacy, including the haughty, cruel, deceitful, and impolite as well as those who were every inch the lady even when confronted with the enemy. The depth of a woman's affection for the Confederacy could not be measured by her vituperation, although many did not seem aware of this. While most Southern women disliked the Northern soldiery collectively, many respected and some came to love a specific individual. The attitude of one party often determined the behavior of the other, and those who were brazenly rude in defiance often discovered that other Southern women were among their sternest critics. One ardent young Confederate condemned the women who shouted invectives and spat upon the soldiers. "I hate you," she confided to her diary and asked, "Do I consider the female who could spit in a gentleman's face, merely because he wore United States buttons, as a fit associate for me?" She concluded that they were uncouth because they wanted "to attract his attention."[4]

No military mandate pertaining to women aroused as much indignation on both shores of the Atlantic as General Butler's "Woman Order" directed to any New Orleans "female [who] shall show contempt for any officers or soldiers of the United States." Such a person was to "be regarded and held liable to be

4 Dawson: *Diary*, pp. 78–79.

treated as a woman of the town plying her vocation." While it is not clear what kind of reception the conqueror expected, it is apparent that he did not receive it. This largest Confederate city fell unexpectedly, and according to General Lovell it was surrendered because he did not wish to jeopardize the safety of the women and children; therefore, when the Federals took over they found thousands of hotheaded secessionists whose favorite pastime was insulting the enemy. They flounced off public conveyances and out of public rooms when a Federal entered, drew their skirts aside so as not to brush against him, tilted their noses in the air, sneered and uttered insulting asides as he approached, and used countless other feminine means to show their derision. Equally irritating to many men bent on making friends were the women who simply ignored their presence. Julia LeGrand, a witness, drew a distinction between the "upper classes" who treated the Federals "with greatest haughtiness" and the "lower classes" who were "rude." Sarah Morgan tried to rationalize the "unladylike" aloofness of many as being due to "the odor" of the soldiers, which she had heard was "unbearable." But whether or not other Southern women opposed these tactics, they condemned Butler's order as barbaric and insulting. Mrs. Chesnut was furious when she heard that he was "turning over the women of New Orleans to his soldiers!" Instead of trying to restrain "the brutal soldiery," she said, "this hideous cross-eyed beast orders his men to treat the ladies . . . as women of the town; to punish them . . . for their insolence."[5]

Northern women seemed generally unconcerned about the order, but many abolitionists, including Anna Dickinson, did not permit the proclamation to dim their regard for its author. Butler became a kind of martyr to many Northerners after his removal. The Northern press usually construed the order to mean that contemptuous women would be imprisoned, not treated as prostitutes. One journal condemned Butler's transfer from New Orleans on the grounds that "the morals and manners of no class of women in the world were ever so rapidly improved as have been

[5] Kate Mason Rowland and Mrs. Morris Croxall (eds.): *The Journal of Julia LeGrand* (Richmond, 1911), p. 44; Dawson: *Diary*, p. 37; Mary Boykin Chesnut: *A Diary From Dixie*, ed. Ben Ames Williams (Boston, 1950), p. 224.

those of the Secession women of New Orleans under the stern but *admirable regime* of General Butler."[6] A few Southern newspapers agreed that if the women were conducting themselves as alleged they should be punished, but the overwhelming majority were incensed. The order created conversation throughout the Confederacy, although many mothers tried to keep it from the ears of their young daughters. Men who had boasted about sheltered Southern womanhood discovered the women and girls to be less naïve than they had supposed.

Union soldiers were intrigued by Southern women and for a variety of reasons wanted to make friends with them. They often mentioned them in their letters, the more sensuous and vulgar comments being reserved for other men. A husband had to be careful what he said about the "secesh" ladies when writing to his wife, for feminine jealousies and suspicions were natural during a long separation. An officer commented at length about the "strutting . . . very handsome and . . . *sweet*" Savannah women and then decided it might be wise to assure his wife she had no reason to be jealous. "I am not in love with any of them," he said, "so you need not be alarmed."[7] Reassurances did not always erase a woman's doubts, however, for the press frequently reported that soldiers were wooing and wedding Southern girls. The New York *Herald* asked if there was "no way to prevent . . . officers in our army from walking arm in arm with open-mouthed secession women," and later the paper told of men in the Army of the Potomac who were "being grabbed up in consequence of having yielded to the fascination of Southern female eyes." Late in the war another journal reported that "several female rebels" in Missouri had avoided expulsion into Confederate lines by "marrying Union soldiers," and hundreds of similar stories were read by anxious wives and sweethearts back home.[8]

A Northern nurse, commenting on the number of soldiers who married Southern girls, accurately stated that many were "*sham* marriages" but erred in saying that the brides were always from "the poor white trash" and were "miserable, vile, filthy, cringing wretches."[9] A Nashville girl wrote her brother in the

[6] *Frank Leslie's Illustrated Newspaper*, Dec. 13, 1862.
[7] John A. Logan to Mary Logan, June 8, 1865, Mrs. John A. Logan Papers.
[8] New York *Herald*, Sept. 22, 1861, Aug. 19, 1863; *Frank Leslie's Illustrated Newspaper*, Apr. 1, 1865.

Confederate Army that the local belles were "dropping off into the arms of the ruthless invader." Among them was a girl who at first had worn "a large Beauregard pin" and sung " 'Maryland, My Maryland' with so much pathos." Another had once slept "with the Bonnie Blue Flag under her pillow and looked pistols and daggers at the invaders"; while a third, who had carried a stiletto and threatened to emulate Charlotte Corday should the enemy ever reach Nashville, had "gone the way of all flesh and married an officer with that detestable eagle on his shoulder." She was sorry to report that her brother's old sweetheart was now singing "Rally Round the Flag Boys" and "The Union Forever" with Federal officers who called on her every evening. She warned him that when the Confederates came home they would find very few eligible girls, for "the watchword is marry who you can."[1]

No union of the "Blue and Gray" had greater repercussions than the marriage of Eleanor Swain, daughter of the president of the University of North Carolina, to General Richard Atkins of Illinois, who was garrisoned in Chapel Hill late in the war. North Carolinians were infuriated when the engagement was announced, and old friends in the village boycotted the wedding, although the women were more conspicuous by their absence than the men. Eleanor was to be forever after *persona non grata* in the state. The marriage has also been cited as the primary reason for David Swain's being forced out of the presidency and for the closing of the university when the indignant people refused to support it. Cornelia Phillips Spencer, a long-time friend of the Swains, said that "plenty of people" believed for the rest of their lives that "Ellie was married in finery which General Atkins had taken from North Carolina ladies" as he rode through the state with Kilpatrick's cavalry. Ten years after the marriage, Mrs. Spencer wrote Mrs. Swain that a former professor and his wife who had returned to Chapel Hill had *"not yet forgiven"* Eleanor for marrying "a Yankee."[2]

Southern women were known to attend hospitalized or im-

[9] Frank Moore: *Women of the War* (Hartford, 1867), p. 224.
[1] Marie ——— to her brother Tom ———, Jan. 29, 1865, quoted in the Washington *Chronicle*, Apr. 9, 1865.
[2] Cornelia Phillips Spencer to Mrs. David Swain, June 26, 1869, Aug. 23, 1875, Cornelia Phillips Spencer Papers. See also Hope Chamberlain: *Old Days in Chapel Hill* (Chapel Hill, 1926), pp. 94-100, 139-40, 169-70.

prisoned Federal soldiers, and some nursed them in their homes, although this was discouraged. There were secessionists, and especially those in Union lines, who cared for them as they would Confederates. Angelina Tyler, niece of the late ex-President, nursed a New York soldier whom she married at the end of his convalescence, and the event was noted in the newspapers, early reports stating that the bride was the daughter of John Tyler, an error hastily corrected by his widow. When General Butler heard of the betrothal he wrote Mrs. Tyler that she need no longer fear for the safety of her niece in Federal lines now that the young lady had "a U.S. soldier" as protector.[3]

Sanitary Commission workers reported marriages of Southern women not only to their patients but to prisoners of war. Anna Holstein remarked on those in Andersonville who brought their Southern brides North, and she was especially interested in two girls who had been cotton mill workers in Macon and had managed to slip food and cloth to the men while they were imprisoned. Many Southern women who had no intention of finding a husband in the group pitied them and did what they could to ease their suffering. Eliza Frances Andrews told of her own and her sister's compassion for the Andersonville prisoners who were removed during Sherman's Georgia maneuvers, and not until the Northern press and military authorities criticized the treatment of the men without noting what Southern women had tried to do did Miss Andrews become indignant. She then pointed out that after Sherman's troops had finished with the state the Georgians had difficulty feeding themselves and the Confederate soldiers, but this did not imply that they deliberately tried to starve the imprisoned Federals.[4]

Soldiers wanted the company of women, and Southern girls complained bitterly about the scarcity of escorts, so it was natural that the two should get together after a time. As a Confederate officer noted, "a soldier will make love wherever he goes, for the girls all expect it," and he found that when men were in enemy territory those who "made love to the girls got along

[3] New York *Herald*, Aug. 12, 18, 1864; Baltimore *Loyalist*, Aug. 13, 1864.
[4] Anna Morris Holstein: *Three Years in the Field Hospitals of the Army of the Potomac* (Philadelphia, 1867), p. 126; Eliza Frances Andrews: *The War-Time Journal of a Georgia Girl*, ed. Spencer Bidwell King, Jr. (Macon, 1960), pp. 59–60, 70–79, 131, 371–72.

well." A Federal soldier wrote that "a man of perseverance" could very easily kindle a secessionist's "love through her hate," and another thought that "treason, somehow, heightened their beauty . . . [for] disloyalty is always pardonable in a woman." Some Virginians refused to walk under the Federal flag or listen to Northern songs but could be seen any evening walking "arm in arm with dashing Lieutenants and Captains." It was true that they "elicited a great deal of gossip" and feuded "among themselves" to possess the men, often coming to "hate each other more than the common enemy." While this sort of bickering is apt to occur at any time, it was more pronounced during the war when there was a scarcity of men on the home front. Lacking beaux with Southern sympathies, many girls turned to the enemy, and as an older North Carolinian said, found that they were not "so opposed to the Union after all."[5]

Much of the trouble between Southern women and Northern soldiers stemmed from the ladies' failure to understand that the men enjoyed teasing the fiery secessionists. A New Orleans lady overheard one soldier say to another, "I wonder if these Southern girls can love as they hate? If they can it would be well worth one's trying to get one of them." Soldiers were sometimes justified in thinking, as did a Kentuckian, that women facing the enemy quite alone were "of easy virtue or they would not have been left by white men"; but only a new recruit early in the war would have assumed this to be true of many women for a veteran would have understood why proper women might have no protection. Soldiers often expressed the desire to meet "nice girls." One stationed in Florida wrote his father, "I am in the most abject want of sweetheart," and a short time later reported having met a "secessionist with large lustrous eyes" which had a "very serious effect upon the weak points of my disposition." He anticipated great times ahead "provided neither falls in love." Soldiers frequently complained that Southern girls talked too much, were spoiled, and had some habits of which they did not approve, that of chewing tobacco and smoking pipes being most often

[5] Harry Gilmer: *Four Years in the Saddle* (New York, 1866), pp. 119, 178; Junius Henri Browne: *Four Years in Secessia* (Hartford, 1865), p. 39; George Alfred Townsend: *Campaigns of a Non-Combatant* (New York, 1866), p. 227; Eliza Thompson to Ellen Thompson Hedrick, Oct. 8, 1865, Benjamin S. Hedrick Papers.

condemned. One stationed in North Carolina was attracted to a young widow who suffered from "slavery on the brain" and was obsessed with hatred of Hinton Rowan Helper, whom she wished "in hell." Since their differing views made it impossible to carry on a normal conversation, he got satisfaction out of "making her rave at any time."[6]

Confederate belles used their feminine charms to get what they wanted and many proved expert in the art of deception, but these tactics sometimes involved them in embarrassing situations. One young miss dated a Federal officer for many months so that she might get provisions, presents, and other favors which only the victor could bestow, and in order to keep the supplies coming she promised to marry him after the war. When she failed to keep the bargain he threatened to publish her love notes and let the world know of "her fond and devoted attachment" to him. Although so distraught at the prospect that she sought advice from a few intimates, the girl apparently received little assistance or comfort from this source.[7]

Some Confederate women presumed that their sex would make them immune to punishment. The vivacious, teen-aged Sue Ramsey was expelled from Knoxville for many reasons, including her refusal to accept "the attention of the U.S. officers" or to walk under the Union flag. She had been warned repeatedly to desist but assumed that nothing would be done to one of her tender years.[8] Other women were banished into Confederate lines if their conduct displeased Federal authorities, if they were in contact with the Confederates, or if they refused to take the oath of allegiance to the United States. Those known to be Confederate sympathizers or to have men in the Confederate service were often banished in retaliation for others' acts of violence against Unionists or destruction of Federal property, and the homes and

[6] Rowland and Croxall: *Journal of Julia LeGrand*, p. 86; Joseph C. Breckinridge to Robert J. Breckinridge, Dec. 21, 1862, Apr. 2, 19, June 14, 1863, Breckinridge Family Papers; John A. Hedrick to Mrs. Benjamin Hedrick, Sept. 17, Nov. 14, 22, 1864, Benjamin Hedrick Papers.

[7] Mrs. Willis Jones to Issa Desha Breckinridge, Dec. 1, 1865, Breckinridge Family Papers.

[8] James Gettys McGready Ramsey Autobiographical and Genealogical Notes; Sue Ramsey: "Women in the War," MS, James Gettys McGready Ramsey Papers, Southern Historical Collection, University of North Carolina.

other possessions of the Confederates were most likely to be commandeered for military use. But known Unionists within Confederate lines met with similar treatment from both the army and their neighbors. In order to protect their property many women felt justified in using any means at their command—tears, feminine charms, empty promises. When a Nashville woman suspected of Confederate sympathies was asked to give cause why she should not be banished from Federal territory, she cited her assistance to Unionists in the area and her friendship with several high-ranking military officials. Fearing this might not be sufficient proof, she invited the provost marshal and other officers to dine with her and was permitted to remain.[9]

Thousands of women voluntarily left occupied areas rather than submit to the enemy's will, but not all who remained within his lines were turncoats or professed loyalty to the Union. Although the oath of allegiance was required in some towns, this policy was not consistently enforced. While many were banished for refusing to take the oath, others swore allegiance with tongue in cheek or complete honesty, thereby being permitted to remain and hold their property. Those who remained sometimes proved friends in need to refugees by storing their prized possessions, paying their taxes, and preventing their property from being confiscated. Displaced people could never be sure of the fate of their homes and possessions, but those who knew they had a place to go after the war were thankful for small favors. James D. B. DeBow and his family were refugees from New Orleans and for most of the war lived in South Carolina. The journalist had lost his Louisiana property and would have been more deeply concerned about providing for his brood had his mother-in-law not saved her place in Tennessee. "Here will be an asylum after the war," he wrote, and while "the late battles were fought on her grounds and her house was under fire . . . the old lady remained true grit and never moved an inch. What stuff she is made of!"[1]

Women who wanted to stay at home despite the danger were not always permitted to do so. After all the men in her

[9] Mrs. Aaron V. Brown to John Gibson Parkhurst, Jan. 27, Mar. 25, 1865, John Gibson Parkhurst Papers, Manuscript Division, Duke University.

[1] James Dunwoody Brownson DeBow to Charles Gayarré, Feb. 3, 1865, Grace King Collection, Department of Archives and History, Louisiana State University.

family had fled, a Georgian stayed on the farm, determined to hold the property. She had "complete confidence in Gen. Johson [*sic*]," she later wrote, and not until the battle lines extended from her front door "clear across the farm" and she was caught in the crossfire did she "runn" from the house. Like many others who waited too long, she had only the clothing she wore, and unable to return home or find her menfolk, was in a pitiful condition. She had done all she could to hold her property, but when the "bullets and shells were flying all around," Confederate officials ordered her to go far beyond the battle area, and she was displaced for the duration of the war.[2]

Life in Federally occupied cities might not be pleasant for Southern sympathizers, but it usually promised greater security, since there was law enforcement and business flourished, thus affording more numerous employment opportunities. These cities were generally better supplied with necessities, and the indigent had a better chance of receiving assistance from charitable agencies, but to be eligible for that dispensed by the Federals one usually had to take the oath. Much was said at the time about women who hypocritically subscribed to the oath to get provisions and used various means to collect more than they were entitled to receive. Hundreds in New Orleans were accused of having "cursed" the United States in 1861, but a year later they were defrauding the same government by collecting sufficient stocks of food "to start a business"—at the same time teaching their children to hate the Federals. Many women saw nothing dishonest in this, reasoning that anything was fair in war. Not all who sought aid attempted to conceal their convictions, however, and a journalist was shocked to see twenty "secesh women" ride into a Virginia camp, ask for food, and in the same breath praise the Confederate cause. He concluded that after nearly "four years of . . . bitter experience, [their] sentiments had changed in only one way,—they were more embittered against the Union" then ever.[3]

While Confederate soldiers fought in the field, their wives fought starvation at home and those confronted with it had to be

    [2] Mrs. Martha Williams to —— Briant, Oct. 2, 1864, Hulda Briant Letters, Manuscript Division, Duke University.
    [3] Marion Southwood: *"Beauty and Booty," the Watchword of New Orleans* (New York, 1867), pp. 104–5; New York *Herald,* Nov. 13, 1864.

practical. If taking their families into Union lines would assure food, then mothers were inclined to make the move. While not all had this choice, those living near an occupied town were tempted to move in that direction, although this did not mean they were abandoning their cause. Most men regretted circumstances which made the move necessary but understood the family's plight better than one Louisiana officer who compelled his displaced wife and children to wander aimlessly over the state and endure severe hardships rather than permit them to go to New Orleans where friends could care for them. He went so far as to tell his wife that if she did go into Federal lines he would divorce her as soon as the war was over.[4]

Most Southern women who had endured wartime hardships were too bitter in defeat to look at their situation sensibly, but Jorantha Semmes was an exception. Although a New Yorker by birth, she supported the Confederate cause and her officer-husband throughout the conflict, having voluntarily left their comfortable Memphis home so that she and the children might be within Confederate lines. Like all refugees she encountered many difficulties, but by January 1865 she realized the South was doomed to defeat and the time had come to swallow one's pride. For more than two years neither she nor her husband had received word from their daughter Julia, a student in the Ursuline Convent in Columbia. Now that the Federals were headed in that direction, she sought her husband's permission to ask her friend, the Federal General John A. Dix, to inquire about the child. She looked on Dix as a father, having lived in his home and met Benedict Semmes there, and she hoped memories of happier days would cause her husband to grant her request; but he positively forbade her getting in touch with the "enemy." She wrote Semmes, "When you remember that Julia may before long be placed under Yankee rule, you will no doubt see the advisability of keeping friends on both sides," and she promised not to implicate him in any way, but he remained adamant.[5]

---

[4] Louis Amede Bringier to Stella Turead Bringier, Apr. 22, 1864; Joseph Lancaster Brent to Stella Turead Bringier, Apr. 29, 1864, Louis Amede Bringier Papers, Department of Archives and History, Louisiana State University.
[5] Jorantha Semmes to Benedict Joseph Semmes, Jan. 30, Dec. 10, 1865; Jorantha Semmes to John A. Dix, Aug. 2, 1865; Benedict Joseph Semmes Papers.

Conditions were so deplorable in the South and the suffering so great that by the last year of the war a great many women with relatives in the North wanted to go to them at the first opportunity and Unionists thought it in their best interests to follow the Federal armies out of the community. Their neighbors were often shocked and nearly always critical of the departing women, some of whom were only now revealed as Unionists or lukewarm Confederates. Mrs. Chesnut was indignant on hearing that "a born lady" had ridden out of Columbia with Federals, but she refused to give her name "for the very shame of it." She could have been referring to any one of several women, including Mrs. George Crafts, Northern-born and married to a prominent Charlestonian, who was reported to have departed with her three children "in one of Sherman's baggage wagons." The local gossips worked overtime on this topic, but friends who had tried to dissuade her reported that Mrs. Crafts had always said if the Federals came to Columbia she intended to take her children North where relatives could care for them.[6]

Also riding out of Columbia were Mrs. Amelia Sees Harned Burton Boozer Feaster and her daughter Marie Boozer, both known to have been Unionists. Mrs. Feaster had been estranged from her fourth husband since his enlistment in Confederate service, and as neither she nor her daughter were looked upon locally as conformists, their departure was no surprise. Mrs. Chesnut twice referred to the women, both before and after their departure, and in neither instance was she complimentary. Their arrival in the North was heralded by the press and Mrs. Feaster was generously compensated by Congress for her support of the Union, the money making it possible for mother and daughter to enjoy the gaiety in New York. The beautiful Marie has never been forgotten for her escapades, the like of which she could never have enjoyed in the devastated South; and while some of the stories told have been proved fabrications, those which have been authenticated indicate that her career was bizarre and colorful. Unproved is the story of her marriage to a released prisoner whom she was said to have deserted in Wilmington, and she did not, as one Columbian predicted, "marry the entire

⁶ Chesnut: *A Diary*, p. 506; Daniel Huger Smith *et al.: Mason Smith Family Letters* (Columbia, 1950), pp. 181, 183.

Yankee army"; but she did have at least two husbands, one a wealthy New Yorker, John S. Beecher, whom she divorced on grounds of infidelity. In 1876 she married Count de Pourtales-Gorgier, a French diplomat. The couple traveled in Europe, Central America, and Asia, and at the time of her death Marie was living in Italy. Fantastic stories have been told of her involvement with Tsar Alexander II, a Russian nobleman, and the Prime Minister of Japan, and she and her mother have been the subject of novels and countless legends.[7]

Some Southern women supported the Confederacy yet felt no deep-seated hatred for Federal soldiers until they met them, after which they were vindictive. As Sherman was fighting his way toward Atlanta, Gertrude Clanton Thomas confided to her diary, "I don't know why . . . but that man Sherman has interested me very much—perhaps it is . . . that all women admire successful courage and . . . [he] has proved himself to be a very brave man. Our enemy though he is, I can imagine that *his wife* loves him." Yet when he and his men swept past her door en route to Savannah, Mrs. Thomas resented his and other officers' behavior more than the damage to her property. She criticized both Sherman's and Kilpatrick's morals and wished "the women of the North no worse fate than will befall them" when their faithless men compelled them to "drink from the bitter cup of humiliation" after the war. She objected to Kilpatrick's "good looking mulatto" companion's being brought to a friend's house, not because of her race but because she was a concubine. And she wrote Sherman's wife a spiteful letter apparently never mailed. She told Mrs. Sherman that he had "found a woman to replace her," a colored woman referred to as "Sherman's wife,"

[7] Chesnut: *A Diary*, pp. 466, 502; [Julian S. Selby]: *A Checkered Life: Being a Brief History of the Countess Pourtales, Formerly Miss Marie Boozer of Columbia, S.C.* (Columbia, 1878), *passim*; [Yates Snowden]: *The Countess Pourtales* (Columbia, 1915), *passim*; Mrs. Thomas Taylor, *et al.: South Carolina Women in the Confederacy* (Columbia, 1903, 1907), I, 259; Francis Simkins and James Patton: *Women of the Confederacy* (Richmond, 1936), pp. 62–64, 271; Washington *Chronicle*, May 8, 1865; Augusta *Chronicle*, Aug. 18, 1927; James W. Patton: "Mary (Marie) Sarah Amelia Boozer Beecher, Countess de Pourtales Gorgier," unpublished paper in the author's possession. In 1959 Elizabeth Boatwright Coker published *La Belle*, a novel based on Marie Boozer's life; in 1958 Nell Graydon published *Another Jezebel* in which Mrs. Feaster is the central figure.

but assured Mrs. Sherman that most officers had taken a mulatto woman "as a 'companion de voyage'" and her husband was no worse than the others. She brought her long, vindictive epistle to a close by saying, "I pity you," which was the one thing no woman would want to hear under these conditions.[8]

While Mrs. Thomas and countless others had late and brief contact with the enemy, women in the border areas were never free from battles, raids, and all other dangers accompanying a protracted war of invasion. Both armies came and went and each found supporters in divided communities. A lady in Cynthiana, Kentucky, said that the situation was so tense that women in each camp were afraid to speak to each other, and because she was a Unionist she lived in fear of a Confederate attack. She wrote her father one day that she was positive the Confederates would never reach the town and twenty-four hours later was in the streets attending the wounded. The surrounding countryside was infested with guerrillas and pillagers, and she never knew a day when she was not afraid. Her husband decided that she could "no longer be subjected to this sort of anxiety" and considered taking the family elsewhere. Nor did the Confederate sympathizer Issa Breckinridge find it pleasant living under Federal rule. "Everytime I look at a Yankee, and our streets are full of them," she wrote, "I feel as though I am looking at a murderer," and she believed that the Federal occupation would "degrade" everyone before it came to an end. She resented references in the Lexington papers to Confederate women as "Rebel She Devils" and implications that "*not one* is virtuous," and not until she went to Canada did she know "a feeling of personal safety and freedom."[9]

Those who chanced to travel in both the North and South during the war could not help being impressed with the vast difference between the two sections. When Issa Breckinridge was en route to Canada she was surprised "to find how little the

[8] Ella Clanton Thomas Diary, MS.
[9] Sally Morrison to Robert J. Breckinridge, Nov. 23, 1861, July 17, 19, Nov. 8, Dec. 28, 1862; George Morrison to Robert J. Breckinridge, July 19, 1862, Oct. 30, 1864; Robert J. Breckinridge to —— Birnie, June 9, 1865; William C. P. Breckinridge to Robert Breckinridge, July 15, 1862; Issa Desha Breckinridge to William C. P. Breckinridge, July 15, Aug. 5, 1864, Breckinridge Family Papers.

people of the North feel this war" and envious to discover "everything so prosperous—everybody so happy." While Mary Livermore was in Memphis she answered a secessionist's charge that Northern women were not sacrificing as were Southerners by saying, "This war is not impoverishing us as it is you. Our women can afford to wear silk and jewelry, and yet provide everything needful for the soldiers." Confederate women had less contact with Northern women than with Federal soldiers, but when women from both sides confronted each other, harmony was difficult. As one woman from Wisconsin facetiously remarked, after she and other officers' wives had been involved in a spat with Confederate women, "We quieted them down . . . by making them believe it was unconstitutional for women to quarrel and fight."[1]

Although there is little basis for comparing Northern and Southern women's reactions to enemy soldiery, what is known of Northerners' behavior in an invasion indicates that they would have reacted much like the Southerners had the situation been reversed. And as Mrs. Livermore noted, had it been necessary they also would have made as great sacrifices. To appreciate the war's effect on Southern women it is necessary to understand contrasting conditions in the two sections both during and after the war, for the women of the South were compelled to drink the bitter dregs of defeat, devastation, impoverishment, and reconstruction. As Mrs. John A. Logan noted fifty years later, while 1865 ended the "agonies, anxieties, and labors" of Northern women, those in the South were "entitled to credit for a longer period of endurance through the unspeakable trials during the years of reconstruction."[2]

[1] Issa Desha Breckinridge to Mary C. Desha, July n.d., 1864, Breckinridge Family Papers; Mary Ashton Livermore: *My Story of the War* (Hartford, 1889), pp. 290–92; Ethel Alice Hurn: *Wisconsin Women in the War* (Madison, 1911), p. 105.

[2] Mrs. John A. Logan: *The Part Taken By Women in American History* (Wilmington, 1912), p. 308.

12

A Grand Convulsion in Society

BEWILDERED CONTEMPORARIES often referred to the innumerable changes in the women's world as a social revolution, but a Washington matron more aptly described the upheaval as "a grand convulsion in society."[1] The alterations in woman's position, attitude, behavior, and image were spasmodic and erratic, and while some proved permanent, many women at the time considered the temporary and trivial to be of far greater importance.

The activities of two groups of women were widely publicized during the war. There were the selfless ones whose energies were dedicated entirely to serving others, women who saw only the seriousness of the struggle and denied themselves even an occasional good time. At the other extreme were the selfish, extravagant, and sometimes immoral epicureans who seemed oblivious to the war except as it made their lives more exciting. Although these two groups were spotlighted, they represented only a small percentage of American women. The overwhelming majority fell somewhere between the extremes. In varying degrees they possessed human frailties and virtues, and while willing to

[1] Caroline Eliot Kasson: "An Iowa Woman in Washington, D.C., 1861–1865," *Iowa Journal of History*, LII (1954), 79.

make sacrifices they found no reason for altering their usual way of life more than necessary. They saw no harm in participating in lively social functions or indulging an occasional selfish impulse, for as long as they contributed some of their time to charitable work why shouldn't they get some joy out of life? Most women found it impossible to change their personalities overnight, and many could not bring themselves to defy customs and conventions.

The press had an important part in changing woman's image. A journalist lauded hard-working, self-sacrificing women and condemned others for any attitude which did not meet with his approval. He seldom distinguished between the immoral and the indiscreet, the social butterfly and the woman or girl who attended an occasional gala social function. Whether praising or reprimanding, newsmen tended to generalize, and as the war continued they became increasingly critical of women. They expressed their views in such a straightforward manner and in such bold language that no one could misconstrue their meaning. Because they no longer showed the slightest reluctance to discuss immorality, Mrs. Chesnut's "prudish female . . . who would rather die [than acknowledge] . . . the improper half of the world" could no longer feign ignorance of its existence.[2] And the widespread publicity given those involved in crimes and scandals served to weaken the pedestals on which ladies had been placed. Never had women been lectured by the press as they were during the Civil War.

Typical of hundreds of wartime editorials was one published in the Washington *Chronicle* on February 6, 1865, entitled "The Ladybird's Mission," a "ladybird" being characterized as lazy, self-centered, and "diametrically opposed to the strong-minded woman" whom ironically the same paper had severely criticized in the prewar years. The "ladybird" was a wealthy, frivolous, fashionable creature who thought only of the "pleasant excitement" afforded by the war, and this was a disgraceful attitude in an age when "every female" was expected to rise to "true womanhood." The editorial raised this question, "What is the mission of such women as these?" The Confederate press was no less

[2] Mary Boykin Chesnut: *A Diary From Dixie*, ed. Ben Ames Williams (Boston, 1950), p. 466.

vehement in denouncing Southern women—a departure indeed from antebellum practice. On April 16, 1864, the Mobile *News* implied that if the war was lost it would be because of the "trivial and light conduct . . . of our women who adorn their persons for seductive purposes . . . tempting our officers to a course alike disgraceful and unworthy of women whose husbands and brothers are in our armies." The writer further stated, "The demoralization of our women is . . . fearful" and suggested that the "frail sisters [and] fast women" be banished from the Confederacy. If the romanticists were not converted to realists during the war it was not the fault of the journalists.

Washington and Richmond, the social as well as political centers of the Union and the Confederacy, mirrored the worst and finest aspects of American society. The eyes of the people were specifically on those who moved in official circles. These set the example for wartime social activities and attitudes. The Washington leaders followed tradition and continued to entertain lavishly lest the government lose face, while those in Richmond determined that their society should shine just as brilliantly so as to gain prestige for the young government. Both groups were criticized for their extravagance but Richmond officialdom was more severely censured because the majority of Southerners were suffering so acutely. Both cities were endowed with gracious hostesses who set the social pace, but in neither capital was the First Lady the most popular. Although most of the social belles did some sort of war work, this did not make as interesting newspaper copy as their parties, gowns, and feuds, thus the general public had reason to assume they were uninterested in the conflict.

The Washington social scene changed drastically in 1861 when secession caused many of the most renowned hostesses to journey South, and the first Republican administration brought hundreds of new faces to town. Also arriving on the scene were wives of high-ranking military officials and the overdressed, ostentatious *nouveaux riches* who were often referred to as the "shoddy." The presence of the latter, said Mrs. John Kasson, brought "a wonderful turning up of noses" from the aristocrats, who had "nothing left but 'good old blood' to boast of," but unlike many in official circles she thought the "grand revolution" long overdue. "The world is wide enough for everybody," she said and therefore extended her blessings to "Mr. and Mrs. Shoddy, and all the little Shoddies." This was Mrs. Kasson's first experience with Washington society and like many others she found the prescribed social routine "an unmitigated bore" and the "butterfly life" out of place in wartime, but there was nothing to do but conform. This sensible, practical woman never ceased to be amazed by the city's gaiety, extravagance, and wickedness, yet nothing disgusted her more than the "strong-minded" women who came to town during the war. Encountering one in "Bloomer costume," apparently Dr. Mary Walker, and espying at the same moment a picture "of the five-legged calf," Mrs. Kasson was so offended by "two such uncouth phenomena" that she "could not do justice to either." She recorded the innumerable social changes which took place in the capital throughout the war; even during the last winter "every hour of every day" continued to be filled with activity, although so many were in mourning that a somber note was injected.[3]

Mary Todd Lincoln's emotional instability would have made it difficult for her to be a popular First Lady in any age, but her Kentucky background and divided family subjected her to suspicion in time of war. Born into a slaveholding family and having a brother, half-brothers, and brothers-in-law in the Confederate service, she was vulnerable to the charge of disloyalty; and because she came to Washington from the Illinois frontier, many presumed she was ill-prepared to carry out the duties of First Lady. Yet Mary Lincoln was a charming hostess. She was in a position to command the presence of leaders at her social affairs but was never more than the titular head of capital society. Her irrational outbursts, consuming jealousy, domineering tendencies, and susceptibility to flattery were favorite topics for her critics, who seldom paused to consider that she was in poor health, buried a son, lost relatives in the service, worried about her divided family, and was constantly concerned about her husband's heavy burden. Yet Mrs. Lincoln was her own worst enemy. Her love of beautiful clothes, jewels, and other luxuries sent her on buying sprees that became the talk of the nation and plunged the family deep into debt. No woman was in a better

[3] Kasson: "An Iowa Woman in Washington," pp. 61–90.

position to encourage economy and moderation in dress and entertainment and none did less; for not only did she set an example for extravagance, but to the disgust of many Washington women she often decreed formal attire for White House functions which could well have been informal.[4]

Several Washington ladies outshone Mrs. Lincoln, but none was more popular and ambitious than Kate Chase, a beautiful, talented, sparkling young lady with one purpose in mind—to see her father President. Mrs. Lincoln neither liked nor trusted Salmon P. Chase, and his vivacious daughter was a thorn in her flesh, for Kate managed to be the center of attention at every social function she attended, including those given by the First Lady. Kate lacked only the necessary funds for lavish entertaining and these she acquired by marrying the millionaire industrialist and former Governor of Rhode Island, Senator William Sprague. From that moment she was Washington's most brilliant hostess and basked in the spotlight Mary Lincoln so desperately coveted.

The extravagant dress of the capital's social leaders made the city a logical place to organize a dress reform movement, and in April 1864 a group of women under Ann Stephens united to discourage the importation of expensive fabrics and other luxuries. Mrs. Stephen A. Douglas and several other prominent women were among the sponsors but when Mary Lincoln was asked to sign the pledge she refused, ostensibly on the ground that the program would decrease Federal revenue at a time when it was most needed. Many Congressmen opposed the movement for the same reason, but by May the crusade had spread to New York and thereafter extended to other cities. "Strong-minded" women, including Susan Anthony, supported it.

The press generally opposed the idea or viewed it as impractical and unrealistic, but the Washington *Chronicle* supported it from the beginning. The New York *Herald* at first favored the movement but pointed out that it would have no effect on the "shoddy" who were for the first time wearing "diamonds . . . silks . . . fine velvets and magnificent hats." No one, said the editor, "is equal to the task of reforming the war millionaires," but he com-

[4] Ruth Painter Randall: *Mary Lincoln: Biography of a Marriage* (Boston, 1953), pp. 196-438.

plimented the ladies for "working a field quite as new to them as to the general public." Within a few weeks, however, the *Herald* labeled the movement as "humbug . . . an offspring of sham patriotism, [probably] . . . fostered by secessionists"; and by fall the paper called it a "farce" and commented on a few women's wearing cotton dresses which they adorned with jewels. *Harper's Weekly* was more enthusiastic, noting that Northern women had not "felt seriously enough the necessity of individual sacrifice, and . . . [this] would be a kind of test of national earnestness." *Leslie's* approved the idea but doubted that the movement would succeed.[5] Again woman's best-intentioned efforts were ridiculed by the same press that condemned their extravagance.

Richmond's high society was a strange medley of folk—the families of officials, most of whom were less than hospitably received by the city's old families, and proud but poor refugees from the invaded areas and border states, notably Maryland. The Richmond aristocrats had not wanted their city to be the capital for they realized it would bring a cross section of humanity to town and alter their way of life. As thousands of strangers from all walks of life poured in, the citizens and press became increasingly critical of officials, whom they blamed for all social and economic problems. The residents were especially indignant that officials appeared to be living so well and entertaining so lavishly while they had less than ever before, and they were resentful that recently arrived speculators and blockade runners were making fortunes at their expense. Richmond, like Washington, had its "shoddy" although fewer grew rich from the war. The Richmond *Examiner* was the most caustic of the papers in blaming all the city's woes on the "rag, tag and bobtail," which included officials, refugees (especially Marylanders), thieves, prostitutes, speculators, and Negroes—all of whom the editor would have his readers believe had arrived since the outbreak of war. The *Examiner* was brutal in its comments on women and when it once reprimanded them for planning five balls in a single week while flour was selling for $125 a barrel, Mrs. Chesnut noted that the writer "went for the merrymakers, the party-goers, the prompters and

---

[5] Washington *Chronicle*, Apr. 26, May 2, 3, 23, 1864; New York *Herald*, Apr. 26, May 16, 17, 23, 27, Sept. 3, 23, 1864; *Harper's Weekly*, May 21, 1864; *Frank Leslie's Illustrated Newspaper*, May 28, 1864.

attenders of festivities." She added, however, that no one paid the slightest attention to his rantings. Nor did they heed the *Whig* references to Richmond's "adulterated society" which entertained "as though peace and plenty blessed the land."[6]

Judith McGuire was more hurt than angry to see so much ugliness in Richmond, but she was indignant in referring to the speculators, "a peculiar class," she said, "of which I neither like to speak, think or write; they are objects of my implacable disgust . . . They are with us but not of us." She wondered how they would be able to live with their "ill-gotten gains" after the war, but a more realistic woman predicted they "would roll by in their splendid carriages and throw the dust of insolence in the faces of the old aristocrats."[7] Mrs. McGuire was also disturbed by the gaiety of officials and their friends whose elegant feasts should better be sent to Lee's regiments, and whose merrymaking went on unabated even as men were dying in the city's hospitals. Mrs. McGuire had every right to attend these social functions, for she was from an old respected Richmond family and now returned as a refugee, but to this lady the war was too heartbreaking to sanction revelry.

Mary Chesnut was more discerning than most in her social set, and she saw "the handwriting on the wall" long before the Confederacy collapsed. On New Year's Day, 1864, she wrote, "God help my country! I think we are like sailors who break into the spirits closet when they find out the ship must be sunk. There seems to be a resolute determination to enjoy the brief hours and never look beyond the day. I now have no hope." She was criticizing herself as well as others in Richmond society who became more extravagant in the last year of the war, but like many women Mrs. Chesnut followed her friends. When her husband decreed "no more feasting" in his home, she confessed that he was the "master of his own house," but the parties nevertheless continued. Her social life was typical of that of most women in official circles as she attended lavish functions and an occasional "starvation party" where no refreshments were served, and

[6] Richmond Examiner, Nov. 24, 1863, Jan. 9, May 3, 1864; Chesnut: A Diary, p. 354; Richmond Whig, Dec. 24, 1864.
[7] Judith Brockenbrough McGuire: *Diary of a Refugee* (New York, 1867), pp. 325–26, 328–29; Sallie Brock Putnam: *Richmond During the War* (New York, 1867), p. 193.

spent countless hours calling on and receiving friends while de-
voting relatively few to hospital or other war work. She enjoyed
Richmond for the same reason both single and married women
preferred it—there were more men than in other communities. In
the spring of 1864 she reported "generals galore" in town, fourteen having been spotted in a single congregation on Sunday
morning. Young unmarried women elsewhere in the Confederacy
were envious of the Richmond belles who had a choice of eligible
escorts while they sat out the war in a manless society. One wrote
her cousin in Richmond, "I wish you could be condemned for a
week to our . . . evening social gatherings,—small feminine tea
fights. We absolutely stagnate."[8]

Varina Davis had many of the problems familiar to Mary
Lincoln, including aristocratic critics who considered her unsuited for the position since she was "Western" and who chose
to ignore her years as a Washington hostess. She was accused
of being domineering, meddling in politics, and having a barbed
tongue, and like Mrs. Lincoln she lost a young son during the
war. But Varina Davis shocked many old Richmond families
when she opened her receptions to everyone and greeted all with
the same cordiality. Although once falsely accused of giving
secret information to a Federal spy, she was not charged with
disloyalty to the Confederacy, but in the nineties some unrecon-
structed Southern ladies questioned her loyalty to the Lost
Cause when she left the South to reside in New York. During
the war faultfinders noticed that she did not visit hospitals, but
this was because her husband preferred her to confine herself to
other war work, and she chose to assist the indigent families of
soldiers. She was not criticized for her extravagant dress but was
occasionally reprimanded for purchasing material and other
blockaded goods at inflated prices; and while never guilty of
ostentatious display, she was a possession-conscious woman. Endowed with greater emotional stability than Mrs. Lincoln, Varina
Davis was an enigma to many women, primarily because she was
an astute politician and an intelligent conversationalist. She
could forcefully argue a point and hold her ground with the best
of men.

[8] Chesnut: *A Diary,* pp. 335, 343, 392, 394; Hetty Cary to Constance
Cary, Nov. 7, 1861, Burton Harrison Papers.

Mrs. Davis seemed unconcerned that she had social rivals and adored two of her younger competitors, neither of whom had such political aspirations as those of Mrs. Lincoln's nemesis, Kate Chase Sprague. Hetty Cary was the reigning belle in Richmond, popular with both men and women; and her cousin Constance was a great favorite of the Davises, who encouraged her romance with Burton Harrison, private secretary to Davis. Marrying after the war, the couple remained Mrs. Davis's lifelong friends, and to Burton Harrison she often turned for advice.

As a Confederate matron noted, Southern women's love of pretty clothes may have been "scotched" but was "not killed" during the war. Those in Richmond were just as interested in the latest styles as Northern ladies, and any fashion magazine penetrating the land blockade was studied by scores of style-conscious women who hoped they might renovate their old garments according to the latest vogue. Their preoccupation with clothes sparked some of the sharpest journalistic reprimands, and even the staid *Southern Literary Messenger* accused women of bowing "to fashion's shrine" as the Confederacy was "writhing in the throes of mighty agony." They were primarily responsible, it stated, for supporting the speculators who would be bankrupt except for their patronage. Richmond papers repeatedly assailed women who crossed into enemy territory to purchase finery, the *Enquirer* going so far as to say that some sold "their honor to invest the proceeds in all the paraphenalia [sic] of women's wardrobes and vanity." When a Northern newsman read this he asked what terrible conditions in the Confederacy could make this "organ of Richmond leaders . . . turn upon its own women in this way."[9]

The seasonal style showings in New York attracted throngs of Northern ladies and buyers, and to their great delight secession enabled the spring shows to be scheduled a month later than usual, since light clothing was not needed as early in the North as in the South. Nor do reports indicate that Southern customers were missed, for Northern prosperity increased the sales to an all-

[9] Mrs. Virginia Clay-Clopton: *A Belle of the Fifties* (New York, 1905), p. 225; *Southern Literary Messenger*, XXXVIII (1864), 127, quoting the Mobile *Advertiser and Register*, n.d.; Richmond *Enquirer*, Sept. 26, 1864; New York *Herald*, Oct. 9, 1864.

time high. Styles increasingly reflected the military spirit in the use of brass buttons, gold braid, epaulets, and military jackets. The most popular jacket for a time was the Zouave. *Harper's Monthly Magazine* in February 1862 described it "as much in favor" and stressed as one of its advantages that it could be made from a variety of materials. The "Bloomerites" saw in the war an opportunity to campaign for their favorite costume by pointing out that it was practical for the active woman and insisting that it was economical and therefore patriotic. They convened in Rochester in 1863, at the moment Lee's army was heading toward Pennsylvania, and a New York paper suggested that their time could be better spent if they sent their men to Gettysburg "to defend the drygoods on hand." As usual the Bloomer costume was ridiculed, and while a few women adopted a modified version it was no more popular during the war than earlier. The most controversial style change of the war years was the low-cut evening gown which Mary Lincoln helped to popularize. Conservative ladies were shocked when young women wore them and disgusted when the middle-aged and elderly appeared, as a New York matron described them, "bare to their waist and dressed for show." One of her older friends dared to attend a ball in a gown which left "her poor neck and arms bare," and to make matters worse, with pink roses in her "faded hair" which should have been covered by "a nice matronly cap." Women conservative in all other matters often threw their inhibitions to the wind where fashion was concerned.[1]

The war had a pronounced effect on social activities, the shortage of men steadily growing more marked on both home fronts but especially in the small towns and rural areas where many women were compelled to endure the most monotonous years they would ever know. In cities there was a greater variety of entertainment, yet because "nice ladies" did not venture out at night without male protection, many were denied the privilege of attending evening affairs. The war did furnish ladies with a social outlet in the form of aid societies, fairs, and amateur theatricals, and late in the war "calico balls" were held in the North and "homespun balls" in the South to raise money for worth-while

[1] Harold Earl Hammond (ed.): *Diary of a Union Lady, 1861-1865* (New York, 1962), p. 331.

projects. A few women worked so hard for these projects that their health was impaired, and the deaths of Mrs. Dudley Field and Mrs. Caroline Kirkland were attributed to overexertion in planning the New York Metropolitan Fair. Most, however, derived social satisfaction from the work. Girls tended to look upon these events as a godsend; it gave them an opportunity to escape "anxious mama's observation" since they were usually permitted to participate in the preparations unchaperoned. A Washingtonian noted that fairs and bazaars gave young lovers an opportunity to meet clandestinely while ostensibly interested in patriotic service. How many romances flourished at these benefits will never be known, but young women like Kate Stone met their future husbands at them.[2]

A family or other small group could participate in such simple pastimes as euchre, backgammon, chess, checkers, charades, conundrums, fortune-telling, group singing, and impromptu dancing. Women often had to dance with each other, but many more did this than attended parties and balls. Of course they relied on conversation to fill many an empty hour; and while they continued to discuss the usual feminine topics, they also became more interested in political and current affairs as their interests now extended far beyond their homes and neighborhoods. A teen-ager summarized the favorite subjects of those in her age group when she wrote a friend who was soon to visit her, "we will have as nice a time as we can . . . talking over books, men and the war."[3]

Southern women who enjoyed reading complained bitterly about the lack of books and magazines, especially those Northern and foreign periodicals to which they had grown accustomed. Mrs. Chesnut admitted having thrown away her money in renewing subscriptions to *Blackwood's*, *Harper's*, and the *Atlantic* in January 1861, for "everything stopped with Fort Sumter" and she was denied the privilege of "looking out into the world." Kate Stone was irritated that "good" Southerners were not supposed to read "Yankee" writings, for she thought this prejudice unjustified

[2] Hammond: *Diary of a Union Lady*, p. 293; Kasson: "An Iowa Woman in Washington," p. 72; John Q. Anderson (ed.): *Brokenburn: The Journal of Kate Stone* (Baton Rouge, 1955), pp. 320–22, 328–32, 334, 336, 241–48.

[3] Lillie B. Chace to Anna Dickinson, May 22, 1865, Anna E. Dickinson Papers.

even in war. "Northern literature," she said, was to her "what 'the flesh pots of Egypt' were to the wandering Israelites," and her Confederate convictions did not keep her from reading anything that came into her hands. Occasionally a Northern book went begging in the Confederacy, however, and that was likely to be true of Harriet Beecher Stowe's works. A woman caught in the Vicksburg siege went into a bookstore and found one lone volume standing on the shelves, Mrs. Stowe's *Sunny Memories of Foreign Lands*. This the dealer offered to sell at a discount since her books did not have a market in the South. Despite the dearth of reading materials in the Confederacy, literary groups met to discuss books and encourage talent. Constance Cary organized a club in Richmond composed primarily of refugees and including both men and women who had an interest in writing. It was at these meetings that she and Burton Harrison became interested in each other, and after the first meeting he was her steady escort. They wrote and read poems to the group, but each also wrote confidential poetry to the other.[4]

The theater and lecture platform afforded entertainment for many people, the cities offering everything from opera, Shakespearean readings, intellectual discourses, and political harangues to burlesque, and many of the smaller towns being visited by traveling companies and individual performers. As in all other instances, however, the war determined where and when Southerners would enjoy this form of entertainment. New York, Richmond (after the fall of New Orleans), and San Francisco were the theatrical centers of their respective regions, and each offered a variety of programs. Eastern audiences proved as rowdy as Westerners had long been, and increasingly patronized raucous entertainment familiar on the West Coast. Many theater managers made a deliberate attempt to capture the patronage of soldiers and others who expressed their enjoyment of earthy presentations by shouting insults at the performers. Ladies usually stayed away from theaters of this type or were denied admission, but newspapers reported that hundreds disguised themselves as

[4] Chesnut: *A Diary*, p. 162; Anderson: *Brokenburn*, p. 280; George Washington Cable (ed.): "A Woman's Diary in the Siege of Vicksburg," *Century Illustrated Monthly Magazine*, XXXVIII (1889), 797; "Poems," MS, Burton Harrison Papers.

men, attended the vulgar performances, and were arrested if detected. How many were never apprehended can only be surmised.

Actresses and dancers, like lecturers, increased in numbers during the war. They had to be careful to say or do nothing that would indicate they were not in sympathy with the views of their audiences, and this was not always easy for those traveling from town to town in an area where people's loyalties were divided. Lotta Crabtree toured the mining camps and frontier towns in the Far West expressing her Unionist sympathies in word and song and was usually enthusiastically received. Once, however, when she was appearing in southern Oregon, her entrance was greeted with rebel yells, but nothing her frantic manager could do kept Lotta from going ahead with her usual program. When she completed her numbers there was no applause, and the ominous silence so frightened the company that all of them hastily fled the town. The war offered Miss Crabtree her first opportunity in the East and in 1864 she made her debut in New York, but the "Toast of the West Coast" was too rowdy and uninhibited to win favor with a select Eastern audience. After a few months in New York, followed by a tour of the Midwest, she again made a bid for recognition in Eastern cities by playing the role of a vivandière. Unfortunately she took the show to Boston, where she shocked her audience by pulling up her hose as she ran on stage, rolling off sofas showing "more than her ankle," smoking, and sitting on tables in short skirts with her legs crossed. Whatever effect the war had on Eastern decorum, it had not prepared Victorian theater-goers for Lotta Crabtree, who eventually returned to California.[5]

New actresses appeared and old favorites returned. Laura Keene delighted audiences for three years in *Our American Cousin,* the play President Lincoln was attending at the time of his assassination. Kate Dean was among the popular vocalists who entertained on the home front as well as in camp and hospital, and Fanny Kemble came out of retirement to give Shakespearean readings for good causes in both America and England. Charlotte Cushman, "in the autumn of her life," returned briefly

[5] Constance Rourke: *Troupers of the Gold Coast, or the Rise of Lotta Crabtree* (New York, 1928), pp. 190–205.

from Europe to perform in behalf of the Sanitary Commission. The elite of Washington, including the Lincolns, attended her performance of *Macbeth*, and this performance along with those in Baltimore, Philadelphia, New York, and Boston netted the Commission more than $8,000. She was unable to perform in St. Louis and Chicago for the Northwestern Sanitary Commission but asked Henry W. Bellows to share the proceeds with this branch. "I know no distinction between North, South, East or West," she said, adding, "it is all my country." When Bellows refused to grant her request, the hurt Charlotte Cushman embarked for Europe.[6]

The war brought varied types of recognition to actresses. Caroline Chapman, long past her prime, had returned to California four years before the war and was living in San Francisco when a group of Southern sympathizers honored her by naming a Confederate brig *The Caroline Chapman*. Actresses received much mail from lonely soldiers who professed admiration or love and pleaded with the lady to write. While the Confederate actress Laura Waldron would have expected letters of this sort in any other period, some she received could have been written only during a war. A lieutenant, who had written twice without a response, assured her that she would "incur no risk" in corresponding with him since he belonged "to one of the first families of Georgia" and was the son of a "distinguished jurist" who had helped "to draw up the ordinance of secession." He told of his service to the Confederacy and implied that no woman could ask for more than the qualifications he had to offer. He closed with a statement as old as time: "Until I saw you I was a gay, reckless young man . . . but since I saw you, I've been a changed man."[7]

"Every girl in Richmond is engaged or about to be," wrote Phoebe Pember in February 1864, and Mrs. Chesnut recognized this but also noted, "An engagement . . . means so little."[8] We may add to these statements the hundreds of references by con-

[6] Washington *Chronicle,* Oct. 18, 1863; Charlotte Cushman to Henry W. Bellows, Oct. 31, 1863; Henry W. Bellows to Charlotte Cushman, Nov. 9, 1863, Charlotte Cushman Papers, Manuscript Division, Library of Congress.

[7] Rourke: *Troupers of the Gold Coast,* p. 152; Walter Rogers to Laura Waldron, Feb. 3, 1863, Laura Waldron Papers, Manuscript Division, Duke University.

[8] Phoebe Yates Pember to Mrs. Jeremy Gilmer, Feb. 19, 1864, Phillips-Myers Papers; Chesnut: *A Diary,* p. 372.

temporaries to the "marrying craze" in all areas. While many encountered only the usual problems and joys en route to the altar, the war changed time-honored traditions and altered for better or worse the lives of hundreds of thousands of women. Couples often rushed into marriage before the man went to the front or while he was on leave; and women sometimes chose to be married in camp, often in hastily planned ceremonies and without their families present. The war shifted men into new areas where they married girls about whom they knew much less than convention would have dictated before the war, yet the girls usually knew even less about the soldiers' backgrounds. Friends and relatives of each often worried about these "strangers" marrying. Many girls left behind had experiences like that of a young Louisianian who promised to marry her childhood sweetheart as they had always planned, when he came back from war, only to find that he married a Virginia girl who nursed him! The Louisiana girl had defied her father and gone to Richmond to attend him but heard the truth from "rumor's thousand busy tongues."[9] But girls also did their share of rejecting. Thousands of war brides became war widows, some still in their teens, and many of all ages were left with families to support.

The question whether a girl should marry a handicapped soldier was long debated. Some did not let the loss of an arm or leg stand in their way, but many confessed that they kept their promise because they felt obligated to do so, and others who had sent a healthy fiancé to war refused to wed the returned amputee. A Mississippian professed her love for a soldier until he lost a leg. While he was still in the hospital she tactlessly informed him that she could "never marry a cripple" and had decided to accept the proposal of a neighbor who was strong and could take care of her. Mrs. Chesnut was disgusted that the question was so often discussed by groups of ladies at the dinner table or over the teacups or wherever people gathered. She was shocked by the lighthearted way in which her friends joked about the matter and indignant that thoughtless people asked personal questions of her friend Sally Buchanan Preston, who was engaged to General John B. Hood, an amputee. When Miss Preston was once asked

[9] Putnam: *Richmond During the War*, p. 74; Mrs. Burton Harrison: *Recollections Grave and Gay* (New York, 1911), pp. 49–51.

what it was like to be engaged to a "lame lover," she said that "the cause glorifies such wounds," and to this her questioner replied, "I fear it will be my fate to marry one who has lost his head."[1]

The press, pulpit, and politicians were known to remind women it was their obligation to marry handicapped veterans. Even while the war was being fought, Jefferson Davis became obsessed with the idea. "Take the one-armed soldier who has proved his fidelity and manhood," he told the North Carolinians. "When choosing between the empty sleeve and the man who has stayed home and grown rich," he advised the Georgians, "always take the empty sleeve." However, mothers of young girls were among the sternest critics of this policy. A North Carolinian saw her daughter and other girls marry veterans whom the war had changed in various ways; many returned as alcoholics. She wrote an older daughter, "Girls have married men they would never have given a thought of had it not been thought a sacred duty. You would never believe," she continued, "how our public speakers . . . excite the crowd to this thing."[2] It isn't surprising that many of these marriages turned out badly. How many women spent their days with chronic alcoholics will never be known, for scores who left personal records indicate that this was their problem, but many were too proud or humiliated to discuss it with others.

Weddings were eagerly anticipated social events, adding as they did a happy note to the sad times. There were brilliant matches like that of Kate Chase to William Sprague, bizarre ones like that given the "Tom Thumbs" by Phineas T. Barnum, and simple ones like that of a Virginia girl wed in an old gray homespun dress. Yet brides were still radiant. Referring to the Virginia girl, the Prussian Heros von Borcke said that she was "most beautiful in von spunhomme dress," but not all women guests concurred.

Many brides economized either because they had no choice or thought extravagance out of place in wartime, and daytime

---

[1] Fannie Beers: *Memories* (Philadelphia, 1889), p. 206; Chesnut: *A Diary,* pp. 395-96.

[2] Richmond *Enquirer,* Sept. 26, 1864; Macon *Telegraph,* Sept. 24, 1864; New York *Herald,* Oct. 9, 1864; Eliza Thompson to Ellen Thompson Hedrick, July 2, 1867, Benjamin Hedrick Papers.

dresses were recognized as proper wedding attire although formal gowns were still preferred. Southern brides were usually compelled to wear borrowed finery, old dresses, or gowns made from any available material including draperies and curtains; while Northern women seldom had to go to these extremes, they often had to limit their trousseaux. Ellen Wright could have had an elaborate wardrobe but preferred to renovate her old clothes, for she had no intention of "shining forth in new apparel in these hard times." Although she requested her friends not to send gifts, she received many, some of which were reminders of the war, including statuettes of "The Wounded Recruit," "The Wounded Scout," and "The Contraband." Confederate brides received few gifts but their friends made the wedding feast as memorable as times permitted. When LaSalle Corbell married General George Pickett, dozens of friends had a hand in the dinner, including Mrs. Robert E. Lee, who made a "wartime" fruit cake, and Mrs. Maria Dudley, who gave one she had been saving for her own fiftieth wedding anniversary. After the feast, guests danced "as only Richmond could dance in the Confederacy," wrote Mrs. Pickett years later; "if people could not dance in the crisis of life the tragedy might have been darker." She was married at the front and others were wed in predawn ceremonies, a wartime innovation made necessary when the couple had to take an early morning train to camp.[3]

Mock weddings were the rage during the war but were condemned on moral grounds by many. The New York *Herald* criticized ministers who officiated at these ceremonies, thereby making the union "as legal . . . as could be solemnized under the laws of the State." A mock wedding performed at a Christmas party in Charleston in 1862 had serious repercussions, since it was performed by an ordained clergyman who read the complete Episcopal service. News traveled over the state to Spartanburg, where a displaced Charlestonian noted that "in the opinion of many people this was a real wedding." When Sarah Morgan vis-

[3] Harrison: *Recollections*, p. 135; Chesnut: *A Diary*, pp. 396, 460; Mary Elizabeth Massey: *Ersatz in the Confederacy* (Columbia, S.C., 1952), pp. 88–90; Ellen Wright to William Lloyd Garrison II, July 23, 25, 26, 1864, Garrison Family Papers; Katharine Jones (ed.): *Heroines of Dixie* (Indianapolis, 1955), pp. 244–47; McGuire: *Diary*, p. 329; *Harper's Weekly*, Apr. 4, 1863.

ited Columbia four years later she found the affair still discussed and the bride doomed to "a life of single blessedness" since too many people knew of the affair for it to be "hushed up." She was told that "gentlemen like to flirt with her but were afraid to go beyond," for the "groom" was considered to have legal claim to her and her property and unless he formally withdrew those rights "she would not be free to marry." Sarah was disgusted and admitted that the "frightful law" would have made her "afraid to step over a twig in the presence of gentlemen" if she were a resident of the state.[4]

Conservatives were forever being shocked by the rapid changes in conventions. The 1864 leap year parties did not escape censure, for those of the "old school" thought it disgraceful for women to plan and pay for men's entertainment. Mrs. John Daly was only one among many who assumed the "what's the world coming to" attitude, and even a sleigh ride and supper given by the choir women of a Hartford church for the men of the congregation brought press comment. Women increasingly criticized men who no longer paid them little courtesies, and the men countered that women were more careless about expressing appreciation when doors were opened and seats relinquished for them. It was a lady journalist, however, who reminded her sex that their own scandalous conduct was responsible for "the decay in men's manners."[5]

Women were losing their femininity, said the critics. Not only were they adopting military styles; they were becoming much too interested in weapons of war. "I wish to God the war were finished," said one lady, for "I hate to hear the gentle-hearted ladies admiring swords, guns, and pistols." Frequent mention was also made of women's profanity, brutality, and vindictiveness. Although Northern newspaper accounts of Southern women who collected bones of Union soldiers were grossly exaggerated, there were some who did. A Confederate nurse told of a Richmond woman who kept "a pile of Yankee bones" where she could see them every morning on first awakening, and she reported that

[4] New York *Herald*, Mar. 6, 1864; Meta Morris Grimball Journal, MS, John Berkley Grimball Papers; Sarah Morgan Dawson Diary, MS, Manuscript Division, Duke University.
[5] *Frank Leslie's Illustrated Newspaper*, Feb. 6, July 9, 1864; Washington *Chronicle*, Apr. 25, 1864.

another had asked if she could "get her a Yankee skull to keep her toilette trinkets in." An increasing number were accused of taking up smoking and dipping snuff; and a long, rollicking rhyme was widely circulated on the subject, the author saying that while he did not like to see a woman "smoke, dance, and skip," he disliked most of all "to see one chew or dip." A soldier was astonished to see a woman bite into a plug of tobacco but nauseated "to see her spit," and a Louisianian was shocked when a Texan asked her if she didn't "dip . . . chew, nor nothing." Northern papers thought women seen smoking cigars, drinking, and disguised as men especially newsworthy. Scores of women were arrested for posing as men; some were traveling with a man to whom they were not married and some with another girl. Reported less often were men disguised as women, but one widely publicized case was that of a deserter caught living with a teen-aged girl in a Cleveland hotel.[6]

Both scandal and divorce increased during the war, and the press was eager to report them. Peter Strong's suit for divorce against Mary Stevens Strong, daughter of a highly respected banker, shook New York society when it was revealed that Mrs. Strong had been having an illicit affair with the plaintiff's brother, Edward Strong. Almost as shocking to some, however, was the Stevens family's refusal to withdraw from the public gaze and "bend . . . with true show of humility to this terrible chastisement." Although divorce was frowned upon in proper circles, it increased to the point "of getting to be quite fashionable," according to a journalist who reported that three decrees had been granted in New York City on the preceding day and a fourth denied because the wife had not proved her husband's infidelity to the satisfaction of the court. While Nevada was as yet in the territorial stage, a newcomer from the East found it "a great country for divorces—fully equal to California." She wrote her parents that fifteen cases were pending in Carson City and

[6] Hammond: *Diary of a Union Lady*, p. 73; Phoebe Yates Pember to Eugenia Phillips, June 25, 1863, Philip Phillips Papers; Robert Blackwell: *Original Acrostics* (St. Louis, 1869), pp. 17–18; O. H. Bixby: *Incidents in Dixie* (Baltimore, 1864), p. 72; Mrs. Robert Pugh to Robert Pugh, Dec. 18, 1862, Robert Pugh Family Papers, Department of Archives and History, Louisiana State University; New York *Herald*, Aug. 1, 1861, Sept. 23, Nov. 3, 1863; *Frank Leslie's Illustrated Newspaper*, Apr. 23, 1864; Cleveland *Leader*, Feb. 13, 1865.

that a woman in Virginia City had been married twice in six months by the same minister. This, she thought, "must require some elasticity of conscience."[7]

Contemporary public and private records make mention of illicit relations, abortion, and the birth of illegitimate children, but many relevant personal records are as yet carefully guarded by the writers' descendants. While these problems are not peculiar to any age, the press had theretofore given them less attention. Numerous instances have been found of unmarried girls, many· from respectable families, who had children by soldiers; and while references in letters are usually delicately phrased, their meaning is clear. The woman was often said to have been "cruelly deceived," as in truth she often had been; and instead of the word "baby," phrases such as "the poor little thing" were customarily used. Northern papers were especially brutal in reporting such incidents and some had no hesitancy in citing names. After identifying one woman who appeared at an induction center to see her lover off to war, a reporter noted that her "condition precluded all doubts of her fondness for her affianced" and surmised that after bidding him farewell the girl went home to await "her expected visitor." The reader of metropolitan newspapers was kept informed on gruesome abortion cases, and here too the women were usually identified. A typical story related to a soldier's wife who had not seen her husband for more than a year when she died as the result of an abortion performed by another woman; both women were named, and the dead woman's brother told the reporter that she had been drunk at the time of her seduction by a stranger. Lonely, depressed women often were reported to have committed suicide and many were soldiers' wives or widows. One of the latter, only seventeen, impoverished, and unable to find a job, moved in with a man who promised to support her. But he was sadistically cruel and she was so ashamed and desperate that she made a futile attempt on her life. When brought into court, she said that her only regret was that she had not succeeded.[8]

[7] Hammond: *Diary of a Union Lady*, pp. 280–81; New York *Herald*, June 18, 1864, Mar. 29, 1862; Ann Loomis North to Mary and George Loomis, Nov. 9, 1862, John Wesley North Papers.

[8] New York *Herald*, Nov. 7, 1864, Sept. 3, 1862, Feb. 7, 1863.

Foreign observers were quick to note the decline in moral standards. George Sala reported that "Boston absolutely swarms with strumpets" and New York "has at least two hundred and fifty supper and concert saloons, which are dins of prostitution." An unsuccessful if halfhearted attempt was made during the war to rid these places of so-called "waitresses," but this Sala failed to note. He did, however, mention the daily insertions in newspapers by "dissolute young men who slyly advertise for mistresses, or abandoned women who advertise for keepers." He concluded that American prostitutes did exceedingly well, especially those who moved to California, posed as war widows, and made or married a fortune, after which they traveled in Europe and managed "to wiggle into some kind of society, and die in the odour of respectability." American prostitutes had a better future, said Sala, than those in England, for the United States was so large they could "clear out" of a community where their sins were known and "go to another quarter."[9]

The increase in prostitution can by no means be blamed entirely on the camp followers, for the low wages which had always contributed to this problem were also a factor during the inflationary war period. The Boston *Post*, on April 30, 1862, reported a girl of sixteen arrested "for improperly soliciting men on the street," and she told the court that as a "sewer of button holes" she could not earn enough money to support herself and her mother. Thousands of similar cases were brought to light in other cities across the nation, and many girls scarcely more than children were becoming prostitutes. A student of the problem states that one, whose diary he was privileged to see, was only fourteen when she started "catering to the finest carriage trade" in Richmond. Not only did she amass a fortune, but after the war she married into a "prominent" Richmond family.[1]

Periodic raids on the bawdy houses were graphically described in the press, conspicuously one in Chicago in the summer of 1864 which resulted in five suicides, two attempted suicides, and the frantic flight of at least 118 prostitutes to Cincinnati, St.

[9] George Augustus Sala: *My Diary in America in the Midst of the War* (London, 1865), II, 58–61, 162–63.
[1] Robert W. Waitt, Jr.: "Kinsey Report on the Civil War," unpublished paper in possession of the author.

Louis, and Pittsburg. One of the girls who committed suicide was identified as being from a "respectable" Connecticut family; another had tried previously to take her life because she had no home, could find no other work, and "was not eligible for charity." The police were not alone in raiding houses of ill fame, for indignant women like those in Brooklyn "demolished" the establishments and sent the terrified inmates scurrying to safety, and others like some in Richmond signed petitions and testified against specific individuals.[2]

Washington and Richmond were noted for their dens of iniquity. There had been approximately 500 prostitutes in the Federal capital before the war, but the number increased to more than 5,000, not including those in Georgetown and Alexandria. By 1862 there were 450 "registered houses," but records of the provost marshal's office indicate that others were continually being uncovered that were not registered. Not included in the above figure were the concubines whom Margaret Leech describes as "set up in their establishments by officers and men," sometimes passing as their wives. Some Washington women were aware of the immorality in high places, among them the observant Mrs. Kasson, who at first had been reluctant to report to her Iowa readers that Washington was "a more dangerous city, morally speaking, than almost any other." She was shocked to find in "this terrible Washington" women so goaded by ambition that they sacrificed their families' welfare and turned to "opium eating, . . . whiskey drinking," or worse only to become "victims of their follies." Princess Salm-Salm thought the city "abominable." She knew many prominent women who had an eye "on gain rather than virtue," and some were all too ready to sell their "charms [for] ready cash."[3]

Those remaining in either capital for an appreciable period stressed that matters grew worse, not better. By the last year of the war conditions were deplorable in Richmond, as newspapers, local officials (especially Mayor Joseph Mayo), and court records testified. Mayo repeatedly ordered raids on houses of prosti-

[2] Chicago *Post,* Aug. 8, 9, 1864; New York *Herald,* June 15, 1865; Richmond *Examiner,* Oct. 11, 1864.
[3] Margaret Leech: *Reveille in Washington* (New York, 1941), p. 261; Kasson: "An Iowa Woman in Washington," p. 89; Agnes Salm-Salm: *Ten Years of My Life* (London, 1875), I, 25–26.

tution and one madam reported seven houses visited by the police in one evening, but she forwarded fifty dollars "in metal" to "Rednose Mayo's" headquarters and dared him to interfere with her establishment.[4] Hundreds of prostitutes were arraigned, but those arrested on the charge of "cohabiting with niggers," as the press expressed it, were more numerous than might be assumed. They were usually reprimanded and fined, but when such a penalty had been imposed several times without effect the women were hustled off to jail. And as in Washington, "kept women" moved in the best circles. As early as September 4, 1862, the *Examiner* reported that " a large number" of beautifully attired "pimps" could be seen any evening dining in the city's finest hotels.

In some instances crime was relative, depending on whose side the women were. This was true of those who mastered the art of smuggling contraband through the lines. If they did it for themselves or for the Confederacy a question might be raised as to the right or wrong, but if the smuggling was for speculative purposes it became more clearly criminal. Yet in the eyes of the Federals all smugglers were breaking a law of war. There was no doubt, however, that women who bootlegged liquor in camp, served it in unlicensed establishments, or stole government property were breaking the law. Hundreds in both the Union and Confederacy were found guilty of these crimes. Theft increased during every year of the war and women were among the thieves. When caught, many expected to be handled gently because of their sex, like a New Yorker who when caught in the act of stealing lumber said to her captor, "Surely you wouldn't shoot a poor woman that's breeding for the Union."[5]

Drunkenness and vagrancy charges against women also increased, and according to the 1863 report of the New York Commissioners of Public Charities and Corrections, 8,425 of the 10,753 vagrants sent to Blackwell's Island were women. Several women were involved in a counterfeiting ring operating in the Midwest during the war, and others participated in a variety of frauds. None served to disillusion generous, compassionate peo-

[4] Waitt: "Kinsey Report on the Civil War."
[5] Records of the Provost Court, Department of the Gulf, Adjutant General's Office, Records Group 242; Records of the Office of the Provost Marshal, Washington, War Department Records, National Archives; Martha Wright to Eliza Yarnell, Aug. 26, 1864, Garrison Family Papers.

ple more than those who, posing as innocent victims of the war, pleaded for assistance they did not need. A married couple, professing to be mistreated Southern Unionists who had lost everything when driven from their home by Confederates, won the sympathy of a respected New York clergyman who arranged for them to speak in several churches where the congregation was called on to help them. Not until they had amassed a tidy sum was the hoax detected.[6]

In retrospect, the innumerable complex social repercussions of the war are especially significant in showing women's attitudes to abnormal situations. A tendency throughout history to idealize the women of past generations has sometimes made them appear so perfect as to be positively inhuman, and this has been one of the greatest injustices done those of the Civil War generation. Actually they were like women of any other age. The majority exhibited the finest traits of character known to womanhood, but even they at times reacted to specific situations as "typical" women and not as saints. In the Civil War as in all others, corruption surfaced, increased, and spread through the social structure and women were in part responsible, for without them some of the most prevalent evils could never have flourished.

In publicizing woman's weaknesses and sins, the press helped to change her image; and whether or not the writers realized it at the time, this would eventually help to "emancipate" the sex. Six months after the war, a New York editor reminded his readers that the conflict had "brought all corruptions of the body politic to the surface" but nothing had been done because of the people's preoccupation with the struggle. He called specifically on women to join in a massive reform movement, and they were not slow to respond.[7] Free from their war activities, Mary Livermore, Anna Dickinson, and scores of other energetic women were soon crusading for causes which included temperance, eradication of prostitution, better educational facilities, birth control, and others which they believed would improve society and especially woman's lot. Because evils had been so realistically bared during the war, many people no longer alluded to them in whispers or ignored them; they were compelled to admit their existence.

[6] New York *Herald*, Apr. 7, 1864.
[7] New York *Herald*, Oct. 13, 1865.

13

Women and Negroes

EMINISTS OF THE FIFTIES had often spoken of the status of "women and Negroes," and the phrase was used increasingly as the war altered race relations. More than 3,500,000 slaves were emancipated, and within six years thereafter they were made citizens and the males given the right to vote. For decades "women and Negroes" continued to be compared in status, and as Orra Langhorne noted, the two were often "classed together." This remarkable Virginia liberal realized that they were also thrown together in the South. For more than forty years Mrs. Langhorne worked to improve their economic and social position by trying to develop mutual understanding and appreciation as she emphasized their common problems and stressed the positive effects of the Civil War on both.[1]

Several factors must be considered in appraising the war's effect on colored and white women: Negro women's role in the conflict, the relations of Northern and Southern women with Negroes during and after the struggle, and the effect of emancipation on colored women. Much of the story naturally centers in the South, where more than 4,000,000 white women from all classes and more than 1,500,000 Negro women were caught up in

[1] Charles E. Wynes (ed.): *Southern Sketches from Virginia, 1881-1901* (Charlottesville, 1964), pp. 66, 107.

the social and economic revolution for which neither group was prepared. Although the impact of emancipation was less keenly felt in the North and West, where there were fewer Negroes, repercussions were not entirely lacking. The hopes of various groups were kindled as: Northern Negroes dreamed of economic and social equality with whites; abolitionists retired victorious from a thirty-five-year crusade, trusting they had done more than merely free the slave; and woman's rightists hoped to share in the franchise when it was bestowed on Negro men. When thousands of colored people migrated North and West during and after the war, women who had had little if any contact with the race came to know them as employees, competitors, students, or colleagues.

Negro women in the North were justifiably proud of their wartime services to the Union. In addition to assisting the whites in philanthropic endeavors, they organized their own aid societies, took an active interest in colored soldiers and contrabands, volunteered their services in hospitals, and worked in battle areas. When thousands of contrabands flocked to Washington, it was Mrs. Lincoln's mulatto modiste and confidante, Elizabeth Keckley, who organized and headed the Ladies Contraband Relief Society. In her travels with Mrs. Lincoln she never missed an opportunity to solicit funds for her pet project. In Boston she established a branch of the society, in other cities she spoke in its behalf, and through influential friends she saw that it was publicized in England and Scotland, where a number of people contributed generously to the work. But Mrs. Keckley made her greatest sacrifice when her only son, whose freedom she had purchased, was killed on a Missouri battlefield. Another worker with the soldiers and contrabands in Washington was Sojourner Truth, by then nearing eighty. As articulate as ever, she continued to address audiences—"scouring the Copperheads," she said, as she had once scoured brass doorknobs. But her most cherished memories were of her visits to Lincoln, whom she did not hesitate to advise on matters relating to her people.[2]

[2] Benjamin Quarles: *The Negro in the Civil War* (Boston, 1953), pp. 128–29, 228–29, 233, 246, 331, 341; Ruth Painter Randall: *Mary Lincoln: Biography of a Marriage* (Boston, 1953), pp. 211–15, 299–301, 311–12, 361, 385–90, 409–15; Samuel Sillen: *Women Against Slavery* (New York, 1955), pp. 39–40; Hallie Quinn Brown (ed.): *Homespun Heroines and Other Women of Distinction* (Xenia, Ohio, 1926), pp. 14–15, 147–49. See also Elizabeth Keckley: *Behind the Scenes* (New York, 1868): Arthur Huff Fauset: *Sojourner Truth, God's Faithful Pilgrim* (Chapel Hill, 1928).

Sojourner Truth was among those who favored the use of Negro troops and when the government sanctioned the enlistment of Negroes she and other women became active recruiters. Josephine St. Pierre Ruffin encouraged men to enter military service and also worked with the Sanitary Commission, and Mary Ann Shadd Cary was appointed by Governor Levi Morton of Indiana to help recruit Negroes, while in California Mrs. Priscilla Stewart urged her race to raise a regiment. Frances Watkins Harper delivered patriotic lectures and wrote verse expressing her devotion to the Union. Her persuasive powers were frequently compared to those of Anna Dickinson, and in later years she became her race's foremost feminist crusader and lecturer. The longtime abolitionist Sarah Remond was in England during a part of the war, and there she addressed audiences of mill workers, industrialists, and others on emancipation and the Union cause.[3] For each Negro woman whose work was recognized, hundreds were quietly working behind the scenes.

While some attention was usually commanded by those who helped freedmen in the South, not many of the Negro workers were accorded national recognition. The work of educated women like Charlotte Forten and Mary Peake was known, but scores of semiliterate women who assisted the teachers remained anonymous. Despite laws in Southern states which forbade teaching slaves to read and write, probably 5 per cent of the adults coming into Federal lines had a rudimentary literacy and were occasionally assigned to instruct beginners. A Northerner who noted that their "want of training detracts from their usefulness" mentioned a colored woman who, after a few weeks, brought her class to another teacher because she could take them no further. When Miss Breck was a principal in Charleston, she noted that eleven of the twenty-five Southern Negroes teaching in the city schools were women but did not say whether they were recently emancipated or had been free Negroes before the war.[4]

Colored women were already nursing when the War De-

[3] Brown: *Homespun Heroines*, pp. 15, 95, 100–103, 151, 242.
[4] Edward L. Pierce: "The Freedmen at Port Royal," *Atlantic Monthly*, XII (1863), 307–9; E. P. Breck to M. A. Cochran, June 5, 1865, E. P. Breck Letters, Smith College Archives.

partment ordered that they be employed in the army's general hospitals, and additional hundreds were enrolled as cooks and laundresses. Occasionally some were the subject of human interest stories like one in *Harper's Weekly*, accompanied by a drawing, about "Aunt Charlotte," a woman in her sixties who had been left in New Bern by her white owners. She was employed at six dollars a month to cook for an officer but volunteered to care for sick and wounded soldiers as well. According to the correspondent, her patients testified to her culinary abilities, efficiency, character, and "other virtues that ennoble her position." *Harper's* was more critical than most Northern periodicals of the wage paid contraband women—usually about half that paid the men, who were also clothed by the government.[5] One of the first lessons freed Negro women learned was that, like their white sisters, they could expect to encounter wage discrimination.

The Federals had scarcely arrived on the South Carolina coast when Harriet Tubman appeared on the scene, as anxious to share in the excitement of war as she had been to conduct fugitive slaves along the underground railroad. With less effort than many whites she had obtained passes from high-ranking officials, including Governor John A. Andrew, Generals David Hunter and Quincy Gillmore, and Secretary Stanton. Harriet found many things to do. As a scout she worked alone or led troops deep into Confederate lines, usually returning with valuable information and slaves she had spirited away from their masters. As a nurse she irritated army doctors because she insisted on simple home remedies; but since she cured some patients and had influential friends, the medics gave her little trouble. Harriet Tubman did not know what to think of the South Carolina Negroes and could not understand Gullah, a dialect which she described as "different" from any she had known.

In 1865, as Mrs. Tubman was returning to her home in Auburn, New York, she boarded the wrong train in Washington and was told that neither her military pass nor her half-fare ticket entitled her to ride on the all-white train. She protested vehemently when the conductor forced her into the baggage car, and her arm was wrenched in the struggle. A witness suggested that she sue the line, and giving her his card, offered to testify in

[5] *Harper's Weekly*, Aug. 12, 1862, Jan. 11, 1862.

her behalf. A New York doctor and several friends wanted her to take the matter to court, but since the witness could not be found the idea had to be abandoned. Throughout the winter her arm troubled her so that she could do no work and was dependent on charity. Largely through the efforts of William H. Seward, the town's most prominent citizen, she was given a plot of land on which she built a cabin, and here she lived out her days. For several years after the war, despite her poverty, she and her white friends held an annual fair, the proceeds going to the Southern freedmen; as did the profits from Mrs. Sarah Bradford's biography of Harriet, subsidized by Auburn friends. She and her white patrons were indignant that the Federal Government did not give her a pension for her war services. They and the Empire State Federation of Colored Women were her chief sources of support.[6]

Susie King Taylor won her freedom in the war and immediately turned to helping others of her race. She had been taught to read and write by her master's daughter, and when her husband enlisted in a South Carolina colored regiment she enrolled as a laundress, serving also as a teacher and nurse. One of her most cherished memories was of work in Beaufort with Clara Barton, to whom in her book written forty years later she paid tribute. Caroline Johnson, a former slave, nursed in the Washington hospitals and was once invited by Lincoln to visit the White House.[7]

The services of Negro women were rarely recognized during the war except in the abolitionist press, but afterward if any issue arose involving them woman's rights publications sometimes gave them space. The big tome, *Woman's Work in the Civil War*, published in 1867, paid tribute to more than five hundred Union women who worked on the home front and in battle areas, but no mention was made of the Negroes. This was generally true of works published during the remainder of the century, and since

[6] Sarah H. Bradford: *Scenes in the Life of Harriet Tubman* (Auburn, N.Y., 1869), pp. 42, 45–47; Martha Wright to Marianne Mott, Nov. 17, 1865; Martha Wright to David Wright, Apr. 2, 1866, Garrison Family Papers; Quarles: *The Negro in the Civil War*, pp. 225–27; Brown: *Homespun Heroines*, pp. 55–68. See also Earl Conrad: *Harriet Tubman* (Washington, 1943).

[7] Susie King Taylor: *Reminiscences of My Life in Camp* (Boston, 1902), pp. 5–6, 59–62; Pierce: "The Freedmen at Port Royal," p. 307; Willie Lee Rose: *Rehearsal for Reconstruction* (Indianapolis, 1963), pp. 87, 197, 408.

colored women rarely left records except an occasional ghost-written account of questionable authenticity, contemporary references came primarily from the pens of the whites.

Northern abolitionists were the chief supporters of Negro women's wartime projects. Martha Wright donated so much of her family's wearing apparel to clothing drives for freedmen that the end of the war found the Wrights with a scant supply on hand. "I often think of the freedwomen," she said, "flaunting in most of my wardrobe." Her daughter Ellen reported that Lydia Maria Child was busy "doing sights" for the Southern Negroes and had "denied herself tea, sugar, butter, servants, clothes and thus saved $200" which she contributed to them. This was in addition to her gift of $500 from book royalties. Although Ellen Wright praised this sixty-five-year-old lady's generosity she nevertheless believed "the freedmen would forgive her if she didn't do her own washing."

Many philanthropic Northern women knew very little about the slave except that he should be free, and when he was emancipated they were sometimes disillusioned by his attitude and conduct. Mrs. Wright, whose home had been a station on the underground railroad, wrote her sisters late in the war that she doubted the ex-slave could ever be molded into a useful, decent citizen but thought it unwise to express this opinion unless "only their friends are present." Many Northern whites, she said, were "just emerging from bitter prejudice" and always happy "to hear anything that justifies their prejudice." Like other critics, she blamed the former masters for the Negroes' immorality and other sins, but she also proved that one is more likely to be tolerant of a minority living far away. Although disillusioned about those she had helped, she thought "the worst Negro . . . [was] considerably higher than the worst Irishman."[8] Southern women would have been delighted to know that an abolitionist questioned Negroes' abilities and conduct, and Mrs. Wright would have been surprised to find that many Southern women blamed themselves and their menfolk for the Negroes' worst traits.

Northern prejudice against the Negro did not end with the

[8] Martha Wright to Marianne Mott, Nov. 17, 1865; Ellen Wright Garrison to Martha Wright, Apr. 2, 1865; Martha Wright to her sister, Apr. 19, 1864, Garrison Family Papers.

war, and in many instances it increased as greater numbers of the race came into Northern communities. A New Yorker deplored the violence employed against Negroes during the draft riots but hoped it would frighten them into submission, for she had found them "so insolent as to be unbearable" since the outbreak of war. "I cannot endure free blacks," she said, "they are immoral with all their piety." Mrs. Kasson confessed to being "a good abolitionist," but when she mingled with Negroes socially for the first time she felt as though she was "having a very funny dream." In this instance the colored people to whom she referred were official representatives from Haiti, but she could not resist staring impolitely at them and did not approve of the races mixing socially, nor did they often do so in Washington or any other Northern community. If an abolitionist reacted this way, rank-and-file Northerners could not be expected to welcome the race with open arms. Several ministers in Auburn, New York, decided "to test public opinion" when Frederick Douglass was to be in town for several days; instead of finding accommodations for him in the home of his white friends, they asked other prominent citizens, some professing to be liberals, to entertain him but none consented to do so.

A discussion of miscegenation, a popular topic during and after the war, indicated that most abolitionists had not come around to accepting racial intermarriage. When a Boston abolitionist was asked if she approved of it, she said she would marry a Negro "sooner . . . than a white man who would ask such a question," and this was about as close to the affirmative as anyone came. Abolitionists rarely had a sense of humor where the Negro was concerned, but Ellen Wright was an exception. She tried to entice her friend Lucy McKim to visit her by saying that Lucretia Mott already was there and "ready for any radical emergency," and there were "plenty of colored brothers around, if that's what you want."[9]

Military officials hated to see large numbers of Negro women come into camp, for several reasons: there were fewer

[9] Harold Earl Hammond (ed.): *Diary of a Union Lady, 1861–1865* (New York, 1962), p. 251; Caroline Eliot Kasson: "An Iowa Woman in Washington, D.C., 1861–1865," *Iowa Journal of History,* LII (1954), 177; Martha Wright to Marianne Mott, June 23, 1865; William Lloyd Garrison II to Ellen Wright, March 13, 1864; Ellen Wright to Lucy McKim, July 7, 1862, Garrison Family Papers.

jobs for them than for men, many were encumbered with several children, and they contributed to problems of supply, morale, health, and discipline. Officers repeatedly ordered that they not be permitted to enter camp and that those already there be sent away. General Grenville Dodge stated that the Alabama women "are a burden to us and should stay on plantations," and when others flocked into his camp in Tennessee he ordered that they be returned to their homes, settled on abandoned farms, or "quartered upon known rebels." His brothers-in-arms were equally determined to be rid of them, including General Thomas W. Sherman, who took a very dim view of the "prolific race" in coastal South Carolina. While admitting that Negro men were of some value to the army, he was quick to note that for every "able bodied man, we have five to six women and children," and while men often left when given heavy work the women and children remained to be cared for.

One of the gross understatements of the time was Sherman's observation that the Negroes' "minds are unsettled to any plans." General S. S. Fry often gave vent to his feelings about the "Nigger Woman Question," as he expressed it, and when ordered to "feed and clothe" all coming into camp in the winter of 1864–65 he wrote a friend, "It will be impossible to furnish them shelter and will be an invitation for all Negro women in the region to flock to this camp." Experience had taught him that they created innumerable problems, and he predicted that "disgraceful . . . shameful conditions . . . and obscene and brutal practices" would result from their presence. "I shudder to think of the consequences," he said.[1]

Many Negroes came into Union lines from plantations abandoned by their owners, and others followed the armies who passed their doors, but not until the last year of the war did they begin to leave the whites in droves. Although slaves were sure to hear about emancipation if they came in contact with the Federals, the Southerners did not as a rule tell them they were free until the war had ended and then both Negroes and whites had to decide what could be done. But through most of the conflict the plantation mistress managed to retain at least a few of her domestics and on these she relied. Mrs. Chesnut's devoted and

[1] *O. R.*, XXXII, Part 2, 391; XXXI, Part 3, 198; XVI, 202, 205; S. S. Fry to Robert J. Breckinridge, Nov. 28, 1864, Breckinridge Family Papers.

faithful "Ellen" was entrusted with her mistress's diamonds, and several weeks later the girl returned them "with as little interest as if they were garden peas." Slaves were often made responsible for guarding family treasures and others knew where they had been hidden, and many never divulged the secret. Those left in charge of the property when their owners fled frequently did what they could to protect it, and that many failed was not necessarily their fault. A colored girl in New Orleans reported regularly to her displaced mistress on the condition of the house which had been taken over by a Federal officer's family. The girl stayed on as a maid and tried to keep the place as always. She reported that two Negro women from the plantation had joined her, their husbands having run off with the Federals, and while well taken care of they begged to join their mistress in "exile." Refugees often took with them their most trusted servants. Mrs. Elizabeth Meriwether would have had an even more difficult time in Alabama had it not been for her "Rose" who had the solution for many baffling problems, including the extermination of bedbugs. She nursed the Meriwether baby as well as her own when milk could not be had at any price in Tuscaloosa.[2]

White women and their slaves often drew closer during the war; for when the mistress was left without a white man's protection, the Negroes often sensed that they were needed. When it was known that Federals were headed in their direction Negro women and children begged to be permitted to stay in the "big house," and the mistress was usually glad to have their company. A Georgian later recalled that she was "frightened half to death" upon hearing the enemy was coming, but the slaves came "in flocks for protection," wanting her "to do something for them or with them." They were terrorized by the "Yankees" without knowing for sure just what a "Yankee" was; and when he appeared and they saw he was human, they would rush out to get a better look, and according to one observer, "act like a set of lunatics." Fear of the enemy was not confined to slaves, however; when it was known that the Confederates were marching on

[2] Mary Boykin Chesnut: *A Diary From Dixie*, ed. Ben Ames Williams (Boston, 1950), pp. 531–32; Elizabeth Avery Meriwether, *Recollections of Ninety-Two Years, 1824–1916* (Nashville, 1958), pp. 114–15; Memphis *Appeal*, Dec. 20, 1862.

Gettysburg, the free Negroes hysterically scampered out of town, loaded down with their worldly goods and followed by children who were "trying in vain to keep up with their elders." A resident watched the hegira and heard a mother shout to her children, "*Fo the Lod's sake, you chillun, cum right lon quick! If them Rebs dun kotch you, dey tear you up.*"[3]

Traveling in the wake of a rapidly moving army was especially hard on Negro women, some of whom died of exhaustion, exposure, or foul play. Those who followed Sherman's troops through Georgia and the Carolinas endured indescribable hardships. More than 300 were reported left behind at river crossings in South Carolina, and others were drowned trying to cross on rickety rafts. Bodies of women who had been stabbed or died in other violent ways were seen along the roads, and when eighteen bodies were found in the Camden area it was assumed they had been killed by Federal soldiers who "could not rid themselves of these pests in any other way." But some women were also brutal, and hundreds were reported to have abandoned or killed their children along the line of march rather than be slowed down by them. A Northern teacher of freedmen was horrified to find babies left "exhausted and dying" by the roadside and reported that two women who had been seen to kill theirs were hanged "on the spot" by military authorities. Mrs. Chesnut wryly commented on Negro mothers who "did not spring from block of ice to block" clutching their young to their bosoms, "as Mrs. Stowe fondly imagines," but tossed them aside when the going got rough. She could not but be amused when her aunt's coachman gathered "a wagonload of babies" for his mistress and proudly announced he had "saved" those left "all along the road." In her testimony before a Senate committee, Mrs. George Ward told how Negroes had abandoned their young who were then placed in an Atlanta institution and "bound out" to white women after the war. She had taken one of the girls and kept her for a few years but had to let her go because she was "sadistically cruel."[4]

[3] *Report of the Senate Committee on Labor and Capital* (1883), IV, 342; Tillie Pierce Alleman: *At Gettysburg or What a Girl Saw and Heard of the Battle* (New York, 1889), pp. 19–20; Bell Irvin Wiley: *Southern Negroes, 1861–1865* (New York, 1938), p. 72.
[4] Columbia (S.C.) *Phoenix*, Apr. 4, 1865; Pierce: "The Freedmen at Port Royal," pp. 293–94; Chesnut: *A Diary*, pp. 531–32; *Report of the Senate Committee on Labor and Capital* (1883), IV, 324–25.

Although antebellum critics were justified in condemning the separation of slave families, many Negro mothers were indifferent to their own children. Negroes themselves confirmed this when questioned by the Senate committee in 1883. A colored pullman porter testified that the parents were "to blame" for "a heap" of Negro girls "turning out badly" after the war; and a few years later an elderly colored woman told Orra Langhorne the trouble was that the girls were no longer being "brought up" as in slave days but were "jerked up." The illegitimate, she said, were often looked on by their mothers as a burden and "turned adrift to seek such fortune as the cold world may have in store." This worried Mrs. Langhorne, who had to admit that the "generation . . . born since the war . . . [was], in many cases, greatly inferior to their parents born and bred in slavery." Eliza Frances Andrews told of a family who had belonged to her father; while the older girls who spent several years in slavery led respectable lives, the youngest one grew up "a degenerate of the most irresponsible type." She had "five or six illegitimate children, all by different fathers," and lived to see one of her sons hanged "for the usual crime against a little girl" while the others had records that rivaled "the Jukes family."[5]

Whites who realized they must take a major part of the blame for the low moral standards of Negroes also knew that freeing them en masse would not immediately improve them. The women might bring children into the world but few were trained to raise them properly, for Negro mothers had been childishly dependent on whites and were naïve and confused. To them freedom implied release from all conditions of servitude. They shunned work, and when handouts were no longer forthcoming many resorted to stealing. They revolted against discipline, and even the most efficient often became irresponsible. Most did not want to remain with their former master, nor did those in towns want to live on the property of their employer, for this smacked too much of former days. They segregated themselves in shanties and created sanitation problems which might have been minimized if they had been willing to accept lodging and board as

[5] *Report of the Senate Committee on Labor and Capital* (1883), IV, 5–10; Wynes: *Southern Sketches from Virginia*, p. 123; Eliza Frances Andrews: *The War-Time Journal of a Georgia Girl*, ed. Spencer Bidwell King, Jr., pp. 377–78.

partial payment for their services. The Negroes tended to migrate to cities, and although the Freedmen's Bureau transported more than 30,000 back to the plantations or to other places of employment, many times this number settled miles from their white friends who were more interested in their welfare than were strangers. Regardless of the Negro's capabilities and virtues, a child raised in these deplorable surroundings during the topsy-turvy postwar period was likely to have his progress blocked by virtually insurmountable obstacles.

Family ties were more often weakened than strengthened immediately after the war, since many Negroes interpreted freedom to mean breaking all bonds they knew as slaves. When visionaries insisted that colored people living together be married, they did not always ascertain whether they were already legally wed. A teacher-minister arriving in a Georgia village in the late spring of '65 announced he was there to marry Negroes for a nominal fee, but his interest seems to have been primarily in their money, not their morals. Hundreds of freedmen proceeded to select a mate and the couples were united in a mass ceremony performed in a grove near the village. In the group was Eliza Frances Andrews' maid "Charity," who six years earlier had been legally married in the Methodist Church to a man who was still very much alive. When the legal husband of a colored woman protested against her second marriage, the minister ignored him since "husband number two had the woman and fee on his side."

Testimony before a Senate investigating committee indicated that men more often abandoned their mates. A former governor stated that women thus deserted created a serious problem in the sixties and seventies, especially those left behind when "whole trainloads" of Negro men migrated to Kansas. An Alabama lumberman reported that fewer Negroes were legally wed in the postwar period than in antebellum days; and a Georgian said that Negro men went "here and there," their wives having "no control over them." This helps to explain a South Carolinian's statement before the same committee that Negro women had to be more industrious because many were the sole support of their families.[6] While women often shirked their responsibilities, the

---

[6] Andrews: *Journal*, 346–47, 359–60; *Report of the Senate Committee on Labor and Capital* (1883), IV, 51–52, 103–5, 492, 836.

fact remains that the typical postwar Negro family was matri-
archal.

When Gertrude Thomas's maid announced that she wanted
to marry a field hand, Mrs. Thomas told her she must first divorce the man to whom she had been married before the war.
The girl was sent to an Augusta attorney who explained that a
divorce was slow and costly but for only ten dollars he would
"write them off a paper which would divorce them." Despite Mrs.
Thomas's warning that this was not legal, the girl nevertheless
married the second man; and when Mrs. Thomas asked her husband to intervene in the matter he refused, saying that he did not
want to "lose a good field hand." Like many white women, she
was concerned about Negro morality and acknowledged the
whites' primary blame; yet now that the Negroes were free she
felt the white people should be responsible for righting the wrong.
"We have assisted in retarding their moral development heretofore," she said, but "we now in justice . . . should assist them in
their efforts to do right." The most serious mistake being made by
the Southern whites, she noted, was ignoring their ways and expecting no more of them "than from . . . horses and cows."[7]
This negligent attitude, combined with the visionaries' high ex-
pectations and the mercenaries' exploitation of their ignorance,
created an impossible situation for the Negroes. If the authority
for handling the situation had been placed in women's hands,
some of the evils might have been ameliorated. Certainly the
women were more concerned than the men about Negro morality.

Negro women welcomed emancipation until they realized it
carried greater responsibilities than they had ever known. Most
at first had a merry time going where they wanted to go, doing
what they pleased, and receiving flattering attention from both
Negro and white troops stationed in the South. They imitated
white ladies in dress and manners, wore veils denied them in
slavery, carried parasols, and proudly used their new "entitles,"
as they called their recently acquired surnames, which they
changed whenever they found one more to their liking. Their
antics amused some whites and disgusted others. Eliza Frances
Andrews did not begrudge her "Cinthy's" using scarce flour to

[7] Ella Gertrude Clanton Thomas Diary, MS.

powder her face, and she enjoyed eavesdropping on her engagements with colored soldiers, which were far more entertaining
than "an evening at the Negro minstrels." But Miss Andrews, like
other Southerners, saw nothing amusing in the Negro women's
socializing with white soldiers. In the opinion of white women,
this social mingling of the races was the most distasteful aspect
of reconstruction. But not all Northern soldiers approved, either,
and many who might date Negroes never sanctioned marrying
them. When a private married an ex-slave in South Carolina, his
fellow soldiers tarred and feathered him, and drummed him out
of the regiment; and when a soldier proposed to one in North
Carolina, she rejected him by saying he couldn't "be much" or he
would not have suggested such a thing.[8]

Many white women who had long favored emancipation did
not endorse the freeing of all slaves simultaneously. Ellen Wright
Garrison, whose "hero" was John Brown, was skeptical about
having millions of "the reckless creatures thrown upon society,"
and other Northerners expressed similar feelings, but Southern
women were even more aware of the potential dangers. A Louisianian had been severely criticized when she favored arming
slaves during the war and rewarding them by freeing them ahead
of others. But she was worried that Negroes had been freed "so
suddenly" and predicted trouble, first in the South but eventually
throughout the nation. Eliza Frances Andrews was confident that
the time would come when Negroes would rise, not against either
"Yankee or Southerner" but against the white race everywhere in
the country. She thought that slavery was an evil institution but
explained that the slaveholder had been like the man "who had
the bull by the horns and couldn't turn loose if he wanted to for
fear of being gored." Mrs. Gertrude Thomas approved emancipation and had only the "kindest possible feeling" for all Negroes
until the reconstruction years turned her "against the whole
human race."[9] Southern women were not usually so much concerned about the loss of their investment in slaves as that the

[8] Andrews: *Journal,* pp. 344–45; Huntsville (Va.) *Advocate,* Nov. 19,
1865; "Belle" Thompson to Ellen Thompson Hedrick, Oct. 18, 1865, Benjamin Hedrick Papers.
[9] Ellen Wright to Lucy McKim, July 28, 1862, Garrison Family Papers;
Frances Fearn: *Diary of a Refugee* (New York, 1910), pp. 117, 140; Andrews: *Journal,* pp. 280, 315; Ella Gertrude Clanton Thomas Diary, MS.

naïve, childlike people might be misguided and misused by out-siders and then, when the damage was done, abandoned on Southern doorsteps.

The older Negro women realized that trouble lay ahead. Shortly after the war one cautioned that there would be "awful times among black folks. . . . Some of 'em'll work," she said, "but most of 'em won't without whippin', and them that won't work will steal from them that does, an' nobody won't have nothin." This woman remained with her master until a daughter took her to Philadelphia, but she did not like living in the North and "finally drifted back South, to live with her sons." The older Ne-groes also more often came "home" when they could no longer support themselves; forty years after the war one of Garnett An-drews' daughters was caring for a colony of the family's former slaves who had returned in old age. Cornelia Spencer noted, as did others, that when "in distress or want" the Negro first thought of the "old master or missus," certain that they would help him. Nor did all former slaves wait years to return. An old woman who had belonged to the Chesnuts was soon disillusioned about the great world beyond the plantation and within a few weeks after her departure sent word for them to come for her. When no one went she somehow made her way back, for as Mrs. Chesnut quipped, "after the first natural frenzy of freedom sub-sided, [she] knew on which side her bread was buttered."[1] The former owners could not always support the ex-slaves who came back, but the Negroes knew they would at least be fed before being sent on their way.

Emancipation fomented a domestic revolution in the South as thousands of high-born ladies for the first time wielded brooms and mops, bent over washtubs and hot stoves, and performed other tasks theretofore assigned to slaves. This overturn, begun during the war, was completed in reconstruction when women were demoted from supervisors in the home to manual laborers. In the summer of 1865 the women in Eliza Frances Andrews' family were doing the work previously performed by twenty-five or thirty domestic slaves; and despite her youth, Miss Andrews complained that her "legs ached as if they had been in stocks,"

[1] Andrews: *Journal,* pp. 293–94; *North Carolina Presbyterian,* Aug. 24, 1870; Chesnut: *A Diary,* p. 531.

her bones "felt as if they were ready to drop out," and she was too weary by evening to participate in the social affairs she so enjoyed. Accustomed to sleeping late, she was now out of bed at dawn; and once always groomed to receive callers, she was now so disheveled that she hid when visitors came. "Fanny" Andrews could be thankful that the family's cook had stayed on, for many women had never prepared a meal until they lost their slaves, and she did not have to split wood, milk cows, care for stock, or labor in fields as others did. All these unfamiliar tasks were especially hard on older women, one of whom "fainted dead away" when trying to wash windows, while others took to their beds after scrubbing floors or laundering clothes.[2]

When a group of women were asked in the nineties how the war had most significantly changed their way of life, all said that doing their own work or adjusting to hired Negro domestics was their major postwar problem. Emancipation, said one, had made "mere . . . drudges" out of white women, and another thought it "altogether evil" for this reason. None positively defended slavery, but all emphasized that free servants were more unreliable, disobedient, slovenly, and erratic than slaves, a conclusion reached earlier by Mrs. George Ward who found servants "getting more incorrigible all the time." Those trained in slavery were preferred to those growing up after the war, but by the nineties the older Negro women were rapidly disappearing. Mrs. Ward was not alone in blaming the servant problem on Northerners who tried to reconstruct the South, and she thought all Southern women compelled to endure this "great tribulation" should be assigned a place in the "Celestial City . . . where they could look down on all Yankees." Orra Langhorne and other optimists saw the problems attendant on the domestic revolution as a godsend because they made women more self-reliant. "How much better girls of today are being trained for the realities of life," wrote Mrs. Langhorne in the nineties, but like so many others she regretted that the servant problem had contributed to the disappearance of the famed antebellum Southern hospitality. It was impossible, she said, for a hostess both to prepare and serve a meal and receive guests, for entertaining was still done on a formal scale and there were as yet no "modern" conveniences.

[2] Andrews: *Journal*, pp. 374–78; Grace B. Elmore Diary, MS.

Housewives' problems were further complicated by the huge, rambling, high-ceiling houses they lived in, some of which as yet had the kitchen in a separate building or on another floor. Long after the slaves were freed, white women were compelled to live in homes built for slaves to tend.[3]

Northern women who came South were often more critical of the free Negro than were Southerners. A Bostonian in Charleston decided the "whole race [was] . . . humbug," and she could not understand why "Southern people hug them so closely to their hearts." Laura Comer, Henry Ward Beecher's niece who had married a Georgia planter before the war, would have shocked her abolitionist relatives if they had known what she thought of the free Negro. She was exceptionally generous, kind, and patient with them but found the Negro more ungrateful, irritable, lazy, and "trifling" than he had ever been as a slave. Those for whom she did the most were the least dependable, and because of her postwar labor problems she decided to sell her property and be "released from free Negroes." Frances Butler Leigh, daughter of Frances Ann Kemble, went South to live on her father's plantation after the war and was so distraught because of the Negroes' attitude toward work that she and others in the neighborhood considered trying to find other sources of labor. Her cook drove her to distraction wasting food which was difficult to come by in the postwar years. While Mrs. Comer complained that "freedmen and women will not work unless you are continually with them," Mrs. Leigh found that if she relaxed her guard for a moment they "would get the upper hand."

Among the Negroes' sternest critics were the wives of carpetbaggers, who were usually disillusioned as well as disgusted. From the time that Mrs. John Wesley North joined her husband in Knoxville in 1866 until her departure two years later, she complained that her servants were "stupid," "a trial to the flesh," and so dishonest that she had "to lock up everything." She was shocked by their low morals and fired one who entertained "a male visitor" overnight in her room; and she could not accustom

---

[3] Wilbur Fisk Tillett: "Southern Womanhood as Affected by the War," *Century Illustrated Magazine*, XLIII (1891), 9–16; Wynes: *Southern Sketches from Virginia*, pp. 93, 110, 122; *Report of the Senate Committee on Labor and Capital* (1883), IV, 343–45.

herself to their aches and pains, which invariably gripped them when it rained or company was expected. Having to deal with Southern Negroes "does come hard on Northern women," she said.[4]

Too stunned by the domestic upheaval to search immediately for a solution, women eventually began to offer suggestions. In the late sixties and seventies Cornelia Spencer often mentioned the problem in her weekly newspaper column addressed to "Young Ladies." She suggested that students in girls' schools be given a series of lectures on the management of servants, for this would be of greater importance to future housewives than hearing about "astronomy . . . the nebular hypothesis, [or] the poetry of Wordsworth transcendentally considered." The women of tomorrow must be made to realize, said Mrs. Spencer, that "a great deal of their respectability, influence and happiness . . . will depend on knowing" how to train and retain servants. She knew that the rising generation would not have servants trained in slavery but would have the twofold duty of instructing the individual and helping the race "rise above its previous condition." She also told the young women that their generation must restore harmonious relations.[5]

There were many poor white girls in the South who needed employment, but women were unaccustomed to having them work in the home. Mrs. Spencer reported that her friends who had employed them were not satisfied, primarily because they did not "know how to treat them." When asked why she did not employ white servants, Mrs. Ward declared, "I would not give them room. We would all go distracted if we had them as servants." She and others noted that they were abominable cooks and expected to be treated like members of the family and to work alongside the woman of the house rather than for her. Mrs. Ward saw no future for the poor whites except in industry, and many did find work in the factories which were opened in postwar decades. Negro women less often found employment in

[4] Boston *Traveler*, Jan. 16, 1864; Laura Comer Diaries, Southern Historical Collection, University of North Carolina; Frances Butler Leigh: *Ten Years on a Georgia Plantation* (London, 1883), pp. 87, 89, 128, 139; Ann Loomis North to her parents, May 4, 27, June 10, July 8, 22, 1866, November 4, 1868, John Wesley North Papers.
[5] *North Carolina Presbyterian*, Aug. 24, 31, 1870.

industry although hundreds worked in the tobacco factories, but by the eighties whites were beginning to replace them in the Virginia plants. The two groups did not work side by side in the mills, for integration was not generally popular with either race and was opposed by Southern society.[6]

Other changes in race relations were often more difficult for Southern women to accept than the loss of slaves, but the worst were of relatively brief duration. They especially resented having Negro troops garrisoned in the South, and while not all communities were affected the citizens in some detested even the soldiers who were courteous and well behaved. It was as if salt were being poured in the wound to have them patrolling the streets; and when they were rude, insolent, or obscene the ladies seethed. Some women refused to walk on the streets even in daytime, and others crossed to the other side. When escorted by a man, women feared that the Southerner might construe a Negro soldier's slightest action or movement as an insult and cause a row. Realizing that an incident between a Southern man and Federal soldier, whatever his race, would probably result in trouble for the Southerner, women often refrained from reporting real or imagined discourtesies. The situation was always tense in an area occupied by Negro troops. "Think of it," exclaimed a Georgian, "bringing armed negroes here to threaten and insult us! We were so furious," she continued, "we shook our fists and spit at them from behind the windows . . ." This was childish, she said, but "it relieved our feelings." Negro soldiers committed fewer heinous crimes than Southerners expected, and when their guilt was proved they were usually punished by the military authorities, but Southern women were nevertheless deathly afraid of them. Women resented their effect on Southern Negroes as much as anything.[7]

Southerners had not expected an occupation, and the women were more embittered by the white soldiers' presence during reconstruction than during the war. While the soldiers gained access to many Southern homes, eventually if not at once, anybody

[6] *North Carolina Presbyterian*, Jan. 13, 1869; *Report of the Senate Committee on Labor and Capital* (1883), IV, 345–47; Wynes: *Southern Sketches from Virginia*, pp. 73–74.

[7] Andrews: *Journal*, pp. 261–63; Meriwether: *Recollections*, pp. 172–174.

known to be associating with colored women was not welcome. A lieutenant who had been well entertained in Wilmington, but who was seen entering a Negro school, was thereafter ostracized by local citizens, and a North Carolinian who had seen officers "hugging and kissing" Negro women asked her friend if it wasn't "enough to make a Christian cuss." She wondered how they could expect Southern whites to befriend them, and a Georgian observing similar conduct thought they had no grounds for complaint when "not invited to sit at the tables of southern gentlemen."[8]

A third group of "outsiders" resented by Southerners was composed of teachers, politicians, and agents of the Freedmen's Bureau who fraternized with the Negroes. Southern women seldom protested the Negroes' being educated or converted, nor did they oppose their receiving economic assistance which they were in no position to give. What they did not like, however, was their being taught that the former masters were their enemies and that a Utopia lay ahead for those who did as their Northern friends, and specifically the Republican party, told them to do. Southern women spilled hundreds of thousands of words upon the pages of diaries and letters to express their indignation at the way in which gullible Negroes were being used for selfish ends. "If there had never been any intrusion of false teachers between us and the Negro," wrote Cornelia Spencer, "there would have been but little difficulty."[9]

After the war most Northerners ceased to support freedmen's projects. With the establishment of the Freedmen's Bureau it was assumed that the government would provide for their needs, and those who had contributed to a host of wartime charities contended that as the war was over their obligations had ended with it. Abolitionists who had supported so many of the contraband and freedmen projects now assumed that their battle was won. Woman's rights advocates, many of whom had worked on behalf of the Negro, were infuriated that they had not been given the franchise when it was bestowed on Negro men, and lost

[8] Whitelaw Reid: *After the War, a Southern Tour* (New York, 1866), p. 204; Mary Caldwell to her sister, July 17, 1865, Ted R. Caldwell Papers, Southern Historical Collection, University of North Carolina; Andrews: *Journal*, pp. 267, 288, 291, 323, 344, 378.

[9] *North Carolina Presbyterian*, Aug. 30, 1870.

interest in the former slaves. In 1869 the American Freedman's Union Commission gave as its reason for disbanding that "givers were waxing weary . . . our people no longer care for the matter." After this time economic aid for Negroes came primarily from churches and a few interested individuals. Women were tired of contributing, and many expressed sentiments similar to those of Julia Ward Howe who said that she wanted to hear no more about matters pertaining to "the interests of the Negro race."[1] The depression of 1873 reduced assistance to a trickle, and before the end of reconstruction the Southern whites were left with the problem of rehabilitating both themselves and the Negroes.

Southern women who did not care whether they had the ballot were opposed to granting it indiscriminately to Negro men. In an article on the subject written for Northern newspapers, Eliza Frances Andrews referred to the enfranchisement of Negroes as "the last act of the reconstruction comedy," one that "would be the most laughable ever presented" were it not so tragic. Seated at the polls to observe the proceedings, she saw how difficult it was for the men to identify themselves since many had changed their "entitles" at least once since registration. When she asked one for whom he was voting, he said his "missis" since she was "sure to do what's right." Miss Andrews facetiously remarked that "the radicals made a great mistake" in not conferring the ballot on Negro women, for long after the men "become too wise to be managed with cocks and bulls" the women's vote could be bought with "a red silk parasol and artificial waterfall of fair blonde hair . . . from the most respectable old 'mammy' to the rawest Dinah in the cornfield." "Fanny" Andrews did not oppose qualified Negroes' voting but opposed giving anybody the privilege unless he was literate. Not until the Negro was given the ballot, said a Georgia lady, did the "worst times" come to the South, and in 1870 she wrote, "So long as the negro soldiers guard and the negro men make laws for us, just so long will the feeling of resentment linger in our minds."[2]

[1] *American Freedman*, VIII (1869), 3–5; Julia Ward Howe to Francis Lieber, July 31, 186–, Julia Ward Howe Papers, Manuscript Division, Library of Congress.
[2] Eliza Frances Andrews Scrapbook, Garnett Andrews Papers, Southern Historical Collection, University of North Carolina; Ella Gertrude Clanton Thomas Diary, MS.

Southern white women had a deep-seated fear of the free Negro, and this was often justified. One of the first things that thousands of freedmen did was to arm themselves with guns, razors, or knives, all of which had been denied slaves, and they used them on whites as well as other Negroes. Women who had never been afraid of slaves were terrorized by the freedman. When Frances Butler Leigh first came South she would stay alone on the plantation "without the slightest fear," but by 1868 she "never slept without a loaded pistol" under her pillow. As soon as Negroes started carrying guns Eliza Frances Andrews was "frightened out of her senses," and more women found it necessary to arm themselves after the war than during the conflict. The atrocities committed and the even greater number of rumors circulated unnerved the women, especially those in rural areas. There were instances of rape and assault; and if women tried to protect themselves by brandishing weapons, as did Lucy Vincent of Charleston when a Negro man wanted to "hitch up" with her, they were sometimes arrested. This happened to both Miss Vincent and her mother.[3] Families were known to move into town because the chances of protecting women and girls were better there, and white men organized ostensibly to guard their women although they often went further than giving protection. When the whites moved against Negroes, as in the Memphis and New Orleans riots, Negro women were raped, clubbed, and murdered, and for weeks thereafter the white women feared retaliation.[4]

Some reconstruction policies complicated race relations in such a way as to hurt rather than help the Negro who remained in the South. The typical Southern woman's view was expressed by Cornelia Spencer, who predicted that the civil rights legislation of the seventies would hurt "the poor colored people and . . . shut them out from the kindness . . . sympathy and good will of their white neighbors which they so much need." More surprising, however, was Anna Dickinson's comment in the same period. Miss Dickinson toured the South and was pleased to note the

[3] Leigh: *Ten Years on a Georgia Plantation*, pp. 35, 131; Andrews: *Journal*, p. 315; Myrta Lockett Avary: *Dixie After the War* (New York, 1906), pp. 266–67, 379, 383, 377.
[4] Laura Haviland: *A Woman's Life Work* (Grand Rapids, 1881), pp. 436–37; Meriwether: *Recollections*, pp. 178–182.

progress made by the Negro in many areas, but she was convinced that the carpetbag governments and civil rights legislation harmed rather than helped the freedmen. Many Northerners who came South with the best of intentions were surprised to find how impractical their ideas often were, for as Kate Cumming wrote in the nineties, "This love of the 'colored brother' is so *beautiful* in theory, but how few theorists could stand the practice." She knew Northerners in Birmingham who refused to pass through colored neighborhoods and insisted on doing their own laundry rather than have their "clothes come in contact with darkies." She wondered why more Negroes had not been invited to colonize in the North, but in 1869 a New Yorker had suggested just that and found that women who had been active in the antebellum underground railroad would have no part in the scheme.[5]

Negro women won freedom in the Civil War, but as one authority has noted, "remained for a long time second class citizens" everywhere in the nation. Although some persons did take advantage of the educational and economic opportunities opened after the war, it was never easy for a Negro woman to get ahead. One of the most remarkable of Southern-born women was Ida Wells, a daughter of slave parents, who attended a freedman's school in Mississippi, taught in that state, and in the eighties went to Memphis to teach and to edit the Memphis *Free Speech*, a journal devoted to the elevation of her race. When she dared criticize the city's colored schools, her contract was not renewed; and when she spoke out against lynching, her newspaper equipment was smashed and she was told never to return to Memphis. Because she fought for the Negro she made many enemies both North and South, especially after describing conditions to English audiences. In 1895 she married the Chicago editor and attorney Ferdinand Lee Barnett and lived in that city until her death in 1931.[6]

[5] *North Carolina Presbyterian*, Feb. 26, 1875; James Harvey Young: "A Woman Abolitionist in the South in 1875," *Georgia Historical Quarterly*, XXXII (1948), 240–41, 249; Kate Cumming: *Gleanings From the Southland* (Birmingham, Ala., 1895), pp. 11–12; Martha Wright to William Lloyd Garrison II, Jan. 10, 1869, Garrison Family Papers.

[6] Eleanor Flexner: *Century of Struggle* (Cambridge, Mass., 1959), pp. 186, 188–89; "Ida B. Wells-Barnett," typescript, Smith College Archives.

In the late seventies Frances Watkins Harper was enthusiastic but too optimistic about the progress of Negro women. She was correct in saying that many mothers who were ex-slaves were sacrificing to educate their children, and that women were generally the family's financial "mainstay." She found them everywhere "more industrious than the men" and pointed with pride to their accomplishments in all parts of the country; but perhaps she was hopeful because she viewed the recently emancipated slave against the backdrop of the antebellum period which she could vividly recall. Twenty years later Fannie Barrier Williams, founder of the first school for Negro nurses, spoke before an international gathering at the World Columbian Exposition. While stressing the attainments of Negro women, she had nothing but harsh criticism for the discrimination they were encountering throughout the nation. She charged white women with being primarily responsible and especially those fighting for woman suffrage, some of whom were the abolitionists of old. She reminded these women that whites and Negroes were working toward the same goals, more likely attainable if the two races worked together. "Everywhere the public mind has been filled with constant alarm lest in some way our women shall approach the social sphere of the dominant race in this country," she said. Mrs. Williams had found that whites who were "perfectly sane in all things else become instantly unwise and foolish at the remotest suggestion of social contact with colored men and women."[7]

It is significant that Mrs. Williams was describing conditions across the country, not in any one region. When she spoke in 1893, Northern women were moving "full steam ahead" with innumerable crusades and had for twenty-five years been forming women's clubs throughout the nation; but with few exceptions Negro women were either banned from these organizations or segregated in auxiliaries. The reason for this discrimination could not have been the presence of Southern women, for apart from the temperance movement they themselves were just beginning

[7] Frances Ellen Watkins Harper: "Coloured Women in America," *Englishwoman's Review*, Jan. 15, 1878, pp. 10–15; Fannie Barrier Williams: *Present Status and Intellectual Progress of Coloured Women* (Chicago, 1893), pp. 3–15.

to participate in appreciable numbers. Except in the educational field, Negro women of the nineties had few opportunities in the North which had not been available to them in the sixties. The Southern Negro had gained relatively more from the Civil War than had her Northern counterpart. All Negro women had their freedom but none had complete equality.

14

Uprooted and Floating

As a result of the war and its aftermath hundreds of thousands of Americans found new homes or places of refuge. More than 250,000 Southern residents were displaced during the conflict, and at least half this number moved several times in an effort to stay within Confederate lines, while others fled into Northern or Western states and territories or to foreign countries. Most refugees were trying to escape the enemy, lawless marauders, or foragers, but both armies contributed appreciably to their ranks by driving out thousands suspected of subversion. Relatively few outsiders moved into the Confederacy and most of these were from the border areas, but Northerners interested in commercial ventures established themselves in Federal-held cities throughout the conflict. The wartime migration to the frontier was primarily a continuation of the nation's westward movement, now stimulated more by the Homestead Act than by the sectional struggle; however, postwar conditions pushed people in all directions. For a quarter-century after secession thousands of women felt as did Mrs. Jefferson Davis—that they were "uprooted and floating."[1]

[1] Eron Rowland: *Varina Howell, Wife of Jefferson Davis* (New York, 1931), II, 488.

Frequent mention has been made in this book of displaced women who tried to remain within Confederate lines, and of the problems they created for themselves and others by wandering from place to place and insisting on living in congested cities and along transportation lines. As the war continued their problems increased rather than diminished. When it was over some were miles from their prewar homes, many of which had been confiscated as abandoned property, or looted and destroyed, or left to fall into disrepair in the owners' absence. These things might have happened if the women had stayed home, yet the chance of protecting their property was better when they were there. The Confederate refugees represented all social strata, but a disproportionate percentage of the upper and middle classes uprooted themselves and stayed away for the duration of the war. These were the ones who could finance their flight and relocate themselves in safer areas, and they were also more likely to have widely scattered friends to whom they might appeal. But the affluent risked losing more valuable property and personal possessions than did the poorer folk.[2]

Most women who went North immediately following the outbreak of war were natives of the region, and many were educators and their wives, or relatives of businessmen who had financial interests in the North as well as the South. Frederick Augustus Porter Barnard, the eminent educator and president of the University of Mississippi, wrote a friend that he had hoped to remain in the Confederacy and offer his services to the government but Mrs. Barnard was "dying by inches" in the South and he felt he should take her North.[3] Two years later, in 1864, Barnard became president of Columbia University, a position he held until his death in 1889. Of significance to postwar generations of women was Barnard's battle to get them admitted to Columbia on an equal basis with men; six months after his death Barnard College of Columbia University opened its doors.

Although Southern Unionists went North throughout the

[2] Mary Elizabeth Massey: *Refugee Life in the Confederacy* (Baton Rouge, 1964), *passim.*
[3] F. A. P. Barnard to Burton Harrison, Feb. 7, 1862, Burton Harrison Papers.

war, their numbers increasing greatly during its last two years, not all of the poor who joined the hegira had strong political convictions. Many were hard-working farm folk who would have stayed where they were had wartime conditions not uprooted them. The majority were women and children whose men had left them to go to war or had fled from conscription. Living in remote areas without male protection and confronted with enemy soldiers, hostile neighbors, and ruffians, thousands not surprisingly fled into Union areas in search of safety, food, shelter, and employment. Most were penniless and entirely dependent on strangers for necessities. By 1863 a steady stream of these people were moving northward out of Texas, Arkansas, and southern Missouri. Several trains of frontier folk passed through Fort Smith, Arkansas, every week during the summer of 1864, headed for St. Louis, Kansas, and other Midwestern points. On August 13 the Fort Smith *New Era* reported "the largest train yet," composed entirely of Arkansans who had abandoned their homes and were on their way "to a strange land . . . to begin life over again." None had any intention of returning to the state.

The following day the same paper reported a band of Texans, mostly women and children, who came walking into town, their personal possessions, wagons, and stock having been stolen thirty miles out of Fort Smith. On the same day still another train passed en route to "Kansas and the States of the North West." All of these emigrants were leaving because of wartime conditions.

In the fall of 1864 a St. Louis reporter was surprised to find scores of wagons "overloaded with women and children" crossing the river into Illinois, for other wagons were "going West with hopeful emigrants" and he saw no hope in the faces of these refugees. He surmised that because of the war Missouri had lost a "quarter of its population . . . since 1860," and the unsettled conditions provoked more to leave the state than had formerly come. Women and children arrived in St. Louis on foot, by wagons, and on boats, many transported at least a part of the way at government expense. Pitiful tales were told of the old, sick, and blind who walked a hundred miles or more before reaching a Federal camp. A blind mother was led by her two children for more than 125 miles through the Ozarks to Rolla, where they were given transportation to St. Louis. Upon their arrival in that city the youngsters were cared for in the refugee home while the woman was sent to a hospital for an operation to remove the cataracts causing her blindness. Many of the indigent arriving in Federal lines had no idea where their husbands were.[4]

So many "shelterless and penniless" Southern refugees landed "at all hours of the day and night" in Cairo, Illinois, that the Relief Association was sorely tried to accommodate all. By the spring of 1864 it was estimated that an average of 2,000 a month were arriving, "nine-tenths" women and children "of tender years." They gave as reasons for leaving home that their husbands had been conscripted, their crops destroyed, farms laid waste, stock taken, and houses sacked or burned. When an Eastern journalist heard of their plight he editorialized on the "white refugees," suggesting that Congress turn its attention to them and "give them as well as the black brethren a helping hand."[5]

Eastern cities had their share of refugees, and in February 1864 it was estimated that 25,000 Southerners were living in and near New York City. The *Commercial* noted that they could be divided into three groups, "the secessionists, the no-siders and the Unionists." The writer went on to say that the secessionists were the most affluent and came North to live "more cheaply and better" while at the same time securing their Northern property from confiscation, but he noted that this group was "in the minority of Southern visitors." The majority were Unionists who came from impoverished families in Virginia and the border states. Most were women who had to support themselves and their families by "doing fancy work for the stores, operating boardinghouses," or working at odd jobs outside the home. Some who had come from comfortable homes, he said, were living in garrets and cellars unfit for human habitation. The "no-siders," of whom there were many, included a large number of border state women and Northern-born wives of "deceased planters" whom

[4] New York *Herald*, Nov. 4, 1864, quoting the St. Louis *Post*, n.d.; W. R. Hodges: *The Western Sanitary Commission* (n.p., 1906), p. 11; St. Louis *Democrat*, Mar. 11, 1862.
[5] New York *Herald*, Mar. 12, 1864.

the journalist said were better off than most since they did not seem to care which side won the war. City officials were so concerned about the number of Southerners in New York, especially after sabotage and subversive activities were traced to some of them, that in the fall of 1864 General Dix ordered all to register; but few women bothered to comply.

The arrival of thousands of impoverished Southerners in the last year of the war puzzled authorities who did not know what to do with them, and many had to be housed in buildings on the Battery. But New York was not alone in this problem, for the poor-white refugees coming into other Northern cities increased noticeably late in the war, and by 1864 it was estimated that at least 80,000 had arrived in the environs of Washington.[6]

The Southern press condemned Southerners who left the Confederacy to sit out the war in safer places. After reading about those in New York in the fall of 1864, a Richmond editor blasted the "skulkers" who were passing "the time pleasantly" in the North and Europe while their friends were suffering in the Confederacy. He felt that they should be identified since "*it might be useful for future reference.*" When the war was over, many women who had suffered did resent those who had run away. In 1866 Gertrude Thomas thought a certain woman "pleasant, agreeable and smart" until she learned that she "had been North all . . . during the war"; then she wished to have no more to do with her.[7]

A few Southern women, most of them wives and daughters of Confederate officials or businessmen, found refuge in Europe. Those who were abroad when the war started usually chose to remain, as did Kate Cumming's mother and sisters who landed in England on the very day Fort Sumter was shelled. But refugees left the Confederacy throughout the war. In the summer of 1863 a Richmond official mentioned that a great many women were applying for passports to go abroad. The following fall James Ryder Randall was surprised to find a Wilmington boarding-house filled with New Orleans exiles awaiting passage on a

[6] Petersburg (Va.) *Express*, Feb. 13, 1864, quoting the New York *Commercial* n.d.; New York *Herald*, Oct. 9, Nov. 27, 29, 30, Dec. 2, 1864; Washington *Chronicle*, Feb. 10, 13, 1865.

[7] Richmond *Examiner*, Dec. 4, 1865; Ella Gertrude Clanton Thomas Diary, MS.

blockade runner which would take them to Nassau or Havana, where they could board a ship bound for Europe. Refugees left from other Southern ports, and a great many west of the Mississippi crossed Texas and sailed from Matamoras. A Louisiana woman who took this escape route was urged to stay in Texas but was determined to accompany her husband. "These are heroic times," she exclaimed, "and they call for heroic action on the part of women as well as men." This Louisianian's journey took her first to Havana, where she felt completely at home amid the displaced Confederates and where her daughter met the man she would later marry. The family sailed to France, where they joined the Confederate colony in Paris, and like refugees everywhere they were "drawn . . . together" and tended to be exclusive. A Charlestonian in Tours reported that the Southern expatriates "grow everyday more and more like one family," and when several in the group decided to move to Barcelona she chose to remain in France because she wanted to be near South Carolina friends in Paris.[8]

As mentioned earlier, Belle Boyd married, gave birth to a daughter, and was widowed while living in England. Her wedding in 1864 attracted attention on both continents and was one of the most widely publicized in London. The marriage in Paris of John Slidell's daughter to Emile Erlanger of the banking family was a brilliant social event attended by more than 200 of the cream of society. A reporter noted that the gathering was composed of "beautiful . . . but rebellious daughters of the sunny South . . . English sympathizers . . . Northern secessionists . . . French aristocracy, and those of the same religious persuasion with the bridegroom"—namely, Erlanger's Jewish friends. Other Southern girls married in Paris and one especially incensed Mrs. Slidell by being married in the United States Legation. The Confederacy had no legation since France did not recognize the government.[9]

[8] Josiah Gorgas Journal (microfilm), Southern Historical Collection, University of North Carolina; James Ryder Randall to Kate S. Hammond, Oct. 6, 1863, Randall Letters, Southern Historical Collection, University of North Carolina; Frances Fearn: *Diary of a Refugee* (New York, 1910), pp. 48–49, 88–89, 102–5, 126–28; Charlotte Holmes (ed.): *The Burckmyer Letters* (Columbia, S.C., 1926), pp. 105, 208, 228–229.

[9] New York *Herald*, June 11, 1862, Sept. 26, Oct. 4, 18, 1864.

The last year of the war found several hundred Confederate refugees in Canada, most of them women. Scores of Kentuckians, primarily wives of Confederate officers, fled to Toronto after rumors circulated that they were to be sent out of Kentucky into Confederate lines. In this group was Issa Breckinridge, who wanted to be with her husband but who did not care to be taken down the Mississippi on a Federal transport and "dumped" miles from his camp. She was miserable in Toronto, pining for her husband and the daughter she had left with her parents. Mrs. Breckinridge's only social contacts were with other Confederates, primarily Kentuckians, and she was aloof and rude toward the local ladies. She told those who called on her that she had not come to Toronto to visit, and wrote her mother, "I don't want any *new friends*." Six months later she had returned none of the calls and said she had no intention of doing so.[1] This attitude, typical of many refugees without and within the Confederacy, ultimately hurt them, for very few did not sooner or later need the assistance of local people.

Women entered Confederate lines throughout the war, but those arriving after the first year were usually trying to reach relatives or had been banished by Federal authorities, for the beleaguered Confederacy had little to offer them by way of economic opportunity. Because women going South usually had their baggage limited and searched for contraband, few could take more than the bare essentials but most tried to get through with more. When 450 women and children were transported by boat from Washington to Virginia in January 1863, it took eight inspectors several days to check their luggage and some women were found to be carrying enough clothing "to stock a country store." They had been told they might have two pairs of shoes per person, but some had as many as twenty-five in their trunks. The surplus was confiscated and when these and other refugees arrived "in the realms of Secessia" they had few possessions and little chance of obtaining replacements.[2]

Many more Northern women moved West than South dur-

<hr />

[1] Issa Breckinridge to William C. P. Breckinridge, July 15, 1864, Jan. 31, 1865; Issa Breckinridge to Mary C. Desha, July 15, 17, 19, 20, 29, 1864, Breckinridge Family Papers.

[2] *Harper's Weekly*, Jan. 24, 1863; New York *Herald*, Jan. 8, 1863.

ing the war, but the most interesting expeditions were those sponsored by Asa Mercer in 1864 and 1866. Both were prompted by wartime conditions in the Northeast, the first being planned to attract unemployed cotton textile workers to the Pacific Northwest as teachers and the second to bring Eastern women, especially war widows, to Washington Territory to marry settlers or do a "woman's work." For years journalists and various state officials had called attention to the growing surplus of women in the Northeastern states and the preponderance of men on the frontier, and by 1864 Governor John Andrew of Massachusetts was trying to persuade some of the state's 40,000 surplus females to go West. There they would have a better chance of marrying and would no longer have "to compete for employment fitted for men alone," as they were doing in the East.

Several influential newspapers supported Andrew and one tactlessly suggested that the women should "go where they were needed." When Mercer arrived in Lowell, Massachusetts, in early 1864, he found that much of the propagandizing had been done for him and within a few weeks eleven ladies "ranging in age from fifteen to twenty-five" had agreed to accompany him to the West Coast. They traveled to Puget Sound via Panama and San Francisco, and within a few weeks after their arrival seven were teaching school. One of these died the first summer, another preferred to be an assistant lighthouse keeper at Admiralty Head, and Antoinette Baker was so well qualified that she was appointed to the faculty of the Territorial University. All but three of the eleven were known to have married, and another may have married after moving to California. The remainder spent the rest of their lives in Washington, Oregon, or British Columbia.[3]

This first colonizing venture proved so successful that Mercer decided to return East to recruit 700 women to come West, promising to bring wives "of good character" to all men who would pay $300. This ambitious scheme was poorly planned, inadequately financed, and as it turned out, unfortunately timed, for the war had ended by the time Mercer arrived in New York. Landing on the very day Lincoln was assassinated, he was

[3] Washington *Chronicle*, July 25, 1864; Boston *Advertiser*, July 22, 1864; Flora A. P. Engle: "The Story of the Mercer Expedition," *The Washington Historical Quarterly*, VI (1915), 225–28, 235.

caught up in the confusion and confronted with unexpected problems, not the least of which was getting a ship in which to transport his recruits. During the spring and summer he spoke in more than a hundred Northeastern towns and was reported to have enrolled approximately 400 women by September; but when the departure date had to be repeatedly postponed, more than three-fourths of his passengers canceled their reservations. Some would probably have withdrawn in any event, but newspapers stirred doubts by satirizing and condemning the scheme as dishonest and immoral. And by late summer the cotton mills were reopening, men were returning from the service, and many women and girls erroneously assumed that the end of the war would bring an end to their problems. The New York *Times,* one of Mercer's staunchest supporters, tried to confute the critics by stressing that the women were promised employment at higher wages than they were receiving in the East, and that it was not simply "a matrimonial venture" as implied by some. To support its stand the paper cited the glowing reports of those who had gone West in 1864.[4]

When the *Continental,* a wartime troop transport, sailed from New York on January 16, 1866, there were one hundred passengers aboard, forty-seven of them "unattached females," and the *Times* was sending along its correspondent Roger "Rod" Conant. After a hard three-month trip the ship docked in San Francisco, where thirty-six passengers decided to remain, including two widows and eleven single women. Of the thirty-four "Mercer girls" going to Washington, all but three were known to have married eventually and four wed men they had met on shipboard; among them Annie Stevens who married Mercer, and Mary Martin "in her forties" who married a member of the crew, aged twenty-five. Those who wanted jobs soon found them, most teaching in the territorial schools and two conducting private classes. Libbie Peebles taught for three years before being appointed the first woman clerk in the territorial legislature, a position secured with the aid of a fellow passenger on the *Continental,* and her sister Annie Peebles served for several years as deputy collector of internal revenue; but both girls had married

---

[4] New York *Times,* Sept. 30, Oct. 24, Nov. 6, 1865; Linna A. Deutsch (ed.): *Mercer's Belles: The Journal of a Reporter* (Seattle, 1960), *passim.*

within five years after their arrival. The "Mercer girls" married men from all walks of life—farmers, merchants, craftsmen, saloon keepers, and professional men. Conant reported that one of the Lowell operatives married a man "worth $100,000"; and a widow from Lowell, not finding what she wanted in Washington, went to California and lectured on spiritualism before marrying a man eight years her junior. "She was the lady," said Conant, "who was going to marry an old man with one foot in the grave and the other just ready to go in." Age was no obstacle to matrimony; a seventy-year-old widow, who had accompanied her widowed daughter West, married a Seattle hotel porter after seeing her daughter wed.[5]

The "Mercer girls" were subjected to journalistic insults and insinuations, and some newsmen went so far as to imply they were prostitutes. Anna Dickinson suggested they might as well have gone West with placards reading, "We are for sale and come for some man to buy us," and she saw no difference between them and the one who "sells herself upon the street for bread."[6] But whether the women "married for better or worse," they remained on the West Coast, and most if not all became respected citizens and contributed to the development of their communities. It is obvious that the aspersions cast at the time were soon forgotten on the frontier.

The Western movement in the postwar years was stimulated by the migration of veterans and their families, many of whom returned to Northern cities crippled, unable to find jobs, and so impoverished that their wives and children had to live in charitable institutions. This was the situation in Chicago when Mrs. Mary Bickerdyke returned in the spring of 1866, and while working in the Home for the Friendless for a year she came in contact with the families of poverty-stricken, embittered veterans. As in other cities, they were being encouraged to go West and claim homesteads, but they lacked the necessary funds to transport their families West and start farming. When Mrs. Bickerdyke realized that many of her "boys" wanted to go to Kansas, she went out and surveyed the area, returned to Chicago, borrowed

[5] Deutsch: *Mercer's Belles*, pp. 3–25, 136–57; Engle: "The Story of the Mercer Expedition," pp. 231–37.
[6] Troy Daily *Whig*, Dec. 5, 1865.

$10,000, and arranged with Colonel Charles Hammond, president of the Chicago, Burlington, and Quincy Railroad, to transport free of charge fifty veterans' families to Salina, Kansas.

Arriving in Kansas, the settlers had no trouble getting homesteads around Salina but they were not farmers and had no money with which to buy stock and equipment; their more experienced leader decided to capitalize on her wartime friendship with General William T. Sherman, now commandant of Fort Riley. She persuaded him to condemn a sufficient number of army wagons and horses to get her homesteaders started and asked him to write a letter of recommendation to railroad officials whom she wanted to build a hotel in Salina and appoint her manager. The Salina Dining Hall was soon open for business, but as might be expected, was better known as the Bickerdyke House. While intended to be a business venture it was more of a charitable institution for the 250 veterans and their families settling near Salina over the next two years, for "Mother" Bickerdyke could never bring herself to charge the "boys" room and board.

In 1869 the Arapaho Indians raided the area around Salina, killing forty settlers and leaving thousands homeless. This disaster sent Mrs. Bickerdyke to Washington, where she was given army blankets and requisitions for food to tide the stricken families over until the new crop. She also persuaded the Kansas legislature to appropriate money for seed and other essentials. In her travels and relief work she had used hotel profits which the owners thought should be applied to the mortgage, and she was fired. The irate lady left immediately for Washington, where she became "a one-woman counter-lobby" and helped to defeat the railroad appropriation bill then pending.[7]

The bill's defeat did not restore her job; and when colleagues urged her to go to New York to work with indigent tenement dwellers, she agreed to do so. For four years she was in the employ of the Protestant Board of City Missions; but she could not be said to have been under its jurisdiction, for she used her own methods. During these years her thoughts were in Kansas,

[7] Nina Brown Baker: *Cyclone in Calico: The Story of Mary Ann Bickerdyke* (Boston, 1952), pp. 220–28. See also Julia A. Chase: *Mary A. Bickerdyke, Mother* (Lawrence, Kan., 1896), pp. 88–113.

and when her sons asked her to join them on their Great Bend farm she was happy to accept. No sooner had she arrived than the grasshopper plague ruined hundreds of prospering farmers, and she scampered to Illinois on a foraging expedition reminiscent of those she had conducted during the war. She called on farmers to contribute food and then moved into Midwestern cities to urge that the disbanded aid societies reconvene to make clothing for the Kansans, most of whom, she reminded the people, had come from Illinois and neighboring states. She also appealed to Sanitary Commission colleagues, and from Mary Safford (now a physician) in Boston to Mrs. Eliza Porter in Texas, they responded. In 1874–75, Mrs. Bickerdyke made ten trips East to get aid for Kansas, and as a result of her efforts more than 250 carloads of food, fodder, and clothing arrived in the state. The legislature passed a resolution of appreciation and commanded that a portrait of Mrs. Bickerdyke be placed in the state capitol. All of this activity contributed to a physical breakdown, and her sons sent her to California for a rest.[8]

As soon as she arrived in San Francisco she communicated with her "boys" and learned that many of the crippled, sick, and impoverished were entitled to pensions but uncertain how to get them. They had to satisfy the government that they had served at least ninety days, been honorably discharged, and were permanently incapacitated in the line of duty. They must state exactly when and where they had incurred the disability and submit proof of their claims. Because most had migrated hundreds of miles and lost touch with their friends this was difficult. Mrs. Bickerdyke became their pension agent, went to Washington, and sought out influential politicians whom she had known in war, including Senator John A. Logan, now her devoted friend. Mrs. Bickerdyke searched through endless records, questioned both Union and Confederate veterans to obtain necessary information, traveled thousands of miles, and as usual met with amazing success. She continued with this work even after Logan got her a job in the San Francisco Mint. While in California she also worked with various reform groups, took a personal interest in trying to rehabilitate alcoholic veterans, and was active in the Woman's Relief Corps, the auxiliary of the Grand Army of the

[8] Baker: *Cyclone in Calico*, pp. 233–35.

Republic. In the eighties she returned to her son's home in Bunker Hill, Kansas, and in 1886 Congress finally got around to giving her a $300-a-year pension, one-half that asked by Senator Logan. Among her latter-day accomplishments was the Bickerdyke Home near Ellsworth, Kansas, founded for war nurses, veterans, their widows and orphans, and kept in continuous operation until 1951.[9]

Mother Bickerdyke was not only an extreme example of one on whom the war had a lifelong impact, but her activities reflect many problems of frontier women. One pioneer who went from Illinois to Kansas shortly after the war wrote Mrs. Logan in the eighties to describe the family's hardships. Her husband had fought with Logan, and for that reason she felt she could ask for assistance. He had been crippled while in service; then hard work, crop failures, and discouragement made him "a complete wreck in mind and body," so that for twelve years she had been the family's "sole support." Four children were then at home, and none could go to school because they lacked adequate clothing. She asked Mrs. Logan to send old clothes which could be made into garments for the youngsters. Admitting that she might be able to get help "nearer home," she confessed that "my pride is not all gone yet although I have tried to subdue it."[1]

Kansas, a stormy sectional battlefield in the fifties, received emigrants from all parts of the country during and after the war, among them approximately 50,000 Negroes who left the South in the late seventies and early eighties. They brought tales of brutality, intimidation, and discrimination and arrived impoverished and untrained for any work except farming, manual labor, and domestic service. The Freedmen's Aid Society, headed by Elizabeth Comstock with Laura Haviland as her assistant, aided the Negroes until it went out of existence in March 1881. Miss Comstock collected more than $90,000 in money and supplies. Of this amount $13,000 worth, mostly clothing, was contributed by friends in England; but despite this aid, the Negro settlers endured terrible hardships during the winters. Mrs. Haviland re-

[9] Mary Bickerdyke to L. Hopkins Emery, Dec. 14, 23, 1897, John Page Nicholson Collection, Henry E. Huntington Library. This letter is attached to the copy of Chase: *Mary A. Bickerdyke, Mother* in the collection.
[1] Baker: *Cyclone in Calico*, pp. 253–54; Mary Metcalfe to Mrs. John A. Logan, Oct. 23, 1866, Mrs. John A. Logan Papers.

ported that in one winter in the Topeka area more than a hundred suffered frozen hands or feet for lack of heat, bedding, and clothing. When she returned in 1886, after a five-year absence, she found a great improvement, most of the Negroes "doing as well as any class of people who go into a new country with little or nothing but their hands to do with."[2]

Northern women who came South during reconstruction were seldom prepared for the cold reception they received from the local ladies. Even the wives of Federal officers, other government officials, and carpetbaggers, who would never have been there but for the war, presumed that since the conflict was over it would be immediately forgotten. This was naïve, for the Southern women had lived in the midst of the struggle, suffered much, and become embittered by defeat, impoverishment, and the overturn of the social system. Some Northern women were arrogant and vindictive; but others, like Ellen McGowan Biddle, a colonel's wife, tried to be courteous and forgiving of slights, because as she said, "the victor" could afford to be generous "to the vanquished." Mrs. Biddle joined her husband in Macon, Georgia, and accompanied him on assignments to New Orleans, Natchez, and Brenham, Texas. Only in Brenham did she report making "no friends or acquaintances . . . for everyone stood aloof from the Yankees." In Natchez the residents were at first cool, but after her husband sided with a local judge against the carpetbaggers the ladies were more polite and friendly. Mrs. Biddle was not as critical of Southerners as some newcomers were, but when she first arrived she was surprised to see them avoid her, turn up their noses, nudge each other, and smile derisively.[3]

Southern women looked on army wives as temporary residents, although they remained longer than the natives expected, but the families of carpetbaggers gave every indication of coming to stay and were therefore even more resented. Mrs. John Wesley North was in many ways typical of the better educated group, and by the time she arrived in Knoxville in 1866 she should have been accustomed to settling among strangers. Born in New York,

[2] Laura Haviland: *A Woman's Life Work* (Grand Rapids, 1881), pp. 482–520, 529.
[3] Ellen McGowan Biddle: *Reminiscences of a Soldier's Wife* (Philadelphia, 1907), pp. 18, 25, 32, 36, 65–69.

she was living in Minnesota in 1861 when Lincoln appointed her husband Surveyor-General of the Nevada Territory. She disliked living on the mining frontier, where she found the schools unsatisfactory, the women uncouth, the people so irreligious that they conducted business on the Sabbath, and servants scarce.

North soon resigned his appointment to enter territorial politics and made a small fortune from mining enterprises, but his wife was still not acclimated to Nevada. Then the couple chanced to read "Edmund Kirke's" (James Robert Gilmore) *Down in Tennessee and Back By the Way of Richmond* (1864) and became interested in the Tennessee Unionists whom he described and the natural resources needing development in East Tennessee. This seemed like a good place to make an investment and at the same time live among people sympathetic to the Union. North went to Knoxville and invested in a foundry; his family joined him in 1866.

Mrs. North was a person with strong convictions, especially on the race question. She had been an abolitionist and upon arriving in Knoxville let it be known by word and deed that she favored the education of Negroes and intended to associate with them and their teachers. Her husband shared her views and both were surprised to discover that even those Tennesseans who had remained loyal to the Union during the war were violently opposed to "uplifting" the freed Negro. Mrs. North was critical of the residents and whether or not she spoke out as frankly as she wrote is uncertain, but she made no attempt to adjust to the mores of the community. Through either necessity or choice, or perhaps both, the carpetbaggers were as clannish as the Confederate refugees; thus the Norths associated only with other newcomers who shared their views and with a few local German families. When some of the local women finally got around to calling on Mrs. North she received them without enthusiasm and made no attempt to return their calls. Soon after her arrival, North was attacked by a group of men when he went to the assistance of a Negro being mistreated by "a burly one-armed rebel."[4]

The Norths' fourteen-year-old daughter Emma delighted in

[4] Ann Loomis North to George and Mary Loomis, July 8, Aug. 26, 1866, John Wesley North Papers.

shocking her school chums, especially "Parson" Brownlow's daughter. This young lady was "greatly horrified" to learn that Emma had gone to school with "three colored girls and sat with one." This she thought was "worse than calling on white teachers in a colored school," which the Norths were also known to do. Emma was disappointed to find that all of Governor Brownlow's "women folks were 'Johnsonites' . . ." for she had "expected to find them Radicals" like herself, and she never missed a chance to tell her friends that she was proud to be a "Radical, an Abolitionist, and a Yankee." She had been in the South only a few months when her parents sent her North to school, but during her Knoxville sojourn she could scarcely be called a good-will ambassador.[5] Like other carpetbaggers who failed to understand conditions in the South, North was baffled by many unexpected developments, including the boycotting of his foundry, labor problems, and the resentment of local citizens who ransacked his home and intimidated his family. When he was forced to sell the foundry at a loss and was unable to satisfy his creditors, things looked dark indeed, but the family was soon on its way to California where North helped to establish the community of Riverside.

Not all Southern women condoned the use of violence in handling the recently arrived Northerners, and many who detested them as they never had before the war ignored but did not insult them. There were those who were ladies still, despite the roughening effects of the war and its aftermath. In 1865, Gertrude Thomas proclaimed, *"Today* I am more *opposed to the North* than at any period of the war," and four years later she could not bring herself to "welcome" Northern people, but when two appeared in church she thought the minister "inhospitable and rude" to condemn the "Yankee nation" in their presence. Northern women were often hurt by even Mrs. Thomas's brand of cool indifference, and Harriet Beecher Stowe was unprepared for the lack of cordiality she found when she took up residence in Florida. She was not ostracized so much because she was interested in educating the Negro, for she went South, she said, to rescue

[5] Emma Bacon North to George and Mary Loomis, Sept. 9, 23, Oct. 7, 1866; Emma Bacon North to Ann Loomis North, Jan. 13, 1867, John Wesley North Papers; Merlin Stonehouse: *John Wesley North and the Reform Frontier* (Minneapolis, 1965), pp. 178–210.

him from the "corrupt" radical politicians; her cold reception must be attributed primarily to her *Uncle Tom's Cabin*.[6]

Conditions growing out of the war were responsible for the movements of Southern people years after it ended. Defeat sent many leaders into self-imposed exile which for most ended after a year or so, while the end of the struggle set wartime refugees toward home or another place of residence. The economic, political, and social upheaval in the South caused thousands of former Confederates to migrate to other areas, but their movements followed no set pattern and they went in all directions. Those wanting to start over in the South flocked to Texas or Arkansas, but many who could finance the trip went farther West. As in the North, there was a marked shift of population from rural to urban areas and especially to communities offering industrial and business opportunities. Southerners who had lived on the same farm or plantation for many years pulled up stakes and moved elsewhere in the discouraging postwar period, and single women and widows who doubtless would have lived out their years in the family home, like those of past generations, were compelled to go where they could find jobs.

Eliza Frances Andrews' description of the Confederate leaders' flight through her town of Washington, Georgia, is indeed a classic. They began to arrive in April, most without their families; and while her mother worried about lodging the visitors and making a diet of field peas appetizing, "Fanny" watched the parade of dignitaries whose "necks were in danger." General Arnold Elzey, her favorite, joined his wife in the village but his brother-in-law's wife and six daughters were in Norfolk. General and Mrs. Brickett Fry, General and Mrs. John B. Gordon, Louis Wigfall, and cabinet members Reagan, Mallory, and Breckinridge were among the notables passing through the village. Robert Toombs, whose home was there, dashed in and out, leaving Mrs. Toombs to face the Federals, who threatened to burn her home but decided instead to confiscate it and evict the mistress. Mrs. Jefferson Davis, escorted by Burton Harrison, arrived in late April. "The poor woman is in a deplorable condition," said Miss Andrews; "no home, no money, and her husband a fugitive."

[6] Ella Gertrude Clanton Thomas Diary, MS; Annie Fields (ed.): *Life and Letters of Harriet Beecher Stowe* (Boston, 1898), pp. 302–33.

She rode out of town on May 2 and the following day the citizenry "was thrown into the wildest excitement" by her husband's arrival, but he remained less than twenty-four hours and hastened away to be captured a week later. As "Fanny" Andrews heard "the men all talking about going to Mexico and Brazil," she concluded that "if all emigrate who say they are going to, we shall have a nation made up of women, negroes and Yankees."[7]

Miss Andrews' implication that the women would be left behind, at least temporarily, proved correct in most cases, for their husbands were usually in too big a hurry to be delayed by their wives, and many who went to Latin America preferred to get settled before sending for their families. In the Confederate colonies in Mexico few wives appeared, though probably more would have come had their husbands remained longer. Mrs. Joseph Shelby joined her husband in the fall of 1865, their first meeting since 1861, and settled down to housekeeping in the home of the exiled Santa Anna. Their sojourn was brief, however, and the fall of 1867 found them back on the Missouri farm. Mrs. Sterling Price arrived in the Carlota colony in mid-1866, having traveled on a ship with several other ladies who were joining husbands and sweethearts. After living several months in an adobe hut built by the general, the couple returned to Missouri in January 1867 and through the generosity of friends were able to purchase a home in St. Louis. Beverly Tucker was one of the few expatriates accompanied by his wife, but the couple was robbed five times after entering Mexico and impoverished on arrival at their destination. To relieve their economic situation Mrs. Tucker taught school until they returned home in the early seventies. Matthew Fontaine Maury arrived in Mexico with grandiose plans for colonization and was appointed immigration commissioner by Maximilian; however, Maury insisted that his wife and three daughters go to England in the summer of 1865 rather than come to Mexico. His son and daughter-in-law, Richard and Susan, did join him and after his abrupt departure for England went to Nicaragua. The Maurys stayed more than two years in England, then returned to Lexington, Virginia. Few unmarried women went to Mexico, but the Unionist sympathizer

[7] Eliza Frances Andrews: *The War-Time Journal of a Georgia Girl,* ed. Spencer Bidwell King, Jr. (Macon, 1960), 180–217.

Melinda Rankin was forced to close her school in Brownsville, Texas, and flee to Matamoras during the war. Here she did missionary work among the Mexicans. After the war she established a school in Monterey, but failing health forced her to return to her native Illinois in 1872.[8]

The women who did follow their husbands to Mexico found the life primitive and dangerous, the climate depressing, disease rampant, and the political situation confused and uncertain. Robberies posed a problem for wayfarers and residents alike. A lady traveling in the country reported that women were sometimes forced to disrobe to prove they secreted no valuables on their person. She told of a general's wife who made paper dresses for herself and her daughter, hoping to appear so impoverished that no bandit would be interested in searching them.[9] In Mexico the people were so "different" that homesickness as much as anything sent the colonizers back to the States as soon as they were sure it was safe.

An estimated 10,000 Southerners, not more than 700 or 800 of them women, migrated to Latin America in the late sixties and early seventies, but most of them eventually returned. The largest number went to Brazil, where slavery was still legal, but colonies were also established in Honduras, Venezuela, Nicaragua, and elsewhere. Many who went down to survey the situation returned almost immediately, deciding with Dr. Thomas Waring, a former Confederate surgeon from South Carolina, that it was no place to take a family. He arrived in Venezuela in June 1870 and was so repelled by the "indolence, discomfort, and ignorance" of the natives that he returned home before the end of the year. Poor people, believing a bonanza awaited them in Latin America which they could never find in the postwar South, were usually penniless upon arrival and had no alternative but to remain until they could get transportation back to the States, often at the expense of the Federal Government. The failure of the Venezuela venture has been attributed to "lack of organization, money, and knowledgeable leadership . . . but perhaps the

[8] Andrew Rolle: *The Lost Cause: The Confederate Exodus to Mexico* (Norman, Okla., 1965), pp. 97, 106, 108, 117, 136–37, 142–43, 177, 197–98; Mrs. John A. Logan: *The Part Taken By Women in American History* (Wilmington, 1912), pp. 513–14.

[9] Agnes Salm-Salm: *Ten Years of My Life* (London, 1875), p. 185.

most serious handicap was money."[1] The same factors explain the failure of most Latin American colonies; among others were homesickness, political turbulence, and language barriers.

Although our knowledge of Loreta Janeta Velasquez' involvement in the Venezuelan colonization scheme rests primarily on her own questionable account, the New Orleans *Picayune* announced on January 5, 1867, that she was an agent for an emigration company. In her book she says she visited Venezuela to survey the situation for New Orleans friends and went only because her third husband, an ex-Confederate, insisted. She said she preferred to go West where the opportunities were as numerous and the risks fewer. Her description of the voyage on an overcrowded ship and the suffering of the deluded emigrants left stranded by the agents corroborates accounts that appeared in the Southern press at the time. Madame Velasquez stated that she was "the means of preventing a great number of persons . . . from being swindled by speculators who . . . [took] advantage of the unsettled condition of the South . . . and the discontent of a large portion of the people." South America was "no place for Americans to go," she concluded—which was the consensus of opinion by the time she wrote her book nearly a decade later. After burying her third husband in Venezuela, Mme. Velasquez went West, married a miner in Nevada, and by the seventies was in dire financial straits, a situation which prompted her to write her controversial autobiography.[2]

Eliza McHatton-Ripley's family fled from their Louisiana plantation in late 1862, spent the remainder of the war in Texas and Mexico, and after the conflict went to Cuba, living in Havana before buying a sugar plantation. She found the hotel "overflowing with Southerners," mostly Confederate military and political officials, some accompanied by their wives, and also refugees she had known in Texas. After moving to the plantation, she found the way of life "almost as new . . . as if we had dropped

---

[1] Thomas Waring to his parents, July 5, 1870, Thomas S. Waring Papers, South Caroliniana Library, University of South Carolina; Alfred and Kathryn Abbey Hanna: *Confederate Exiles in Venezuela* (Tuscaloosa, 1960), p. 136; Lawrence F. Hill: *The Confederate Exodus to Latin America* (Austin, 1936), pp. 1–94.

[2] C. J. Worthington (ed.): *The Woman in Battle* (Hartford, 1876), pp. 536–49.

from the moon," for they were up at dawn and worked until dark, yet they were enthusiastic and optimistic until the outbreak of civil disturbances in the late sixties. Lawlessness, insecurity, and corruption prevailed, and as the family was not permitted to arm itself for protection, "life was a burden." They tried to hold on for several years, during which her husband was wounded by an insurgent, but "military exactions . . . ruinous taxation . . . and the emancipation of slaves" forced them to abandon the plantation. The bankrupt couple sailed for New York, and never returned to their prewar home in Louisiana.[3]

Most former Confederates were only temporarily in Cuba trying to decide upon their next move. The island was a springboard to Mexico, Europe, or Canada, and a refuge for those who hoped to return home at the first opportunity. General E. Kirby Smith went to Havana after deciding against exile in Mexico, and Mrs. Smith with their two daughters and the ever-faithful ex-slave "Aleck" made their way from Texas to her parents' home in Virginia. John Cabell Breckinridge, the sixth and last Confederate Secretary of War, went to Cuba, England, and then to Canada to pick up his family and take them to Europe. The family remained abroad until 1868, when they returned to Kentucky after President Johnson's amnesty proclamation.

Women refugees in Canada when the war ended waited for their husbands to join them before returning to the United States, and the men who got pardons usually departed soon thereafter. Issa and William C. P. Breckinridge went back to Kentucky in the fall of 1865, and his sister and brother-in-law left St. Catherine's in October for New York, both men having been pardoned through the intercession of the staunch Unionist Robert J. Breckinridge. Nancy Hines Hunter, one of Issa Breckinridge's friends in Toronto, had to remain in Canada much longer because her husband was not given a pardon, but she had plenty of company among the Kentuckians and others in the area. General and Mrs. George Pickett were among the fugitives who sought refuge in Montreal after the war, the general going first and his wife and infant son following a week or so later. The trip was the most

[3] Eliza McHatton Ripley: *From Flag to Flag: A Woman's Adventures and Experiences in the South During the War, in Mexico and in Cuba* (Boston, 1889), pp. 126–293.

difficult Mrs. Pickett had undertaken. For lack of funds the baby's nurse could not go and the young mother was inexperienced in caring for the child. She felt that it was necessary to travel under an assumed name since her husband had been branded a traitor, and she used her grandmother's name and "oath of allegiance," a necessary identification and travel permit which Mrs. Pickett did not have since she refused to swear allegiance to the United States. Her husband was ill during the winter and the couple's funds were low. Determined to keep her worries from him, Mrs. Pickett borrowed on her emerald necklace and slipped out for two hours every day to teach Latin in a girl's school. He was none the wiser until she bought him an overcoat for Christmas and he demanded to know where she had got the money. In the spring of 1866 they returned to Virginia, stopping briefly in New York where they were feted by the general's men and Southern friends, the most extravagant entertainment they had known since the war.[4]

Montreal's most distinguished Confederate exiles were Jefferson Davis and his family, but the children and their grandmother arrived nearly two years before their parents, for Mrs. Davis remained in the South until Davis was freed from prison in May 1867. These were miserable years for Varina Davis, who spent most of the time as a guest of friends in Georgia and Virginia. Not only was she worried about her husband and children, but in the summer of 1865 she fully expected to be imprisoned in "Old Capitol." She was also concerned about the family's finances, yet the requests for various items and money she sent friends in Savannah indicate that she was not suffering. Among her orders was one for five dollars' worth of "nice French candies," with the explanation that "the only tooth I have is sweet."

After going to Montreal, Mrs. Davis mentioned the high cost of living to friends but tried to keep such worries from her ailing husband. Because their home near Natchez had been destroyed and the property confiscated, the family had no apparent means of support, but they left Montreal and went to England and New Orleans before settling in Memphis in 1868. Davis accepted the

[4] Nancy Hines Hunter to Issa Breckinridge, Dec. 6, 1865, Breckinridge Family Papers; LaSalle Corbell Pickett: *Pickett and His Men* (Atlanta, 1899), pp. 30–85.

presidency of an insurance company, and saying that he wanted to support his family, refused the gift of a house in the city. Not until they moved to Memphis did Varina Davis lose the feeling of being "uprooted and floating." Their stay there was relatively brief, for when the company failed in 1874 they moved to "Beauvoir" near Biloxi, and after her husband's death Mrs. Davis made her home in New York.[5]

Most Southerners who flocked to Europe after the war sought only temporary refuge or were vacationers; but the Judah P. Benjamins remained in England, where he became a prominent barrister. Constance Cary and her mother lived with relatives in New Jersey and New York before going to Paris in October 1866, avowedly for the purpose of giving Constance's education the "finishing touches sadly omitted in war experience." Although she took lessons of various kinds, she spent most of her time enjoying the gay social life with the "southern set." Her mother forbade her to associate with Northerners, although Constance did not emphasize this in her reminiscences written forty years after the war as she did in her diary and letters at the time. John A. Dix, in Mrs. Cary's opinion, had sinned beyond redemption in wearing the Blue during the war; and when he and Mrs. Dix arrived in Paris to represent the United States Government, Constance was not permitted to accept their invitations to legation parties. In reporting this to her fiancé Burton Harrison, she said that Dix and other officials were being snubbed by the "southern set" and she could not afford to offend either her fellow Southerners or her mother. Harrison had by this time been released from prison and chose to establish his law offices in New York, and he did not want his future wife offending important Northerners. While taking pains to say that he admired Mrs. Cary's convictions, he wrote Constance that she must not follow "the great mumbo-jumbo which calls itself the 'Southern Set' in Paris," for they were "a collection of jackasses and geese" and half of them had been speculators during the war. The officials in exile "had done no real honest work to help" the Confederacy and

[5] Varina Davis to Martha Levy, Aug. 18, 22, Sept. 17, 1865 (also two undated letters), Philip Phillips Papers; Varina Davis to Burton Harrison, n.d., 1867, Burton Harrison Papers; Varina Davis: *Jefferson Davis: A Memoir* (New York, 1895), II, 802–12; Eron Rowland: *Varina Howell*, II, 488–534.

were rancorous, self-elected martyrs who stayed in Europe out of egotism and pride rather than "any real fear of vengeance" from the United States Government. If they had loved the South they would have remained there instead of going abroad and "insanely fomenting dead quarrels" in Paris.[6]

Constance Cary and Burton Harrison were married in November 1867, and the bride found hundreds of once ardent Confederates living in New York. The Roger Pryors were there and he, like Harrison, had opened law offices in the city which afforded greater opportunities than the impoverished South. Both attorneys counted among their clients many Southerners who seemed to trust "their own kind," but practice was not limited to this group and Pryor gained notoriety for his part in the sensational Beecher-Tilden trial. Dr. Theophilus Steele, whose Confederate activities had put him behind Federal bars twice in the war, went to New York to practice medicine because of the greater promise of success and also to be "free from molestations of any kind." Before they had been in the city two months, Mrs. Steele reported "people from the South coming here to live" and seeking the services of her husband. The doctor was soon doing well enough to move his family into a spacious home.[7]

The return of Confederate refugees to their homes started before the end of the conflict, for some, like Susan Dabney Smedes' family, were displaced only a few months. But many war-weary fugitives who wanted to go home were unable to do so. Homesick, they dreamed of the day they could return, and as soon as the war ended the movement got under way. The lucky ones like Elizabeth Meriwether found their property intact and settled down with a minimum of trouble, but most discovered their homes destroyed or damaged, fences gone, and the land overgrown with weeds. Kate Stone's family was heartsick to see their once magnificent "Brokenburn" a shambles. For more than two years they tried to make a go of the plantation, but the levees had been cut during the war and the property was flooded sev-

[6] Burton Harrison to Constance Cary, Mar. 8, 1867, Burton Harrison Papers; Mrs. Burton Harrison: *Recollections Grave and Gay* (New York, 1911), pp. 244–62.
[7] Theophilus Steele to Robert J. Breckinridge, Oct. 3, 1865; Sally Steele to Robert J. Breckinridge, Oct. 9, Nov. 20, 26, 1865, Jan. 7, Mar. 4, 1866, Breckinridge Family Papers.

eral times a year. Finally they were compelled to move across the river to Mississippi. Other women found that if their property had been confiscated much legal red tape had to be cut before it was restored. It was more than two years before Mrs. John B. Grimball could leave Spartanburg and return to Charleston, and some women like Mary Curtis Lee never got their property back. Judith McGuire could not return to Alexandria, and Sarah Morgan did not go back to Baton Rouge but remained with Unionist relatives in New Orleans until her brother was mustered out of Confederate service and bought a South Carolina plantation. He soon lost the property and Sarah took a job as correspondent for the Charleston *News and Courier* until in the seventies she married the editor, Francis W. Dawson. After his murder a decade later, she remained in Charleston for a time and then went to France, where she spent the rest of her life. During the war Julia LeGrand was pushed eastward by degrees to southern Georgia and after the struggle went to Texas where she married, never returning to New Orleans.[8]

Some women who had stayed in their homes during the war lost them later when labor problems, taxes, high interest rates, and crop failures made it impossible for even the industrious to prevent foreclosures. Gertrude Clanton Thomas saw her two plantations and her husband's business taken away because of unpaid taxes and foreclosed mortgages in the five years following the war. But it was not only economic problems during reconstruction that uprooted families; the political situation also cast them adrift. In 1861 Joseph and John LeConte were on the faculty of South Carolina College, later the state university, and they remained in Columbia after it closed in 1862, living on the campus and working in the Confederate Nitre Bureau. When the university reopened in 1866, they were again on the faculty and for two years adjusted themselves to local conditions, making friends of the occupation forces and seeming content to remain in a community John LeConte described as "one of the most refined and cultivated" he had ever known. However, after the installation of the carpetbag government, neither LeConte could accept the new situation. They toyed with the idea of going to Latin America but decided instead to join the faculty of the new Uni-

[8] Massey: *Refugee Life in the Confederacy,* pp. 263–80.

versity of California. John and his wife went West first and were followed a few months later by the Joseph LeContes, their daughter Sally, his widowed sister, and her daughter. Sally enjoyed life in Oakland, camping trips to Lake Tahoe, and reacted in a typically feminine way to parties, styles, and young men. She had left behind in South Carolina a fiancé who did not want to marry until he solved his financial problems, and while Sally's father said they were engaged for the seven years they were separated, her diary indicates that it was an "off-again-on-again" affair, complicated by distance, poor mail service, and Sally's friendship with other young men. When she returned East in 1876 to visit her sister, Emma LeConte Furman, the couple decided the time was right for marriage and she closed her diary by writing, "this great event of my life [is] consummated at last & all other beaux consigned to merited oblivion."[9]

As the war generation was uprooted, tossed about, and transplanted, the women had to adjust to new conditions, some better and others worse than any they had known. They had to make a new home and new friends and in the process lost much of their provincialism. While there were exceptions, Southerners who moved to other parts of the country did not cling to their prejudices or stay as bitter as those remaining amid scenes of happier days. Women going into new areas were not so often reminded of the past and were too busy to brood or indulge in false pride. Whether they prospered, failed, became good citizens of a community, or kept floating like nomads depended on the individual and the circumstances, but the war uprooted women and made them face many diverse fates.

[9] William Dallam Armes (ed.): *The Autobiography of Joseph LeConte* (New York, 1903), pp. 235–41; Sally LeConte Diary, MS, South Caroliniana Library, University of South Carolina.

15

The Ground Swell after the Storm

  "In all such revolutions," wrote Cornelia Spencer referring to the Civil War, "the ground swell after the storm is often as destructive as the storm itself."[1] The "ground swell" of the late sixties and seventies was in many way as turbulent as the upheaval which preceded it, and while it is not always easy to distinguish developments attributable to the conflict from those stimulated by other forces, many unfortunate economic, social, and psychological repercussions followed in the wake of war.

  Women everywhere were weary of the struggle long before it ended and some were sick of it before it was scarcely under way. In the summer of 1861, Eliza Carrington of Virginia prayed that "God will put an end to this miserable and unholy war," and a year later Mrs. John A. Logan was convinced that her Illinois neighbors would "go crazy if the war goes on." By the last year thousands felt like Kezia Payne of Texas, who was so "tired of the whole mess . . . [that] victory no longer seemed important," or like Gertrude Thomas, who wanted peace but not "on humiliating terms."[2] When the end came women everywhere were relieved,

[1] *North Carolina Presbyterian*, Sept. 24, 1873; Cornelia Phillips Spencer Papers (1873), typescript.
[2] Eliza Carrington to Robert J. Breckinridge, July 31, 1861, Breckinridge Family Papers; Mrs. John A. Logan to John A. Logan, Aug. 15, 1862, Mrs. John A. Logan Papers; Harold Jackson Matthews: *Candle By Night: The*

but this was the only reaction Northerners and Southerners shared.

The North greeted the fall of Richmond with wild celebration. "Boston is gay," the people jubilant and buying newspapers in such quantities that the newsboys "are amassing independent fortunes," wrote Ellen Wright Garrison. Her neighbor was "blowing soap bubbles . . . bells were pealing, cannon firing and pyrotechnic wonders being exhibited." Throughout the North flags were flown, bells rang, homes and public buildings were brilliantly illuminated, torchlight parades wound through city streets, bands played, and people everywhere were exuberant.

In the South, however, most women reacted as did Constance Cary, "with heavy heart." In Richmond she heard the noises of surrender—explosions, the crackle of flames, the cannons' roar heralding the arrival of the victors, the bands playing "Hail Columbia" and "Yankee Doodle," which Miss Cary said "sounded the death knell" of the Confederacy. She stayed indoors with friends and peered "through closed blinds," first at the victorious Federal Army and then at "the Washington Ape seated in state" in a carriage traveling at a rapid clip "down Grace Street." That evening she attended church, where "the Litany was sobbed out by the whole congregation of stricken women." The city mourned. Throughout the Confederacy the first reports of Richmond's fall and Lee's surrender caused stunned women to ask, as did Elizabeth Meriwether, "Could the report be true?" But they knew that it was, and after the first shock had passed tears flowed. Eliza Frances Andrews was "blue" on hearing of Richmond's evacuation, yet "not disposed to give up" as long as Lee was in the field; but when he surrendered she accepted defeat. Miss Andrews then saw a "new pathos in a crutch or an empty sleeve," knowing that the men's sacrifices had been "all for nothing."[3] War-weary Southern women also realized that their struggles had been in vain.

Nothing more dramatically reveals the despondency of

Story of the Life and Times of Kezia Payne de Pelchin, Texas Pioneer Teacher, Social Worker and Nurse (Boston, 1942), pp. 70–71; Ella Gertrude Clanton Thomas Diary, MS.

[3] Ellen Wright Garrison to Martha Wright, Apr. 3, 1865; Martha Wright to Ellen Wright Garrison, Apr. 6, 1865; Martha Wright to Frank Wright, Apr. 11, 1865, Garrison Family Papers; Constance Cary to her mother, Apr. 4, 1865, Burton Harrison Papers; Elizabeth Avery Meriwether: *Recollec-*

Southerners late in the war and immediately thereafter than the gaps in their diaries. Young Sidney Harding, who had faithfully kept a record throughout her displacement, made her last entry on December 31, 1864. "War still going on," she wrote, ". . . how it sickens the heart to begin another year with this cruel, terrible war still raging . . . my heart feels as if it would break." Sarah Morgan wrote irregularly after going to New Orleans and made no entry in 1865 until April 19, when she recorded Lee's surrender. There followed two brief notations in April and May and nothing more until she left the city. After Kate Stone returned to the family plantation, "Brokenburn," in the fall of 1865, she did not write from November that year until January 1867. Kate explained that this lapse was due to her low spirits and the family's unsuccessful attempts to "make a crop and reconstruct the place." After her return she withdrew from all activities and refused to see old friends, preferring to carry her "burden of defeat" alone. In May 1865, Gertrude Thomas put aside her pen for five months, and Mrs. John Grimball made only one entry in her diary in 1865 and one the following year. The latter was a brief résumé of her life during the ten months following the war and could as well have been written by countless others. She told of the sale of personal possessions to sustain the family, her husband's attempts to reclaim his confiscated property, her humiliation at her daughters' having to work, her sons' dissipation, and the loss of a faithful ex-slave who left the Grimballs to join her husband.[4]

The North's jubilation was brought to an abrupt halt with the assassination of President Lincoln. Although women's opinion of the man varied, all were shocked, most were saddened, many condemned the Confederate leaders as having a hand in the dastardly crime, and the irrational cried out for vengeance against all Southerners. Northerners who had criticized Lincoln were viewed with suspicion, and some met with the fate of a "Copperhead milliner" in a New York village who was forced to

---

tions of Ninety-Two Years 1824–1916 (Nashville, 1958), pp. 158–59; Eliza Francis Andrews: *The War-Time Journal of a Georgia Girl*, ed. Spencer Bidwell King, Jr. (Macon, 1960), pp. 135, 154–55.
[4] Sidney Harding Diaries, MS, Department of Archives and History, Louisiana State University; John Q. Anderson (ed.); *Brokenburn: The Journal of Kate Stone* (Baton Rouge, 1955), pp. 368–69; Ella Gertrude Clanton Thomas Diary, MS; Meta Morris Grimball Journal, MS.

close her shop and leave town. In Rome, Charlotte Cushman could not believe such a thing could "happen in our country in these modern days." When she heard only that the assassin was "a man named Booth," she immediately concluded it was her fellow actor, "the madman John Wilkes Booth . . . a perfectly reckless dare-devil." This, she said, "brings the war home to me . . . my heart feels as if it was cramped in a vise." In a six-page letter to her daughter, she kept referring to this "horrible tragedy." Later she noted its effect on her friends in Rome, who had long referred to "Confederates and belligerents" but now spoke of "Rebels and insurgents."[5]

Coming as it did even before all Confederate forces surrendered, the assassination of Lincoln served to increase suspicion and distrust between the sections. A great many Southern women feared that their lot would be made all the harder because of this deed, and a Louisianian wrote that the "bad feeling" generated by the crime destroyed all hope of a merciful reconstruction and would greatly complicate the process. Northern women also believed it would change policies. Martha Wright thought it would "take a good while to get things running smoothly," and meanwhile she intended to "watch" not only Southerners but Washington. Like many abolitionists and temperance advocates, she despised Johnson and favored his impeachment. Even before Lincoln's funeral cortege had started on its circuitous journey to Springfield, Anna Ella Carroll was busy rearranging the cabinet without Johnson's knowledge, for she was deeply concerned about reconstruction which she believed to be more important "than even the subjugation of the Southern Armies." Some women thought Lincoln would have been the better man for the job, while others favored Johnson, but all seemed anxious that the South be reconstructed rather than rehabilitated.[6]

By the summer of 1865, Southern women were generally too

[5] Martha Wright to William P. Wright, Apr. 21, 1865, Garrison Family Papers; Charlotte Cushman to her daughter, Apr. 28, May 6, 1865, Charlotte Cushman Papers, Manuscript Division, Library of Congress.

[6] Frances Fearn: *Diary of a Refugee* (New York, 1910), pp. 114–15; Martha Wright to William L. Garrison, II, July 29, 1865, Jan. 21, 1867; Martha Wright to Frank Wright, Mar. 17, 1865, Garrison Family Papers; Anna Ella Carroll to Robert J. Breckinridge, Apr. 17, 1865, Breckinridge Family Papers.

burdened with their own problems to draw distinctions between Washington politicians. They hated them all, as well as the troops sent to occupy their communities. Even those who had criticized Jefferson Davis continued to think of him as "their president," and this would be true of some for years to come. When Gertrude Thomas met Davis in Augusta in 1871 she found him excessively prejudiced on some issues but said, "I have had no other President since [the war] . . . and until a Southern man, not a radical, presides in the White House, I will acknowledge none." As time passed, Davis grew in stature in the eyes of many Southern women. After John Eaton, U.S. Commissioner of Education, toured the South in 1881 he wrote Mrs. James A. Garfield that the Southern people were indignant at the assassination of her husband, but he thought she would be especially interested to know that women who had never before expressed loyalty to the Union now spoke of the late Chief Executive as "our President." Yet many irreconcilables continued to refer to Davis in the old terms; and with the founding of the United Daughters of the Confederacy in the nineties, references to him as President increased rather than diminished.[7]

The personal records of Southern women make it apparent that their hatred and distrust of Northerners grew during reconstruction. Most of them became more embittered in the seventies than they had been during the war, and some were never able to overcome their resentment. Even those who went North to visit relatives were regarded with suspicion when they returned. Belle Thompson of North Carolina reported that when a rumor was circulated of her friendships with "Yankees" while she was visiting her sister in Washington, old friends refused to associate with her. Her mother was distressed because the young people were snubbing Belle, who spent several miserable weeks after her return home; but when no "Yankee beau" came galloping into town to claim her hand in marriage she was accepted again, although her friends continued to ridicule her "Yankee ways."[8]

Unfortunately many Southern women carried their preju-

[7] Ella Gertrude Clanton Thomas Diary, MS; John Eaton to Mrs. James A. Garfield, Aug. 12, 1881, James A. Garfield Papers, Manuscript Division, Library of Congress.
[8] Belle Thompson to Benjamin Hedrick, June 29, 1866; Eliza Thompson to Benjamin Hedrick, July 30, 1866, Benjamin S. Hedrick Papers.

dices for years after Northerners discarded any animosity, but this is not difficult to understand since they had the war at their doors, met defeat, and were saddled with innumerable postwar problems which they attributed to the enemy. Only when they realized they were hurting themselves more than anyone else did their hostility gradually subside, but some never could forgive and forget. Their children were reared on stories of diabolical acts perpetrated by Yankees, and these stories more often came from the lips of mothers than fathers. A former Confederate officer was disturbed that his son was being taught "*to hate a Yankee.*" The child's "bread is buttered with hatred, his milk is sweetened with it, his top spins and his ball bounces with it," he wrote. A Richmond woman was heard to say just after the war, "If I ever have any children . . . I shall bring them up in eternal hatred of those who have subdued us," and this seems to have been the determination of countless thousands. Some taught the young to hate all Northern soldiers; others, like Elizabeth Meriweather, concentrated on one—in her case William T. Sherman who had banished her from Memphis. Her son Lee, born in 1862, was carrying his mother's grudge against the general a century later.[9] Many Southern women never seemed to realize that it was possible to bury the real or imagined wrongs of the past without forsaking their convictions, or to be proud of the role their families played in fighting for their principles without taking refuge in hatred.

Stories are legion of young women who for years after the war were forbidden by their parents to marry Northerners or Republicans; and while some defied parental authority, others could not bring themselves to do so. Biographers of the Jefferson Davises cite the case of their younger daughter "Winnie," born during the war and affectionately known as the "Daughter of the Confederacy." Because of her birth in wartime, wrote Eron Rowland, it "was thought that she should be set apart as a kind of shrine at which none but those below the Mason and Dixon line should worship." In the eighties, when she fell in love with a New Yorker, Southerners who "had written 'Lest We Forget' in

[9] William Gale to ———, Aug. 26, 1865, Gale-Polk Papers, Southern Historical Collection, University of North Carolina; Washington *Chronicle*, Apr. 11, 1865; Meriwether: *Recollections*, pp. 87–88. Lee Meriwether was 101 years old on Christmas Day, 1963.

their recessionals" opposed the marriage and the young lady acquiesced to their wishes—and possibly her father's. After her father's death she moved to New York with her mother, who was criticized for leaving the South. Here "Winnie" died in 1898.[1]

Not all Southern women were irreconcilable, however, and some were soon trying to heal the sectional wounds. After receiving a letter from an embittered New York friend, Cornelia Spencer wrote a long conciliatory reply which she hoped would help to bridge the "deep gulf," and she assured the woman the breach would be "filled up . . . in God's own good time." She explained that while she had opposed secession, when war came all her energies were thrown on the side of the Confederacy and she was humiliated by its defeat, yet she did not hate the Northern people. She attributed much postwar hostility to the newspapers in both areas. Their words "did more," she said, "to set us against each other than bullets," and since the war they had served to keep open the wounds. Mrs. Spencer told her friend that she had long since "disgorged" the gross fabrications about Northerners that she had "swallowed," because it was necessary in order "to accept the situation." She hoped that her friend would discount those circulated about Southerners and not blame all for the actions of a few. "The South sinned in her pride, her prosperity, her confidence," wrote Mrs. Spencer, "and God has humbled her."[2]

Southern women lost their "prosperity" and "confidence," but a great many retained their "pride." As thousands were compelled to accept aid from the Federal Army, Freedmen's Bureau, and private agencies, they had to swallow that pride. Distributions by these agencies kept thousands from starving after the war, but at best they represented temporary relief and did not solve the underlying problem or set in motion a rehabilitation program for whites or Negroes. There were also many women too proud to accept handouts regardless of their financial straits. Northerners who chanced to be in the South in the spring and summer of 1865 were appalled by conditions but had no sympathy for those who hid their humiliation under a haughty exterior. Northern correspondents delighted in telling of women who must

[1] Eron Rowland: *Varina Howell, Wife of Jefferson Davis* (New York, 1931), II, 506, 534.
[2] Cornelia Spencer to Eliza North, Mar. 10, 1866, Cornelia Spencer Papers (1866), typescript.

now seek aid from the enemy, but not with the idea of arousing compassion or appealing for assistance but solely in order to ridicule the suppliants. By the fall of 1865 there were a few exceptions, including the New York *Herald* and the *Tribune,* which advocated that something be done for the "poor whites," who by this time included most Southerners. On September 3 the *Herald* told of the widows and orphans of Confederates who were entirely dependent on charity and urged that "the Northern female philanthropists of the abolition school" turn their attention to this problem, since "the Southern blacks have enough friends to look after them." On October 5 the *Herald* made its second appeal, this time inspired by the *Tribune*'s editorial of the preceding day entitled, "What shall we do for the Poor Whites?"

A few Northern groups interested themselves in the impoverished Southerners, and individuals often came to the assistance of friends and relatives in the South. In December 1866 the New York Ladies Southern Relief Association was founded by Mrs. Algernon Sydney Sullivan, who served as secretary with Mrs. James Roosevelt as president. The leaders were primarily Southern-born ladies who had married and gone North before the conflict. In the fall of 1864, Mrs. Sullivan went to Virginia to visit relatives and remained until after the war. She realized the people must have assistance and after returning to New York rendered aid privately before founding the association. During the conflict she had worked with Confederate prisoners as much as she dared, and when these men returned to a hopeless situation at home they asked Mrs. Sullivan to help them in any way she could. It was their letters that convinced her of the need for an organized relief agency. The association counted among its members many socially elite, and much of the money was raised by conducting gala functions. There were dinners at Delmonico's, balls at the Academy of Music, and private parties at the mansions of Mrs. William Price and Mrs. John Jacob Astor. On house-to-house canvasses the women encountered many evidences of hostility toward Southerners, but schoolchildren contributed their pennies, "one large chain store donated the entire profits of one day," managers of theaters gave them over to benefit performances, and transportation companies contributed their services. Between January and November 1867, the association dispensed $71,000 through Southern ministers, primarily in Virginia, the Carolinas, Georgia, Alabama, and Mississippi.

The more than 1,500 extant letters written to Mrs. Sullivan by those aided bear ample testimony to the destitution of once affluent women. Most needy cases were reported by others, but the letters of appreciation for even the smallest gift are heartwarming, like that from a South Carolina girl of the planter class who "danced for joy" upon receiving a new dress. A minister reported once wealthy Southern ladies who had "not a cent in the world and no calling to which they can resort for support" but who refused to ask favors. "I pity these people much more," he wrote, "than persons who have always been poor." Another cited more than 40,000 Georgians left destitute by the war and two successive years of crop failures and reported that he had seen many "women at the plough,—white women . . . hard at work . . . to help make a crop." One of the distributors in Mississippi told of an "educated, refined lady of excellent family" who had owned fifty slaves but now as a war widow was seeking domestic employment in order to support several small children. In 1860, Mrs. Joseph Huger's family had land and slaves worth $200,000, all of which was lost in the war, and in 1867 her sister reported the family's destitution because Mrs. Huger was too proud to do so.[3]

Poverty prevailed within the planter class, for many had lost investments in land, slaves, and Confederate bonds while those who had held their land lacked money for taxes, repairs, crops, and wages. Mrs. Robert Allston of South Carolina, who had done a magnificent job of managing the family's plantations during the war, lost her 600 slaves but determined the land would not go. She opened a girls' school in Charleston and invested the profits in the plantation. Mrs. Grimball reported that several of Charleston's "first families" had taken "inferior positions" in order to support themselves. Mrs. Henry Manigault was matron and her husband steward of the Alms House in Charleston and their daughters taught in Yorkville. Mrs. James Heyward, her sister-in-law and daughters were "taking in sewing," and Mrs. Grimball

<hr>

[3] Anna Middleton Holmes: *Southern Relief Association of New York City* (New York, 1926), pp. 7–78. The manuscript letters are in the Confederate Museum, Richmond.

noted that "all over the state people are making efforts to support themselves."[4]

The difficult postwar years had a strong psychological impact on Southern women, many of whom tried to conceal their problems from even their closest friends while using their diaries as an outlet for their frustrations and innermost thoughts. Especially revealing is that of Gertrude Clanton Thomas who started writing twelve years before the war and continued until 1889. Here can be seen the changes wrought by the war and reconstruction on a refined, educated lady, a tragedy all the sadder because a liberal, tolerant woman of the type so desperately needed in the South was converted into an embittered, critical cynic through no fault of her own. She had every right to blame most of her later problems on the war. It and the postwar pressures changed her husband into a short-tempered, moody person who took refuge in the bottle and resorted to profanity, habits Mrs. Thomas said he had acquired "since the war." Although she was a devoted mother who took great pride in her children, after her baby died in the fall of 1865 Mrs. Thomas confided to her diary, "If I could have you back I would not." One of her biggest hurts was Mr. Thomas's refusal to discuss his "pecuniary embarrassments" with her because she was a woman and "didn't know anything." Whenever she questioned him, for much of the property lost was hers, he became so profane that she dared not quote his statements "verbatim" in her diary. After most of what they owned was gone she feared losing the remainder of her inheritance but realized that husbands resented references by their wives to "*my* plantation, *my* horses, *my* cows," even though they were "as much her own as the dress she wears." She thought it ironic that the state legislature was finally discussing a law to protect "a married woman's property . . . now that most of the women in Georgia had nothing to lose."

Mrs. Thomas skimped and worked hard to help her family but felt her husband resented the fact that she wore "faded calico" instead of being "fashionably dressed." Above all else she wanted her children educated and was heartsick when her son had to quit school to work in the fields. But she compounded her problems by worrying constantly about what people were saying,

[4] Meta Morris Grimball Journal, MS.

confessing, "I am a coward where public opinion is concerned." Humiliation engulfed her with each loss of property, and they came annually for five years after the war, her 800 acres in Burke County being sold in 1870 to satisfy her husband's creditors. "It is an additional calling of the public to notice our degradation," she wrote, and "so humiliating." She taught pupils at the rate of thirty-five dollars a month but had to plead with parents to send their children so that the superintendent would be convinced the school was necessary. She boarded a few students, sold wood to supplement her meager income, and parted with many personal possessions in order to buy magazine subscriptions for herself and the children; and this she was doing fifteen years after the war. After inheriting her mother's home in Augusta, Mrs. Thomas opened a boardinghouse with her daughter, but despite her efforts the financial problems were never solved, to the extent that once in the eighties she could not pay a thirty-five-cent debt.

There were a great many Gertrude Thomases left in the wake of war; and if, as Mary Livermore said, the "disappointed and defiant" women of the South "sat down in the ashes of . . . dead hopes and despair," Mrs. Thomas's case explains why. Not all did "sit down," however, and many worked as hard as Mrs. Thomas to extricate themselves from the slough of despond only to sink deeper and deeper into its mire.[5]

Marjorie Mendenhall has referred to these women of the war and postwar years as "a Lost Generation . . . united in poverty and in a search for a new way of life." Not until the eighties and nineties, when the planter family began to give way to the "merchant-farmer and his wife," did a noticeable transition from the old way of life take place. The most significant trend was the shift of population "away from the country and toward the town," where ideas circulated more freely and where women had greater opportunities for employment, group activities, and leadership.[6] By the nineties they were taking advantage of opportunities seldom afforded those in rural areas. The Southern woman of 1861 had been primarily the product of an agrarian, conserva-

---

[5] Mary Ashton Livermore: *The Story of My Life* (Hartford, 1899), p. 488.
[6] Marjorie Stratford Mendenhall: "Southern Women of a 'Lost Generation,'" *South Atlantic Quarterly*, XXXIII (1934), 334, 336.

tive society and, with few exceptions, a generation behind Northern women in her ideas and organized activities. Instead of encouraging Southerners to be more liberal and progressive, the war, defeat, and reconstruction tended to make them reactionary and in opposition to all things Northern. They at first determined to recapture their old ways of life, which is not unusual after a war, and some never quit trying. Only when a woman realized that the past was dead did she begin to search for a new way of life, and this was of course easier for the younger woman. Her willingness to accept progressive ideas depended in large measure on her own attitudes and personality, but some who endorsed Northern ideas continued to emphasize the differences between the two geographic groups. They were women of the "New South," which they preferred to think had no connection with the late enemy.

Northern women were not without their problems in the postwar period, although they did not have to live amid devastation and face overturned economic, social, and political systems, nor did they have to endure an army of occupation. Theirs was a problem of readjustment rather than reconstruction, and the North had the wealth, resources, and means of production to facilitate the conversion to a peacetime economy. The Federal and state governments were able to assist veterans, their widows and families, while the impoverished Southern states had little to offer the former Confederates immediately after the war. Yet able-bodied Northern veterans as yet had no pensions and the handicapped met with complications in claiming theirs. So did the widows and children of soldiers who had died in the war. Thousands of soldiers returned home only to face long periods of unemployment, and their wives and children either had to support the family or rely on charity. Women who had worked in "men's" jobs were sometimes replaced by returning servicemen, and when they were not it was usually because they worked for lower wages. Women who needed jobs faced greater competition from men than during the war. To make matters worse for women, employers were under pressure by the public to hire veterans, so that the destitute wives of the handicapped and many of the four million widows and orphans were often left in desperate need. Welfare agencies might assist them for a time, but this type of relief was temporary and insufficient. These women were humiliated at having to ask for handouts, and the suffering among those who never sought favors can only be imagined. Much of their bitterness stemmed from the belief that the government and more fortunate citizens were ungrateful for their sacrifices.

Hatred for the recent enemy was not as prevalent among women of the victorious North as among those of the South, but it existed. In May 1865, Jane Grey Swisshelm informed her Minnesota readers, "The wives, widows and children of Northern soldiers . . . are often left to suffer while rations are freely dealt out in Charleston and Savannah to the families of those in the rebel army . . . [who] spit on our flag . . . and curse our Government." So afraid was Mrs. Swisshelm that the South would be too gently handled that she used her meager earnings as a War Department clerk to found and publish a radical newspaper, the *Reconstructionist*. She emphasized the need for a harsh program of reconstruction and consistently opposed everything President Johnson did. Angered by her caustic attacks, Johnson fired Mrs. Swisshelm from her job without bothering to consult the Secretary of War. Left without regular income, Mrs. Swisshelm ceased publication and went to Pennsylvania to write her memoirs and live out her days at Swissvale.[7]

Others nursed a hatred no less deep-seated. After returning from a vacation in Niagara in the summer of 1866, Susan Dickinson indignantly reported that she had seen Northern girls dancing with a former Confederate. And a woman who toured the South in 1866 spoke of the cemetery at Arlington and hoped that "no rebel will ever set his accursed foot within those sacred precincts!" After stopping in Richmond she regretted that the city's "very foundations" had not been "plowed up," with nothing left "to tell that it had ever existed." Everywhere in the South she reported only the "bitterest hate and opposition" among the people, and not once did she express sympathy for their suffering but constantly reiterated her desire to see them punished. Other Northern women who went South for the first time after the

[7] St. Cloud *Democrat*, May 18, 1865; Lester Burrell Shippee: "Jane Grey Swisshelm: Agitator," *Mississippi Valley Historical Review*, VII (1920), 225–27.

war found much to condemn but were less vindictive. Martha Wright had been as critical of Southerners as only an abolitionist could be, but after talking with women who had lost their homes, gardens, and trees, all dear to Mrs. Wright's heart, and seeing the poverty and destruction, she wrote her sister, "Poor things, one can't help pitying them."[8]

Although relieved at war's end and happy with the Northern victory, many women were restless in the spring and summer of 1865. Like Julia Ward Howe, their "whole nature cried out for play," and Mrs. Howe planned parties for her daughters, participated in music festivals "celebrating the close of the war," went on picnics, and crowded her days with the more trivial activities she had abandoned during the conflict.[9] Women who had been actively engaged in nursing or other war duties had a greater adjustment to make than those who had stayed at home. Nurses were mustered out in the summer of 1865, and Dorothea Dix resigned on September 1 to return to the establishment and expansion of mental institutions. This occupied her for another fifteen years, and she did not retire until eighty. Mary Bickerdyke was harder to send home than some and insisted on staying with her "boys" until the last one was discharged in March 1866.

Clara Barton found another task before the war ended and for nearly four years thereafter engaged in the heartbreaking work of tracing missing soldiers. Thousands of soldiers' families knew her by name, and throughout the war she received letters from women requesting information about men who were killed, wounded, taken prisoner, or missing. Early in 1865 she realized that the conflict would soon be over, and she knew that the sooner someone sought to trace the missing men or find and mark their graves, the easier it would be. In March she was authorized by Lincoln to search for missing prisoners of war. Miss Barton had never asked or received pay for her services, but she expected the government to defray the expenses she incurred in so tremendous an undertaking. She could not wait for Congress to make an appropriation, however, and although Johnson approved her plan she met with numerous harassments from the

[8] Susan Dickinson to Anna Dickinson, Aug. 20, 1866; Francis W. Lewis to Anna Dickinson, Oct. 4, 1866, Anna E. Dickinson Papers; Martha Wright to Lucretia Mott, Dec. 11, 1873, Garrison Family Papers.
[9] Laura Richards and Maud Howe Elliott: *Julia Ward Howe* (Boston, 1915), I, 222, 231, 237.

War Department. While in Andersonville in the summer of 1865 identifying and marking graves, she crossed swords with Captain James M. Moore, who had been appointed by Stanton to head the work. When Congress convened in December she hoped to be appointed head of a Bureau of Missing Soldiers, logically expecting it to fall within the War Department. However, a Burial Bureau had recently been established in the department and officials thought this sufficient to handle the problem; moreover, they did not want to give a woman, least of all Clara Barton, a position of authority. In December the Adjutant General reported that her services could not be used and implied that she was one of the "irresponsible agents" who should not "have access to information contained in the records." He further stated, "There is no appropriation or fund . . . out of which so expensive a 'Bureau' . . . could be maintained" and "stringently recommended" that no concessions "be granted to Miss Barton."[1]

By this time Clara Barton was already hard at work on her project, and thousands of circulars and newspaper reports announcing her work and listing missing men had come to the attention of the public. Tens of thousands of letters from anxious relatives had already crossed her desk, and she had no intention of abandoning the work. But she did need financial assistance, having already expended more than $7,000 of her own money. In March 1866, Congress appropriated $15,000 for the project; but when the job was finished in 1869, Miss Barton had not received a penny in salary and had spent approximately $1,750 of her own money. In her report to Congress she stated that she and her staff had received and written 63,182 letters, that more than 22,000 families of soldiers had been given information, and that at least 40,000 missing men were as yet unaccounted for. "In most instances pay or bounty in some form must have been due their families at the time of their disappearance," but nobody could collect until proof of death was given. She asked Congress to declare the men dead and pay "their legal heirs" whatever they were entitled to receive.[2]

This had been a difficult work, for Clara Barton read thou-

[1] Report of E. D. Townsend, Adjutant General, Clara Barton Papers, Manuscript Division, Library of Congress; Isabel Ross: *Angel of the Battlefield* (New York, 1956), pp. 84–96.
[2] *Senate Documents (Miscellaneous, Number 57), 40th Congress, Third Session* (1869).

sands of pathetic letters from women who did not know what had happened to their men or where the dead were buried. Since more than 40,000 more were reported killed than had known graves, the families of most never found out what had been done with the men's bodies. Countless others of the missing were not known to have died, and the women could only hope they would some day return; but uncertainty was harder to bear than the assurance that a man was dead and properly interred. Many who had this assurance also wrote Miss Barton to ask about the manner of death. One who was told that her brother had died and been buried at Andersonville asked, "Is that all we can ever know of our lost darling? . . . Oh, what I would give to know . . . if he had anyone to comfort him in his last moments. . . . His dear mother is heartbroken . . . but feels it would be a great relief if she could hear the particulars." Another man was imprisoned for two years, during which time his mother did not know his whereabouts, and not until a fellow prisoner brought word of his death did she learn what had happened to him. These two years of "waiting, waiting, waiting," she wrote, "were too terrible to imagine." Women were reported to have searched the battlefields hoping to find their men's bodies. An elderly New York woman spent three weeks in May 1865 in the area around Petersburg before finding her son's remains. They were placed in the coffin she had brought and sent North for proper burial.[3] The same anguish was experienced by thousands of Southern women who had no Clara Barton.

Miss Barton sometimes found soldiers who did not choose to go home or inform their families of their whereabouts, but before she was through they knew the contempt she felt for them. The sister of one from Lockport, New York, wrote that the family had heard nothing about him for more than two years, during which time his mother had died from the *great grief* caused by her son's "silent absence." Her dying request had been that her daughter try to find out what had happened to him. His name was inserted in one of the lists of missing men and six months

[3] Mrs. Hannah R. Nash to Clara Barton, Aug. 27, 1865; Mrs. Martha A. Upton to Clara Barton, Sept. 10, 1865; Clara Barton to Mrs. Upton, Sept. 16, 1865; Mrs. T. B. Hurlbut to Clara Barton, Sept. 26, 1865, Clara Barton Papers, Manuscript Division, Library of Congress; New York *Herald*, June 29, 1865.

later he wrote Miss Barton from Illinois demanding to know what he had done to have his "name *Bla*zoned all over the *Coun*try." He said that if his family wished to know where he was "let them wait un*till* I see fit to write them." The irate Miss Barton minced no words in her reply. There was no excuse, she said, for his "unnatural concealment" from those who loved him more than he loved them, and she reminded the man, *"Your mother died waiting."* She let it be known she was informing his sister "of your existence lest you should not 'see fit' to do so yourself."[4]

Women who had worked hard to support themselves and their government during the war had reason enough to feel unappreciated when it was over. Even those like Clara Barton who had made a major contribution were impeded in rendering further service, and hundreds were ignored. Some were dismissed from their jobs, and many industrial workers were being paid less than they had been when the war started. They dared not protest against the deplorable situation lest they lose their jobs. These were the women, wrote "Grace Greenwood," who had given their "brothers, husbands, and sons to the war by sufferance," worked for the soldiers "by sufferance," paid taxes "by sufferance," and continued to "live by sufferance."[5] The state of affairs among working women provoked the New York *Herald,* on September 13, 1865, to suggest that the government create a bureau for women similar to that provided the freedmen. "It is ridiculous," said the writer, for the government to care for the Negro and not these neglected ones. Next day he facetiously commented that it would be unfair to the War Department to assign it this responsibility since the Freedmen's Bureau was under its jurisdiction, but perhaps the "woman's bureau" could be assigned the Navy Department "since old Welles has nothing to do just now." The agency should have authority over "employers, landlords, grocers," and others who took advantage of women, should be given the power to decree divorce "wherever a heartless husband . . . or a drunken one . . . is in the way," and be authorized to "settle all points of women's rights." Throughout the war the *Herald* had been indig-

[4] Eugenia Phillips to Clara Barton, Apr. 17, 1865; Joseph Hitchins to Clara Barton, Oct. 16, 1865; Clara Barton to Joseph Hitchins, Oct. 23, 1865, Clara Barton Papers, Manuscript Division, Library of Congress.
[5] Emily Faithfull: *Three Visits to America* (Edinburgh, 1884), p. 330.

nant at the way the working women were treated, and conditions were growing worse instead of better.

Working women were resentful and bitter, yet not all their indignation was aimed at the groups suggested in the *Herald*'s editorials. They were disappointed that so many reformers were lashing out against other evils and evading their problem. Julia Ward Howe was more concerned about the Greeks, Armenians, world peace, and clubs for intellectuals than about the wages paid factory operatives in her home state; Harriet Beecher Stowe, who had protested against the condition of Southern labor, could not be bothered about New England's mill workers. Mary Livermore and others who emerged from the war experienced organizers were more interested in temperance, prostitution, and women's political rights than in remedying the economic evils of their toiling sisters. Susan Anthony was more concerned with workers than most others in the woman's rights camp, but she and the rest too often reminded them that they could expect little if anything until they had the ballot.

There were organizations to assist the working girls, but as Elizabeth Bancroft Schlesinger has noted, the things that were done tended to be "palliatives for the ills of the few, not curatives for the suffering of many." The workers were sometimes provided with reading rooms, but the opinion of most women in a position to help was that factory operatives and domestics were "riff-raff who should be grateful for any job." Not until the mid-eighties and nineties was much done to remedy the situation, and in the meantime women were hearing all the age-old arguments based on health and morals as to why they should not work in industry, offices, and business. After the invention of the typewriter, there were men who maintained stenography could never be a field for women because it required so much concentration and physical endurance that it "would break a young woman down in a short time." More than twenty years after the invention of the sewing machine it was declared too dangerous for women to operate; and a Boston physician testified that in a survey among sixty-nine of his medical colleagues, forty-four stated woman's physical structure did not permit her to sew by machine without permanently damaging her health. Nor was the outlook more promising in the professions immediately after the war; Dr. Elizabeth

Blackwell was so discouraged about the future in medicine that she moved to England in 1869.[6]

Women wanted nothing more than to earn a decent living, and they were resentful when denied the opportunity. Those who had given breadwinners to the nation and must now support themselves and their families were not nearly as bitter toward Southerners as toward fellow Northerners who refused them jobs. The majority did not want charity, they wanted work. They were not as interested in the franchise as in the full dinner pail and shoes for their children. They might believe that women had the right to vote, but they knew they could starve waiting to be granted the right. Disillusionment was as widespread among groups of Northern women as among those in the South, but it arose partly because they lived in the wealthy area where so many had so much while they had so little.

Hundreds of thousands of personal tragedies were written because of the war, and each was distinctive. While it cannot be assumed that with continued peace the individual would not have met with similar heartbreak, it is safe to say that in many instances unhappiness, physical breakdown, psychological disturbances, or insecurity were a direct or indirect result of the war. The tragic later years of Belle Boyd, Pauline Cushman, and Anna Dickinson might have been different but for their role in the conflict. The same may be said for the neurotic Mary Todd Lincoln, whose erratic behavior, had it taken the turn it did, might at least have escaped widespread publicity. Nor can one be sure as to the exact effect on Mrs. Lincoln of the criticisms and insinuations hurled at her during the war, but the chances are that she would have been happier if she had never been First Lady. It is dangerous perhaps to speculate on the wives of military men who were elected to high political office because of their military careers, but they were required to share the sorrows as well as the pride of office. Julia Dent Grant would certainly never have been mistress of the White House had there been no Civil War, and she was sensitive to the criticism of her husband and his

[6] Elizabeth Bancroft Schlesinger: "Attitude of Society Toward Working Women, 1860–1890," paper presented at Seminar on American Women (1952–53) at Radcliffe, copy in Smith College Archives; Azel Ames: *Sex in Industry: A plea for the Working Girl* (Boston, 1875), pp. 24, 30, 31, 114, 116–17.

administration. The same might be said of Mrs. Andrew Johnson, whose ill-health necessitated her daughter's assumption of most of her official duties.

Many women who led vigorous lives during the war felt the effects in later life. Nurses often had to resign before the end of the war because of physical breakdown, though others did not feel the effects for many years. Clara Barton's collapse did not occur until the mid-seventies, but she attributed her bad health primarily to overwork during the sixties. After two illnesses during the war years, one of them serious, she continued to suffer from gastric troubles but refused to give up. After three years at the front and four years working with missing soldiers and lecturing on her war experiences, she went to Europe for a rest but was soon with the Red Cross during the Franco-Prussian War. Already ill when she returned to the United States in 1873, she found her sister dying, her brother David in declining health (she had lost Stephen a few years before), and her favorite nephew an epileptic. In the fall of 1875 she lost one of her dearest friends when Henry Wilson passed away, for the war had brought them together and Wilson many times interceded to make her task a little easier. The papers of her nephew and biographer, William Barton, in the Smith College Archives, contain letters which indicate that some in her family believed she and Wilson were planning to be márried, and one goes so far as to say that Lydia Maria Child was making her wedding dress. William Barton did not mention Wilson's name in his biography, simply noting that it was thought she planned to marry a prominent politician.

Clara Barton showed signs of physical and mental collapse more than a year before Wilson's death, and some of her actions are difficult to explain in view of the fact that she had been a nurse. Also in William Barton's papers are letters written by and to Miss Barton from physicians, "healers," and clairvoyants from whom she sought advice by mail. When he was preparing her biography in 1917, Barton wrote Clara's great-niece that he "did not want to publish" her correspondence "with physicians at the time she thought herself an invalid." Among the letters is a copy of one, in her handwriting, to Doctor Edward B. Foote of New York, who had assured her that he diagnosed patients "in every part of the civilized world" and would be happy to recommend treatment if she would write him her symptoms. In her ten-page reply she repeatedly referred to hardships endured during the war, her disregard for her health, and the strain of lecture tours during 1867 and 1868. In one seven-month period she "spoke every night but Sundays, crossed the Mississippi 6 times on ice," and by spring was "weak and ill."

During 1874 and 1875 Miss Barton answered several newspaper advertisements of men and women offering to diagnose ailments by mail. She corresponded with at least four in Boston, including S. C. Hewitt and Charles Main, both of whom urged her to come to Boston but when she refused sent her medicine. Mrs. C. M. Morrison said she needed nothing but a lock of Miss Barton's hair, which she would hold while in rapport with the spirits of three physicians, one the Greek Galen "who had been out of the physical for about 1700 years." From November 1874 through the following June, Clara Barton was in touch with Mrs. Morrison, who recommended various medicines and diets. H. B. Storer also promised a cure if she would send a lock of hair, her age, and two dollars, but the medicine he concocted was $2.50 a bottle. In 1876 Clara went to a sanitarium in Dansville, New York, where she was cared for by Drs. J. C. Jackson and Harriet Austin. Her health and mental outlook improved during the next two years, and nearing sixty, she started her twenty-five years' work with the Red Cross.[7]

The end of the war found many women in all parts of the country destitute, despairing, and embittered. They had presumed conditions would be vastly improved after four years of bloodshed, and while there were hopeful signs on the horizon they were distant. People could later look back and see that during the war much had been done by and for women, but those who were hungry, confused, and in mourning could not recognize their gains. To talk to these women about the stronger na-

[7] William Barton to Saidee Riccius, Aug. 2, 1917; Edward B. Foote to Clara Barton, Feb. 23, Aug. 7, 1875; Clara Barton to Edward B. Foote, Feb. n.d., 1875; S. C. Hewitt to Clara Barton, Oct. 15, 25, 1875; Charles Main to Clara Barton, Dec. 2, 1874, Oct. 12, 1875; H. B. Wilcox [for Mrs. C. M. Morrison] to Clara Barton, Nov. 30, Dec. 2, 1874; Feb. 17, 23, 27, June 8, 1875; H. B. Storer to Clara Barton, Oct. 28, Nov. 8, 10, 1875, Clara Barton Papers, Smith College Archives.

tion welded together by the conflict would have been useless. Those who made great sacrifices and received nothing but problems in return took a pessimistic view, some for only a brief time and others for the rest of their lives.

16

A Bold and Active Position

O N MEMORIAL DAY, 1888, Clara Barton told a Boston audience that when the Civil War ended "woman was at least fifty years in advance of the normal position which continued peace . . . would have assigned her." She was, Miss Barton went on, in "a new bold active position" which made it possible for her to advance rapidly. While many of woman's gains between 1865 and 1890 were attributable to the conflict, none were freely bestowed upon her by a grateful public for services during the war. Rather they were achieved by the active, energetic, imaginative woman who, as Julia Ward Howe said, refused "to return to her chimney corner life of the fifties."[1]

In performing unfamiliar tasks and assuming new responsibilities women had acquired skills and self-confidence which made them more independent and anxious to be "up and doing." They had learned to work with others and to support themselves and their families; and in the process they developed new interests and broadened their horizons. Many proved to be so capable that they had won the admiration of those with whom they la-

[1] Clara Barton, "Memorial Day Address," May 30, 1888, Clara Barton Papers, Smith College Archives; Laura Richards and Maude Howe Elliott: *Julia Ward Howe* (Boston, 1915), I, 293.

bored. Blessed with a greater number of experienced leaders and afforded more numerous opportunities by the war, the sex was in a better position than ever before to go forward.

Much of woman's postwar progress may be ascribed to her increased employment opportunities, and to continued business and industrial expansion. How much more acute would have been the suffering of war widows, orphans, and impoverished Southerners if only the jobs available in 1861 had been open to them or if they had encountered as widespread opposition as their predecessors! Many conservatives still did not approve of women working outside the home; but while most women worked because of financial need, the ambitious had greater incentive to excel for their chances for advancement and recognition were more numerous. They no longer had to spend a lifetime dependent on others. They could strike out on their own and go to new communities with less risk of criticism than before, and those who did so were generally more realistic, broad-minded, and receptive to new ideas than their sheltered sisters. The economic emancipation of women was the most important single factor in her social, intellectual, and political advancement, and the war did more in four years to change her economic status than had been accomplished in any preceding generation.

When hundreds of jobs in government offices were opened to women during the war, no one could have predicted how significant this would be. By 1875 the number in Washington had doubled. Federal, state, and local agencies, business firms and institutions were employing women clerks, bookkeepers, stenographers, and receptionists. Foreign travelers were intrigued by the "government girls," and none more than the English feminist, Emily Faithfull, who made three visits to the United States during the seventies and early eighties. She marveled that the Civil War "alone procured women admission to the Civil Service," a vocation which she found among the most interesting in the nation. She was delighted to hear President Grant, Secretary of the Treasury George Boutwell, Francis Spinner, and other officials praise their work, and she thought American women extremely fortunate to have these opportunities. Competition for jobs was keen because wages were higher and workdays shorter than in most lines of work, and it was exciting to live in the nation's capital. A Kentuckian employed in the Post Office Department loved her work but hit upon the greatest drawback of these positions when she wrote, "the trouble is . . . you never know how long you can count on them." There was a certain insecurity in that the employee usually depended upon her benefactor's re-election, but she was usually in no greater jeopardy than a man unless the entire female office force was dismissed to make room for men. Rumors that this might happen were constantly circulated but usually proved false, and with the passage of the first effective Civil Service Acts in the eighties the danger was minimized.[2]

The regular overturn of Federal employees made astute politicians of women long before they had the ballot. After every election, officials were deluged with applications from the "female side of the party," as Thomas Donaldson referred to those who "wanted a slice of the loaf." The personal papers of politicians reveal the increasing pressure put on them by women wanting jobs, many of whom were careful to stress their war services or mention that they were the widows or orphans of soldiers. None was more persistent than Dr. Mary Walker, who pestered scores of Republican Congressmen for an appointment, never letting them forget that she had done her bit in the war. Nor did their demise necessarily silence her, for several years after Senator Logan's death she reminded his widow of promises he had made and pleaded with Mrs. Logan "to listen to a recital of the same."[3]

On April 15, 1883, the New York *Tribune* reported that "a book could be filled with the pathetic histories of the women in the Civil Service," yet their stories would have been even more "pathetic" had it not been for these jobs which enabled war widows and others from all parts of the nation to be self-supporting. Josephine Griffing, Julia Wheelock, and others active in the war had positions in Washington, and Annie Etheridge held one in Detroit until she married. Many once ardent

[2] Emily Faithfull: *Three Visits to America* (Edinburgh, 1884), p. 330; Virginia Grigsby to her brother, July n.d., 1883, Gibson-Humphreys Papers, Southern Historical Collection, University of North Carolina.

[3] Thomas Donaldson to W. E. Chandler, Apr. 21, 1881, W. E. Chandler Papers, Manuscript Division, Library of Congress; Mary Walker to Mrs. John A. Logan, Jan. 7, 1890, Mrs. John A. Logan Papers.

Confederates were working in Washington offices not long after the war, including Mrs. George Pickett, who was left penniless when the general died in 1875 and was only too happy to be added to the Federal payroll. Dozens of Southern Unionists were rewarded with appointments during reconstruction, some retaining them into the twentieth century.

If the *Tribune* reporter had searched every office he could not have found a more pathetic story than that of Mrs. Emma Richardson Moses in the Treasury Department. Described as a person "of education, refinement and . . . all that goes to make a true lady," Mrs. Moses was the daughter of an eminent South Carolina jurist who died in the sixties after having been financially ruined by the war. When she married Franklin Moses shortly before the conflict he gave promise of a brilliant future, but after serving as a Confederate officer he cast his lot with the radicals in 1867, was elected carpetbag governor in 1872, became involved in a number of fraudulent schemes and personal scandals, sank deeper and deeper in debt, turned on his friends, and was later arrested several times in the North for petty crimes. Mrs. Moses obtained a divorce in the late seventies, and needing work, accepted a position in Washington. She was lonely and hesitated to force her company on others who she feared held her "responsible for some of the Governor's misdoings."[4] There were hundreds of women who found in government work a chance to "lose" themselves in Washington and earn a living away from tragic memories.

As the government workers proved efficient, their supporters increased. Robert Porter's report on the 1,100 women employed in the Census Bureau in 1890 is typical of that of many other supervisors. More than half, he said, had scored higher than 85 per cent on the mathematics examination, a field considered by some beyond woman's comprehension, and they computed and "worked the tabulating machines" faster and more accurately than did the men. The women had a "more exact touch, were more expeditious in handling schedules, were more at home in adjusting delicate mechanisms and more anxious to make good

[4] John B. Dennis to Clara Barton, Dec. 12, 1882, Clara Barton Papers, Manuscript Division, Library of Congress; see also Robert Woody and Frances Simkins: *South Carolina During Reconstruction* (Chapel Hill, 1932), pp. 126–27, 370, 545.

records" than their male colleagues.[5] In both business and industry they were often more adept at handling machines, including typewriters and looms, and by the nineties were surpassing men in many lines of work.

Women employees increased in offices elsewhere in the nation, and many Southern postmistresses received their appointments because of conditions arising from the war. President Grant made more than 200 such appointments, including Elizabeth Van Lew and Mrs. Armistead Long, wife of a one-armed former Confederate colonel, whom he appointed postmistress in Charlottesville, Virginia. Many women were given similar positions because, as a journalist noted, they could subscribe to the oath that they had not borne arms against the United States Government, which relatively few men in the South could do.[6] That there were no more postmistresses in the United States in 1870 than ten years earlier may be explained by the fact that not half the prewar Southern post offices had been reopened and Union veterans were often appointed postmaster in other areas.

The "fight" for claims and pension payments opened a new opportunity for women who announced themselves as agents. For decades this was a thriving business; scores of private compensation bills were introduced in every session of Congress, old laws were amended and new ones enacted, until in the nineties the floodgates were opened to include most veterans and army nurses who could prove eligibility. The first pension legislation pertaining to widows and other female dependents of men who died in the service was enacted in 1862 and the last in 1959, when the widow of Confederate soldiers were made eligible for Federal pensions. On June 30, 1964, there were 1,545 widows of Civil War soldiers on the Federal Government's pension rolls, and 572 were Confederate widows also pensioned by Southern states. At this time Civil War widows were living in every state except Hawaii, Alaska, Delaware, and North Dakota, and six pensioners were listed as residing abroad. California had the largest number with 110, five of whom were Confederate, and Texas, Tennessee, Georgia and Virginia each had more than eighty. In June 1964 there were more than 1,545 Civil War

[5] Robert P. Porter to Mrs. John Logan, Mrs. John A. Logan Papers.
[6] *Frank Leslie's Illustrated Newspaper*, March 17, 1866.

widows in the nation, however. Some had remarried and were ineligible to receive a pension, and Southerners whose husbands fought in both the Civil War and Spanish American War were already drawing a pension when the 1959 law went into effect.

Ada Celeste Sweet, daughter of General Benjamin Sweet, was probably the most successful early pension and claims agent. When her father died in 1874, President Grant appointed her to succeed him, and she worked in this capacity until the nineties. Mrs. Emma Smith Porch, who as a teen-ager had served as guide and scout for the Federals in Missouri, spent ten years trying to convince Congress that her physical breakdown in the seventies was caused by her war activities, and in 1884 she was granted a pension of twenty dollars a month. Soon thereafter she became a "claims attorney, with pension claims a specialty," and her letterhead assured interested parties that she had been "Admited [sic] to practice in all departments in Washington, D. C." It is uncertain how many cases she handled before her "business as a claim agent . . . was nearly ruined" in the nineties, but she reported that at this time she "hardly ever got a case allowed" although she "took only good cases."[7]

Republican policies developed after the war period continued to stimulate the nation's economic growth and created additional jobs for women as well as men. With this expansion came urbanization, which had both happy and unhappy effects on women workers whose major problem was maintaining a decent standard of living. In 1865 women's wages were low, the cost of essentials high, and the competition with male workers keen, but by 1870 there was a faint glimmer of hope when men's unions began to realize that as long as women were willing to work for less pay and serve as strike breakers the wages of all would be depressed. A few unions admitted women in the sixties and seventies. But the Knights of Labor, did not admit women until 1881, a significant victory, and a few years later the American Federation of Labor welcomed the women's unions as affili-

[7] Mrs. John A. Logan: *The Part Taken by Women in American History* (Wilmington, 1912), p. 831; Ada Celeste Sweet to Mrs. John A. Logan, Mrs. John A. Logan Papers; Pension Records Number 276,360, Veterans Administration, National Archives; Emma Porch to Senator T. M. Cockrell, Feb. 3, 1896; Emma Porch to Webster Davis, Feb. 22, 1898, Emma Alvira Smith Porch Papers, National Archives.

ates. Women unionists did not entirely lack leaders immediately following the war; but excepting Jennie Collins, who had been a nurse, and Augusta Lewis Troup, who had to go to work after her family's fortune was wiped out in 1865, none of these had been directly affected by the conflict. The most prominent war leaders did not champion the cause of the factory operatives, sweatshop workers, and salesladies, although women laborers needed leaders, organizers, and the cooperation of men.

The New York Workingwomen's Protective Union was one of the most useful agencies created during the war, and its most valuable services were rendered after 1865. The union announced it was ready to assist "seamstresses, dressmakers, teachers and operatives in every branch of labor except HOUSEHOLD SERVICE." Furnishing a model for similar organizations in other Northern cities, it had a threefold purpose: to protect the workers against unfair practices and unscrupulous persons, to provide suitable jobs, and to open new employment opportunities to women. The union worked on the principle that workers needed not charity but guidance, legal assistance, and the opportunity to work. By 1878 the New York agency had taken to court 6,192 cases involving attempts to defraud women of wages, had recovered $20,169.19, and had settled more than 12,000 cases out of court. It made no charge for this or other services since the lawyers and interested parties contributed their time and energies, and all expenses were paid from donations. In the same period the union found work for 37,000 of the 124,000 applicants, and the number desiring but not finding jobs indicates the competition for places. Had it not been for this and similar organizations during the depression of 1873, the suffering would have been very acute.[8]

Newspaper support was essential to the workers' cause, and while a few journalists and other writers publicized the plight of women workers, many more advocates were needed. Susan Anthony and Elizabeth Cady Stanton gave them space in the short-lived *The Revolution;* but Lucy Stone Blackwell, Mary Livermore, and later editors of the *Woman's Journal* took scant

[8] *Plain Facts About Working Women* (Program of the Fifteenth Anniversary Meeting of the New York Workingwomen's Protective Association, 1879), Smith College Archives.

notice of their problems during the paper's forty-seven-year existence. Helen Campbell's series in the New York *Times*, later compiled and published as *Prisoners of Poverty* (1889), was a significant exposure, as were the writings of Elizabeth Stuart Phelps in the sixties and seventies and those of Eleanor Marx Aveling in the nineties. By 1890 more than a dozen states had made studies of the women's problems, and in 1888 the recently created Bureau of Labor published its report, *Working Women in the Large Cities*. States were beginning to legislate on hours and working conditions, but the situation had not appreciably improved by the nineties when Jacob Riis exposed sweatshop conditions and Stephen Crane linked the girls' starvation wages with prostitution. Nor had the evils disappeared when the muckrakers of the early twentieth century opened the public's eyes to a host of economic problems.

The destruction of the plantation-slavery system accelerated the industrialization of the South. While handicrafts and small industries had been developed during the war, the South had fewer factories in 1865 than 1860. During reconstruction some Northern capital was invested in Southern mills, but the real industrial revolution did not get under way until the eighties. By 1890 more than 17,000 women and girls were employed in factories, six times the number in 1870, and while the overwhelming majority came from the poor white class or were Negroes, a few from once wealthy families were driven into factory work. Orra Langhorne reported that the 300 white females employed in Lynchburg cigarette factories in 1886 came from "all classes of society," and several from Virginia's "first families" had found they could earn more in industry than "at the sewing machine." Yet prejudices against women working in factories kept many chained to their sewing machines, as census reports indicate, for between 1870 and 1890 the number of seamstresses increased from 17,860 to 71,319. Despite the feeling against factory operatives, some Southern leaders realized soon after the war that industrialization was needed to give work to war widows and other indigent women. Governor Robert Patton of Alabama stated in 1867 that "the employment of this large class of sufferers is a matter of pure necessity." He estimated that more than 20,000 widows and orphans in Alabama were untrained for other types of employment but might work in mills. In the eighties, however, he told a Congressional committee that it had often been necessary to bring skilled labor from the North.[9]

Although economic necessity compelled Southerners to modify their views on woman's work outside the home, the change in attitude came slowly. Cornelia Spencer rendered a real service by discussing women's need and opportunity for employment in the late sixties and seventies, but she also revealed her inner struggles in adjusting to the new situation. She probably helped to modify the ideas of older women as well as the "young ladies" to whom her column was addressed, and she generally took a progressive view as she stressed the need for looking forward, accepting graciously the changes wrought by the war, and realizing that women must solve their own problems. Mrs. Spencer considered any honest work honorable but reflected her Victorian upbringing by favoring teaching and home vocations. She did not like to see "refined and intelligent women" becoming factory operatives because the long hours, hard work, and personal contacts gave them little time or incentive to pursue intellectual interests. They would "slide downward" rather than elevate themselves when thrown in contact with "ignorance and vulgarity," she said, but if they must work in factories it should be as missionaries bent on raising the standards of their less fortunate colleagues. When readers asked her opinion of their becoming housekeepers or companions to older women, Mrs. Spencer replied that she would much prefer to have them clerk or keep accounts "in some office or store," and in this she was decidedly more liberal than most. A Louisianian was appalled to find an antebellum school friend clerking in a New Orleans department store in the eighties, for she had once been "a lady." "Just think of it!" she exclaimed. Yet hers was not an unusual experience in the postwar period.[1]

Educated women in all parts of the country taught for a

[9] Charles E. Wynes (ed.): *Southern Sketches From Virginia* (Charlottesville, 1964), pp. 73–74; Robert M. Patton: "The New Era of Southern Manufacturers," *DeBow's Review*, III (1867), 65; *Report of the Senate Committee on Labor and Capital* (1883), IV, 47, 537.

[1] *North Carolina Presbyterian*, Jan. 15, 1875; Jan. 31, 1872; Aug. 21, 1872; Mrs. Lucy Humphreys Johnstone to Mrs. Sarah Humphreys, Nov. 19, 1884, Gibson-Humphreys Papers, Southern Historical Collection, University of North Carolina.

living, but many proud ladies found it difficult to accept even this type of employment. When no other position was available Southern women taught in Negro schools, many of which were more adequately supported during reconstruction than those for whites; and it was not unusual for white women to work with Negro superintendents, as did Eliza Frances Andrews, since this position was frequently bestowed on Negro men by the radical state governments. A Negro teacher in Georgia said it was to the colored children's advantage to be taught by "white ladies of the upper class," provided they did not make the youngsters feel inferior, as had one in his school who told the pupils not "to come too close to her."[2] By the late seventies teachers and students had been segregated according to race, and the whites preferred teen-agers to be separated according to sex. Segregation, whether by race or sex, resulted in the proliferation of institutions which worked a hardship on the poorer areas, especially in the impoverished South. It meant that a greater number of public, private, and denominational schools must be supported, and this often meant poor instruction, inadequate library and laboratory facilities, and low salaries for teachers.

The entrance of women into the business and professional world focused attention on their need for training. In 1870, Whitelaw Reid told Anna Dickinson, "The one gospel which you ought to preach . . . is that women need . . . to fit themselves for work they undertake to do. Not one in a score of those who come to me for employment have any such fitness." If they want "to do a man's work," he said, they must prepare, and if they want equal opportunity they must pursue "it steadily and persistently" and not look upon a position as temporary until marriage comes their way.[3] When the exigencies of war brought thousands of untrained women into vocations, their critics were quick to make use of the argument that they were unqualified and should be replaced with men. If they wanted to hold and expand their wartime gains, they must be as well trained as their male competitors. Even those who did not expect to become self-supporting were told they should learn how "to do things." They were

[2] *Report of the Senate Committee on Labor and Capital* (1883), IV, 28–29, 121, 203, 578–80.
[3] Whitelaw Reid to Anna Dickinson, June 17, 1870, Anna E. Dickinson Papers.

reminded that many women who did not plan to earn a living had been compelled to do so and were handicapped by lack of "know-how."

Between 1865 and 1890 an educational revolution was taking place in the woman's world. Among the outstanding women's colleges found in this period were Vassar, Smith, Wellesley, Bryn Mawr, Barnard, Radcliffe, Goucher, Sophie Newcomb, and Agnes Scott. State universities and land grant colleges, often synonymous and the latter made possible by the Morrill Land Grant College Act of 1862, were opening their doors to women. Among the coeducational universities were Cornell, Michigan, Wisconsin, Kansas, Missouri, California, Texas, and Kentucky. Joseph LeConte had his first experience with coeds at the University of California and was so impressed by their abilities that he predicted "before long female talent will be so far recognized that the Professors' chairs will be occupied by ladies." When he wrote in 1871 women were found primarily on women's college faculties and were in the minority even there. Maria Baldwin of Ohio, one of the early university professors, at the age of twenty-one was teaching Latin and Greek at Baker University in Kansas, but she was an exception.[4] As women moved into the field of higher education they asked for admission to graduate schools in America and abroad, and with the increase of coeducational institutions came the demand for deans of women. Other administrative posts were occupied by qualified women, one of the most prominent being Alice Freeman Palmer, a University of Michigan graduate who was president of Wellesley in its formative period and later dean of women at the University of Chicago. Julia Tutwiler, after three years' study in Germany, returned to teach in her native Alabama, became president of Livingston Normal College, led in the establishment of the state-supported woman's college at Montevall, and pressed for the admission of women to the University of Alabama.

To meet the need for teacher training and vocational courses institutions were founded throughout the nation. The George Peabody Normal School opened in Nashville in 1875, made pos-

[4] Joseph LeConte to Emma LeConte Furman, June 19, 1871, Joseph Le-Conte Papers, Southern Historical Collection, University of North Carolina; *Frank Leslie's Illustrated Newspaper*, Mar. 3, 1866.

sible by Peabody's contribution of $3,500,000 to establish the Southern Education Fund. A part of the South's educational rehabilitation was financed by philanthropy from outside the region, a necessity if higher education was to meet postwar demands since the war had swept away endowments. In the eighties state-supported "normal and industrial colleges" for women were being chartered, Mississippi taking the lead; but in most states these institutions for the poorer girls were founded after the overthrow of the conservative Bourbon governments and in some about the time land grant colleges for men were established. In the seventies summer institutes for teachers were first conducted on university campuses and were open to both women and men even when the institution refused to admit girls in the regular academic session. Most Southerners agreed with Cornelia Spencer in opposing coeducation, but approving it in the summer institutes. Mrs. Spencer was enthusiastic about those held at the University of North Carolina and reasoned that they were quite proper since the men and women attending them were more mature and serious-minded than the average undergraduate. After reconstruction segregation was practiced in Southern colleges and universities, excepting Berea College in Kentucky, but by 1890 thirty-two institutions for Negroes were open to women.

The need for practical education was emphasized by many prominent women in the postwar period, among them Anna Dickinson. Mary Livermore preached the same sermon for an even longer time, lecturing more than 800 times on "What Shall We Do With Our Daughters?" and "Superfluous Women." She declared that as the excess of women in sixteen Eastern and Southern states precluded marriage for many, they must prepare for remunerative work. Even those who did marry might find it necessary to support the family, and the age had dawned when women were combining marriage with a career. She advocated domestic science, vocational, professional, and physical education courses, and she favored coeducation. Mrs. Jennie Cunningham Croly ("Jennie June"), an eminently successful journalist, feminist, and club woman, not only stressed the need for vocational training but also advocated keeping girls in school until their middle teens. She was one of the most outspoken critics of child labor. Before women in poorly paid jobs could advance, said Mrs. Croly, they needed two things neither of which they were receiving—a suitable education and the understanding and assistance of "more fortunate women." Though Mrs. Livermore, Anna Dickinson, Susan Anthony, and others emphasized the ballot as essential to educational and economic progress, Mrs. Croly believed that "work is infinitely more important than a vote and infinitely better."[5]

As previously noted, the war's effect on the medical profession was not immediately apparent. Since most nurses returned home feeling unappreciated, they were doubtful of their future and that of the profession. After 1863, when the War Department authorized the Surgeon General as well as Miss Dix to appoint nurses, she became little more than a figurehead and this was a blow to her pride and to the prestige of women nurses in general. Throughout the war the army surgeons had ridiculed, ignored, and harassed the women, most of whom at some time felt unwanted. No group had made greater personal sacrifices and none was more unceremoniously damned with faint praise. Those whose health had been impaired because of their service had to fight for a pension and the fortunate might collect a small monthly compensation; but not until 1892, after the Civil War nurses had organized and the Woman's Relief Corps assailed Congress, were the majority eligible for pensions.

There were nurses who seemed undisturbed and found postwar work to do. Cornelia Hancock and other Union nurses worked for years with the freedmen, and the Confederate Kate Cumming remained in Mobile until she accepted a teaching position in the new industrial city of Birmingham. Mary Phinney von Olnhausen, Princess Agnes Salm-Salm, and Clara Barton nursed in the Franco-Prussian War, and Hattie Noyes and Hannah Shaw of the Christian Commission went to China as medical missionaries. Women were being called into this field, and Jane Hoge as president of the Woman's Board of Foreign Missions encouraged many wartime colleagues to give serious thought to missionary

[5] Mary Ashton Livermore: *The Story of My Life* (Hartford, 1899), pp. 407, 491–94; Mary Ashton Livermore: *What Shall We Do With Our Daughters?* (Boston, 1883), pp. 133–45; *Report of the Senate Committee on Labor and Capital* (1883), IV, 605–15.

training. When Clara Barton, with the support of President Garfield, founded and headed the American Red Cross she inspired women to prepare themselves for work in the organization. It cannot be said positively to what extent the autobiographical writings of war nurses and Sanitary Commission workers influenced young ladies to follow in the "Florence Nightingales'" footsteps, but their publications and lectures on their war experiences probably interested many in making a career of medicine.

Educational opportunities for women in medicine increased in the quarter-century following the war. By the mid-eighties there were twenty-two schools for nurses in the nation and the number of medical colleges had increased. Before leaving for England, Elizabeth and Emily Blackwell established the New York Medical College for women, and in 1870 the Woman's Medical College of Chicago was founded. Even more encouraging was the fact that a number of men's medical schools admitted women. In 1871 the University of Michigan Medical School was opened to them, and while required to take the same course of study as men, the women were taught in separate classes. By the nineties more than a dozen medical colleges were coeducational, including those of Syracuse, California, Iowa, and Howard Universities. State medical societies began to lower their barriers in the seventies, the Kansas Medical Association being first in 1872; and quite by accident the American Medical Association in 1876 accepted the credentials of one Dr. S. H. Stevenson of Chicago, only to discover this was Sarah Hackett Stevenson. But walls tumbled slowly in these associations and prejudice remained strong against women physicians long after the beginning of the twentieth century.

No women were more aware of the medical profession's prejudice than the war nurses, who realized that to earn a degree was but half the battle, for they then had to establish a practice. Yet nurses did find their careers in the war and determined to become doctors despite the obstacles. Nancy Hill took her degree from the University of Michigan Medical School and opened an office in Iowa. Mary Safford completed her medical studies in the United States in 1867 and spent a year in Vienna before joining the faculty of the Boston University School of Medicine and practicing in the same city. She was one of the foremost women surgeons in the country and is credited with being the first of her sex to perform an ovariectomy. Belle Reynolds, decorated for war work, became the resident physician in the Home for the Friendless in Chicago, engaged in Red Cross work in the United States and the Philippines, and practiced for more than thirty years in Santa Barbara, California.

Women who agreed with one another on little else credited Anna Dickinson with clearing the path for feminine speakers, and in the seventies Emily Faithfull found the United States "a great field for lady lecturers." When Olive Logan was trying to get started she asked Anna for a recommendation to use in her advertising since she was encountering competition ranging from "the lofty poetess to the little newspaper scribbler, from the actress to the working woman and from Washington lobbyists to women preachers."[6] Anna's emulators dreamed of financial success, for in the late sixties and early seventies she was making more than $20,000 a year; but they did more than earn a living. As they crusaded for a host of reforms and expressed a variety of opinions, they gave insight into postwar problems and developments and stressed woman's needs in the changing times. So promising was public speaking that young ladies were soon taking elocution courses in schools and colleges, and if they failed to succeed on the platform they could always try their hand at teaching the subject.

The end of the war made it necessary for Anna Dickinson to find a new set of lecture topics and the woman's rights advocates helped solve the problem. They needed all the attractive talent they could recruit, and Anna was ripe for conversion. For ten years after the war she included suffrage speeches among her offerings. "Idiots and Women" was one of the first, the title alluding to women's classification with "paupers, criminals, and idiots" in being denied the ballot. A Brooklyn editor said the speech should have been entitled "A Plea for Women's Rights," but Anna was in the business to make money and was wise enough to know that any such title would have had an adverse effect on box-office receipts. For the same reason she found it profitable to lecture on sensational subjects. In the seventies, she spoke on "A Woman's Opinion of It," which sounded like a harangue on woman

[6] Faithfull: *Three Visits*, p. 295; Olive Logan to Anna Dickinson, Oct. 8, 1865, Anna E. Dickinson Papers.

suffrage, and audiences were small until word got around as to the contents. She actually condemned "this savage civilization and infidel Christianity" for its double standard and declared she was doing so because no one else would. But many people were shocked to hear a woman hurl at mixed audiences such words as prostitution, rape, seduction, and adultery. Journalists said the subject was "unsuited to the lecture platform," and one thought it should have been entitled "Stirring the Dunghill," but even the most caustic had to admit that she "held her audience's attention." When she spoke in New York, Theodore Tilton, Roger Pryor (without his wife,) and Victoria Woodhull were in the audience, and it is safe to say that Mrs. Woodhull, herself an advocate of free love, was not among those shocked by Anna.[7] While she was delivering this lecture, her earnings reached an all-time high.

When Anna Dickinson embarked on her Southern tour in 1875, she included neither of these speeches in her repertoire but spoke instead on "Joan of Arc," "For Your Own Sake," which stressed woman's duties as opposed to her rights, and "What's To Hinder?" which emphasized that women no longer had "to work in silence and obscurity in the home" since there was now nothing "to prevent a woman from doing what she will." The last most startled Southerners, and one critic of the Richmond *Enquirer* reported that "some of the sentiments she uttered have seldom been heard in this community before." The press made it clear that women lecturers were a curiosity in the South, frowned upon by most, but at the same time reporters obviously tried to be polite and some managed to manifest enthusiasm. A Petersburg, Virginia, paper noted that lecturers had never been popular but confessed, "It will require great genius to inaugurate a fashion which will be popular with our people." Criticism of Anna was more often mild than sharp, but the *Southern Home* warned Charlotte citizens that she was "a female rightist," one of those "shriekers whose doctrines . . . have done so much to unhinge and demoralize even the best Northern society," and had "never been a friend of the South."[8]

[7] Brooklyn *Daily Mirror*, May 13, 1868; Boston *Post*, Nov. 6, 1867; Hartford *Evening Post*, Feb. 25, 1875; New York *Daily Tribune*, Mar. 6, 1875; Brooklyn *Daily Eagle*, Mar. 6, 1875.
[8] Richmond *Enquirer*, Apr. 3, 1875; Charleston *News and Courier*, Apr. 16, 1875; Savannah *Morning News*, Apr. 17, 1875; Petersburg (Va.) *Daily*

The response of Southerners to women lecturers had changed little since antebellum days. Typical of the older women's attitude was that of Mrs. Garnett Andrews. When Eliza Frances, her daughter, returned to Georgia after teaching in Mississippi, she was asked to speak in a local school but Mrs. Andrews opposed the idea because "it was too much like Olive Logan and Anna Dickinson."[9] Miss Andrews later developed a mind of her own and not only advanced with American society but moved ahead of it in permitting herself to be listed as a Socialist during World War I. In 1926 when she declined an invitation to address the International Academy of Science in Italy, age rather than decorum was responsible for her decision —"Fanny" Andrews was eighty-six at the time.

Clara Barton's speeches immediately following the war and most she delivered later stressed her personal wartime experiences and the conflict's effect on women. Between 1866 and 1869, Miss Barton addressed hundreds of audiences on "Work and Incidents of Army Life," "The Moral and Religious Effect of the War Upon the Soldier and the Country," and "How the Republic Was Saved, or War Without Tinsel." Her fee ranged from $100 to $150, except when she spoke to veterans' groups for less. She always opened her address with "Gentlemen and Ladies," and while a friend of many suffragists, especially of Susan Anthony whom she defended with tongue and pen, she never crusaded for suffrage or for temperance.

Annie Wittenmyer, Laura Haviland, and Mary Livermore were among the war workers who supported the temperance movement, and Anna Dickinson was accidentally involved when she was called to the platform of the National Temperance Convention in 1875; but it could hardly be said that she aided the cause. She tactlessly told the gathering that woman needed the ballot, not prayer, to fight liquor, for they could "pray until the crack of doom, but there would scarcely be a drunkard less." This offended many in the audience, for the temperance crusade was

---

News, Apr. 16, 1875; *Southern Home* (Charlotte), Apr. 12, 1875; James Harvey Young: "A Woman Abolitionist Views the South in 1875," *Georgia Historical Quarterly*, XXXII (1948), 241–251.

[9] Mrs. Garnett Andrews to Rosalie Andrews, May 15, 1871, Garnett Andrews Papers, Southern Historical Collection, University of North Carolina.

supported by churches, and many conservative women, including Southerners, were active in it long before they participated in other movements. Anna's statements nearly broke up the meeting, as women rose to proclaim that she had "degraded prayer" by putting it in the same category with politics. One who said that "prayer was the greatest of all reformers" asked Anna if she thought she could have ascended the lecture platform and remained there without women's prayers.[1]

Mary Livermore was a professional crusader and included both suffrage and temperance among her causes, often using one to support the other, but she could not have held out as a public speaker for thirty-five years if she had been indifferent to her audiences' views. No woman of the Civil War generation lasted as long on the platform as Mrs. Livermore. Beginning immediately after the war by telling of her experiences with the Sanitary Commission, she later advocated a host of reforms from the rostrum. After Anna Dickinson went into decline Mrs. Livermore advised her to renew her strength by allying herself with the Woman's Christian Temperance Union, saying that if Anna was "careful" she could expect to follow her career for many years. At the time Anna was forty-one and Mrs. Livermore sixty-three and still going strong.[2]

Kate Field, four years older than Anna, in many ways resembled the egotistical, nonconforming Miss Dickinson. While known primarily for her journalism and other writings, she had done some lecturing during the war and was later lauded for her rollicking, vigorous, humorous presentations, but like many lecturers of the period she was inclined to overwork the pronoun "I." Among her subjects was one popular with Anna Dickinson and other strong-minded feminists, namely "Mormonism," a creed most women could not endorse. Although Miss Field could claim few other "firsts," she was the first person to lecture in Alaska; her audience was composed of miners, her subject "Charles Dickens."[3]

In 1865 no crusaders were more confident of immediate vic-

[1] Chicago *Tribune*, June 4, 1875.
[2] Mary Livermore to Anna Dickinson, Dec. 18, 1883, Anna E. Dickinson Papers; Livermore: *The Story of My Life*, p. 473.
[3] Helen Beal Woodward: *The Bold Women* (New York, 1953), pp. 201–14.

tory than woman suffrage advocates, for they expected to ride to the ballot box with the Negroes, whose emancipation they had supported. In 1866 their organization was rechristened the Equal Rights Association, and they fought desperately to get the word "male" deleted from the Fourteenth Amendment, which defined citizenship and included all men excepting Indians. Failing in this they concentrated on being included in the Fifteenth Amendment which gave Negro men the right to vote. But many Northerners as well as most Southerners doubted the wisdom of conferring the franchise on those so recently freed from bondage, and this the politicians knew. To include two unpopular groups in the amendment, women and Negroes, would further endanger its chances of passage and ratification. At this moment the women lost several longtime male supporters, including Horace Greeley, Wendell Phillips, and Frederick Douglass, who maintained that this was the Negro's "hour" and after he gained the vote women would be next. By 1869 troubles had developed within the association, and when it became apparent that women were not to be included in the Fifteenth Amendment the organization split. The Anthony-Stanton National Woman Suffrage Association (no men allowed) pushed for a sixteenth amendment granting suffrage to women and the Blackwell-Livermore-Howe American Woman Suffrage Association concentrated on obtaining the franchise through state legislation. The schism continued for twenty years and weakened the movement, but it is doubtful that it could have succeeded in this period even had the women held together.

Susan Anthony never ceased to believe that had the war not come women would have won the ballot in the sixties, but she imagined it nearer a reality in 1860 than it actually was. The women had just begun to press their cause in the fifties, and many woman's rightists did not think this the primary concern of the group. Had the measure reached Congress it is doubtful that a majority of the free state congressmen or any from the slave states would have supported it, and even had it passed Congress as an amendment it would not have been ratified. Because so many suffrage advocates were abolitionists too, and assuming that slavery would have continued during the sixties had there been no war, it is safe to say that the fifteen slaveholding states would not have ratified the amendment. The best hope of the suffragists lay on the traditionally democratic frontier; and while they lost their battle in Kansas just after the war, women were given the vote in Wyoming Territory in 1869. However, Wyoming's admission as a state twenty years later came only after heated debate on the woman suffrage article in the state constitution. Then in the nineties Colorado, Utah, and Idaho were admitted with the same provision. There is little reason to believe that without the war and the injection of the Negro question nationwide woman suffrage could have become a reality before the nineties at the earliest. The woman's rightists were unquestionably the victims of reconstruction politics, but they also misjudged the public's attitude.

New faces appeared at the Equal Rights meeting in May 1866, and there is no doubt that potential strength lay in the aggressive, active, independent women of the war generation, yet many who had worked the hardest and sacrificed the most during the struggle made no claim to having earned the right to vote. In the late sixties most were too preoccupied, indifferent, or weary to give it a thought, and in the seventies and eighties many opposed it. The Boston Committee of Remonstrants, founded in 1882, circulated propaganda against suffrage, petitioned Congress and state legislatures to block it, and published *The Remonstrance* to offset the *Woman's Journal*. Similar groups were organized elsewhere; and while few women went to this extreme, many thought woman suffrage ridiculous. When Martha Wright tried to circulate a petition favoring the idea one exclaimed, "Perfect Nonsense!!!" Mrs. Wright hated to "paddle around" trying to get signatures because so many "irate" women "sneered" at her, but she reasoned philosophically that "as the world moves they can't help moving with it."[4]

In the South a few women joined Susan Anthony and others in trying to vote in 1871 and 1872, among them Elizabeth Meriwether, but the overwhelming majority living through the war and reconstruction felt with Augusta Evans Wilson that "politics at best was slightly degrading, and . . . noisy women reformers were not a credit to their sex." She held the same opinion of those who joined the temperance fight and is reported to have said, "If

[4] Martha Wright to William Lloyd Garrison II, Dec. 16, 1868, June 10, 1869, Garrison Family Papers.

358

women attended to their privileges, they would not need to be keen about their rights." Eliza Frances Andrews opposed woman suffrage in the press and spoke for thousands when she said that woman's "business is to refine and elevate society . . . her mission is moral rather than intellectual, domestic rather than political." As for woman's needing the vote before they could advance economically, she pointed to their entrance into many new fields and concluded that "female suffrage would not affect the matter one way or the other." She hoped that the question would be submitted to "women only," in which case she was positive that it would "never become a *fait accompli*" and would have to be forced on Southerners like Negro suffrage. This would mean, she said, that "Bridget and Dinah will have it . . . a charming picture of equality for Southern ladies to contemplate." Yet a few colored women did vote in local and state elections during reconstruction and were encouraged to do so by Negro election officials.[5]

There were faint but optimistic signs that women were becoming more vote-conscious by the seventies. In 1872 the National Woman Suffrage Association had members in every state and eleven of the forty (!) vice presidents were in the South, most of whom supported the Republican party. More to the detriment than advantage of the movement, Victoria Woodhull ran for President in 1872. Frederick Douglass was nominated for Vice President on the same ticket, but he viewed the proceedings as impractical and "hastily extemporarized."

It was at this time that Grant told Emily Faithfull he championed the economic advancement of women but opposed "female suffrage."[6] During the eighties new recruits joined the ranks and by the nineties temperance women were interested, including a score or more in every Southern state, among them Caroline Merrick and Belle Kearney, both influenced more by Francis Willard than by the old-line suffrage leaders. In all areas of the nation younger, active women were becoming ardent exponents of equality for their sex, and when the two suffrage or-

[5] William Perry Fidler: *Augusta Evans Wilson, 1835–1909*, (Tuscaloosa, 1951), pp. 163–64; Eliza Frances Andrews Scrapbook, Garnett Andrews Papers, Southern Historical Collection, University of North Carolina; Benjamin Quarles: "Frederick Douglass and the Woman's Rights Movement," *Journal of Negro History*, XXV (1940), 33–44.
[6] Faithfull: *Three Visits*, p. 38.

ganizations came together the movement gained new strength and life. Woman suffrage would, however, have to await another war before becoming the law of the land.

Some reform groups were kept intact during the war, but little attention was paid them by the preoccupied public. As soon as the war ended, however, they regrouped their forces, and as a journalist noted, there was "a revival of the 'isms' . . . socialism, freeloveism, Bloomerism, and a score of like doctrines." The Dress Reform League convened in June 1865, hoping to find that the war had made trousers acceptable female attire; but if the members thought Clara Barton and other workers at the front would continue to wear the modified Bloomer costume, they were doomed to disappointment. The conflict had an indirect effect on dress reform when it forced women to work outside the home. As the working girl daily battled the elements, got on and off public conveyances, walked great distances, crossed muddy or dusty streets, waded through gutters and pools of water, and worked on rainy days in soaked dresses and petticoats, she was ready to shorten her skirts a few inches well before decorum said she might. This and the postwar emphasis on physical education and women's sports did more than the Dress Reform League had ever done to alter styles. Croquet, tennis, roller skating, and bicycling gained favor soon after the war, and while cycling was eventually approved by most as healthful and moral, there were critics who proclaimed it as both dangerous and licentious. The Women's Rescue League was organized in Washington to fight the bicycle because, as it maintained, "the temptations of the road were daily swelling the army of outcast women" and the costume worn by cyclists was shocking.[7]

Dr. Mary Safford and other women favored simpler, more comfortable dress but these sensible women are not to be confused with those like Dr. Mary Walker who insisted on male attire, or Cecelia Whitehead who wore men's clothing for two years despite the "great mental strain." She told a Senate committee that the "two necessary factors" for woman's advancement were dress reform and the franchise. Mary Walker was the most

[7] New York *Herald*, June 26, 1865; Foster Rhea Dulles: *America Learns to Play: A History of Popular Recreation, 1607–1940* (New York, 1952), pp. 194–95, 266–67.

widely publicized of the nonconformists because she was most frequently arrested for wearing male attire and persistently refused to relinquish her right to do so. She was also a professional reformer who advocated woman's rights, temperance, and the anti-tobacco crusade. Even her writings were sensational, but her *Unmasked, or the Science of Immorality* (1878) did such a thorough job of "unmasking" sex that it shocked even the uninhibited. Whatever might be said in her favor, Mary Walker was so eccentric that she injured rather than aided the reforms she supported. She was more favorably received during her lecture tour in England than in the United States, where she became an object of ridicule.[8]

Reformers had less to say about divorce in the immediate postwar period, although they realized it was on the increase. Woman's rights advocates continued their fight to liberalize the divorce laws so that women could rid themselves of good-for-nothing husbands, and temperance workers were convinced that "demon rum" was the root of the problem, as it often was. Rid the country of liquor, they said, and there will be fewer divorces, an argument advanced by many in the temperance ranks who were themselves wives or relatives of intemperate men. Elizabeth Stewart, a war nurse who joined the temperance movement, had seen soldiers become alcoholics and was convinced that many postwar family problems could be attributed to rum. Most Americans of the period were, as Emily Faithful said, either abstainers or heavy drinkers—they did not "practice moderation." But whatever the causes of divorce, the public was shocked to be told by Labor Commissioner Carroll D. Wright that between 1867 and 1886 divorce had increased 150 per cent.[9]

The increase in prostitution had been spotlighted throughout the war and was discussed by the reformers, including the temperance women. Hannah Tatum told the 1875 temperance convention that prostitution was "chiefly due to liquor"; and Missouri Stokes, one of the organization's most active crusaders in Georgia, fought not only for anti-liquor laws and temperance

[8] *Report of Senate Committee on Labor and Capital* (1883), II, 919–20, 924; Charles Snyder: *Dr. Mary Walker: The Little Lady in Pants* (New York, 1962), pp. 51–87.

[9] Sidney Herbert Ditzion: *Marriage, Morals and Sex in America* (New York, 1953), p. 277; Faithfull: *Three Visits*, p. 92.

education in the public schools but also for a state-supported home for "fallen women." Mary Livermore told her audiences that prostitution and alcoholism were linked, but she also asserted that if girls were trained so that they could obtain jobs much would be done to eradicate prostitution. What she failed to note was the connection between low wages and the evil. In speaking on prostitution Julia Ward Howe directed her remarks primarily to men by saying, "You men have created for women a hideous profession whose ranks you recruit from the unprotected, the innocent and the ignorant. This is the only profession, so far as I know, that man has created for women." Anna Dickinson emphasized the problem in her speech on the double standard, and all over the nation women discussed the matter openly as never before the war. Some strove to destroy the evil by trying to rehabilitate prostitutes, and one of "Mother" Bickerdyke's activities in San Francisco was working with them in the city's red-light district. A young San Franciscoan wrote a friend about "this awful prostitution in our midst which only feminine moral force" could eradicate.[1] Yet only the most naïve would ever suppose that either alcoholism or prostitution could be successfully legislated out of any society.

Helen Hunt Jackson championed a cause in which few people were interested, the American Indian. After her husband, Major Edward Hunt, suffocated in an underwater vessel he was testing during the war, she supported herself by writing, always hiding behind a pseudonym. In 1875 she married the wealthy railroad executive William Sharpless Jackson and moved to Colorado, where she soon became interested in the Indians. While visiting in Boston she heard Chief Standing Bear speak of the plight of the Ponca Indians and forthwith determined to tell the American people about the injustices done the race. In 1881 she published *A Century of Dishonor,* one of the most significant volumes to come from a woman's pen in the postwar period. Exposing the government's mistreatment of its "wards," she sharply assailed its policies and those of the Interior Department and Carl Schurz in particular. Mrs. Jackson made no attempt to

---

[1] Chicago *Tribune,* June 4, 1875; Richards and Elliott: *Julia Ward Howe,* I, 308–16; Coelia Curtis to Anna Dickinson, Jan. 18, 1870, Anna E Dickinson Papers.

be objective, for she wanted to arouse the American people. The year after her book appeared the Indian Rights Association was established, and six years later the Dawes Act became law.[2]

Prison reform caught the attention of reformers, but in the South the convict lease system presented a special challenge. This was a direct outgrowth of the war, which had destroyed many penal institutions, and of emancipation which removed the whites as disciplinarians of the Negroes. After Southerners assumed control of the state governments the system became involved in politics and in many states was a disgrace. Men and women convicted of crimes were leased by the states to individuals and companies, for whom they worked for the length of their sentence. Politically influential men could lease a large labor force and supply the workers with nothing more than food to sustain them and sufficient clothing to cover them, and they were kept in chains and crowded together in compounds without any thought to decency and health. At best the system was bad and at worse deplorable. Negroes more often than whites were convicted on little or no evidence and given unreasonably long sentences. Many women opposed the system as cruel and indecent, but two stand out. Julia Tutwiler, in addition to being an eminent educator, was also active in the Woman's Christian Temperance Union, peace organizations, and women's clubs. She campaigned for prison reform and abolition of the convict lease system and was instrumental in bringing about reforms and in getting schools set up in labor camps. Rebecca Felton of Georgia also opposed "the notorious convict lease" which she called "a foul blot on civilization." She told of convict camps where men and women were chained together, and of unfair sentences imposed on Negroes, citing as an example a young girl who was sentenced to five years for stealing fifty cents. Mrs. Felton reported that of the 1,200 persons sentenced in 1880, "only 112 were white." She was among the first Southern women to advocate equal rights, was an ardent temperance worker, and the first woman to sit in the United States Senate when given an *ad interim* appointment upon the death of Tom Watson in 1922.[2]

The postwar club movement clearly shows that American

[2] Rebecca Felton to Mrs. John A. Logan, Jan. 1, 1881, Mrs. John A. Logan Papers.

women had no intention of staying at home. In all the nation's history prior to 1865 not as many women's clubs were founded as in the quarter-century following the war. It is impossible to give attention to all, but they reflect the greater activity and interests of the late-nineteenth-century women. Mrs. Jennie Croly organized the Sorosis in New York as a protest against women's exclusion from a banquet tendered Charles Dickens by the all-male New York Press Club; and in the same year, 1868, Julia Ward Howe and others founded the New England Woman's Club. Similar organizations sprang into existence across the nation and in 1892 the General Federation of Women's Clubs was formed with affiliates in every state. From the beginning they refused to mix in politics, and not until 1914 did the federation endorse woman suffrage. Mrs. Howe made it clear that it would not pit "East against West, or North against South," but the members would "meet as citizens as one common country . . . to love and serve the whole as one.[3]

It was the Sorosis and New England Woman's Clubs that launched the Association for the Advancement of Women dedicated to their social, economic, and cultural advancement. In 1914 more than 5,000 local clubs were "federated," and at least twice as many similar groups were not, for by no means all were invited to affiliate. Even more exclusive was the American Association of University Women, which grew out of a meeting of eighteen delegates from eight colleges in Boston in November 1881. And in June of the next year sixty-five delegates met in New York, and over the protests of Lucy Stone Blackwell but with the encouragement of Alice Freeman Palmer the Association of Collegiate Alumnae was organized. The name was later changed, but the purpose was the same: to bring together women graduates of recognized colleges and universities for furtherance of educational work. By 1900 the graduates of twenty-three American colleges and universities from Massachusetts to California were eligible for membership, but no groups were formed in the South.

Urban women had innumerable opportunities to affiliate with clubs, and with the organization of the Patrons of Hus-

---

[3] Richards and Elliott: *Julia Ward Howe*, I, 265–68, 295; Nell Orgel to Anna Dickinson, Dec. 6. 1869, Anna E. Dickinson Papers.

bandry, or the Grange, rural women across the nation were given their opportunity. Oliver Kelley, a government clerk, toured the South in 1866 and returned to Washington convinced that farm families needed social outlets. While the social aim became secondary to economic and political interests in the seventies, to most women it remained the primary advantage of membership. They paid dues of only fifty cents a year and not only attended meetings which combined business with social activities but received other benefits. A South Carolinian said that membership in the Grange brought her into contact with "outside ideas," including those related to women's "work and wages" and other matters of which she had "no experience or observation." Previously she had no idea that men and women were in economic competition with each other. It was at Grange meetings, she said, that "the world's woman dawned on me, the woman beyond and outside the prayer meeting and home."[4]

When the Civil War veterans organized it was only a matter of time before their womenfolk would come together in auxiliaries or separate groups, but even before they founded regional associations the ladies had established the custom of observing a memorial day on which they decorated soldiers' graves and held commemorative services. The Confederates chose May 10 and the Union women May 30, the latter ultimately designated the national Memorial Day, although specific Southern groups continue to conduct services on Confederate Memorial Day. In the eighties interested Northern ladies affiliated with either the Ladies of the Grand Army of the Republic or the Woman's Relief Corps, and in the nineties local and state societies were brought together as the United Daughters of the Confederacy.

These organizations interested themselves in a wide range of activities, including the perpetuation of war legends and memories, interest in war widows and orphans, and other educational, social, and philanthropic projects. The members have derived social satisfaction from their regular meetings and conventions and have at times been criticized for the conservatism always found among some members of organizations dedicated to romanticizing the past. While these groups tended to emphasize

[4] Sally Elmore Taylor Memoirs, typescript, Southern Historical Collection, University of North Carolina.

regional differences, the Daughters of the American Revolution, founded in the nineties, brought together ancestor-conscious women from all parts of the country. In many instances this was the first national organization with which Southern women affiliated, many of them also members of the United Daughters of the Confederacy. They began tracing their family trees, often with greater enthusiasm than they had done anything since the war; and by 1912, 87,000 women had found among their forebears a Revolutionary soldier who had fought on the "right" side. Southern women who had refused to have anything to do with the Centennial Exposition of 1876 because it was "Yankee" were now reunited with Northern sisters through the American Revolution.

The Civil War was a mere episode in the lives of some women, a gay interlude for a few, a profound experience for most, and a catastrophe for many. It reached out to touch unborn generations as it hastened the "emancipation" of the sex, not only by affording more numerous opportunities but also by creating greater need, for it was necessity which compelled many to assert their independence. When sheltered timid women came out of their homes to join with others in patriotic endeavors, when bold resourceful ones stepped into the "man's sphere" and did his work, when determined, courageous, or foolhardy ones ignored masculine criticism and Victorian decorum, the individual was inevitably affected, but more important, she was helping to change the position and image of all. Experience acquired during the four years of conflict equipped women for their "war of independence" and enabled them to prove their capabilities as they could never have done, according to Clara Barton, during "continued peace."

There were many reasons why not all the American women moved shoulder-to-shoulder at the same pace, among them the age-old differences between rural and urban societies, for despite urbanization the United States remained primarily rural. Also important was the greater prewar progress made in some areas than others, as well as contrasting circumstances in the victorious and defeated sections. More important by the nineties than any differences was the uniting of so many women from all parts of the country in national movements and organizations; and while not all sectional bitterness had disappeared, the younger, active women were less inclined to brood about the past or get lost in self-pity.

By the nineties women were "fifty years in advance of the normal position" they would have reached had their progress come through the slow evolutionary process rather than the revolutionary. Whatever else may be said for war, changes come rapidly in time of conflict. Even constructive change encounters those who determine to maintain the status quo, and women faced innumerable obstacles as they sought to advance, but their progress indicates that they too had learned to "fight" during the war. A comparison of women's advancement during the seventy-eight years between the end of the American Revolution and 1861 with the forty-nine years between 1865 and the outbreak of the First World War shows that in the latter period they outran and outdistanced their predecessors. The Civil War provided a springboard from which they leaped beyond the circumscribed "woman's sphere" into that heretofore reserved for men. While the country was slow to express its appreciation to the feminine "veterans" of this war, the nation entered another conflict in 1917 confident that its women were much better equipped to do their part than their ancestors had been in 1861.

Acknowledgments

S CORES OF PERSONS have assisted me in the preparation of
this study and I wish it were possible to mention each one
individually, for I am grateful to all. Allan Nevins and Bell I.
Wiley have offered many valuable suggestions and constant encouragement during the research and writing; and Fletcher M.
Green, my teacher and longtime friend, has been an inspiration
in this undertaking as in all others. My students and colleagues
have shown patience and understanding during the years "the
book" took precedence over all else, and I am especially grateful
to Charles S. Davis, Walter D. Smith, Alvin L. Duckett and the
staff of the Winthrop College Library for their cooperation. John
Pomfret, Ray Billington, John Steadman, Mary Isabel Fry, Anne
Hyder, Mrs. Malcolm Bean and others at the Henry E. Huntington Library made my months of research in San Marino both
pleasant and profitable. Margaret Grierson, Elizabeth Duvall and
their associates in the Smith College Archives extended me so
many special privileges and the Sophia Smith Collection proved
such a "gold mine" that I remained in Northampton much longer
than I had intended. James Patton, Anna Brooke Allan and Caroline Wallace of the Southern Historical Collection at the University of North Carolina, and Mattie Russell and Mrs. John Grey of

3 6 9

the Duke University Manuscript Division once again showed an abnormal interest in my work and assisted me in innumerable ways. Equally cooperative were the staffs of the Library of Congress and the National Archives, but I am especially indebted to Percy Powell, Bruce Fant, Elmer Parker, Albert Blair, Henry Beers and that gracious "storehouse of information" at the Archives, Mrs. Sarah Jackson.

I shall always remember friends who helped me with especially thorny problems. Merlin Stonehouse devoted many hours to the compilation of material relating to the John Wesley North family, information which he alone possesses; and John Hammond Moore called to my attention several manuscript collections which I might have overlooked. Eleanor Flexner and A. Elizabeth Taylor shared with me their findings on the woman's rights and suffrage movements; and Mildred Pendleton Newton and J. Ambler Johnston supplied family records relating to the postwar life of Judith Brockenbrough McGuire. Robert Waite, Jr., permitted me to quote from one of his unpublished papers on a seldom-studied aspect of the war, and the late William Best Hesseltine suggested a number of sources used in this study.

I am especially grateful to those officials who assisted me in collecting information on the living Civil War pensioners,— Edward R. Silberman (Veteran's Administration), W. C. Hoffman (Florida State Board of Pensions), J. Harmon Smith (Georgia Department of Archives), Peter Wheeler (Georgia Department of Veteran's Service), Ruben King (Alabama Department of Pensions and Security), E. C. Rhodes (Comptroller General of South Carolina), Roy S. Nicks (Tennessee Department of Public Welfare), E. D. Cox (Mississippi Department of Public Welfare). H. G. Jones of the North Carolina Department of Archives and History showed exceptional interest in this and other problems and supplied a tremendous quantity of information.

E. B. Long's criticism of the manuscript is greatly appreciated, as is the careful editing by Ashbel Green and the editorial staff of Alfred A. Knopf, Inc., and Polly Chill, all of whom have made the publication of the book a pleasant experience for the author.

Research grants from the John Simon Guggenheim Memo-

Acknowledgments

rial Foundation and the Henry E. Huntington Library, and financial assistance from Winthrop College enabled me to take an extended leave from academic responsibilities so that this study could be made. All illustrations used in this volume were photographed at Huntington Library and are used with the permission of the librarian.

A full citation of each title is given when first mentioned in each chapter, and the location of manuscript collections is found in each citation except those used often. They are:

Duke University Library (Manuscript Division)
Ella Gertrude Clanton Thomas Diary
Benjamin S. Hedrick Papers
Henry E. Huntington Library
Lincoln Clark Papers
John Wesley North Papers
Library of Congress (Manuscript Division)
Breckinridge Family Papers
Anna E. Dickinson Papers
Burton Harrison Papers
Mrs. John A. Logan Papers
Philip Phillips Family Papers
Smith College Archives (Sophia Smith Collection)
E. P. Breck Letters
Garrison Family Papers
University of North Carolina (Southern Historical Collection)
Grace B. Elmore Diary
John Berkley Grimball Papers
Meta Morris Grimball Journal
Phillips-Myers Papers
Benedict Joseph Semmes Papers
Cornelia Phillips Spencer Papers

Because the Clara Barton Papers at Huntington, the Library of Congress, and Smith College Archives were used, the repository is designated in each citation.

Index

i

Index

Index